THE AUTHOR: Edward Seidensticker was born in Colorado. He attended the University of Colorado, and at the outbreak of the Pacific War was assigned to the Navy Language School, where he studied Japanese. After further work at Columbia and Harvard, he settled in Japan in 1948, and spent over ten years there, the first two as a diplomat. After a spell of teaching at Stanford, in 1966 he became professor of Japanese at the University of Michigan, and it was during the following years at Ann Arbor that most of *The Tale of Genji* was translated. He is currently professor of Japanese at Columbia University, teaching for half the year, and living the remaining half in Tokyo and Honolulu.

Among his other translations are a number of works by Tanizaki Junichirō, Kawabata Yasunari, and Mishima Yukio. In recognition of his role in the introduction of Japanese literature abroad, Mr. Seidensticker was awarded the third-class Order of the Rising Sun—one of the Japanese government's highest honors.

His latest publication is *Low City, High City: Tokyo from Edo to the Earthquake* (Knopf, 1983).

This Country, JAPAN

EDWARD SEIDENSTICKER

KODANSHA INTERNATIONAL LTD.
Tokyo, New York, San Francisco

*Distributed in the United States by Kodansha International/
USA Ltd., through Harper & Row, Publishers, Inc., 10 East
53rd Street, New York, New York 10022. Published by Ko-
dansha International Ltd., 12-21 Otowa 2-chome, Bunkyo-ku,
Tokyo 112 and Kodansha International/USA Ltd., 10 East 53rd
Street, New York, New York 10022 and Hearst Building, 5
Third Street, Suite No. 430, San Francisco, California 94103.
Copyright in Japan, 1979, by Kodansha International Ltd.*

Paperback edition, 1984   LCC 74-77958
                            ISBN 0-87011-641-x (U.S.)
                          ISBN 4-7700-1141-5 (in Japan)

CONTENTS

ACKNOWLEDGMENTS

The author wishes to thank Mr. Kobayashi and Mrs. Mishima for permission to quote passages here quoted for the first time, and to thank the following for permission to reprint essays and articles earlier printed under their auspices:

Journal of Asian Studies ("Review: *Madly Singing in the Mountains*," 1971)

The Japan PEN Club ("On Being Faithful to Murasaki Shikibu," 1973)

Journal of Contemporary History ("The Japanese Novel and Disengagement," 1966)

Harvard Journal of Asiatic Studies ("The 'Pure' and the 'In-Between' in Modern Japanese Theories of the Novel," 1966)

The Asiatic Society of Japan ("On Kawabata Yasunari," *Bulletin*, 1970)

Hudson Review ("Mishima Yukio," 1971)

Kenyon College ("Redskins in Japan," *Kenyon Review*, 1960; "The Business at Hand," *Kenyon Review*, 1961)

Encounter ("Tokyo," 1957)

Yomiuri Shimbun ("Selections from 'This Country,' 1958–1962")

INTRODUCTION

This is a miscellany. Save for the fact that all the articles are about Japan, it would be difficult to think of a single subject to which they all belong. It seems to be thought a violation of academic propriety, and evidence of shallowness, to venture from the field of specialization listed in the faculty directory. Perhaps it is so. The collection does in any event range rather far afield from the proper subject, writers and writing, though that is the subject that fills the largest number of pages. It ventures into society and culture and ideas and history, and political commentary represents the point of farthest departure from propriety.

Most of the articles have been published before, but four have not: the first two, that on translating "an exotic language," and that on Kobayashi Hideo. The article on Mishima Yukio's *Sea of Fertility* has appeared in Japanese but not in English. Of an earlier essay on Kobayashi Hideo, published by the Princeton University Press with other papers from a conference held in 1966, only quotations remain. It has come to seem unworthy of an important subject, the finest Japanese literary critic of this century. This one too may come to seem inadequate. If so yet another must be written; and someone must some day do a book or so of translations from his work.

The articles in the collection were written over a period of almost two decades. There have been deletions from and minor revisions of the articles here republished, the deletions chiefly to avoid repetition. Annotation has been left very much as it was at the time of first publication. Because some editors are more tolerant of notes than others, it is uneven.

"Tokyo" is the oldest. It was written and published in 1957. The city has been through great changes and even disasters, among which might be listed the Olympics, the anti-prostitution law, the cancerous growth of the southern and western districts, and the destruction of the old Imperial Hotel, the Frank Lloyd Wright one. People are always asking, and clearly hoping for expressions of shock and dismay in reply, whether the changes after a few months' absence are not perfectly astonishing. They are certainly noticeable, but they are uneven, affecting the affluent south and west far more than the plebeian north and east, and it always seems far more astonishing that so much should remain.

The main purpose of the article was to convey a sense of the vitality of the city. It is the most important thing, and it remains. An article from more than two decades ago perhaps does more to convey that sense than an article from but yesterday, because the best quality of the city is still present, and gives promise of surviving yet further changes and disasters.

My one published exercise in the art of fiction, "The Business at Hand," is here restored to its original form. The editors of the *Kenyon Review* were puzzled at the conclusion and asked that it be made more explicit, and so it was. I have never liked the brief passages added at their behest, and here make bold to delete them. Readers to whom the conclusion is puzzling are referred to the *Kenyon Review* for summer, 1961. I usually find that the changes which editors suggest are good ones; but here I do think that I would have been well advised to hold out against them.

The cluster of short pieces at the end of the book is selected from the hundred or so which I did for the English *Yomiuri* between 1958 and 1962. Like most fugitive pieces, they have dated, but they inspire in me considerable nostalgia for those polemic-filled days, the days of the grand anti-American fiesta, or, as it is called in one of them, "the hate-America drive." I hope that they will have the same effect on other persons, now middle-aging, who were witness to it all. The final piece, announcing my departure from Japan, may now seem somewhat overcharged, but it seemed at the time an indispensable conclusion to the whole episode and series.

(March 1979)

THE JAPANESE AND NATURE, WITH SPECIAL REFERENCE TO *THE TALE OF GENJI*

It is not easy to say "flower" in Japanese. The difficulty has to do with the Japanese insistence upon the specific in the observation and description of nature. In the best short dictionary of the Japanese language, the first definition of *hana*, informing us that it refers to the reproductive parts of higher flora, seems to satisfy the need for a general term. The second definition is an extension of the first, covering the branch at the end of which the *hana* appears. It is with the third and fourth that trouble begins: *hana*, without qualification, becomes the cherry blossom and the plum blossom.

In modern Japanese the former is dominant. One goes "flower viewing" in early April when people are doing it everywhere, and, like everyone else, expects to find cherry petals in one's cup. There are general terms for "flowering grasses" and "flowering trees," but "flowers" is difficult to isolate. Elucidation and explanation are needed.

Dr. Kenneth Pike, the eminent linguist, likes to tell of how, in just this context, a Japanese once made things difficult for him. His most famous and popular lecture is a demonstration of how to get into an unknown language without resorting to the devices of a known language. He first establishes a small vocabulary of nouns by showing his informant, a speaker of an unknown language who is assumed to speak no English, a number of objects and inviting vocal equivalents. The demonstration failed to get started when the informant was a Japanese, because he quite refused to give the word for "branch." Instead he gave the name of the tree from which the present branch had come.

The incident illustrates again the truth about the Japanese view of nature that is present in dictionary definitions of *hana*: that it is specific and detailed. In the very earliest graphic representations of nature there are stylized trees which could be almost any broad-leafed variety, but from the twelfth century down to at least the nineteenth scarcely a single unidentified branch of tree or blade of grass is to be found in Japanese painting. In the twelfth-century *Genji* scrolls, every detail of Murasaki's garden as she lies dying is specific and realistic. It is only in the nineteenth century that a similar specificity comes into European landscape painting. In the *fête champêtre* of the eighteenth century ladies swing and flirt and play blindman's buff under trees that look vaguely like elms or walnuts but could be almost anything of considerable stature and a foliate nature. Some flowers, notably the rose, can be identified in medieval tapestries, but more cannot. They tend to look vaguely like daisies.

It is possible that the insistence upon the specific asserts itself even earlier in Japanese literature, though one cannot be certain, since more literature survives than art. The insistence is, in any event, present from at least the eighth century. It has survived down to the very recent past. Though the generalized and non-discrete landscape is not absent from Japanese literature, there has down until very recent times been firm adherence to the tenet that it is not enough to mention classes, that specifics are required. Only in very recent years have we had novelists for whom a bird is just a bird and a tree is just a tree (when you have seen one, you have seen them all). If the loss of the specific is symptomatic of altered receptivity, then the change may be profound. The feel of the amalgam from which man emerged and to which he presently returns—the feel of the universe—may have changed.

In the greatest Japanese fiction nature is a constant and very specific presence. *The Tale of Genji* contains synoptic passages in which seasons and years are lumped together, and there are passages in which the time of the year seems to be deliberately suppressed and obscured; but it is not often through the whole enormous length of the work, perhaps two-thirds or three-quarters of a million words, that we are unaware of the season and the phase of the moon.

There is probably no comparable work in the whole cosmopolitan corpus of literature in which nature is such an immediate and continuing presence. In the English novel nature is a very sporadic presence, something which the novelist can bring in from time to time when a higher force is needed to veto or ratify the arrangements made by man. In *Bleak House*, perhaps two-thirds the length of the *Genji*, season and natural setting tend to be absent, and then suddenly it is summer, so that dear little Esther may have the best journey into Lincolnshire ever imagined, or winter, so that Lady Dedlock may die in particularly distressing circumstances. The seasons do not flow, as in the *Genji*. They pop in and out, and the characters seem as unaware of them as the reader is required to be.

In the *Genji* the seasons float by and the characters float with them, a single continuum. The origins of *fūryū*, a very ancient word indicating elegance and the life of taste, do not seem to have much to do with the characters with which it is written, "wind" and "flow." That is a pity, because in the Heian period *fūryū* was very much that, life with the breezes and the waters of the seasons. Nature is very rarely an adversary in *The Tale of Genji*, although there is one memorable typhoon. When nature pops in and out of an Austen or Dickens novel, it is more likely than not to be in the role of adversary, making it impossible for people to meet or subjecting them to discomfort. But it is scarcely there at all, a fact which is more to the point. It is rejected by the interior habits of the Austen set and the urban habits of Dickens's characters. Murasaki Shikibu's ladies have even more uncompromisingly interior habits than Miss Austen's, who do from time to time go strolling in the shrubbery, and like Dickens's they live in the world's greatest city (Kyoto probably was just that in those days). But they live the *fūryū* life, flowing with the breezes.

Of the *Genji* chapter titles, some two-thirds contain references to nature. It is true that the references are sometimes ambiguous or general, and sometimes but indirectly natural. "The Paulownia Court" is a place, and "Bamboo River" is a song. Even so, chapter titles that have a specific reference to nature are in a solid majority.

Nature is in all of the first eleven chapter titles. The frequency is lower in the following dozen or so, and the imagery tends to be somewhat generalized. From the twenty-third chapter, "The First Warbler," down to and including "Evening Mist," the thirty-ninth, only one title, "The Flute," contains no natural image, and even there the flute is linked to its origins in the bamboo grove. "Flares" and "The Cypress Pillar" are references of course to fabrications and not to natural objects as such, but summery connotations are strong in the former, and the latter does contain the tree from which the pillar is fabricated. Dickens sometimes gave his chapters titles, but to provide such a sequence he would have had to be a different sort of novelist.

In the last chapters the incidence of natural imagery is lower. Nature is present in under half of the last ten titles, and in only under a third is it so specific that the season is immediately apparent. Efforts to find broad significance in this rhythmical emergence and withdrawal of nature are hampered by the fact that we do not know when and at whose hands the chapter titles came into being. The fact that the very last chapter is the least specific of all the fifty-four, however, has been advanced as evidence that the *Genji* is complete. The decreased frequency of natural images in the last titles is beautifully symbolic of the gradual falling away of the phenomenal world as one last sad lady is left alone with her fate. It would not have been symbolic of anything at all had nature not been such a constant and emphatic presence over such an extended sequence of titles only a few chapters before.

The *Genji* is often described as the first novel in the literature of the world. An elusive word, "realism," tends to figure in attempts at definition of that elusive word "novel." In some very important ways the *Genji* is undoubtedly realistic. The action takes place in believable, mundane circumstances with very little intervention of the marvelous and the supernatural, and a broad and varied illusion is created of human individuality. The characters are individuals and not types. The individual makes his first appearance in English literature with Shakespeare, and in English fiction not much earlier, perhaps no earlier at all, than Jane Austen.

Yet there are ways in which the *Genji* is other than realistic. Its predecessor, *The Tale of the Hollow Tree* (*Utsubo monogatari*), has much more the feel of actual life in its randomness and diffuseness. The *Genji* is the more carefully shaped of the two, and in the shaping is unreality. Selection and elimination are apparent, and there is a bending of the action to the natural setting that is by no means realistic. Dickens seems to remember that there is nature out there somewhere, and to provide a summer day for an excursion or a winter twilight for a death. In the *Genji* it is as if the reverse were true, as if nature were the ubiquitous condition to which the action must be fitted. The pace is now slackened and now hurried that the most effective mating of nature and incident may occur. Because in real life events tend to scatter themselves haphazardly across the seasons, this is not realistic.

No one of importance, which is to say no one of central importance to Genji himself or to his reputed son Kaoru, dies in the summer. There are three considerable deaths in the spring, and one of them, that of Fujitsubo, is very important indeed. The other major characters who die in the spring are Princess Ōmiya, the mother of Genji's first wife, and Kashiwagi, who has had an affair with the Third Princess, Genji's young wife. We have no account of Princess Ōmiya's death. It occurs between chapters, and only when the first anniversary comes round do we learn that it took place in the Third Month, at the radiant height of spring. What we learn of Kashiwagi's decline and death is unusual, for it is not very firmly attached to seasonal and natural background. At the beginning of the thirty-sixth chapter, "The Oak Tree," we are informed that the New Year has come, and we are soon afterward informed that the Third Princess has borne a son, Kaoru, as a result of the affair with Kashiwagi. With the fiftieth-day celebrations in Kaoru's honor we know that the Third Month, the time of the blossoms, has come, and soon we find Yūgiri enjoying them in the garden of Kashiwagi's widow. Somewhere in the interval, in early spring, Kashiwagi's death has taken place. If the death of Ōmiya, slipped surreptitiously between chapters, does not figure directly in the narrative, that of Kashiwagi is also made to stand apart, cut off from the chronicle of the seasons that is almost as important as the chronicle of human affairs.

These are in any event deaths-once-removed from Genji's own life. Princess Ōmiya is the mother and Kashiwagi the son of his good friend Tō no Chūjō. The former is charged with the rearing of his son, Yūgiri, and the latter becomes the father of Kaoru, but neither is so close to Genji himself that the death jars and dislocates his life. With the single exception of his father, only women have the power to do that; and only one of the women in his life, Fujitsubo, dies in the spring.

She is very important indeed, a sort of mother-surrogate for Genji, who early lost his mother. In the treatment of her story are many eccentric details and devices, as if to emphasize that importance. The seasonal setting for perhaps the most significant events in

5

her life, her trysts with Genji, are obscure, in a work in which attention to the passing seasons is for the most part so unwavering, and her death too is exceptional, the one genuinely important death to occur in the spring.

The possibility cannot be completely denied that it is in fact a fortuitous exception. A close reading can defeat its own purposes, because almost anything can be made by misplaced attention to seem exquisitely artistic. There can be scarcely any doubt at all about the mortuary significance of autumn and winter. They are the seasons in which important people die (and it may be remarked that the boundary between the two is less clear than the boundaries between the other seasons).

The earliest events in the narrative are synoptic and not closely tied to seasons. It is summer when Genji's mother goes home, fatally ill, from the palace. The most beautiful scene in the chapter, and its most important scene, when the emperor sends a messenger to the home of the dead lady's mother, is autumnal. There is a setting moon as the messenger leaves to return to the palace, and there are songs of autumn insects. The following scenes are again synoptic, and no seasonal setting is offered for the death of Genji's grandmother. We learn only that Genji is six years old.

The next significant death is in the fourth chapter, "Evening Faces." It is elaborately autumnal. The air is chill and the moon is full when Genji takes the lady of the evening faces from her house in Gojō. She dies the following night, and her funeral takes place under an autumn moon two nights past full. It is the eighth moon of the year, the harvest moon, the most beautiful of all.

Genji's first wife Aoi dies five chapters later. It is the Eighth Month again, later in the month this time. Again there is a moon for the funeral, called especially to our attention when Genji remembers it after the death of Murasaki, the great love of his life. Because the phases of the moon are as important in the *Genji* as the passing of the seasons, and because Aoi's death affects Genji less than do the others—the deaths of Murasaki and the lady of the evening faces—one sees purpose in having the moon at the end of its cycle, late to rise and only a diffident presence. The moon emphasizes important events, and when there is specific mention of a moonless night, as when Kashiwagi first visits Genji's young wife or Niou last visits Uji, it is likely to be the setting for clandestine, furtive happenings. A waning moon clearly remembered at Aoi's funeral is contrasted with a bright moon erased by tears at Murasaki's, and so the moon is made to convey Genji's feelings with more directness and force than generalized statement would have been capable of.

In the next chapter Genji's father dies, in late autumn or early winter. The period of mourning extends through the darkest time of the year and ends at the close of the year. The failure of the New Year to bring comfort and renewal emphasizes the intensity of the grief.

When the Rokujō lady dies it is again late autumn or early winter. There are high winds and sleet in the days following her death. Five chapters later comes the death of Fujitsubo, the springtime departure from the series.

In the third chapter after Kashiwagi's death there is another death-once-removed, so to speak. Kashiwagi's widow, with whom Yūgiri is somewhat comically seeking to become intimate, loses her mother. Again it is the Eighth Month.

In the next chapter comes Murasaki's death, the saddest of them all. Once again it is the Eighth Month. The last great affair at which Murasaki is present, a reading of the Lotus Sutra, is in the spring. She languishes through the hot months, and when the *hagi* is in bloom and the most beautiful of autumn moons is near full, she dies. There is a full moon for her funeral, and Genji is too blind with tears to see it.

In the Uji chapters there are two important deaths and an attempted suicide. The Eighth Prince, Genji's uncle and the father of the Uji princesses and Ukifune, dies in the Eighth Month. It is late autumn or early winter when the older Uji princess dies, in the next chapter. In the city the last great festival of the year is taking place, and the contrast with the more rapid assaults of winter upon Uji, where the princess languishes and dies, is very telling. There is no mention of a moon at the princess's funeral, and we have been informed, when Kaoru is visiting for the last time, that clouds have darkened an already dark sky. Afterward we learn of cold snows and an icy river. There is a gale in the night when Kaoru next comes to Uji, and there are storms at the end of the year.

But spring is the time for the only attempted suicide in the whole long tale. We have been informed, in delicate touches here and there, that spring is Ukifune's favorite season, and her last meeting

7

with Niou takes place when, in the harsher sequence of seasons at Uji, winter snow and spring blossoms come together. A year has passed and again it is high spring when suspicions begin to filter back to the city that she is still alive. Autumn, Murasaki Shikibu seems to be telling us, is the time when people die with a certain serenity, falling away with the fall of the natural cycle. Suicide runs against nature, at the rising of the cycle. Ukifune's attempt at suicide is unique, in any case, as, in its different way, is the death of Fujitsubo, and the two are the great exceptions to the autumnal rule.

There need be nothing so very unnatural about a certain tendency for events to occur in the pleasanter seasons, the spring and autumn. It is then that people arrange for things to happen. It is quite unnatural, barring disasters and epidemics, which do not occur in the *Genji*, for natural deaths to be clustered in a single season, and it is highly improbable that the deaths of three of Genji's most important ladies should occur from the middle to the end of the Eighth Month. These things do sometimes happen in the real world, with its wild coincidences, but in artfully contrived fiction and especially fiction in which the natural setting is so important, they must be attributed to conscious intent. The season controls the most important of all matters in the development of the plot, when people are to depart.

We do not learn in what season Genji's own death takes place. It too is slipped between chapters.

Most events other than death are to an extent voluntary. An emperor can choose the time for his abdication, and Genji, anticipating forcible exile, can choose the time for his departure to Suma. Yet here too the massing of events in the clement seasons is remarkable.

Not many things happen in the summer. There are grand readings of the Lotus Sutra, presumably so that they may occur when the lotuses are in bloom, and one such reading, in the third chapter from the end, is the last important public observance in the whole vast narrative. In Genji's personal life, summer events of some significance have to do largely with the affairs of lesser ladies. The famous "rainy night's discussion" in the second chapter, listing the varieties of ladies and amorous experiences, takes place in early summer, and Genji's visits to the governor's wife in that and the following chapter are also warm-weather events. His visits to the lady of the orange blossoms in the eleventh and fourteenth chapters occur during breaks in the summer rains, and his encounter with the aged and comical Naishi in the seventh chapter also takes place in the summer. There are two brief summer chapters in the sequence following Genji's removal to Rokujō.

The fact that the list of summer events is so scant leads to interesting questions about events that do take place or seem to take place in the summer. The very first and the very last seasonal references in the *Genji* are summery. It is summer when Genji's mother leaves the palace in the first chapter, and in the last chapter we have Ukifune looking out at fireflies among the trees at Ono. Then there is the mysterious matter, already touched upon, of Genji's trysts with Fujitsubo. The first such meeting is completely surrounded in mystery, and the one that results in the birth of the Reizei emperor is fairly mysterious too. There is a gap in the fifth chapter, with no seasonal references between Genji's visit to the northern hills, when the cherry blossoms are in bloom, and Fujitsubo's return to the palace in the Seventh Month. Nor can we with confidence reckon back from Reizei's birth to his conception, because his birth is anticipated over a span of six or eight weeks. Everything considered, it seems likely that the crucial tryst occurs in early summer.

When there seems to be artistry in the massing of events in the clement seasons, one wants to find artistic intent too in the assigning of important events, only rarely so assigned, to an inclement season. Fujitsubo's death takes place in a season not meant for deaths, and these other events take place in a season not meant for much of anything at all. May it not be that the remarkable role which Fujitsubo plays in Genji's life is made more emphatic by manipulation of the seasonal background? As for the fact that summer opens and closes the tale, the summeriness of the last chapter is one of several considerations which in sum may be taken to support the view that it is just that, the last chapter—that Murasaki Shikibu intended it to be the last, and so the *Genji* is finished.

As for winter, it has been noted that there are important hibernal deaths. Winter too is a time in Genji's personal life for visits to lesser ladies. When in the sixth chapter the safflower lady's nose is first observed, the rufosity is emphasized by cold and snow. He visits his cousin Asagao on a night of snowy moonlight. There is snow on the night of his engagement to his niece, the Third Princess, but this is in the spring, after the advent of the New Year. The snow on the occasion of Niou's last meeting with Ukifune is also spring snow. If there is an association of Fujitsubo with improbable seasons and thereby a heightening of her uniqueness, there seems to be something similar in the case of Genji. We are told that he is unusual in his liking for cold winter nights, and it does not seem improbable that this unusual taste was meant by Murasaki Shikibu to emphasize his unusualness in other respects as well. Another character, the Akashi lady, is especially associated with the winter by being assigned the winter garden at Rokujō, and she is of Genji's ladies the one whose influence lasts longest. Through her Genji becomes the grandfather of an emperor (this we may assume, though he is still crown prince at the end of the story), and she is in effective management of the Rokujō complex after Genji's death.

There is a winter chapter in the review of the seasons after the move to Rokujō. There is also winter in a second review of the seasons, following Murasaki's death, and Genji is last seen as the New Year approaches. The beginning of the year is much more important in the *Genji* than the end of the year, and the fact that Genji himself should last be seen at an unlikely time, like the fact that the *Genji* comes to a conclusion in an unlikely season, may be taken as evidence of conclusiveness. One may imagine that Murasaki Shikibu meant him to be seen last at the close of the first full year of his bereavement, and that the chapter describing his death, held by long tradition to have been lost, was never written.

Most of the other important events take place in the spring and the autumn. To list them all would be as tedious as that dullest of documents, a plot synopsis. A very rough assigning of events to seasons reveals that there are far more springtime events than the combined total for summer and winter, and even if events which occur along the shadowy border between autumn and winter are assigned to the latter season, there are more autumnal events than vernal. If the *Genji* as a whole is to be assigned to a season, then the season is autumn. This seems most fitting. The beauty of the *Genji* is of a melancholy autumnal sort. There is a bittersweet quality about its happiness, an awareness of transience and insubstantiality. It is symbolized in the passing of the seasons and in the particular fondness for the season when the flowers and grasses are dying.

In two sections of the *Genji* the natural background seems to come forward as the chief matter of the narrative: the first complete year at Rokujō and the year following Murasaki's death, the last in which

Genji himself is seen. The Rokujō sequence, if such it may be called, extends over seven chapters, and the sequence following Murasaki's death over a single short chapter. The latter is like a sad, plaintive echo of the former. The seven Rokujō chapters are among the happiest and the most lyrically beautiful in the tale. The second sequence is also very beautiful, but the mood is of intense sadness. Formally it is like a return to the *utamonogatari*, the "lyrical episodes" which are among the literary origins of the *Genji*. There is consummate artistry in this return to origins even as the brilliant career to which we have been witness is about to end.

As in most Heian narrative literature, there is in the *Genji* a vocabulary of natural images for use in elegant social and amatory converse. The more important ladies in Genji's life are associated with flowers. The lost Tamakazura is a wild carnation, as also is the young Murasaki. The adult Tamakazura is given bright floral associations, the *yamabuki*, a yellow-flowered shrub related to the rose, and the *hōzuki*, sometimes called "Japanese lantern." The Akashi lady is likened to the orange blossom, and a lady especially associated with the orange blossom is to be found in the northeast quarter at Rokujō. Genji's only daughter is likened to the wisteria. We are more than once told that spring is Murasaki's favorite season (her last public appearance is in the spring, when the cherries are in bloom), and she is more than once likened to the *kabazakura*, a delicate and retiring variety of wild cherry. Genji so dominates the story that he is not captured in any one natural symbol, but a particular significance may perhaps be seen in his fondness for cold winter nights. In them is his own cold majesty—for despite repeated assurances about his warm charity and steadfast affections, he emerges as a chilly person.

The *Genji* is a feminine book, describing a feminine way of life as sedentary as ever was a Turkish harem. It was written by a woman, chiefly about women, and in the first instance for women—the early history of *Genji* criticism is in large measure a process of breaking the sexist barrier and making a womanly romance acceptable in proud manly society. Yet nature is so constantly and intimately present that one is not being merely whimsical in describing it as a book of the outdoors. The action floats upon the seasons as Huck and Jim upon the Mississippi, and indeed it is to the American novel that one turns in search of a Western strain in which nature is as constant a presence. "The Japanese *Huckleberry Finn*"—one could add it to the list of Japanese Shakespeares and Japanese Venices, and by no means only with intent to amuse. The great difference is that for Huck and Jim nature is an undifferentiated expanse, and for Murasaki's people it is carefully observed and chronicled in all its minute seasonal shadings. One cannot think of a book in the great English tradition which is as lacking in walls as either the *Genji* or *Huckleberry Finn*.

The first great woman novelist of the Western world (and perhaps the first great Western novelist) tells us, by contrast with the first great woman novelist of the Eastern world (and most definitely the first great novelist), how firmly indoors her tradition is. Jane Austen's ladies spend much of their time strolling, and Murasaki Shikibu's ladies do not stroll at all, although one of them, Tamakazura, makes an arduous journey on foot. When they know that they are being observed, they take great care not even to get to their feet. Yet it is the Jane Austen characters who live the indoor lives, with nature felt, out there beyond the walls, as a change in temperature and little else. Early in *Emma*, Jane Austen's finest novel, we are made aware that the weather is cold, and perhaps a quarter of the way through the book Christmas Eve comes, and a fall of snow, so that an excuse is present for avoiding a difficult encounter with the vicar at Christmas services. Three-quarters of the way along, "June opened upon Hartfield." There are two memorable outdoor scenes in high summer, and it is summer when Knightley proposes to Emma, and the year has come almost full circle by the time all the weddings have been attended to.

There is no compelling reason that it need have, other than that the cozy habits of Emma and her father do not permit a scene large enough for a climax to take place in their parlor. It must be out of doors, and so the season must be summer. Aside from the snow, there is very little detail to make us attend to the passing seasons. Mr. Woodhouse has his "great fire" and Miss Bates her tippet and spencer to attest to the English chill, but only once, to our knowledge, does Emma look at the hedges and think that "the elder at least must soon be coming out." There are strawberries to be picked at Donwell Abbey—that is why people were invited there in the first place—but "a broad short avenue of limes" is the only other feature of park or garden of which there is specific mention. Emma as an observer of nature seems to prefer somewhat bookish and contrived generalization. "I shall gradually get intimately acquainted with all the hedges, gates, pools, and pollards, of this part of Highbury," she muses as she and her friend Harriet pass the vicarage. Half of her little medley gives us nature quelled and caged by the eighteenth century, and the other half is a play upon the sound of words. And when, radiantly happy after Knightley's proposal, she sits down to tea, she observes "the same shrubs in the lawn . . . the same beautiful effect of the western sun." Generalized plants and generalized light—and nature itself is a generalization making its presence felt upon the elegant order of the parlor only to dictate whether the fire shall be great or small. One could come up with a considerably more detailed list of nature's contributions to Emma's diet than to her sense of the beautiful. Whole books, by contrast, are devoted to cataloguing the flora of the *Genji*, and what we learn of the *Genji* table suggests an overabundance of starch, and little else.

In both Jane Austen and Dickens the emphasis upon extremes of temperature is notable. It may be argued that this is necessarily so, since England has a single pleasant season and three chilly to cold seasons. Yet when Dickens sends Martin Chuzzlewit to the New World, the inclement again predominates. Martin is in America for a full cycle of seasons, returning to England a year after his abortive emigration. The seasonal pattern of mid-Atlantic America corresponds fairly well with that of Kyoto. It is the reverse of the English: one of the seasons, the summer, is most unpleasant, two of them are very pleasant indeed, and the winter is far from as unpleasant as people make it out to be. Yet the principal memory which Martin takes home seems to be of unbearable heat. The season which for Murasaki's characters is the most inactive, the nearest thing to a period of dormancy, is for Martin the season of the most intense activity. Murasaki's characters live in accommodation with nature, Martin in conflict.

The American chapters in *Martin Chuzzlewit* are probably Dickens's lengthiest excursion into the field of naked satire, in which such concerns of the novelist as character and probability are abandoned; but it happens also to be the passage in which a Dickens character is in a position to observe the nearest approximation to the seasons of the *Genji*. He seems to be aware only of the temperature. If it is aberrant Dickens, and to the minds of many of us bad Dickens, by its neglect of the novelist's proper concerns, it is all the same very typical Dickens in its treatment of nature. Neglect may be said to be the most marked characteristic of that treatment.

In *Great Expectations* Pip is seen down in Kent in "summer-time, and lovely weather," telling Biddy that he wants to be a gentleman. "Oh, I wouldn't, if I was you," the wise Biddy replies. "I don't think it would answer." He goes down to Kent again to see Miss Havisham, and "winter had now come round." A hundred pages of the Everyman edition, or some fifty thousand words, or about the first five chapters of the *Genji*, over half of the way to the exile—and one would have to search very hard, and probably in vain, for overt mention of nature along the way. In the earlier instance it is very generalized nature in any event, only the feel of the summer air and the waters of the Thames "rippling at our feet"; and to find another reference to nature one would probably have to push all the way back to the chill Christmas Eve of Pip's great fright, at the very beginning of the novel. For the visit to Miss Havisham nature is even more general, only winter and nothing more; and for further recognition that nature exists one must push ahead another fifty pages, when it is summer again, and Pip goes down to Kent for his sister's funeral. Only these four bits and nothing more through three hundred pages, or a hundred fifty thousand words, or not a great deal less than the *Genji* down to Tamakazura's flight from Kyushu. There are almost two hundred items on my own listing, down to that point, of references to or descriptions of nature in the *Genji*.

Nature is most explicit in the last of the four, with Pip in Kent for his sister's funeral.

> It was fine weather again. . . . For now, the very breath of the beans and clover whispered to my heart that the day must come when it would be well for my memory that others walking in the sunshine should be softened as they thought of me. . . .
>
> And now, the range of marshes lay clear before us, with the sails of the ships on the river growing out of it; and we went into the churchyard, close to the graves of my unknown parents, Philip Pirrip, late of this parish, and Also Georgiana, Wife of the Above. And there, my sister was laid quietly in the earth while the larks sang high above it, and the light strewed it with beautiful shadows of clouds and trees.

Aside from the lark, which in its figurative sense is a sort of leitmotif for Joe Gargery and therefore frequently present, we have only sensible, useful beans and clover.

So too it is in *Bleak House* when Esther Summerson goes down to Lincolnshire and the description of nature is, for Dickens, specific and detailed.

> It was delightful weather. The green corn waved so beautifully, the larks sang so joyfully, the hedges were so full of wild flowers, the trees were so thickly out in leaf, the bean-fields, with a light wind blowing over them, filled the air with such a delicious fragrance! . . .
>
> O, the solemn woods over which the light and shadow travelled swiftly, as if Heavenly wings were sweeping on benignant errands through the summer air; the smooth green slope, the glittering water, the garden where the flowers were so symmetrically arranged in clusters of the richest colors, how beautiful they looked! The house . . . and lying heaped upon the vases, there was one great flush of roses. . . .
>
> The old lime-tree walk was like green cloisters, the very shadows of the cherry-trees and apple-trees were heavy with fruit, the gooseberry bushes were so laden that their branches arched and rested on the earth, the strawberries and raspberries grew in like profusion, and the peaches basked by the hundred on the wall. Tumbled about among the spread nets and the glass frames sparkling and winking in the sun, there were such heaps of dropping pods, and marrows, and cucumbers, that every foot of ground appeared a vegetable treasury.

Down in Kent we had, for the funeral, the most obvious of diurnal birds; and here in Lincolnshire we have the most obvious of flowers and that same obvious bird, and the only decorative tree for which anyone in *Emma* has a sufficiently lingering eye to permit identification. Everything else is edible, or unidentified. When there is a list of decorative plants at the end of *Bleak House*, with the description of dear little Esther's dear little cottage ("woodbine, jasmine, and honeysuckle"), one feels that Dickens has in mind not nature but a greeting card. As he leaps from summer to winter and back again and notices nothing between, nature is for him either something to eat or something to resent and put back in its place, firmly out of doors, as soon as possible. There really is no indoors in the *Genji*, and edible nature is a small presence indeed.

Nature is given the most perfunctory notice by these the greatest of English novelists. If one chooses to look at the positive side of things, not the shortness of the shrift but the relationship between novelist and character on the one hand and, on the other, nature which does not after all go away and must be implicitly present, one sees the shadow of the preoccupations that have been with Western man ever since he turned his attention to these matters. Is there purpose in nature, he has asked, and if so does that purpose have to do pre-eminently with man? Why yes, of course, replies Dickens; there is winter, when sensible people get themselves indoors, and there comes summer, always in its time, when nature can be eaten. The dichotomy is the great difference from the *Genji*: the Dickensian resists in the winter and eats in the summer, and in both cases nature stands apart as the object of man's endeavors. The good disciple of Murasaki Shikibu accommodates and fits in, and floats along with nature—again it is *Huckleberry Finn*, among the remotest of novels from Heian elegance, that comes to mind as the nearest Western approximation, or at least as a Western novel that provides appropriate images.

Dickens probably never gave the matter much thought, but there all the same is the ancient line of speculation about nature. Murasaki Shikibu was a much less "thinking" kind of novelist. Although great messages can be derived from her book, it is not a speculative or even an intellectual book. Had she been a more thoughtful writer than she was, she would not have had a speculative tradition to turn to. Careful observation and sympathetic, carefully realistic depiction of nature was already by her time a venerable and glorious tradition. It did not, however, set man apart from nature, making him now seek to tame and now seek to conquer, and leaving him constantly and fretfully curious as to his own position in this strange, fascinating dichotomy.

The language in which Murasaki Shikibu wrote would not, indeed, have been up to articulating the dichotomy. *Shizen* is the word that would spring to everyone's lips to answer a demand for a translation of "nature." *Shizen* has been very busy this last century helping render into Japanese all manner of unfamiliar Western concepts, such as *jus naturel* and *Naturwissenschaft* and "natural selection" and the like. Before the West came sweeping in with this proliferation of neologisms, the adverbial sense seems to have been dominant when the word was used at all. The Japanese-Portuguese dictionary of the early seventeenth century offers the sense of "spontaneously" or "without external agency," but the nominal sense, setting man off against everything else and subsuming the latter under a concept of "nature," seems to have been absent.

Murasaki Shikibu would have had altogether as much difficulty assimilating the Rousseauesque "return to nature" as some of us have had assimilating her own nebulous intuitions and pronouncements. When in "Of Birds and Beasts" Kawabata Yasunari has a character musing upon the workings of nature, the Kawabata instinct for the unchanging leads him to a more venerable word, *zōka*, akin to "creation." There is a trinity of creators, up there on the High Plain of Heaven, in the oldest chronicles; but having done their work in a phrase or two they are heard from no more. Nature goes on without them, gods and men all in it together, and *zōka* would not have been a very useful weapon for Murasaki Shikibu in her struggle with Rousseau. Even today, looking through the columns and columns of compounds beginning with *shizen*, one feels that it is an abstraction from a great parcel of Western abstractions, and not from the real natural world.

In the poetry of perhaps a century and a half preceding the *Genji* there is apparent, under a continental influence, a radical separation of man from nature. One wants to describe it not as dichotomy but as solipsism, however, for there is not the restless attack upon and questioning of nature that is the Western tradition. There is rather a withdrawal into amorous moodiness for which nature provides a set of objective correlatives. Perhaps, though it dominated poetry for a very long time, it was like Pip's gentlemanly aspirations: it did not answer. It was fun for a while, but it got too stubborn and straitening a hold, and the old art of drifting along with nature was frustrated. One feels somehow that if the proper, orthodox poetry of the *Kokinshū* period had never existed it would not really have been missed, but that the deeper urge, blocked while the continental dalliance continued, could not be denied forever. In this fact, or possibility, may be the best explanation for the remarkable flowering of prose at the hands of women from the tenth century into the eleventh. Victims of propriety and orthodoxy, men went

17

on writing what would not have been missed if it had not been written, and to women was left the writing of what had been dreadfully missed all through it.

In the Middle Ages sensitivity and accommodation to nature emerged once more in poetry. Continental dalliance became the thing in prose narrative. A celebrated example is the Chikubu episode exactly midway through *The Tale of the Heike*. It is by someone who was stuffed full of continental texts and would have thought of them and not of the scene before him even if he had taken the trouble to visit Chikubu. Again one feels that it would not have been greatly missed if it had not been written, whereas the meditative poetry of the day, which like the *Genji* flows along with nature, demanded to be written.

In the Middle Ages drama first reached heights of elegance permitting it to be called art. If the *Genji* may be described as of an outdoor character in the sense that outdoors and indoors are one, so may the premodern drama. A Nō play begins out of doors and usually stays there. Some scenes, the last scene of *Mochizuki*, for instance, seem to take place indoors, but as in the *Genji* the line between outdoors and indoors is not a clear one. A Kabuki interior is always a part of an exterior, and slipping in and out of footwear is among the most sophisticated branches of Kabuki dramaturgy. Missteps and stumbles are not permitted, and it takes great skill to avoid them. There are no stuffy dolls' houses on the Kabuki stage.

The closed interior was among the more revolutionary importations of the late nineteenth century. We need not feel deprived of knowledge, for a great deal has been said in the matter, of how it felt for an actor to talk carelessly of this and that in the Western parlor manner after all those centuries of prancing and growling, or of how helpless he felt when deprived of music and musical intonation; but not much has been said about how it felt to be suddenly shut up in a Western room with no suggestion of nature anywhere in sight. It must have been suffocating, like going down with a disabled submarine. Perhaps, indeed, the drawing of a line between indoors and outdoors was the most revolutionary thing of all, the genuinely radical break with tradition.

A certain difficulty in breathing is produced by a great deal of recent fiction as well, and the causes are similar. The old accommodation with nature, the old awareness of the outdoors, has disappeared. Abe Kōbō has one of his heroes wandering through a nightmare of a city, and so in a formal sense almost everything is outdoors. Yet the time and place are so general that the outdoors as something seen and felt is scarcely there at all. Mishima Yukio was the most erudite of novelists, widely conversant with Western and Japanese literature; but there seems to have been a very important part of the Japanese tradition that did not interest him at all. A bird in one of his novels is only a feathered creature, possibly a duck if near water, quite likely a sparrow or a pigeon if not. A break with tradition contains many elements, and a feeling that a kind of writing is deracinated doubtless has many causes; but preeminent among them in the case of the modern Japanese novel must be the shutting of doors and the cutting off of nature.

The old awareness has not entirely disappeared, although it is a rare element indeed in the writings of the men to whom, in the common view, the future belongs, the cosmopolitan set led by Messrs. Abe and Ōe Kenzaburō. Until but recently it continued to be virtually "the mainstream."

In literary histories the mainstream (shuryū) of modern literature flows grimly down a course known as naturalism and held to be strongly under the influence of the West and addressed to the existentialist discomforts of modern man. It seems not improbable, however, that if the best of the naturalists are read a hundred years from now it will be as sensitive regionalists, gifted chroniclers of the "wind and earth," the ancient term for ecology, that produced them. This is especially true of Shimazaki Tōson, who occupies the grandest place of them all in the literary histories. His social awareness now seems sentimental and his self-awareness adolescent, but his sketches of the moods and seasons of his native Shinano are very beautiful. One comes upon them in his novels, having pushed dutifully past all the significant things, as one comes upon a vase of flowers in a corner of a grimy railway station. He wrote novels because that was the modern thing to do, but he did not really understand the genre, and was at heart an impressionist poet with strongly traditionalist tendencies.

Nagai Kafū was a kind of metropolitan regionalist. Edith Wharton might perhaps be called a metropolitan regionalist, but she did not have the affection for New York that Kafū had for Tokyo. He observed the moods and seasons of the city with wonderful sensitivity and conveyed them with wonderful finesse. It is sometimes possible to tell from the titles of his stories and sketches, as from chapter titles in the *Genji*, the season in which they are laid. Lacking a sense of the dramatic and quick to assign the simplest and least charitable of motives, he was not a remarkably gifted novelist, but perhaps more than any other modern novelist he was heir to the old awareness of and accommodation to nature.

Along with the minutely specific detail, one is aware of the acceptance. It is perhaps most apparent in *A Strange Tale from East of the River*, written in 1936, the masterpiece of his late years. Only marginally fictional, *A Strange Tale* is an effort, eminently successful, to convey the totality of a setting and a season, a licensed quarter east of the River Sumida from summer into early autumn. The mosquitoes too are a part of the season and the setting, and they are welcomed and accommodated.

> If one but goes east of the River Sumida, the hum of the mosquitoes by the ditch is even now as it was some thirty years ago, singing the melancholy sweetness of the further reaches of town; and how great, even in these last ten years, has been the change in the speech of the city!
>
> "A clearing in the litter, room for a mosquito net. . . ."
>
> "Autumn comes to a close, and the net will be turned into wine."
>
> These slight epigrams of mine came back to me one evening when I found a mosquito net hanging in one of O-yuki's rooms.

In the writings of Kawabata Yasunari the distance between success and failure is a very short one, because when he succeeds it is at something precarious and unstable, a blending of actor and scene in which they seem constantly on the point of fusing. Two memorable scenes in *Snow Country* center upon women's faces reflected against a natural background, and the marvel is that these substanceless wraiths should be memorable humanity, the matter of substantial and believable fiction. Not a confessionary sort of writer, Kawabata made at least one celebrated confession: the defeat of 1945, he said, was for him an event of such moment that it left him capable of writing only elegies. During the war years he was strongly drawn to the *Genji* and to the poetry of the late Middle Ages, in which the quiet pursuit of natural subjects brought serenity in the midst of civil turbulence. "The Tōkaidō," a small gem among Kawabata's writings, lost and rediscovered, was in 1975 published for the first time in book form. It was serialized late in the war in a Mukden and a Dairen newspaper, and discontinued as the end of "Manchukuo" approached. Albeit obliquely, Kawabata's own feelings in that time of great turbulence are stated as affectingly as anywhere in his writings.

There are delicate touches of fiction here and there, but for the most part it is a discursive essay looking ahead to the Nobel lecture. The protagonist, more wraithlike than most Kawabata characters, is a professor who undertakes to enlighten his daughter and students in the literary history of the Tōkaidō, the Eastern Road from Edo to Kyoto. The most beautiful passages, indeed the nearest thing the "novel" contains to sustained narrative, have to do with Sōgi, the fifteenth-century master of linked verse, and Ashikaga Yoshihisa and Sanjōnishi Sanetaka, two sensitive and talented men whose public careers were laid waste by the political turmoil of the fifteenth century.

"It may almost be said," muses the protagonist, "that without a reading of the *Genji* there can be no understanding of Muromachi culture. Shōtetsu lectured on the *Genji* for the shogun Yoshimasa, and the shogun Yoshihisa had Sanetaka lecture on the same subject. One may almost hold the *Genji* responsible for the fall of the Ashikaga shogunate."

In another famous statement from soon after the surrender, Kawabata said that he found in the sadness of the Orient nothing akin to the bleak nihilism of the Occident. Central to this view must have been a sense of affinity with the great nature poets of the late Middle Ages and their affinity, in turn, with the *Genji*. In the peace they make with the universe is a delicate sensitivity to the world around them, and quiet resignation and acceptance. It was exactly such qualities in Kawabata himself that made him seem the least suicidal of men. An element of uncertainty yet remains, and one goes on thinking that perhaps he did not after all commit suicide, and that if he did, it must have been impulsive, an act committed in a moment of great weariness. Some writers, observed in person, are utterly unlike their writings, and some are the very images of it. Kawabata was of the latter sort. Just as his characters seem constantly on the point of falling back into nature, so he seemed to live on intimate terms with extinction. He did not court it, but he seemed fond of it. In the final merging with nature, as of a life in the *Genji* flickering to an end in the autumn, there seemed to be, for him, a consummation. A medieval sensitivity to nature is very closely akin to an acceptance of and even a certain fondness for death, accepting but not actively seeking, and therefore not suicidal.

It is the lack of thresholds that seems important. The outdoors went into the depths of the secluded women's quarters, and the cloistered nun lived an outdoor life like everyone else; and there were no trumpeting archangels and pearly gates to make of death the crossing of a great divide. The difference is not to be described in terms of pleasure and pain. William Blake seems to have welcomed death with exultation, and most Japanese, like most of the rest of us, seem to fear death. It has to do rather with the degree of emphasis upon difference. The outdoors is a much more immediate and accessible presence for the Kabuki actor leaping gracefully in and out of his footwear than for the Western shut-in. Death too seems more accessible and less absolute.

These are difficult, remote matters. It is not easy to know one's own feelings about death, since the days are got through by not thinking about it; and in the endeavor to imagine how someone else feels is an arrogant kind of rashness. Yet one *will* imagine, in full knowledge of the arrogance, and the imagining leads to a strong feeling that for those who have made the old accommodation with nature, disasters are of less magnitude than for others who have not. In the years of the great trauma, 1945 and after, it was a marvel to watch the Japanese refusal to fall into a heap. Much of the wonder was in the fact that for them the trauma did not seem as awful as it would doubtless have seemed for us. It was one of those things, momentous but not final; personal defenses seemed to remain after social defenses had fallen away.

So the possibility that the old awareness of nature may be disappearing suggests very great changes indeed. For the young writer who does not care a great deal whether the feathered creature is a duck or a sparrow, a trauma like that of 1945 might indeed be the end of everything. With the loss of social identity and security nothing would remain.

The road ahead is not going to be easy for any of us. Almost the only certain thing is that we are presently going to run out of fuel, and the empty tank will bring greater unhappiness to those for whom it is everything than to those for whom it is just one of those things. The implications of the anthropocentric rejection of nature so far advanced in the writings of Abe and Ōe are great and ominous. To hold that the duck and the sparrow are interchangeable may well be to cast off the best defenses.

Yet perhaps it is not really happening. Abe and Ōe may be aberrations, strays and not harbingers. The department stores are full of ingenious gadgets for destroying mosquitoes, scentless and noiseless and (of course) harmless; but it is one of the signs that summer is coming when the neighborhood pharmacist stocks up on the coils, made from a kind of chrysanthemum, that send forth a pungent odor and keep mosquitoes at a distance but do not destroy them. It is a sign not only of the summer but of a way of looking at summer. Old Kafū's way is with us yet, and how pleasant to know that it is.

(1975)

THE CONSERVATISM
OF THE JAPANESE

The conservatism of the Japanese is a matter which should be commented upon whenever possible, because evidences of their radicalism are everywhere so apparent. Radicalism is present in the most conventional sense, the political and ideological, and many other senses too. If one were to draw up a list of violent political happenings over the past century, it would establish the Japanese as among the most violent and erratic peoples in the whole world, and certainly in what is known as the "developed" world. In recent years the number of victims claimed by feuding among radical student factions, all of them claiming to be the true heirs of Marx, must be several times the combined total for Western Europe and North America. Perhaps the most striking thing about the radical student movement is that the behavior of its more energetic partisans makes adjectives like "rightist" and "leftist" lose significance. Their blind loyalty, their preference for muscle over mind, their noisy penchant for verbalization so sterile that it really signifies denial of the spoken word—in all these respects student activists show closer kinship with movements of the radical Right in their own country than with movements of the radical Left anywhere else.

Then there is also what might be called a radical receptivity. That the Japanese are clever imitators is one of the first facts every Occidental schoolchild learns about the non-Occidental world. What the imitative faculty must depend upon is, of course, an assumption that there are things worth imitating. The Chinese have tended not to make this sort of assumption, because among the earliest facts implanted in the brain of the Chinese schoolchild is that everything good and valid, save in recent years Marxism, originates in China. The Japanese have for a very long time been aware of vast areas from which to borrow and vast numbers of things to borrow. Sometimes they have outdone their lenders, and upset balances of payments, and sometimes they have done less well, as when they have assumed that they have mastered the art of English composition. The grand result, of recent years, has been the superficial Americanization of the great cities which so upsets the tourist. He has been brought across all that water to look at the quiet beauty of Japan, and has found himself instead in the richest and most teeming of supermarkets.

Something else is there, all the same, if he will look for it, even though "quiet beauty" may not always seem the best way to describe it. The Japanese are the world's great conservers. This radical receptivity means that they are always finding amusing and interesting things to bring home, but it does not mean that they recklessly throw away the things that are already there. Room can always be found for more, and indeed home does not seem home unless new things are constantly being added to the accumulation. The very essence of home is to be found in that great clutter, given form and identity by one grand, undeviating principle, that room must be found for each amusing and interesting new thing, but that old things need not be pushed aside in the process.

This principle shows itself in the basic devices for ordering reality. The Japanese language is a mad, thoughtless jumble of new things, but it is as extraordinary for its fundamental conservatism as for its friendliness to novelty and change. The bright little Americanism on television tonight is part of the language tomorrow, and will be for the next few days at least, and one must know it if one wishes to communicate. Such turns of expression are then likely to be abbreviated or become acronyms, and these too must be a part of one's life for the span of their own lives. Even advertisements which reduce everything to the lowest denominator are incomprehensible unless one is abreast of the neologistic flood. It is all very exhausting and very fascinating, and the overall impression is of an utter want of *shutaisei*. The big Japanese-English dictionary, coining a neologism to translate a neologism, says that *shutaisei* means "subjecthood." What it means in more conventional English is a sense of one's irreducible identity and inviolable integrity, the line beyond which one does not retreat. It is what the language, so madly and promiscuously accommodating, seems to be lacking. But the vessel and vehicle, for all the accommodating, does not change. The Japanese language is surely among the most conservative in the world. Very early it rejected borrowings for the purposes recognized to be the highest, those of lyric poetry, and it is very rare indeed for a borrowed word to make its way into the conjugated core of the language, which does not change. Where else in the world is it possible for a remark heard on the street today to coincide with a remark set down a thousand years ago? It does not happen very often, to be sure, but still it does happen: a remark heard on a Kyoto street can, without being in the least quaint or erudite or antiquarian, be straight out of *The Tale of Genji*.

It was in the eighth century or thereabouts that the decision was made, and no one knows how it came to be made or whether in fact it was ever debated and articulated, that pure native speech must be used for native lyric poetry. It was at a time when the flood of foreign borrowings was probably as overwhelming as it has ever been. Prehistory had some two or three centuries earlier given way to history, and the transformation had been wrought by confrontation with one of the oldest and richest of traditions. Native things seemed very poor and primitive compared with foreign things, and the urge to discard feelings of inferiority by becoming completely foreign was powerful. Already in the eighth century the grand principle proceeded to operate at the very center of things. Not only would the language of the tribe not be abandoned in the rush to become foreign, it would be divested of foreign elements as it addressed itself to the most distinguished and refined forms of communication.

This principle asserted itself in matters of belief as well: a wealth of theological and doctrinal speculation was suddenly there, undeniably superior to the poor and primitive works of the native mind. This was to be mastered—but the native product need not be thrown away in the process. The story of how the Sun Goddess was called upon to help consecrate the greatest of eighth-century Buddhist images is well known. One feels in the presence of something very marvelous, the decision, probably never articulated, that the native should not be allowed to go under in the flood of foreign borrowing. It means specific and explicit preservation in the face of what must have been an almost irresistible urge to destroy. It is conservatism at its grandest and most mysterious, and a conservatism that has continued to operate through the millennium since.

By the time *The Tale of Genji* was written, in the eleventh century, the grand principle was firmly established. The *Genji* is the most remarkable single document showing how the Japanese go about things, and among the most fascinating things it shows is the working of the principle, which is there in the very language itself. There are almost eight hundred poems in the purest of Japanese. There are fragments of Chinese poetry, which contributed to the intellectual and aesthetic paraphernalia of the day, but there is no extended exercise in Chinese poetry, and no original Chinese poetry at all. Similarly there are imported religious appurtenances requiring the occasional use of an exotic word, usually Chinese, but the flow of the story is in the shifts and changes at the conjugated heart of the language.

The principle is also at work in the institutions of religion as the *Genji* describes them. Buddhism is everywhere, its doctrinal niceties providing everything that the rational faculty needs to keep itself busy. Buddhist views of the unchanging and the inevitable are accepted with no apparent doubts. Buddhism offers everything to everyone, and the claims of the native gods seem laughably naive by comparison; but though the Good Law of Buddhism might in the end have its way with everyone, with us and with them as well, it was not the way of the native mind to reject those native gods. Probably no one ever said so and probably no one ever had exactly the thought in exactly those terms, but the essence of the native mind was in the refusal to reject.

The Tale of Genji is a very religious book. Because of its psychological subtlety it is often compared with Proust, but in its spiritual preoccupations it might better be compared with Dostoevski. Once, while reading the *Genji*, I made note of every detail that might be described as explicitly religious. There were in the end more than a thousand notes. Not even this high frequency quite tells how constant a presence religion is, and it may be that in the West an urge to secularize, arising from the altogether proper wish to establish the *Genji* as the first novel in the literature of the world, has had the effect of diluting and diffusing the religious presence. In England the novel is a very secular form, so strongly so that the absence of religion may be among its distinguishing characteristics, and the man who brought the *Genji* to the West was an Englishman.

Though Buddhism is the new, imported religion, some Buddhist notions and assumptions are as constantly present in the *Genji* as the air that supports life. Chief among them are the complementary and somewhat contradictory notions of evanescence and karma, the one averring that only change is unchanging, and the other saying that there is something else unchanging too, the rule that the consequences of our acts do not leave us, in this life or in other lives. When it is explicit and manifest, Buddhism tends to take on dark shades. The Good Law itself is made subject to the workings of evanescence, and so the world is seen to be in decline. The great things are in the past, the future is one of progressive spiritual emaciation. If the consequences of our acts do not leave us, we may yet seek repose by withdrawing from and avoiding the entanglements that add new consequences. Whatever it may be in other lives, this last possibility is rather cold comfort in this, having as its reasonable conclusion lovelessness and isolation.

Still, the *Genji* is not an insistently despairing book. An ill or aged person sometimes compounds the grays of Buddhism into black and withdraws completely, but for the most part a gentle awareness of evanescence only adds to the beauty of the passing moment. Then there are the Eight Million Gods of Shinto, who also have their ways. Indeed they are what Shinto means, the Way of the Eight Million, which is the standard number, mostly, one suspects, because in the native pronunciation it has such a cheerful resonance. Shinto may not be as constant a presence as Buddhism, but it too is present in quotidian life, providing altogether easier and more matter-of-fact ways to keep in harmony with things. The most common and the most pleasant is merely to keep clean. A useful device for making one's way through this dewy vale (a Buddhist image) is to keep one's face washed (Shinto). It also provides Murasaki Shikibu with a useful technical device. Two or three favored Buddhist notions are so continuously present as to be reality itself, but the writer of fiction differs from the writer of a philosophical tract in being compelled to give them concrete manifestation. Very often a belief or observance more anciently Japanese than Buddhism will provide the occasion for action or inaction, and so for the symbolic happenings which make a novel a novel, disengage it from abstraction. In this regard Shinto conveniently provides such ready and pleasant ways of keeping in harmony with the Eight Million as being well scrubbed.

If the objection is raised that literary conventions and religious beliefs are rather different things, answer may be made that a writer as intent on imitating life as Murasaki Shikibu does not resort to conventions which are not acceptable to her readers. She may sometimes have gone beyond her own ability to believe, and there is evidence that she did indeed do so in the matter of ghosts and malign possessions, but the reader's credulity must not be put in jeopardy. Ritual purity, which is exceedingly ancient, must have been very important to him. Though Shinto writ is a complex amalgam of the native and the imported, some things do seem to rise from very deep in the racial memory and cognition. Among them is the notion that defilement lies at the beginning and the end of life and on numerous occasions between, some of them foreseeable and some of them not, and that it must be lustrated away before one is readmissible to the clan councils.

The *Genji* is a very well washed book, perhaps the best washed in the whole canon of the world's classics. There are many clean books in the sense that no speck of dust is allowed to fall on our hero and heroine, but there are probably no others in which spots are so constantly being rubbed away. Many of the grand climaxes are brought into being by the need to cleanse, or, more rarely, the need to refrain from it because of the ceremonies and taboos surrounding it. Doom closes in on Ukifune in the fifty-first chapter when her mother is not permitted to take her away from the mess she has made of her affairs, and a defilement is not only the pretext that thwarts the mother, it is the only one that would have been sufficient and effective in the circumstances. Two chapters earlier, the poor girl's misfortunes are set upon their way because of a hair washing. Heian ladies were so encumbered with hair and clothes that they must have looked like inventories of switches and swatches, and washing the hair would have been something of a secular ritual in any case. A sacerdotal element was added by the fact that hair washing was forbidden through a rather long period in the autumn when Shinto rites were numerous. On an evening when she does not expect to see her husband, Ukifune's half sister has her hair washed, because it cannot be washed for many weeks to come. The husband comes visiting anyway and finds no one to entertain him, for getting the hair dry again occupies the attention of almost the entire household. Wandering here and there in his boredom, he comes upon Ukifune, and so the misfortunes begin.

Often a defilement is only an excuse. Nothing has really happened, but who is to be sure? The exigencies of purification are always given absolute priority. Both Buddhism and Shinto thus provide refuges from too social a life. If it gets to be altogether too much, a lady or gentleman can always go into a nunnery or hermitage, and if more temporary relief is needed it can always be said, and no one can prove the contrary since the possibilities for fabricated detail are infinite, that a defilement has occurred. Until the defilement has been cleansed, all visitors must stay away and all appointments must be canceled.

If the deities of Buddhism preside over the universe, certain of the Eight Million preside over the clan, and so once again something very ancient has survived. The earliest Shinto writ is a family chronicle, establishing the most eminent genealogy in the land. The gods are not creators but procreators. When they have done the important thing asked of them, they withdraw from the scene. They are not constantly with the clan and the tribe, guiding the way through wildernesses and presenting tablets upon high places; but they continue to live, dwelling somewhere off where dead ancestors also live. It is wise and polite to accord them respect, even as the living head of the family is accorded respect.

The sense of the clan councils, where there were seats for the corporeal members and for the non-corporeal as well, is very powerful in the *Genji*, and it derives from the most ancient of native beliefs. Genji behaves like a perfect cad after offering a home to Tō no Chūjō's waif daughter, Tamakazura; he takes full advantage of the fact that as foster father he has all the prerogatives but not all the inhibitions of a natural father. When he undertakes presently to desist from so comporting himself, it is not because he has undergone a change of heart, but because he does not want to cause trouble between Tamakazura and the grand head of her clan, the god of Kasuga. She must announce herself by her proper name, and she must do honor to a grandmother who is shortly expected to die. She avoids unpleasantness by frequent ritual cleansing, and she does so too by being polite to the members of the clan seen and unseen. Genji can no longer pretend that she is his daughter. Her existence and whereabouts must be made known to her real father and to her remotest ancestor.

A rather more dramatic device for bringing concrete happenings forth from the laws and forces of abstract reality is to place a character in the power of a malign spirit. It is very difficult here to separate the domestic from the imported, since the notion of entanglements and commitments which keep a spirit from moving on to other lives is Buddhist. Sometimes, however, it seems as if dissatisfied and resentful spirits, as well as gods, might be members of the clan. When Genji's first wife is dying she is seen to be the victim of possessions, and as they come forth and announce themselves we are made aware that, just as old and noble families have their ancestral gods, so too they have their hereditary ghosts. Among the spirits that emerge in the process of exorcism are some who, like butlers and stewards, have been with the family for a very long time. What established them initially in that role is not made clear, and it does not seem that they mean any dreadful harm. They are the viruses that account for the minor indispositions.

The family feeling, so to speak, between ghosts and the objects of their sometimes capricious behavior suggests once again the oldest of native beliefs. So does a reducing of the distinction between the living and the dead. The most important element defining the relationship between Tamakazura and the god of Kasuga, for instance, is not the negative one that they are not both incarnate, but the positive one that they are both of the Fujiwara clan. So too the most important fact about a possessing spirit does not have to do with the death and disappearance of the flesh. It may belong to someone still living. Buddhist priests are always called in when a spirit, living or dead, is causing unpleasantness, but certain devices for keeping a potentially errant spirit at home have the look of home remedies. These are suggested half whimsically, but in poetic language which assumes and requires a knowledge of folk beliefs. The most likely explanation for the currency of these devices, and for their availability at crucial turns in the *Genji*, is that very ancient beliefs have been reinforced by doctrines imported more recently. If the grand conservative principle sometimes has the effect of tolerating complex incompatibility, it also sometimes orders the selection of novelties so that the interests of compatibility may be served.

There is evidence from certain poems not found in the *Genji* itself that Murasaki Shikibu did not really believe in possessions. Whether she did or not probably does not matter a great deal, since she clearly assumed that her audience did and since she turned that assumption to most marvelous artistry. There are possessing spirits which (like procreating gods) have their time and go, not to be heard from again, but there is one that is central to the action until Genji himself disappears. The spirit of the Rokujō lady, the widow of a former crown prince, loved for a time by Genji, takes possession of other ladies while she is still alive, and goes on doing so after she is dead. It is jealousy that sends her spirit forth on its predatory expeditions, at which she is as horrified, when she is made aware of them, as anyone else. Proud and contrary and sensitive and infinitely accomplished, she is one of Murasaki Shikibu's triumphs, and perhaps the very earliest of them. She is at the heart of one of the great *Genji* mysteries, because the reasons for her jealousy are not established until the ninth chapter, whereas its workings are already apparent in the fourth. Eminent scholars have argued very persuasively in recent years that the ninth chapter was written before the fourth. If this is so, then the splendid festival scene in the course of which vague resentment is turned to uncontrollable anger and jealousy is the earliest of the great *Genji* scenes, and the Rokujō lady becomes Murasaki Shikibu's first considerable characterization, richly ambiguous and contradictory, as superior fictional characters should be.

The novelist Enchi Fumiko, who in 1973 finished her rendition of *The Tale of Genji* into modern Japanese, has said that her favorite among all its ladies is the Rokujō lady. One can see why. In an earlier romance the Rokujō lady would have been no more admirable than a witch out of Grimm. The terror and the beauty are indistinguishable, an amalgam which we may sometimes welcome and must always accept.

Defilement and the appearance of ghosts and possessing spirits are relatively frequent but still irregular happenings. The pattern of more rhythmical happenings having to do with the stages of life is remarkably similar in the *Genji* to that which persists today. Buddhism stands at a terminal point, when someone is at the end of his affairs and prepared to retire to a monastery, or at the end of life itself. Buddhist priests are called in to administer the tonsure and the vows, to pray for the desperately ill, and to preside at funerals. But when the matter has to do with new life, something more atavistic takes over. Buddhist priests are summoned to pray for safe delivery, and we are told that another of Tō no Chūjō's waif daughters, the Ōmi lady, acquired her deplorable speech patterns from a Buddhist priest who was present at her birth; but the ceremonies that follow a birth seem close to rural ceremonies today in which the infant is presented to Shinto gods and their good offices are invoked toward establishing its fragile existence.

As for nuptial ceremonies, there is little to suggest that the Buddhist clergy had much of anything to do with them, and the taking of rice in several forms establishes an affinity with the sacred rhythm of the fields. (It seems to have been thought altogether proper for a young man to be drunk at his wedding, even as his ancestors would have been drunk at a shrine festival.) In the *Genji*, as now, the time of planting and the time of the harvest are preferred for weddings, and not only, one feels, because of the clement weather. If weather were the chief consideration, the mild, sunny winter, when the honeymoon resorts can be delightful, would have a great deal to recommend it; but that is a time of agronomic dormancy.

Genji's son Yūgiri is finally permitted to marry in the thirty-third chapter, in which Buddhism is almost nowhere and Shinto is everywhere. The chapter stands at a climactic point, midway through the enormous tale, when the younger generation has been seen through its turbulent years and the time is approaching for the older generation to depart the scene. There is mention at the beginning of the chapter of Buddhist services in memory of a generation already departed, that of Genji's parents. The only other detail explicitly Buddhist is a reference to observances on the birthday of the historic Buddha. With the wisteria in fine bloom, Yūgiri has a bride bestowed upon him. As spring moves into summer Genji and Murasaki go off to enjoy the Kamo Festival, and Genji reminisces upon that earlier Kamo Festival in which the most subtle and difficult woman in his life, the Rokujō lady, was so grievously affronted. In the fullness of early summer the affairs of Genji's only daughter are put in triumphant order. She is sent to court. Her mother gives silent thanks to the Shinto god or gods of Sumiyoshi, whose especial protection the girl's maternal grandfather invoked at her birth. Toward the end of the chapter, Yūgiri is seen in residence with his bride at the house where Genji made Murasaki his bride, and, finally, Genji's own career comes to a triumphant climax when the emperor and the only living ex-emperor pay ceremonial visits. The chapter comes at the end of the happiest section of the tale, a cycle of a dozen chapters following upon Genji's removal to a splendid new mansion at Rokujō. Another pattern asks to be detected: Buddhism has on the whole a rather melancholy cast to it, and joyous affairs tend to be Shinto to the extent that they are religious at all.

People with petitions can take them to either Shinto or Buddhist deities, indiscriminately, it almost seems. Sometimes both are called upon in the same breath. In the great storm that sweeps over Genji's place of exile all manner of foreign and native gods are invoked. When Tamakazura, having returned to the capital from the far provinces, is casting about for a way to claim her birthright, her advisers send her off to seek the help first of a Shinto deity and then a Buddhist. It is the latter who proves effective, but in that fact is to be seen nothing denigratory of Shinto deities. Sometimes one thing works and sometimes another, and it is not prudent or realistic, not, indeed, well mannered, to turn from any of the gods, native or foreign.

But perhaps the services of the gods are not, after all, sought quite indiscriminately. There seems to be another pattern, which does not lend itself very well to precise statement or definition. At crises of an intensely personal or private nature, such as a grave illness, Buddhist priests are called in; but when the crises have to do with family there is a strong likelihood that Shinto will be given a part in them. When at the bleakest point in his career the exiled Genji is visited by the ghost of his father, it is to the saving power of a Shinto god that he is instructed to give himself up. On the coast of Suma and Akashi that is his place of exile, the whole life of the former governor, soon to become his father-in-law, is given over to blind faith in the future of his one daughter, and it is to a Shinto deity that the future is entrusted. The supernatural force is the same in both cases: the god or gods of the Sumiyoshi Shrine in the present city of Osaka. The most elaborate episodes of joyous thanksgiving are pilgrimages to the Sumiyoshi Shrine.

Genji makes a progress to Sumiyoshi in the fourteenth chapter (and it seems more than chance that in the course of all the joy professional ladies of pleasure make their only appearance in the whole long tale). In the thirty-fifth chapter there is another grand pilgrimage to Sumiyoshi, this time because the last of the old man's hopes has come true: his granddaughter has become the mother of a prince who enjoys every prospect of one day becoming emperor. His vows have been so grand that Genji has been amused by them, in a lofty way, thinking them somewhat beyond the reach of a retired provincial governor; but there is reason in them. If the god does what is asked of him, why then of course the old man will have at his disposal resources beyond his own. Things work out even so. Genji is the grandfather of the little prince, and he arranges a thanksgiving progress to Sumiyoshi, with the ex-governor's wife as an honored guest. The old man cannot be so honored himself. He has given himself over to Buddhist asceticism, for lingering worldly ties would hinder his pursuit of salvation. A pattern which is in general rather vague and blurred is here rather clear: the destinies of the family have been entrusted to a Shinto deity, but for personal salvation the old man has turned to Buddhism, as does everyone in the tale who cares to be saved. Probably no one ever thought of it in quite those bifurcated terms. There were feelings which tended in those directions, and an instinct which urged what seemed a harmonious ordering of things.

A similar bifurcation governs holiday observances. Here it becomes somewhat difficult to decide what is religious and what is not. There is probably no other work of fiction in which nature is so constantly present. "Nature worship" is so vague an expression that one hesitates to use it, and yet there are grounds for thinking that this constant awareness of nature approaches an animistic kind of worship. It has been noted that the presence of Buddhism is little felt in the happiest part of the tale, the dozen or so chapters leading to the jubilee when Genji turns forty. Many interesting and amusing and sometimes poignantly sad things happen to the second generation, whose difficult years are being seen to a conclusion and whose affairs are being put in order; but the passing seasons are as much its real matter as any of the incidents. Genji moves into his splendid new Rokujō mansion in the twenty-first chapter. In the next chapter Tamakazura is brought back from Kyushu and takes up residence at Rokujō, where Genji's principal ladies have preceded her. There follows a review of the Rokujō seasons, from early spring to winter. Then we have the high points of the next year, and, with the weddings of Genji's children and the jubilee, the book moves into a new phase. When it is over and the older generation has departed or is making ready to depart, there is another review of the seasons, quick and muted, in the last chapter in which Genji figures. It occupies only a tenth as many pages as the earlier one, and the only real matter, besides the shifts of nature, is Genji's grief. The effect is of primordial cycles falling back into silence, almost of a twilight of the gods, as if the Eight Million were succumbing to forces more powerful than they.

It may be that these are not religious matters, although so steady a gaze at nature has about it the feel of a religious vigil, and although rather similar tendencies are commonly thought to be religious when (as in Zen) they are described not in implicit and atavistic terms but rather in explicit and Buddhist ones.

When holiday observances are without doubt religious, some are more private than others, and again the private ones tend to be Buddhist. Of these, the greater ones center upon the Lotus Sutra. Other Buddhist texts are mentioned from time to time, but the preeminence of the Lotus Sutra is clear. A solemn reading of the Lotus Sutra was the Buddhist equivalent of a jubilee mass or of a requiem mass—or rather a succession of masses, for it is about as long as the New Testament and a complete reading requires several days. Very detailed planning and very lavish spending went into a grand reading, and all the subtleties and complexities of good taste, which was in the Heian period taken to scarcely bearable heights, were on display.

Sometimes the occasion was a happy one. In the fourteenth chapter, upon his return from exile, Genji commissions a reading which is ostensibly in memory of his father but which carries strong overtones of thanksgiving. In the fifty-second chapter, when the lotuses are at their finest, the empress commissions a joyous reading of the Lotus Sutra. It is the last flutter of joy before the whole vast story comes to a somber, muted end. And sometimes the occasion is sad. In the tenth chapter, in which gloom gathers with the abdication of Genji's father and the approach of Genji's exile, the first of Genji's great loves, Fujitsubo, commissions a reading the ostensible purpose of which is again memorial, but the real purpose of which is to announce her withdrawal from the world. The first conspicuous act of the Third Princess, Genji's young wife, a score or so chapters later when she repents of her sinful ways and becomes a nun, is to have a reading of the Lotus Sutra. It is perhaps of all the readings the one that strikes the best note, not too happy and not too sad, quietly, serenely melancholy. It occupies a crucial place in the last chapters in which Genji figures. The happy and even comical alternates with the sad; the princess's sutra reading introduces a chapter of quiet melancholy which precedes a happy chapter and the saddest of all, the fortieth, in which Murasaki dies. In that same fortieth chapter is the saddest reading of all. Murasaki knows that she is dying and commissions a reading of the Lotus Sutra. She shows the world for the last time what a gifted and sensitive lady she is, and the world, knowing as well as she the significance of the occasion, comes to take its leave.

Whether happy or unhappy, readings of the Lotus Sutra, like other Buddhist observances, tend to be private affairs. Sometimes they are rather public in that everyone longs to be invited and everyone who is invited attends. Genji's sutra reading after his return from exile and the empress's when the lotuses are in bloom are the talk of the court and the whole court assembles. Yet they are private affairs in the sense of being arranged for someone's private purposes, and they take place at home. Great holiday affairs which are of a public nature and which take place outside the house are Shinto. The greatest are the Kamo Festival in late spring and the observances attendant upon the beginning of a new reign.

There is a most wonderful sequence of events reaching through two longish chapters just before Genji's departure for exile. A number of strands are brought together, and at the center, like the tree that supports the vine, is Shinto. In the ninth chapter there is a Kamo Festival and the incident that sets the Rokujō lady's anger to burning out of control. The festive mood is evoked with marvelous skill, and because of it the wound is more telling. In all the happenings of a glorious spring day there is scarcely a touch of the imported religion. The tribes have gathered to honor the gods they have had from the beginning.

In the same chapter Genji's father the emperor abdicates, and the most immediate matters that concern his successor, Genji's half brother, have to do with further propitiation of the old gods. He must send off near relatives to be high priestesses at Kamo and Ise. The lovely, contrary presence of the Rokujō lady continues to demand our attention and Genji's. Her daughter, first cousin to the new emperor, is to be high priestess of Ise, chief handmaiden to the grand ancestress of her clan, the Sun Goddess. In the ninth chapter are the diurnal color and joy of the Kamo Festival. In the tenth, as the Rokujō lady and her daughter prepare to depart for Ise, the mood is nocturnal. Ancestral mysteries are being celebrated. Genji visits the temporary shrine where the daughter is making ready for her journey and investiture. The scene is one of austere, occult beauty.

> The autumn flowers were gone and insects hummed in the wintry tangles. A wind whistling through the pines brought snatches of music to most wondrous effect, though so distant that he could not tell what was being played. . . . A low wattle fence, scarcely more than a suggestion of an enclosure, surrounded a complex of board-roofed buildings, as rough and insubstantial as temporary shelters.
>
> The shrine gates, of unfinished logs, had a grand and awesome dignity for all their simplicity, and the somewhat forbidding austerity of the place was accentuated by clusters of priests. . . . The fire lodge glowed faintly. It was all in all a lonely, quiet place, and here, away from the world, a lady already deep in sorrow had passed these weeks and months.

The feelings of the new priestess herself and of her mother, who defies precedent by going to Ise with her, are delicately complicated. Both know what must be done, and they do it. The needs of the Sun Goddess must be seen to, and the task has been assigned to them. It is not a happy task. For a Heian lady the far corners of the earth lie just beyond the limits of the city, and for these ladies there is the added difficulty of going beyond the pale of the Good Law, Buddhism. For a time their attention must be occupied by less than the most important thing. For the daughter there is no real conflict. The thought of not fulfilling her obligation does not occur to her. For the mother there is conflict, because in going with her daughter she is in fact choosing the less easy course. Back in the city after a stay of some years at Ise, both mother and daughter are intent upon making amends for having neglected the Good Law in their absence. On her deathbed a few chapters later the Rokujō lady takes Buddhist vows and prays incessantly. An air again as of a twilight of the gods hangs over her acts. The native gods have been served even though the laws of Buddhism will eventually have their way. In the end we will all be dead, but while we and the gods are alive and active, at Ise and Kamo, their needs must be seen to.

There is another memorable Kamo Festival in the thirty-fifth chapter (the Rokujō lady returns to the city in the fourteenth), but this time the reader is not taken to see the fun. It is a roar in the distance while melancholy events take place at home. The two matters that throw dark shadows over Genji's later years have their beginnings at the same time. They are the illness of Murasaki and the infidelity of the Third Princess, which makes Genji feel that inexorable retribution is at work, punishment for having loved his own stepmother. The festival is under way and the Third Princess's seducer mopes in his rooms: "He heard the festival roar in the distance as if it were no part of his life and passed a troubled day in a tedium of his own making." Shortly afterward Murasaki has what seems to be a fatal seizure. She is taken for dead but presently revives, and Genji's grief anticipates the inconsolable grief in which we last see him. We soon learn that it is the last day of the festival, a time of wistful joy throughout the city, we may imagine, when ordinary days are about to resume. It is very delicately done, the contrast between public joy and private sorrow. There is a similar contrast in the forty-first chapter, the last in which Genji appears: sounds of the great spring and autumn festivals come in upon Genji's house of mourning. In the forty-seventh chapter the oldest Uji princess lies dying in her remote "mountain village," as it is always called, while in the city, some miles away, it is the time of the harvest festival. "The festival would be reaching its grand and noisy climax. At Uji it was a day of wild storms and winds. . . . Darkness came over an already sunless day." In all these instances Buddhism dominates the house of sadness, while the world outside is given over to the happy excitement of a Shinto festival.

The last ten chapters push events almost a quarter of a century beyond Genji's disappearance from the scene and treat of the love affairs of two young men, Niou and Kaoru, in the third generation from Genji. The Uji chapters, as they are commonly called, are much darker than the chapters that precede Genji's death. There is sorrow in the former, but there is happiness too, while in the Uji chapters there is very little happiness at all. If Buddhism tends toward melancholy all through the tale and if the religious background for happiness and excitement tends to be explicitly or implicitly Shinto, it need not be a surprise that Shinto rather disappears from the last chapters. It has its moments even so, and they are important ones. There are flickers of Shinto at the beginning and end of the Ukifune story, the muted conclusion to the whole long tale.

A delicate reference to Shinto ceremonial apprises us of Ukifune's existence and introduces the water imagery that mounts in intensity as she is driven to attempt suicide. At the end of the story, when Kaoru has succeeded in ruining her life, he tells himself that they may perhaps meet in some other life, and the spirit realm in which he postulates a meeting is not one of the Buddhist paradises but rather the Yomi of very ancient belief. There is in the thought little of the solemnity with which people who have meant a great deal to each other anticipate reunion in the same lotus garden. "Oh well, there is that other place too," he almost seems to be saying. The Land of Yomi itself seems like a temporary, but only temporary, asylum from the workings of the Good Law.

The shift of the action to Uji would probably in any event have required that there not be a great deal of Shinto. Shinto observances, being of a social and communal nature, would at Uji be the concern of classes too low for the well-born principals to note. For similar reasons there are no Maypoles in the novels of Jane Austen; and the Tokyo intellectual, though given to thinking himself the embodiment of the people's best impulses, does not participate in neighborhood shrine festivals. There is also the fact that the action at Uji is of a more constricted and private sort. All through the *Genji* the principal action takes place in the women's quarters, but the court and public affairs are there across the street, so to speak (almost literally in the earlier chapters), for people to move in and out of. But when a gentleman goes to Uji he is on vacation from public affairs, and when a princess lives there it means that the greater world has passed her by. Private observances have always tended to be Buddhist, and so, again, the eclipse of Shinto need not surprise.

There are more momentous reasons for this muffling of Shinto. The darkness and loneliness of the last chapters mean confrontation with the ultimate word, and the assumption throughout has been that the ultimate word is Buddhist. A pathetic girl becomes tragic as the world falls off about her layer by layer, and she is left alone with terrible forces. It is an awesome way for a book to end, as if we were being projected eons hence, when the incidents that have been brought forth from abstract reality must fall back again. In the meantime they have their existence, and so do the forces that brought them into being. The emergence and the falling back are what the whole grand tale has been about.

The Eight Million survived the crisis of the eighth century, when the Japanese so eagerly imported Chinese culture. Another such crisis did not come until the nineteenth century. The Middle Ages, a convenient label for the Kamakura and Muromachi periods, were a time of eager and sometimes indiscriminate foreign borrowing. Japanese art, even the best of it, seems in the Middle Ages the nearest thing to provincial, the recasting locally of what was done some time before in the great metropolitan centers. The vast collection of everything from housekeeping accounts to lyric poems known as *Gozan bungaku* ("Literature of the Five Temples") is in Chinese. Yet never is there a suggestion that, for instance, the presence of the local gods will no longer be recognized. The *Jinnōshōtōki*, probably the most respected of Shinto documents after the very earliest, also dates from the Muromachi period. Though no individual thinker set out to establish the principle of conservatism in the first place, by the Muromachi period it was so firmly established that no one would have thought of discarding it.

The nineteenth century was rather like a revamping of the seventh and eighth centuries. If in the eighth century the tradition challenged by something new was the body of naive domestic works, in the nineteenth century it was the whole Oriental tradition, accumulated over the centuries under the twin impulses to borrow and to save. Though it was a very sophisticated tradition, the problem for those who had to think what to do next must have been rather as in the eighth century: the claims of the new were next to irresistible. Why not take all of it? Why not overcome feelings of inferiority to the foreigner by becoming foreign? There were suggestions for discarding the native language and for discarding native womanhood, and beyond these it would be difficult to go. In its essentials the decision presently arrived at by the rulers of the land was similar to that reached by Genji when he sent his son off to the university: the native spirit would have at its disposal foreign techniques.

Indeed the decision was given rather extreme and ugly application, for it was made into a program, a scheme, a set of concepts. And if its purpose had been to demonstrate that those are the very things to which the Japanese spirit lends itself with the least grace, that purpose could scarcely have been realized more emphatically. As a basis for action—counseling the acquisition of new things to suit fancies or fit needs but demanding also the conservation of old things—the Japanese spirit is rather marvelous, among its more remarkable aspects being its ability to survive these challenges. When, however, the national essence is stripped of foreign accretions and made into a kind of litany, it becomes silly; and a silly litany presided over by a not very sensitive or cultivated priesthood in the form of a bureaucracy can drive away grace and beauty. "Life here is absolutely intolerable. . . . The curs are yelping," said a wise and serene Englishman, Sir George Sansom, writing to Lady Sansom from Tokyo in 1940. "I've never known anything like this atmosphere. There are no standards of behavior left."[1] It was a tragic thing, for the strength of the grand principle lies in the act and not in the thought, and when standards of behavior go there is little left.

The principle itself is still there, to have another try in another crisis. It had come so easily through the Meiji Restoration that extremes in its application had turned good into evil. To say that because of the extremes a war was lost is probably to exaggerate, for even the most benign sort of moderation would not in the circumstances have done much better; but certainly the puritanical and self-righteous victors of 1945 thought that national essence turned into litany had been responsible for the war in the first place and that it had to go. The crisis of 1945 might not, if there were a way of quantifying these things, emerge as more considerable than its predecessor in the nineteenth century, but the result was that now the grand principle could show itself only in the act. Formulations about the national essence and national polity and that sort of thing were forbidden.

One may say a quarter of a century later that the principle has survived. A great many things seemed on the way to rejection in the confused years after the surrender, and no doubt some things did get lost; but on the whole the time-honored arrangement proved remarkably workable. A place was found for all the amusing new things which the aloha-boy was bringing to the Ginza, but his activities did not mean that something had to be shoved through a trap-door to make room for his new acquisitions.

Shinto, the great demon for the puritanical victors, was of course the heart of the matter. The institutions and especially the codes were looked upon with stern disapproval, but Shinto modes of conduct survived all the same. Respect for the emperor as head of the family-state survived in most remarkable fashion. Not very impressive as a concept in any case, it is important in the form it takes in conventional behavior. The intellectual Left, the *interi*, outdid the Americans in simplistic notions of what had caused the debacle. Emperor worship must be destroyed, and the emperor proved disarmingly obliging: he composedly announced himself to be devoid of worshipful attributes. The *interi* had control of some powerful weapons, including what everyone said was the most respected and influential newspaper in the land and some of the most important magazines; but the most important thing of all, the air of silent dignity in which the emperor moves, was untouched. It did not matter very much that he had divested himself of godliness, because Shinto gods are not absolute, terrible beings but creatures whose heads emerge above the crowd. Such a creature the emperor continued to be. Nor were his ancestors much disturbed. Intellectuals demanded that fictions about the founding of the empire, which no one really believed anyway, be expunged from textbooks, but no one tried to do much about the tombs assigned somewhat fictitiously, down on the Yamato and Settsu plains, to prehistoric emperors.

It was with a pleasant sense of incongruity that one noted on the front page of the morning newspaper violent attacks on the emperor's faithful bureaucracy and was informed, on an inner page, in the most ceremonious language, that the emperor himself had discovered a new crustacean down in Sagami Bay, or that the empress, vacationing up in Nasu, had passed another milestone. A special form of

43

address was scrupulously adhered to and it showed that the grand principle yet operated: the old might have to move over just a bit to make way for the new, but it did not have to disappear.

Some aspects of Shinto as the religion of the fields were perhaps in even more danger of extinction than state Shinto and veneration of the imperial institution. Shinto festivals depend very heavily on the young, and the young, with the great fear the young have everywhere of seeming old-fashioned, did not wish to be a part of anything so unmistakably agrarian as a shrine festival. To "smell of mud," as the expression has it, was the end, the loss of the respect of one's peers. Year by year the great Shinto festivals took on more and more the look of dying embers. One and then another of the portable shrines was left behind in the storage sheds on festival day, and sometimes there was the pathetic spectacle of a portable shrine being taken on its rounds, so that the most basic forms might be perilously preserved, in a pickup truck.

Then a few years ago the tide turned. The adventuresome few came forward to bear the shrine on their shoulders, and were joined by others, and the storage sheds were empty once more on festival day. Today there are bands of young people who go from festival to festival, and fall into melancholy when other bands have preceded them and there are not enough portable shrines to go around. It may be that this is a symptom of a dangerous nationalist revival. Many think so. The point can be made even so: Shinto as the animistic religion of the farms is doing very well these days in the large cities.

Out in the country it has never gone into eclipse. Back against almost any range of hills, where the populace lived before venturing out onto the plains, there is certain to be a big shrine or two, very ancient, and still very prosperous. The prosperity of Buddhist temples is usually no mystery: it comes from cemeteries, funerals, and tourists, or some combination of the three. Tourists also contribute very heavily to some of the grander Shinto shrines. But there are Shinto shrines neither mentioned in any tourist guide nor included in any of the economy routes of the National Railways, and these are shrines which teem with life and are a nightless din of new construction.

There is for instance the Kobu Jinja in the hills a few miles south of Nikkō, which one comes upon by accident, having been made aware of its existence by none of the travel literature. It has public rooms which, given the dim lights and the low ceilings, seem as vast as dirigible hangars. The matter of its budget would perhaps be mysterious except for the fact that only one source of income seems at all likely: contributions from the crowds by which it is overrun. They do not have the look of sightseers, and common sense would proclaim that they could not be, for the Japanese are uncompromising in their insistence that for a sight to be a sight it must be designated as such by the accepted authorities. If no authority has even deigned to notice the existence of this shrine, the visitors must be worshipers, a congregation assembled from many miles around, people who wish to ask something of a god, or are taking out a kind of insurance by showing their respect—or are merely doing what they have always done, not really thinking about it in these terms at all. There are no forced exactions, and yet the evidences of prosperity are everywhere, and huge. They all must come from voluntary contributions the only reason for which can be certain feelings of respect for a very old god and a very old way of doing things.

We have all learned, and learned it well, that the Japanese are not a religious people. It is one of the statements that are made early in any introductory course on Japan, and it is one of the statements the Japanese are always making about themselves. At the very least it can be said, however, that Shinto has shown most extraordinary powers of survival through the centuries and that it seems to have survived the crisis of the last decades, too, so sturdily that the prediction implicit in the last chapters of *The Tale of Genji* seems to have been wrong in both its parts: the Eight Million are cheerful and well, and the Good Law is in a sad and perhaps fatal decline. Where traces of Buddhist vigor remain they are in the encapsulations of the Sōka Gakkai, which all along have glorified action and which have not given much thought to the niceties of the Good Law.

Definitions of the word "religious" have a way of working against the Eight Million. To toss a coin in the direction of a shrine is not to be religious, it is to take out a kind of superstitious insurance. So also is to hang a votive picture before a shrine in hopes of passing a university entrance examination. If there were a parade of students in and out of St. Patrick's Cathedral seeking divine help in their efforts to be admitted to Columbia, it would be hailed as a religious revival. The equivalent in a primitive society—the offering of images, let us say, for the taking of handsomer enemy heads—would unquestioningly be accepted as religious. The trouble is that in an "advanced" society it is expected that the gods be lawgivers. The Eight Million are rather simple beings from whom the giving of law is about the last thing that can be expected, and so it is merely superstitious to make obeisance to them or to ask their help. A great many of them do not even have names that anyone has heard of. Often when they do, their chief claim to divinity is in being dead. They may have done eminent things while they lived, and now they are out of it all, free of petty, everyday concerns, and therefore prepared to turn the whole of their attention to helping us into the schools of our choice. When the god has no achievements at all to his credit and no career about which gospels may be written, then he need not be the creator of a mountain or the revealer of truths about that mountain, but rather the mountain itself.

This last of course is animism. When animistic tendencies survive in the modern world it is very difficult indeed to separate the religious from the secular. It seems unfair, in any event, that crediting things with having souls, as the animist does, is merely superstitious, when meditating upon the illusory nature of those things, as the Buddhist does, is religious.

If the attitudes toward nature evident in a Zen garden are to be thought religious, and they do seem to be commonly so thought, then one is tempted to describe a modern cherry-blossom party as of a vaguely religious nature. Among its chief characteristics is that the object of worship is, like most of the outward manifestations of Shinto, reticent. It sometimes shows itself fleetingly, and sometimes not at all. A gale may sweep the blossoms away the night before Cherry Sunday; but that does not matter. The crowds gather anyway, and show no sign of disappointment. They gather for a rite of spring, and the cherry blossoms have but set the date. They gather to mix with the Eight Million, who are being companionable again after the unfriendliness of winter. There have recently been attempts to show that the cult of the cherry blossom is just another importation from China, but they are not convincing. Cherry Sunday, like Easter Sunday, comes but once a year, when the sap is rising. Nature does not permit the cherry blossom more than one Sunday a year, and so provides the perfect occasion, ephemeral and unique, for a rite of spring.

There is a similar blurring of the distinctions between the religious and the secular in matters having to do with the family. Although the tolerant nature of Shinto is among the common explanations for the success of Buddhism in Japan and the symbiosis that has endured through the centuries, the muteness of Shinto is a more probable explanation. At heart Shinto is, if not intolerant, certainly very exclusive. It venerates the most exclusive of institutions, the family, and makes of it a mystical assemblage with divine origins. One sees blue-eyed, black-robed Buddhist priests collecting alms in Asakusa or conducting peace demonstrations in Hibiya and one does not think more than a couple of times about them; but somehow a blue-eyed, white-robed Shinto priest is very hard to imagine, and that is because the Shinto priest presides over a congregation whose credentials are acquired by birth and in no other way. One tries to think what it is in the Japanese that resists conversion to Christianity, and the Good Law of Buddhism somehow does not provide much of an answer. In speculation upon what it was that made the leader of the land, four centuries ago, suddenly turn with implacable hostility upon Christianity, the claims of the Good Law again seem beside the point. It may be that the resistance and the hostility are somehow related to the cohesiveness of the Japanese industrial and trading company that is the marvel of the "advanced" world, and that it is among the things that Shinto is mutely about.

As it is with what the Japanese resist, so too is it with what they turn to. When a year or two ago the novelist Setouchi Harumi shaved her raven locks and told the world that she had become a Buddhist nun, something did not seem quite right. One would not wish to assign unworthy or less than pristine motives, nor would one wish to accuse her of prevarication when she described her spiritual liberation to all the reporters. The trouble was that it just did not, somehow, seem the sort of thing that a Japanese lady with advanced views is likely to do. Japanese ladies become Buddhist nuns for reasons of family or duty, most commonly a combination of the two, but the intensely personal sort of conversion that Miss Setouchi professed to have had went out a long time ago. Curiously, it would have been more fitting if she had become a Catholic nun, submitting to the religious community as a sort of family surrogate—a different thing from entering a nunnery, as ladies from the old court aristocracy are still known to do, because they have accepted the priorities assigned by the natural family.

Miss Setouchi is said to have been strongly influenced by another novelist, Kon Tōkō, who is a Buddhist priest, and whose vocation—like hers—seems not quite right. Integrity is wanting, in the sense of true commitment—of *shutaisei*. Kon makes a great thing of rejecting puritanism and of being a carnal sort of priest, and in the end seems to protest too much. It is one thing to do as Shinran did, to make a place in religion for the terrible and beautiful urgings of the flesh, and another to go rutting about town in priestly garb as if with intent to shock. The difficulty in both cases, Miss Setouchi's and Mr. Kon's, is that there are certain marks of affectation. The deed was done, undeniably, but the heart did not quite seem to be in it.

When a belief in the occult and the spirit world is not Buddhist, it has a way of seeming more genuine. I am convinced that Kawabata Yasunari believed in ghosts. He accepted them, admitted their presence without comment, as he admitted that of his neighbors. Kobayashi Hideo once remarked upon the uncommon "receptivity" of his great benefactor, Kikuchi Kan, and Kikuchi's faculty of admitting things without comment or interpretation or other intellectual mediation. On a lecture trip to Hokkaido, said Kobayashi,[2] Kikuchi was visited at his inn by a lady ghost. "He told of the incident without elaboration, quite as if to tell of it were a tiresome duty." Somehow the story has the feel of Kawabata about it. With Kawabata too, ghosts and travel went together. There is a strange Kawabata story in which a weird visitor describes a meeting on a journey that never took place. The turn of the screw is that we never quite learn whether or not she is a ghost, but a most ghostly aspect hangs over both visitor and journey, and the story seems autobiographical. Once when we were traveling together Kawabata remarked at breakfast upon having "seen" a writer whom we had both known, dead some years. Not wishing to seem incredulous or to make a great thing of a remark striking for its casualness, I did not ask what he meant, but the suggestion was certainly very strong that he had seen a ghost in the night. "Seen" was the verb he used, and not "dreamed." He never told me, as he seems to have told others, of being visited by Mishima after Mishima's death, but I am sure that there would have been not the smallest mark of affectation in remarks he might have made on the subject.

To the question so often asked about the "emperor worship" of

Mishima's last years, the answer must be that it responded to very deep needs. He did not worship the emperor regnant, a sweet old man whom it would be hard for anyone, however hard he tried, to worship, and whose disavowal of godhead rings true because he looks so very ungodlike. Mishima did, however, have a very strong sense of the community at the head of which the emperor stands. One must be aware of that community if his suicide is not to be dismissed as an aberration. It is a very old community and it is very Japanese. The bond which Mishima felt resembles the sense of clan felt by members of the Fujiwara family in *The Tale of Genji*. Genji, a non-member, accepted its claims, as we must accept the claims of Mishima's "emperor worship," properly understood.

The problem of whether or not the Japanese are religious becomes to a very great extent a matter of definition, complicated by the impossibility of distinguishing the religious from the merely superstitious, and by the survival of modes of behavior which, whatever they may be now, once had in them strong elements of the ritual and the occult. The sense of family is among them, and so is a faculty for transferring family attitudes to other social units and to the nation itself. This last distinguishes the Japanese from other people who have been under the influence of Confucius and suggests the survival of something pre-Confucian. One understands the displeasure of Chairman Mao with Confucius, because in China the family has provided the ultimate sanctions and so become an obstacle to wider endeavors. In Korea the family is the heart of factionalism, and factionalism was perhaps the chief reason for the cataleptic reaction of the Koreans to the Western challenge a century and more ago. The Japanese have been remarkable for their ability to transfer and sublimate family relationships.

The rites on Cherry Sunday are similarly pre-Confucian, and so is the bathhouse as community center. The Japanese do go on scrubbing most vigorously. A strong reluctance to send forth a body odor was prevalent long before the cult of the deodorant was imported from the West. There is a single Japanese word covering the concept and phenomenon of armpit odor. Standard English has not succeeded in being so concise, although the big dictionary does offer "B.O." as an equivalent; and where there is a word there is a concern.

In Mishima's last novel disparaging thoughts about Japanese cleanliness are put in the head of a sour old man: "But in Japan, beauty, tradition, poetry had none of them been touched by the soiled hand of sanctity. Those who touched them and in the end strangled them were quite devoid of sanctity. They all had the same hands, vigorously scoured with soap."[3]

Mishima may have been somewhat distraught when he wrote the passage, for he was even then getting ready to kill himself. Yet he must have realized, whether or not he was prepared to admit that soap too can be sacred, that he was contradicting a very large part of his last tetralogy—and denying as well the final consummation for which he was preparing. The cult of purity is at the very heart of the second volume, *Runaway Horses*, in which Mishima enacts his own suicide. The hero has an obsession with purity that comes to seem insane and monstrous, and makes the book a failure precisely because Mishima himself so obviously loved it. He was probably closer to this last hero than to any of the others, and for that character cleanliness, on several levels, was not next to godliness, it *was* godliness.

These several strains may or may not be religious, but they are very old, and in their survival is evidence of a very strong conservatism. If the Good Law of Buddhism, on the other hand, is among the things that have been allowed to fall into a decline, it may be because the Good Law has had too much to say about itself. Buddhist writ gives an impression of enormous volubility, of an inexhaustible urge to say everything several times over. Shinto writ, such as it is, suggests a kind of inarticulateness. There are anecdotes for several occasions, and that is all, and the abstractable content tends to be concerned with the least articulate of virtues, loyalty. Shinto has taken on many Buddhist accretions over the centuries. There are heavily decorated Shinto shrines, and there is anthropomorphic art, Shinto not having shared the Judaic and Mohammedan horror of the graven image. Most Shinto sculpture derives from the more realistic strains of Buddhist sculpture, and some of it seems to have an almost irreligious bent, as if to demonstrate that the gods are even such as we, and that the cheerful innocent is welcomed more warmly into their service than the heavy-headed intellectual. Much of the cleanness of Shinto today, girls in white kimonos and scarlet skirts sweeping across sand-strewn courtyards, is a result of the Meiji determination to cleanse the native essence of foreign accretions. If Buddhism was a great clutter of gold and brocade, all heavy with incense, then the simple thing for Shinto would be to have a lot of simplicity and fresh air. Yet simplicity has always been the distinguishing mark of Shinto. When all the trappings of Buddhism were brought in, simplicity was the essential native quality that was not thrown away to make room for them. The sanctuaries of Shinto have not departed very far from the animistic origins of the religion. The Ise Shrine is an awesome and worshipful place, but what it is for the most part is a grove of venerable trees. Removed from its grove, the Inner Shrine would look rather like a container waiting to be loaded at a railway siding.

Of Japanese understatement in art too much has already been said by too many people. The fact that the aesthetics of restraint received their most subtle expression in the Middle Ages is not to be denied, but because of it continental influences are too easily ascribed. The Middle Ages were a time of vigorous borrowing from the continent, and in religious matters Zen was perhaps the most conspicuous borrowing. To Zen is given credit for the understatement that goes by the name *shibui*. There were similarly intuitive and meditative strains in earlier Buddhist schools, however, and the fact that Shinto held its place against Buddhism by appealing to the simplifying urge is the best explanation for Japanese friendliness to Zen, when presently it came along. The crudeness of the medieval tea bowl informs us, under the influence of Zen, that there is eternal verity in the clod of earth from which it was fashioned, and so does the *torii*, the "bird-perch" of unfinished wood, at the entrance to the Rokujō lady's shrine.

Because of the inability or reluctance of the Eight Million to speak up and tell us what they are about and to lay down the law, the Japanese reticence in literary and artistic matters is easily established, and in a world rather short on simplicities, this becomes the most cherished thing about the Japanese. But a noisy exuberance is just as much a part of the tradition. Overstatement is there along with understatement. If there is art in which the blank spaces apparently say as much as the painted spaces, there is also art which seems always to be running out of space, demanding more for the swelling richness of its colors. If there is the Nō drama interposing realms of silence between the act and its representation, there is also the Kabuki theater wringing everything out of the act and abhorring silence. Over Nō hangs an air of great austerity, as if the actors

51

were on leave from some impossibly ascetic monastery and re-produced like ferns. Over Kabuki hangs an air of great indulgence and permissiveness, as if the actors and musicians (especially, somehow, the latter) might be prepared to arrange almost anything for a fee. The great tradition may be silent and pure, but it is also noisy and dirty. It is the noise and the dirt that one sometimes wants to talk about when everyone else has been talking about the silent beauty. The dirt and the cleanness, the noise and the silence, are not antithetical but the face and reverse of the ancient lack of faith in concepts. The Good Law made the mistake of trying to tell us precisely what it meant. Neither silence nor all-destroying noise makes that mistake. The richness of the Japanese language in ono-matopoeia is here to the point. Onomatopes are the most immediate and least conceptual of words, and incidentally among the words that most stubbornly defy translation. The Japanese reputation for humorlessness may derive in some measure from the fact that so much of their humor is onomatopoetic and therefore untranslatable.

In clean sanctuaries at Ise and in the Imperial Palace, the grand mysteries of Shinto are celebrated in the dead of night, cleanness itself; but a shrine festival in a village or one of the many villages that make up the great cities is a kind of deification of noise and good, clean dirt. It is an invitation to get rid of those encumbering clothes and a few layers of detergent cleanness as well and to slosh naked through the mire. The symbolic lotus has been reversed. In Buddhist lore it signifies the emergence of the blossom from the mire. In a Shinto festival the direction is downward, back into the clean earth. The great Kabuki actor Kanzaburō is said to be fond of telling janitors to desist from their sweeping. Kabuki does best, he holds, on dirty floors. A good deal of Japanese literature has liked dirt too. The short fiction of the elegant Heian period is well supplied with literal and figurative dirt, and even The Tale of Genji has a ribald strain. The Iris Festival, the symbols of which continue to be masculine even though it has been an epicene Children's Day since the Second World War, provides the occasion for poetry of a distinctly phallic nature. When a mollusk enters a poem the intent is very likely to be thecal.

The dirty side of Kawabata was almost certainly overlooked by the Swedish Academy, and those strictures against soap suggest how important the dirty side of the Japanese tradition was to Mishima. "We find the pure Japanese only in the slums and in the underworld," says the sour old man in the last novel, "and we may expect them to be more and more narrowly circumscribed as time goes by. The poison known as the pure Japanese is thinning, changing to a potion acceptable to everyone."[4] Some pages earlier there are these thoughts in the mind of the same character, about the dilettantism of an aging lady friend: "However assiduously Keiko might refine her knowledge, it was not up to plumbing the darkness where stretched the deepest roots of the Japanese. The dark blood springs that had agitated Isao Iinuma were far away. Honda called Keiko's store of Japanese culture a freezer full of vegetables."[5] Iinuma is the young political assassin of the second volume. To point out that Iinuma means "rice swamp" may be to make the common critical mistake of finding great significance in the random and accidental, yet Mishima would probably have approved of the accident, if accident it was. Here too is the reversal of the lotus image, the roots reaching down into the darkness, and not the blossom emerging from the mire. Novelists are very slippery people, constantly evading responsibility for the thoughts and acts of their characters; but if ever Mishima seems honestly committed it is when he is describing Iinuma's violent behavior—those dark blood springs—and the ruminations of the old man turned nostalgically upon the days before all the antitoxins and cleansers had been put to work.

For Nagai Kafū, who made his literary debut at the turn of the century, the whole business of being Japanese was highly sensual. He roamed the slums and the pleasure quarters of Tokyo to find the culture of the Edo townsman. It was an anti-Confucian culture. Inarticulately if sometimes rather noisily in rebellion against the stiff code of the military aristocracy, it made almost a religion of a sad eroticism, and its hagiography was in stories of love suicide. The wail of the Shinnai ballad to the sometimes angry and sometimes disconsolate plunking of a samisen was the native voice emerging from the sanctuaries it had made for itself. The Kabuki there on the edge of town, sharing its music with the pleasure quarters, was one of them. A delicate air of eroticism and disreputability still invests Kabuki; hence the vague feeling one has that the musicians may be moonlighting in all manner of interesting ways. In one of Kafū's masterpieces an ambitious mother refuses to let her son become a samisen musician. It may seem to you and me a harmless enough ambition, but the mother knows where she must take a stand. She is a representative of the neo-Confucians, he of the native sensualists. "In those days," said Kafū on another occasion, "you never saw artisans reading newspapers on streetcars, and socialist propaganda had not yet reached the back streets of Fukagawa. . . . All of one's neighbors had been born in this run-down part of Tokyo, and all of them lived secure in a world of superstition and ancient customs."[6]

If the Edo townsman could work himself into the desperate tantrums of Shinnai balladry, there was much in his tradition in which a cheerful pragmatism was dominant. Most art forms have their more contorted flights—even Mozart sometimes agonizes— and then, still themselves, they come back down again. The best of Edo erotic art has a kind of matter-of-fact realism which seems to announce that the important thing is to do without self-reflection and self-consciousness. The Edo graphic eroticism best known outside the country comes from very late in the period and resorts to grotesque distortion. It was a bad time for Japanese culture in general, when a withdrawal from reality was among the marks of decay. The greatest erotic works of the seventeenth and eighteenth centuries are notable for an unstrained and unstriving kind of realism. Here is this garden, the artist seems to be saying, and here are these young people, and just see, if you will, what they are doing (the most natural thing in the world). In a garden or pastoral setting is an elegant couple whose dress suggests a most exquisite sense of color, and in the composition as a whole there is an undeniable sort of elegance. The finest Japanese erotic prints can be obvious and open imitations of Chinese originals, and yet something other than the dress reveals their origins unmistakably. In seeking to characterize the difference, one is almost tempted to suggest the absence of Confucianism from the Japanese product. It may seem odd to suggest that there can be Confucian content in an erotic work, but it does seem to be so. Chinese erotica seem unfleshly, and coldly intent on making a point and perhaps teaching a lesson of sorts. In a good Japanese print the moment is sufficient unto itself. There is neither apology nor edification.

Nagai Kafū almost went to jail once when the police were having a spasm of righteousness. He wrote a little story in elegant literary language, sprinkled with onomatopoeia, about stamina and various ways of putting it to the test. An unauthorized edition fell into the hands of the police, who affected displeasure. The story has refused to disappear, although it has never made its way into an edition of his collected works. A recent reprint displeased the public prosecutors, who took the publisher to court. Perhaps what it shows more than anything is how intimately good pornography is of its time and place, and in so being gives the time and place identity. I once had a try at translating it, and very soon gave up. The difficulty was not with the elegant literary language, which would have had to go in any event, there being no equivalent in English save perhaps the unreal rhythms of the King James Bible. It was with the vocabulary. The original contained no words nominal or adverbial that seemed either coarse or unnatural. There were words, to be sure, which asked for a certain tolerance, but there were none the very presence of which flung the action into the gutter. Kafū was doing what the Ukiyoe artist had done, adding to the list of pleasures, and the vocabulary thereof, in a rather matter-of-fact fashion. It could not be done in English; the equivalent vocabulary jumps madly between the coarse and the unnatural. Hence the great pity: the Japanese would be very good, if the police would only let them, at demonstrating that standards other than explicitness can be applied in deciding which wares are acceptable.

It is nothing very new, but it is sad all the same, that the institutions charged with preserving the social fabric should keep tearing holes in it. In the Tokugawa period the Confucian orthodoxy drove the Japanese spirit—which in the Heian period was so calmly in charge of things—into the pleasure quarters, and today the police permit the flourishing of a coarse and vulgar foreign product but not the native product in which the plebeian Edo tradition survives. Perhaps it survives even now, somewhere, and waits to come forth again. Writers much younger than Nagai Kafū, among them Mishima Yukio, have been credited on good authority with commendable erotic works. The old tradition survived for a very long time, that new things may come but old things need not go; and the conservatism which is its ground yet survives.

The tradition has its symbols. The geisha, the cherry blossom, and Mt. Fuji are the ones that appear all in a row when the Japanese are seeking objective correlatives for their Japaneseness or taking exception to the ones which foreigners have found. Two of the three seem rather obvious and wanting in overtones. The geisha, calling up a wide range of gracefully sensual happenings if she is properly understood, is complex and suggestive, on the whole a rather adequate symbol. But an even better symbol comes to mind, the drum. Sometimes banging away madly, enjoining festive abandon, and sometimes enjoining silence as one of the Eight Million is about to descend, it has in it both sides of the ancient, perdurable tradition.

(1975)

1. Katherine Sansom, *Sir George Sansom and Japan*, Tallahassee, Florida, 1972: 114, 115.

2. *Collected Works*, Tokyo, 1955–57, IV: 43–44.

3. *The Decay of the Angel*, New York, 1974: 57.

4. *Ibid*: 110.

5. *Ibid*: 49.

6. *Collected Works*, Tokyo, 1948–53, XIV: 252–53.

REVIEW: *MADLY SINGING IN THE MOUNTAINS*

The subtitle of the volume under review tells us exactly what it is: an appreciation and anthology of Arthur Waley. All of the seventeen persons who contribute appreciations, including the editor, Professor Ivan Morris, seem to have known Arthur Waley personally, and most of the contributions were either written especially for the book or offered to the editor for first publication. The anthology, which, with appendices and introductory materials, fills some three-quarters of the book, is for the most part an assembly of old acquaintances it is nice to have had assembled, but it also includes some hitherto unpublished material: a ballad from Tun-huang, a poem by Kublai Khan, an autobiographical sketch by Akutagawa, and excerpts from Waley's remarks on Dr. Morris's *World of the Shining Prince*.

Few readers will like every small detail in the book. Some of the contributors of appreciations tend to gush a bit: Edith Sitwell, for instance, when she becomes all tinklingly tea-table British and says to Waley, "I *can't* dream how you do it." A few specimens of Waley's own writing fail to support the contention implicit in so much of the first section that Waley was a man of unerring taste. I suppose what bothered most, by its archness, was his translation of "A Chinaman's Description of Brighton in 1877."

But since it is always and only in the heart of the reviewer that the ideal anthology exists, the anthology in which he finds little of the exceptionable is a good anthology, and this is such a one. The appreciators also succeed, most of them, in their assigned task, to demonstrate that Waley was an admirable and widely admired man.

And indeed he was a most extraordinary man. The words "poet" and "genius" may appear so frequently in the appreciations as to become a bit monotonous and perhaps somewhat mannered. (On one page Mrs. Waley uses the word "genius" three times in the space of eight lines, juxtaposing it with an unfortunate play on "genes" that makes it stand out the more emphatically.)

But so be it. That Waley wrote damned well, to put the matter less ethereally, is not to be denied, and it is quite proper that appreciator after appreciator should say so, and if each of them in turn wishes to use the word "poet" in his testimonial, that is fine too. And "genius": it is an evasive word, but it must have a great deal to do with originality, and originality in turn must contain a strong element of courage, a willingness to venture where no one has been before. What really sets Waley apart, makes him so extraordinary that we will not see the likes of him again, is what set Columbus and Newton apart: he did it first, and in a manner that required a most uncommon daring. Professor Donald Keene in a sense exaggerates when he says that Waley was "our only predecessor," in view of the fact that Poundians are not Waleyites, and there are signs that the Poundians are the fashionable ones these days in translation of poetry. But there is justice in the remark all the same. Waley was the man who ventured into the wilderness, and however hard the rest of us may work, there is one thing we cannot do, make it a wilderness again.

So, blessed be appreciators and editors of appreciations, and perhaps a most particular benediction should go to Dr. Carmen Blacker, who is first among them by virtue of having a name that begins with a *b*, but might also be first by virtue of having brought into her little essay a most affecting sort of elegiac lyricism.

And now, our justification being the fact that Waley was such an extraordinary man, and that we have his own precedent as a writer of reviews, as exemplified by the posthumous one in this anthology, let us move on to matters not strictly speaking a proper part of a review at all. Let us talk not about the book Dr. Morris has given us, but about several other books that he or someone else ought to give us some day.

Other reviewers have remarked upon how much one learns about Waley from this book. I hope I will not sound ungrateful when I say that for me the striking thing is the number of interesting matters that keep dodging out of sight. We come away wanting to know a great deal more about the man as a man, and about how he worked. Perhaps he was a poet; but then what is a poet? Professor Jacques Barzun, on the publicity flyer distributed with the book, tells us that Professor Morris is "another scholar-poet," whereas Professor Jonathan Spence, writing in the *New York Times Book Review*, informs us from the loftier vantage point of the historian that we are none of us post-Waleyites poets. Waley himself seems to have thought that Whitman was not a poet. Perhaps my most vivid memory from my Columbia days is of being told by Professor Lionel Trilling that anyone who fails to see the poetry in Whitman's "I am the man, I suffer'd, I was there" simply does not know what poetry is. So there we are. We come away warm with the assurance that Waley was a poet, but with a feeling too that we have not acquired great knowledge thereby.

We come away wishing to know more about the man as a man. It may be base of us, but we do wish to know all about extraordinary men. We wish to know more about Henry James's unfortunate accident, and exactly how Wordsworth and Dorothy spent those long northern evenings. We wish to know about Waley's curious domestic life, with Miss de Zoete, evidently for years Mrs. Waley in all but name, dying upstairs while Mrs. Robinson, soon to become Mrs. Waley, manages the pantry below. It is all somehow reminiscent of Thurber's first Mrs. Harris and *present* Mrs. Harris, and just when we hope most for enlightenment the collection before us tends to take on a sort of clubbish propriety. ("For though no one speaks of it, every one knows," to borrow the words of another fine poet, Edward Lear.)

And it would be good to have a little professional advice about the queer bundle of complexes Waley seems to have been. Not a great deal emerges here, and what does tends to be rather contradictory. Thus the devastatingly witty Waley does not quite come across. When Georgia Sitwell asks whether Waley would not think it fun to have a try at a musical comedy and Waley replies, "No," presumably we are supposed to be amused; but something is missing, something does not come across.

As for Waley's celebrated erudition, there can be no doubt that he was a most learned man, the breadth of his erudition being further testimony to his bravery; but the displays of it to which we are granted audience do not dazzle so much as disconcert. When Waley tells Dr. Blacker that he knows of no instances of ambiguity in Japanese, we suspect that he is fibbing; and when he begins a conversation with a remark on the use of the verb "to say" in the *Tao tê ching*, we sense the very antithesis of the urbanity that is supposed to be so typical of Waley. He seems rather like the bridegroom in *Edo kobanashi* groping desperately for something to say to his new father-in-law.

One wants to know more, because he did such uncommon things in every sense of the word. If it is proper that his friends should honor him, it is perhaps natural that we who were not among them should come away from the testimonial dinner feeling dissatisfied, out of it, ever so gently snubbed. "Oh, you know Arthur!" one can hear them saying after having Mrs. Sitwell's account of her own delicious little snub. But of course we the outsiders did not know him.

With his work it is the same. How did he do it? What were his principles? The last question may seem to be a silly and useless one, since his principles, it may be retorted, are there in his work, spread open in all its radiant clarity. Yet the evidence in the translations is, once again, contradictory, and when we do have something akin to an explicit statement of principle or guiding rule, it seems at variance with the practice. Waley's brother tells us that "scorn for the over-ornate was the key to Arthur's preferences at that time and perhaps long after." The statement is an elusive one, for we do not know how long a period of Waley's life it is meant to cover, and of course everyone is opposed to what, in his view, is "over-ornate." Yet the thought that immediately comes to mind is of the young Waley's most ambitious translation, *The Tale of Genji*, which is a very ornate piece of craftsmanship. When Professor Morris uses the adjectives "plain" and "spontaneous," similar thoughts come to mind, though he does not profess to be putting words into Waley's mouth.

One of the "Waleyesque remarks" offered by Professor Walter Simon seems to have been very effective in cutting off a tiresome debate on translating Chinese. "Would it not be better still," said Waley, "to translate it right?" Yet there are countless passages in Waley's *Genji* in which the likely explanation, certainly the most charitable explanation, is that he quite consciously departed from what he knew to be "right" in the sense in which he must here have used the word.

The most interesting glimpse we have of Waley's working habits comes in Professor Keene's article, the matter at hand again being the *Genji*: "He would read a passage over until he understood its meaning; then, without looking back at the passage, he wrote out an English assimilation. He would later consult the original again. If the content of the translation was the same, he would let it pass, even if some words had been added or deleted."

The trouble is that again the practice seems at variance with the principle.

Waley's mistakes have nothing to do with the case. In a pioneering translation of such length and difficulty there are bound to be mistakes, and on the whole they make little difference. The marvel is that, given the materials he had to work with, there are not more of them. (Here too, however, there are mysteries, perhaps chief among them the extent to which he made use of the worthy ladies and gentlemen we have grown accustomed to calling, and he would no doubt have loathed calling, native informants.)

Nor is there a great deal of point in going into his bold excisions, though they do not seem to square, really, with the principle enunciated to Professor Keene. They have been well enough remarked upon already. It seems a pity that the lovely moon-viewing scene in "The Bell Cricket" and the scene of Murasaki's funeral in "The Rites" should be missing, but one can on the whole understand what it was that made Waley so impatient, and it is always possible, as people keep saying, that he improved by abridging.

But though the deletions may not be worth dwelling upon in themselves, they do raise an ethical question. One would like to have asked of this fastidious Englishman: "Why did you not tell us, sir, what you were doing?" In an exchange with Herbert Giles on a Po Chü-i translation, Waley admits that he "ought perhaps to have notified the reader" of omissions. This in 1920. During the *Genji* years he would have had many, many opportunities to make amends, but the fact is that he rather cunningly misled the reader. At the beginning of "Wakana: Part Two" in the Waley *Genji* we have this footnote: "This jump, which may read as though it were a 'cut' made by the translator, exists in the original." What reader would not take this as assurance that the translator would not dream of cutting anything without due notice and leave?

Far harder to understand than the deletions, in the light of the principle passed on to us by Professor Keene, are the additions. Waley embroiders rather marvelously, and the embroidery is more than a matter of an obtrusive little stitch here and there. A footnote in the "Wakana: Part One" chapter, in which Waley offers a not very tenable theory as to why Murasaki cannot consider herself Genji's principal wife, has been much discussed, but perhaps the most curious thing about it is that it footnotes a passage which does not exist in the original (there is no sanction for it in the several texts used in the Ikeda variorum edition). Immediately after the sentence in which Genji agrees to accept responsibility for the Suzaku emperor's young daughter, the action of the original moves on to a congratulatory banquet. Waley cuts the banquet, for such affairs are among the things he obviously could not abide, but adds a paragraph all his own, in which Genji's forthcoming domestic arrangements are predicted (and forsooth they do turn out that way).

Sometimes a piece of Waley's embroidery has a way of changing the whole pattern. In "The Flute" we have Yūgiri visiting Princess Ochiba, the widow of his friend Kashiwagi. Here is Waley's description of the impression her rather melancholy dwelling makes upon him: "There was a dignity, a severity about the place; and looking round him he felt that he who broke in upon this flat tranquillity with so much as a hint of common passions and desires, who fluttered this decorous stillness by any coarse vehemence or unwarranted familiarity, would be guilty of a breach of taste, for the condemnation of which no word could be strong enough."

All the original says is: "Though the garden had been neglected, an air of courtly refinement still hung over house and garden alike. The flower beds caught the evening light in a profusion of bloom and the humming of autumn insects was as he had imagined it in an earlier season."

Waley has put thoughts into Yūgiri's head for which there is no sanction in the original at all; and they must be described as rather pompous thoughts. Might it be that Waley wishes to strengthen the impression we have elsewhere of Yūgiri as a bit of a stuffed shirt? But this is not the place to do so. "The Flute," the chapter in which the passage occurs, is one of the best in the whole long narrative, and a good part of its appeal has to do with the fact that Yūgiri emerges as such a thoroughly likable person, however intent upon killing joy he may seem as he grows older.

I have been talking about a book which Professor Morris did not choose to write. On one score, the book he did choose to write, or edit, may be taken mildly to task: it implies strongly that, since the garden Waley cultivated was perfection, only fools will venture in upon it. "Later I realized," says Professor Morris himself about the Waley *Genji*, "that what enabled him to do this was a rare mastery of style and a self-assurance that allowed him, after he had thoroughly understood a Chinese or Japanese text, to recast it entirely in supple, idiomatic, vibrant English, rather than stick to a phrase-by-phrase or sentence-by-sentence rendering, which might convey the surface meaning but would inevitably mar the artistry of the original."

Inevitably? That does discourage a person; and a person suspects that Waley, prepared to admit that Sam Houston Brock's translation of *Sotoba Komachi* might be superior to his own, would not have approved of such prejudging.

(1971)

ON BEING FAITHFUL
TO MURASAKI SHIKIBU

Let us assume that the translator wishes to be "faithful." This probably means that he has in mind translators, perhaps of the work
which he proposes himself to translate, who have been less than
ideally faithful.

There are limits to fidelity which he must at the outset accept. If
he is translating out of Heian Japanese, he has before him a language
which tends to make clear (sometimes not very clear at all, but that
is another matter) the doer of a certain act through the honorific
level of the verb or adjective which is the decisive word in the
clause or sentence. If he is working into modern English, he has
ahead of him, at the end of the process, a language which is very
stubborn about assigning specific subjects to its verbs, and which
cannot force those verbs up and down a ladder of honorifics. This
means that the translation, based on matter-of-fact subjects and
objects, must automatically have a rather different air from the original, which drifts along, somewhat dreamily, from verb to adjective
to verb.

There are perhaps two conditions under which the basic structure of the second language can be tortured into accommodating
that of the first. One is when the document to be translated wields
an awesome power, not to be resisted. In English we have such an
instance in the King James Bible, the language of which is unlike
any other variety of English. The second is when a country has a
long tradition of translating into a special translators' language,
unlike anything ever heard spoken on the translators' home soil.
Perhaps we have an example of this in Japan, where an artificial

language was long ago put together for translating Chinese.

Few, I think, would make bold to attempt anything of the sort in translating *The Tale of Genji* into English. We are accustomed to dotting our speech at measured intervals with subjects, and we have very few honorifics; and so our Genji must move in a more business-like world, and no doubt a less courtly world, than Murasaki Shikibu's.

If there are these changes which must be made because of basic differences between two languages, there are changes which cannot be permitted. No translator can be perfectly, literally faithful; but there are some who seem unconscionably unfaithful. The temptations to be unfaithful are very strong in the case of *The Tale of Genji*. It is an uneven work, magnificent in sum, magnificent in most but not all of its parts. Murasaki Shikibu would seem to have had her bad days and her bad ideas. It would be a pleasure, thinks her translator, to improve by cutting and rewriting. "Is it ungrateful to add," says Sir George Sansom of Arthur Waley's translation, "that perhaps it does more than justice to the original—not because of any short-comings in Murasaki, but because modern English is incomparably richer, stronger, more various and supple than Heian Japanese?"

Yes, Waley *does* do "more than justice," and the matter has to do with more than the nature of modern English. Murasaki, despite Sir George's generosity, sometimes proceeds rather uncertainly, and Waley is not at all averse to covering up for her. But this should be the work of an editor, not of a faithful translator. Many a fine writer has needed an editor, and to say that a work as long and varied as *The Tale of Genji* has its defects is to say the obvious. The point is that it is the function of the faithful translator to show Murasaki Shikibu on her bad mornings as well as on her good. Sometimes it can be difficult work, even painful work—rather like watching one's beloved when she has stayed too long at a party and refuses to go home.

So far, matters are fairly easy. There are changes which must inevitably be made, unless the translator is prepared to use the language of the translation in a most unnatural way; and there are changes which the translator must refrain from making, if he is to be faithful. In between lies the really difficult region, where the translator of the *Genji*, let us say, finds himself faced with decisions on every page, where the decisions, after they are all made, may seem inconsistent one with another, and where, alas, a certain amount of rationalizing may seem to creep in as the decisions are reviewed and most of them allowed to stand.

In a very general way, it may be described as the realm of linguistic propriety. Passages which may seem exaggerated or sentimental or repetitious or downright long-winded in modern English apparently did not seem that way in Heian Japanese. Things that are apparently in good taste (can one imagine Murasaki Shikibu ever being guilty of consciously bad taste?) in one language are, if not precisely in bad taste, still not in the best of taste when reproduced in another.

What would have bothered Murasaki Shikibu most, one wonders, had she had a modern English or American novel before her, and a contract to translate it? One thing, no doubt, would have been the openness. Heian Japanese preferred not to come right out and say things. The word *monosu*, which means something like "to do it," and which is one of the favorite Heian ways of not coming out and saying a thing, appears some six hundred times in *The Tale of Genji*. And Murasaki might well have been startled at the fact, and wondered what to do about it, that even the best-placed people in Western novels go about with their names hanging out in public. In her own great work, to have a name that could be spoken in public without damage to the amenities meant to have a certain underling status.

To return to translation in the other direction: there is repetitiousness in *The Tale of Genji*. It is there, for instance, in the physical descriptions. A word that appears far more frequently than any of its equivalents would in a good English novel, however massive, is *rōtashi*. It means something like "pretty" or "winsome" or "petitely charming" or "demure." With related and variant forms it appears in *The Tale of Genji* close to two hundred times, in thirty-four of the fifty-four chapters. One may perhaps argue that Heian Japanese had a paucity of adjectives, however versatile those adjectives may have been in accounting for unnamed subjects. Yet somehow it is enough, and often more than enough, to tell us a single time in a good English novel that a young lady is petite and demure. We have seen too many bad novels in which stereotyped characterization is glossed over by physical description, and we know of masterpieces in which there is scarcely any physical description at all. We prefer to have the characters speak and act for themselves, and if they are well done, an impression of demureness, if that is what is intended, will somehow form itself in our minds. Murasaki Shikibu was a master of just such characterization. We readers in English *know* that the other Murasaki, Genji's great love, had to be *rōtashi*, and we resent being told so three and four and five times.

It is a matter of the proprieties. What in modern English becomes a displeasing intrusion was apparently quite acceptable in Heian Japanese. Would we not be doing Murasaki Shikibu a favor, even while remaining faithful, to have her conform to the English proprieties? The temptation is certainly strong.

The problem of repetitiousness is akin to the problem of exaggeration. It may seem curious that a lady who writes in a language of evasion and circumlocution should also write in a manner which, translated into another language, may seem exaggerated and even sentimental. Yet there is no contradiction. Things that are said are said over and over again, and, probably to avoid monotony, they are heaped with intensifiers and hyperbole. The most nagging problem is that of tears, and their inevitable accompaniments, soggy and rotting sleeves.

I can think of two ready justifications for cutting the volume of tears. One is that every culture has its conventions, and they tend not to correspond from culture to culture. The Japanese theater has two conventions for indicating grief, the extremely restrained one of Nō and the extremely emphatic one of Bunraku and Kabuki. The convention of the *Genji* tends toward the latter. One's observation is that in practice Japanese grief finds expression somewhere between, and so no doubt it was in Murasaki's time as well. Genji was a practical politician, and so was his father-in-law, the Minister of the Left, and it is unlikely that either of them would have wasted many working hours weeping over the political crisis presented by the death of Aoi, the Minister's only daughter. The point is not that Murasaki lied to us; it is that she inherited a set of stock literary responses to grief, and saw no need to banish conventions that functioned well enough. In the West artistic representations of grief have for a very long time been more realistic. Might one then seek correspondences, and keep Genji's weeping within limits appropriate to one of his station?

There is a more technical justification for mopping up some of the tears. We may imagine, although of course no document survives in her hand, that Murasaki Shikibu did not have the benefit of punctuation marks; and we know that she had to rely principally upon verbal and adjectival suffixes to indicate, in passages of dialogue, who her speakers were. So, to avoid overusing the verbs *notamō* and *iu*, which in any case take up close to twenty columns of the Ikeda concordance, she resorted to variations, frequently of a lachrymose nature. The result often goes like this: " 'Never before in the history of our realm or of realms beyond the sea has there been such grief as mine, and I think that all the ages will be required to stanch the flow of tears that soaks my sleeves.' He was in tears." The second mention of tears obviously serves a purpose, since without something of the sort we would not be sure who had spoken, or even that what we had just made our way through was a speech. Since the same purpose is served, for us, by the convenient devices of subjects and quotation marks, might we not do away with the tears?

These are rationalizations, perhaps; but when the choice is between verbal fidelity which strikes the wrong note and a certain propriety which requires a departure from strict fidelity, the decision may occasionally be in favor of the second. It is always a painful decision, and it is one with which the faithful translator is constantly faced. Excesses of tears may present the most striking difficulty, but it is only one among several. Most negative emotions, resentment and chagrin and the like, seem to demand that well enough not be left alone. An absolutely literal translation ends up studded with passages like this: " 'I hate you, I hate you.' She seemed resentful."

Another problem has to do with what have been called "unnecessary words." Every language has them. There is an article on them in Fowler's *Modern English Usage*, under the rather stronger title "meaningless words." "Words and phrases are often used in conversation," says Fowler, "especially by the young, not as significant terms but rather, so far as they have any purpose at all, as aids of the same kind as are given in writing by punctuation, inverted commas, and underlining." He finds "actually" and "you know" to be meaningless words in the British speech of his day.

It is no peculiar failing of Heian Japanese, then, to have unnecessary words. Of particular interest is the fact that Fowler should have found them to be a part of conversational English. That he was speaking of a rather more limited problem than the broadness of his title would suggest has something to do with the matter, of course; but might not the absence of punctuation marks in Heian Japanese, already touched upon, also have something to do with it? And I have often thought that many of the difficulties of Heian Japanese, and most especially the *Genji*, have to do with a certain colloquial quality, as if the author were addressing her audience directly, and not through the medium of the written word.

In any case, the *Genji* abounds in such expressions. Here is a mere beginning of a list: *warenagara* (which must mean something like the English "if I do say so myself," but which usually contributes as little to the meaning as does that highly colloquial expression); *ikaga oboshikemu* (the rather chattily colloquial "whatever may he have been thinking?" comes to mind as a possible equivalent, and again the contribution to the meaning seems negligible); *onajiku wa* ("if it is all the same"—and generally it goes without saying that it *is* all the same, and would not everyone be surprised if it were to turn out otherwise?); *onozukara* (a more dubious and complicated case, though it tends to go with verbs that already carry within them the autogenous significance); *hitoshirezu* ("unknown to anyone," presumably, but since it commonly goes with a concealed yearning or frustration, the privacy of the emotion or experience does not need stating).

With some feelings of uncertainty, I would venture to suggest that the suffix *beshi* and the particles *sae*, *dani*, and *nado* are frequently meaningless in *The Tale of Genji*. Intensifiers like *itodo* often seem to intensify the already superlatively intense; and might it not be that occasionally a person would do as well to let that slipperiest of expressions, *sasuga ni*, elude him?

As with repetition and exaggeration, the problem of encompassing such locutions has to do with linguistic proprieties. Every language has its essentially meaningless words, which are scarcely noticed save, perhaps, when they are missing—and then it becomes apparent that they should have been there, for reasons of rhythm or timing or something of the sort. They are a little like the sounds people make on a level more elementary than the verbal. In one culture a person sucks his teeth to indicate deference or eagerness to serve, in another belching is the proper response to a superior meal—and in a third both sounds rather intrude. Might not the translator of *The Tale of Genji* essay to filter the tooth suckings from his translation?

There is no ready answer, nor do there seem to be ready rules of thumb; and the uneasy feeling remains that much of what has been said is rationalization, an attempt after the fact to justify decisions made on the basis of something other than reason. It is by no means easy to be faithful after a fashion.

(1973)

ON TRANSLATING
AN EXOTIC LANGUAGE

The problems of translating from an Oriental language are fundamentally no different from those of translating from a European language, and fundamentally they are so simple that being asked about one's philosophy of translation is rather like being asked one's philosophy of breathing. All the translator must do is seek to understand what the original says and then seek to imitate it in the language into which he is rendering it.

The first half of the statement needs no further comment, because people who do not comprehend the languages from which they wish to translate should either change the wish or look for someone competent to help them, and because there are by definition no languages which are by their nature incomprehensible. It is a defensive measure among the peoples of what are called "developing" countries to say that they may not have much but they do have their mysterious languages, forever beyond the grasp of those arrogant, grasping imperialists. It is not true. There is no language the mysteries of which are beyond the foreigner even of rather advanced years who is willing to work hard at solving them. Perhaps because of a history of cultural subjection in which a century of Western domination was preceded by a millennium of Chinese, the Japanese will go on thinking the underdeveloped way, however affluent and industrialized they become. They will go on saying that it is very brave of foreigners to seek to translate a language which of course they do not understand, and proposing committees as a solution to the problem. It is true that the Oriental languages are for the Westerner very exotic and very difficult; but they are difficult for

Orientals too. The difficulties are of somewhat greater magnitude for the outsider only because he commonly comes to them later in life than the insider.

It is the second half of that very simple statement of principles which presents the complications, but once again there is no fundamental difference between a European language and an Oriental. Most of the complications come down to the basic fact that a translation can only be judged in terms of what it purports to be. If a translator wishes to produce a lucid and economical set of instructions on how to operate an elevator, he will produce one sort of translation. If he wishes to convey all the subtleties of a deliciously subtle novel or poem and is prepared in the process to use a great many more words than the original and risk ending up with something not delicious at all, he will produce another sort. And if the deliciousness is what he wishes to convey, in something like the same number of words, and inevitably the number must be similar if that is his wish, since tempo plays an important part in these matters—then he will produce yet a third sort of translation. And of course the number of possibilities is not limited to three. Permutations and combinations make possible as many sorts of translation as there are hybrid orchids.

If it is true, however, that the Oriental languages are, for reasons having to do largely with the scripts with which they have traditionally been written, more difficult than European languages, it is also true that the difficulty of translating them into a European language is greater by a considerable degree than is to be accounted for by the greater difficulty of the languages themselves. The works to be translated are in difficult languages which are the product of exotic cultures. A look at the literature about translation is enough to establish the point. It is almost entirely about the Mediterranean world, as if the Old Testament, looming off there in the Levant, were too large to permit of viewing anything beyond. There may be references to translations from the Japanese, but the probability is that they will be concerned only, and that very briefly, with the most famous of such translations, Dr. Arthur Waley's *The Tale of Genji*.

A part of the problem of remoteness is just that, physical and measurable: the Orient is a very great distance away, and Orientals live among unfamiliar flora and fauna and manufactures. Even when

Oriental plants have become familiar in the West, they tend, except when the old names have been retained, to have heavy, cumbersome names deriving from the names of the men who brought them or of people whom those men wished to flatter, or compounded of donnish classical elements. Tea still happily and unobtrusively bears its original Chinese name, but the camellia, the wisteria, and the paulownia bear respectively the names of a German Jesuit, an American anatomist, and a Russian princess, and are all for the translator inadequate imitations of Japanese originals because they look artificial.

"Chrysanthemum" is a familiar enough word, certainly, but it rather galumphs along while the Japanese *kiku* is skipping and dancing. To the translator of prose it does not perhaps matter that this should be the case, but the translator of poetry must sometimes wish that "mums" were proper style. Even in prose translations awkward floral designations have a way of appearing in particularly noticeable spots. "Paulownia" is at the very beginning of *The Tale of Genji*, in the title of the first chapter. Arthur Waley chose to do nothing about it, leaving "Kiritsubo" in the original Japanese as if it were what it is not, a personal name.

To leave things in the original with perhaps a footnote is one way, and the temptation is strong to do just that with many a floral thing. After deliberating "bush clover" and "lespedeza" as possible translations for the delicate, lacy *hagi*, so beautiful a symbol of the autumn, it may seem best to call it *hagi*, with an explanatory footnote. Another possibility is to seek an approximation. The great love of Genji's life has traditionally been known as Murasaki, but unfortunately that is not her name, and she is rarely called it in the original. It is a sort of sobriquet deriving from a poem about a little plant of the gromwell family used in making a purple dye. One surely cannot call her her "Little Miss Gromwell," though an early translator called her "Violet," and a case might be made for "Miss Lavender" or "Lady Lavender," using a word which, like *murasaki*, designates both a plant and a shade of purple.

There are these three possible ways of managing exotic flora: to use English equivalents, which may sometimes seem very cumbersome indeed; to leave the names in the original, with or without footnotes; and to seek approximations. There is another possibility, to make up words. "Mugwort" is not to be found in any save the most exhaustive dictionaries of English, but it seems rather splendid for evoking a lanky and voracious weed that quickly takes over a neglected garden. One cannot really talk of a "philosophy of translation" in these matters. Expediency rules, and all that can be expected of the translator is a certain consistency. It may not seem like much to ask that *hagi* be consistently "lespedeza" and "lespedeza" consistently *hagi*, but in fact it is rather a great deal, because one thing may "sound" right one time and another thing another. Perhaps codified rules of style are less important than the feelings of propriety of the person who is after all closest to the problem. The pulse and the flow may be more important than consistency.

Subhuman fauna do not present as many problems as flora. Quadrupeds present scarcely any at all, though their habits may seem strange at times. So common are both rats and hollow ceilings that a rat scampering about in a hollow ceiling is likely to bring to a Japanese not a shudder of horror but feelings of homey coziness, and if the Western reader does not know what is meant in *The Tale of Genji* by the expression "Chinese cat," well, neither does the Japanese, and the matter can there be allowed to rest. The creature which in folklore is fond of thumping its belly and playing deceitful pranks is usually called a badger, though in fact it is a kind of wild dog; but its habits are more important than its name, and mistranslation has probably not misled people enormously.

Insects present complications sometimes. The Japanese have a fondness for them which we do not share. Usually, because the fondness arises from the sounds they make, a brief description of a similar sound or two serves the purposes of a literary text. Fish too may present passing problems, but only passing ones, since they tend not to be lingering presences in poems. Sometimes a translation must be rough, since Japanese ichthyological distinctions are more refined than English, and sometimes it must be rather ugly. "Goby" somehow does not seem to fit any context.

Serious and lingering problems are presented by birds. Probably the most popular of all birds—popular because it has a pretty song and delightful associations with the spring, and also, one suspects, because its name has five syllables and therefore precisely constitutes a line of Japanese verse—must be translated "cuckoo" because it *is* a cuckoo and there really is no other way to translate it; but its most pleasing song, for the poet and the romancer, comes at night, and it carries none of the associations of daffiness that go with the English word. The translator has a choice between retaining the original Japanese, the rather lovely *hototogisu*, and hoping that the reader will come to accept the cuckoo as a nocturnal harbinger of spring.

It is of course the bipeds that present the really difficult problems. The flora and all the other fauna are but occasional stage properties. An alien way of life presents a more complicated and varied set of stage properties that are by no means occasional. A modern Japanese of traditional inclinations lives in a house that is familiar to an increasing number of Occidentals, though probably not to all of them. A Japanese of a thousand years ago lived in a house not in its fundamentals much different, but his way of living in it was in some ways different. Then, as now, indoor life was lived on floors, one of the more undeviating of Japanese tendencies being to reject chairs; but the life of wellborn women, at least, was kept even closer to the floor than it is today. They were not expected to stand up and walk when in the presence of men. They remained seated or kneeling, and when required to move did so by pulling themselves, great heaps of robes, in a sliding motion across smooth floors.

Here most translators feel compelled to become revisionists. To have a gentleman make his way secretly and illicitly into a lady's chambers and attract her attention by pulling at the hem of her skirt seems to suggest that he is groveling on the floor. In fact both lady and gentleman have been on the floor all along and it is the hem of her skirt, some distance from the lady proper, which first comes within reach. It seems better, all in all, to have him tug at her sleeve, or perhaps tap her on the shoulder. And when ladies move about, it is at first surprising, and presently ludicrous, to have them come sliding across the floor. Possible substitutes for "slide" only make things worse. There is "crawl," for instance, permissible just occasionally, when a lady is in great distress or trying to make an escape, but it will not do for ordinary entry and egress. Again compromise and revisionism seem called for.

Waley adapted very boldly in his translation of *The Tale of Genji*, making over most of the exotic caparisons and appurtenances into more familiar things. He had trouble, when for instance a lady's "couch of state" had to be hauled and shoved across the floor that she might receive a gentleman at a "window" (when of course nothing in the original had to be moved—the lady slid her way across the floor to an aperture only remotely resembling a window); and he had trouble, too, being consistent. If one reads his translation with care it sometimes seems that his ladies wear farthingales and live at Hampton Court, and sometimes as if they were odalisques in Constantinople. There was justification for what he did, since not very many people knew much about Japan and its curious ways when Waley was working almost half a century ago. Perhaps it is justified today, too, if it makes things easier for even a few readers. An amount of adaptation does seem called for. The crawling and the slithering simply do not sound very good in English.

More difficult than the problems presented by an alien setting are the notions of propriety and beauty which have grown up in an alien tradition. Sometimes they are concerned with a very clear reaction to what is materially and physically present, and therefore not to be denied. A good instance is a mouth darkened either naturally by tooth decay or artificially by blackening. When we are told in *The Tale of Genji* that an old-fashioned grandmother has refrained from blackening her little granddaughter's teeth as a more normal sort of grandmother would have done, or in *The Tale of the Heike* that a young warrior dazzles his adversary with the beauty of his black-toothed visage, we are likely to think the Japanese inexcusably exotic; and when we learn in the same *Tale of Genji* that teeth brown from decay add wonderfully to the charm of a young crown prince, we are likely to feel a shudder of revulsion.

The reaction in the first instance may have been briefly out of keeping with that intended by the author, but in the second the two are hopelessly at odds. An anthropologist might argue that this is not really the case; since a certain morbid and sick sensibility is common in some measure to all peoples, and Heian Japan had it in rather full measure. We have it on the authority of the great contemporary novelist Tanizaki Jun'ichirō, however, in one of whose most beautiful essays the matter figures prominently, that blackening of the teeth was meant to intensify the whiteness of the skin, and a white skin has an important place in Japanese notions of physical beauty; and so the cult is not of sickness or decay in itself, but rather of the clean whiteness which the decay sets off. It is thus very difficult to see the foreign reaction as other than opposite to that intended by the original author. There is a kind of scholarly translation in which a little essay appended as a footnote may be relied upon to put the matter right; but editors and publishers who hope to make a profit from a book are not tolerant of voluminous annotation. So the choice is between cutting, as Waley did in the instance of the crown prince just mentioned, or hurrying over the matter as quickly as possible and moving on to matters less discordant. Neither solution is ideal, but the translator who thinks himself a faithful sort may in the end feel less troubled by the second than by the first.

A far more serious problem is provided by what might be called the bounds of the sentimental. Sentimentality is a matter of propriety, having to do with what are deemed the proper limits and degrees of emotional expression. When an emotional outpouring seems large out of all proportion to the occasion to which it is a response, we are in the presence of the maudlin or the sentimental. If the limits of propriety were the same for everyone, then there would be no problem, since everyone's sense of when they have been exceeded and sentimentality has begun would be the same.

It does seem to be the case, however, even today, that the Japanese penchant for tears, at least in the symbolic and imitative situations presented by fiction and the drama, is greater than our own. The problem is not likely to be as serious in a modern novel, but the sobbing in a Kabuki play can be deafening and exceedingly long drawn out, and when we are told in a Heian romance that a gentleman or lady has wept so copiously that his or her pillow is about to float away, the effect becomes merely ludicrous. Even without going to this extreme, the translator can quickly produce an effect on his reader which it is altogether reasonable to assume was not produced upon the reader of the original. Why must these people be forever mooning over themselves, the reader in English is likely to be asking, long before the reader in Heian Japan, we may assume, or the reader in modern Japan was or is likely to ask—and indeed it sometimes seems that for them no amount of self-commiseration ever becomes intolerable self-pity. Clearly, then, a "literal" translation becomes a dubious imitation, because the effect upon the beholder departs from the effect of the original upon the original beholder.

What is to be done? There is no answer that will please everyone, and so there can be no translation that will please everyone. But it can be argued rather persuasively that a discreet refusal to mention tears more than perhaps once or twice in a situation in which their presence is not at all surprising need not apologize for itself even when they are more frequently called to the reader's attention in the original; and that, for a reader not accustomed to being confronted with floating pillows, and not familiar with a world in which the source of the flow is as likely to be masculine as feminine, it may be well to tone down the hyperbole, and perhaps substitute a misted-over eye for a river of tears, a trembling lip for a night of racking sobs, a handkerchief touched briefly to an eye for a sleeve, the Heian equivalent of a handkerchief, sodden and rotting away from tears.

The task for the translator of poetry is at once greater and less than for the translator of prose. It is greater because for a period of perhaps three centuries, centering upon the day of *The Tale of Genji*, tearful, unrequited love was the overweening concern of the poet, almost the only concern, one is tempted to say. To diminish the flow is almost to do away with the poetry, and presumably anyone sufficiently interested in it to translate it would not wish to do that. At least one eminent critic, presented with manuscript translations, called the poetry of the period sentimental slush. The problem may be less for the translator, therefore, because there can be no diminishing of the hyperbole. There can only be agreement between translator and critic to disagree. It is easier too because many readers are better prepared to accept this sort of hyperbole in poetry than in prose, and therefore less quick to call the poetry sentimental. What will pass in a mad flight of fancy will not in realistic narrative, and the best Japanese prose narrative tends to be in some sense "realistic." Murasaki Shikibu was more interested in observable and believable life than in histrionic posing, and that is precisely why the plethora of tears in her great work presents such problems.

Certain other excesses, by our lights, in Japanese fiction, as for instance a fondness for coincidence and a willingness to let characters destroy themselves for what seems inadequate cause, present more considerable problems in a modern novel, which is supposed to be "realistic," verisimilitude all the way, than in a premodern piece, which may be called a "romance" or a "tale." The presence of the latter word in the title of the greatest of all Japanese stories prepares us, perhaps unconsciously, to accept departures from the quotidian.

We are now, of course, in the realm of convention, and it is some comfort to think that if responses on the far side of the ocean present impossible problems for the translator on this side, it is very likely indeed that responses on this side of the ocean present similar difficulties for the translator on the far side.

There is a rather different sort of convention which might be called the technical convention, and which without question presents greater problems for the translator of poetry than the translator of prose. It has to do with decorative language. The problem is compounded by the fact that there no longer exists a poetic diction in English. There did until the early years of this century, but more recently we have been made to accept the principle that the poet is not to use overt linguistic signals, such as inversions and antique forms, to inform his readership that he is being poetic; and so anyone, including the translator, who does make use of these conventions becomes not poetic but "poetic." Since the conventions of Japanese poetry are so very different from even those of "poetic" poetry in English, even a translator who lards his translation with locutions like "believe thou me" has not conveyed a great deal of the original.

Without doubt the most trying convention in Japanese poetry is punning. It is all-pervasive, but it is also very conventional, so that from the tenth century or so anyone who saw the word for "pine tree" almost automatically read into it a second meaning, "to wait"; and incorporated in mention of the autumn was almost invariably a sense of boredom and satiety. Very rarely can a pun be translated with a single word, although the meanings in English of "pine" as a noun and as a verb do happen to correspond rather closely to the two Japanese senses. Usually the translator must make a choice: either he will explicitly translate both halves of the pun, frequently resorting to simile, or he will not. If he chooses the latter course he must leave out half the meaning of the original; and if the former he takes a considerably longer time in saying what must be said than did the original poet. The translator who makes it appear that there were no puns in the first place is obviously sacrificing a great deal of contrivance and textual density, and the translator who scrupulously conveys all the subtleties of diction is sacrificing the rhythm.

Some will think that the ideal solution is to do the one thing sometimes and sometimes again the other, and some will think this the worst possible solution. There can be no solution that will seem to everyone ideal. Professor Geoffrey Bownas and Mr. Anthony Thwaite, in *The Penguin Anthology of Japanese Verse*, have emphasized rhythm at the expense of diction, and so accomplished the remarkable feat of keeping the syllable count of their translations down fairly near that of their originals; but it may be argued that their bland and uncomplicated surfaces are very imprecise imitations of a very rich fabric. Professors Robert Brower and Earl Miner, in *Japanese Court Poetry*, have let no small turn of diction escape them, but it may be argued that something else rather important has escaped them when, as is sometimes the case, they use more *words* in their translations than there are *syllables* in their originals. The Gakujutsu Shinkōkai translations from the *Manyōshū* are neither as sparse as the one nor as intricate as the other, and may therefore invite the charge of falling between two stools. In all poems which are to be found in the three versions, the Brower-Miner version uses the most words and the Penguin version the fewest, but the divergence is not as wide for some poets as for others. Some made more elaborate use of decoration and poetic diction than did others, but this fact does not necessarily make them better poets. It may therefore be argued that poetic diction is not everything. To cut it away as if it were nothing, however, is perhaps another matter. Opinions will vary as to which of the three sets of translations comes nearest to solving an insoluble problem.

Japanese poetry may tend toward the consciously poetic in the sense of making fairly consistent use of decorative language, but it is not written in language which announces the sex or station in life of the speaker or actor, or his or her relation to the person spoken to or acted upon. It is not honorific. Classical prose, and especially the prose of the Heian period, tends to be elaborately honorific, and thereby presents its own set of insoluble problems. Verbs and adjectives, the conjugated parts of speech, can be so subtly honorific that they contain in themselves both subject and object, neither of which needs to be mentioned overtly. It of course follows that an English translation, since an attempt to do without subjects and objects may be amusing for a while but cannot be endured for long, must necessarily become clearer and more businesslike than the original, and therefore an imperfect imitation.

There is another change that is perhaps even more important:

English translation results in a loss of courtliness, a very great loss indeed when it is remembered that some such quality is the very essence of Heian prose. The problem is in large measure one of tempo. When a monarch appears on the scene, for instance, the verbs and adjectives slow down to a stately march; and when it is one of his ministers, who may well be the hero and therefore on the scene a good deal of the time, the march is only a little less grand. There may be ways of imitating the effect for brief intervals, but they presently become mannered and tedious, and therefore fail as imitations. There is some comfort in the knowledge that translators from Heian Japanese into modern Japanese face similar problems. Some very well known writers have had a try at translating *The Tale of Genji* into modern Japanese, and some suggestion of what the process implies is to be found in the fact that they must occasionally resort to antique verbs in their efforts to convey the sonorously honorific quality of the original. Modern Japanese is simply not as ceremonious as Heian Japanese was, and the translator is faced with a choice between leaving some of the ceremonious verbs and adjectives in premodern forms and therefore not translating completely, and speeding up the tempo, and so, like the translator into English, imitating somewhat imprecisely.

There is another element of the untranslatable in a kind of Japanese, preeminently that of the Heian romance, and it is a mysterious one. The very heart of the language is of a certain ineffability, and the change wrought upon it in the process of translation is in the direction of clarity and clean focus. In reading a Heian romance one must read so slowly, pausing constantly to consider who may be acting and who acted upon, as to marvel that a sentence containing no unusual words can be so opaque and that the same sentence can have been read aloud and understood immediately. Again it is some comfort to know that the difficulty is very little if at all less for the modern Japanese. At the end of a long and defeating bout with a Heian romance, one sometimes sits back in great discouragement and wonders whether all men are in fact brothers, whether human thought processes are in fact universal, whether the signals might not be different for a Heian Japanese on the one hand and an American or a modern Japanese on the other, even as they are for the American and the modern Japanese on the one hand and a bat on the other.

It is not so, of course, and the solution to the problem may be merely to recognize that the signals were transmitted in different circumstances. What we know of the circumstances in which Heian romances were "published" suggests that it was a very intimate process, with the romancer and her audience (the feminine pronoun is applicable for the best of Heian fiction) going over the agenda together. It would be wrong to say that the process was one of oral transmission, but the author or some substitute for the author was present to make queries of, and so the signals may have been set down on paper in a less complete form than would have been the case for, say, a nineteenth-century English novel. Even when they were set down completely the possibilities for burying them all in a single word, usually a verb or an adjective, was much greater in Heian Japanese than in modern Japanese or in English. It is almost impossible to imitate in English the dreamy, inchoate, half-articulated quality of Heian Japanese. The bravest attempt to do so must presently be given up, for English, even at the hands of a Joyce, tends to be a no-nonsense language, and inchoate translations do not find publishers and readers.

There is a series of delicate balances to be maintained, then, in translation from Japanese, and especially from classical Japanese. The translator may feel compelled to elaborate, but elaboration can go too far. There must be a compromise between the substantive demands of the original and those of its rhythm and tempo. And so on. What can be asked is a certain resolve in adhering to principles more strongly felt, perhaps, than clearly defined.

(1974)

THE JAPANESE NOVEL
AND DISENGAGEMENT

It has been reported by an eminent literary critic that shortly before
the novelist Takami Jun died, in the summer of 1965, he expressed
a wish to die as a member of the Communist Party. More than one
important Japanese writer has made an improbable deathbed revelation about himself, but this one seemed more improbable than most.
In his last years, Takami's influence, less as a novelist than as an important member of the literary establishment, had seemed generally
anti-communist.

But once the first surprise wore off, the news came to seem not
improbable at all. Takami was born in 1907, and he was a child of
his age. In the years when he was a university student, Russian-
inspired radicalism was having its last fling and the decade of the
militarists and the assassinations was in sight. He was active in the
proletarian literary movement. Like many comrades in that movement, he presently went to prison. He emerged some months later
a "reformed man." (The Japanese word *tenkōsha*, of which this is
an attempt at translation, carries a suggestion of "turncoat.") The
work with which, upon his release, he established himself as an
author is in some ways like Mary McCarthy's most widely read
book; the "group" of ex-proletarians it describes is a forlorn and
demoralized one, given over to commercialism and carnal indulgence and self-derision now that its guiding star has been lost.

The signs were there all along and need not have surprised a
person when, in Takami's last days, they came into the open. He
was like many other intellectuals of his time and circumstances: the
"reform" had not been right, and the injury to his conscience never

healed. There had not been enough resistance, the decision to change had come too easily. Although there was one convenient instance of a writer apparently killed by the police, stories of police brutality were not sufficient justification. It was a well-known fact among left-wing intellectuals that methods which quickly brought them to heel were far less effective with rightist bully-boys. In short, they had been weaklings. They had failed.

The failure was the important fact in the lives of people like Takami. One could feel in them something akin to envy for the one novelist, Kobayashi Takiji, who does in fact seem to have died as a result of extreme police methods, and something like yearning for the companionship of the sturdy few who stayed prisoners and stayed Communists through the war years. It is not at all likely that the Japanese Communist Party would have admitted Takami to the companionship had he made formal application. Since the Sino-Soviet break it has been energetically purging itself of important writers. His deathbed wish was symbolic, rather, and the way he chose to reveal it suggests that he meant to make public confession. A youthful failure to follow a political commitment through meant that the commitment dominated his life. When it came time to make his last accounting to his peers, politics were what he wanted to talk about.

Although Takami was of his time and circumstances, it would make much too neat a story to say that everyone was like him. Some writers declined in the first place to succumb to the system imported from Russia and so were not vulnerable to "reform." Others had brushes with it, but for one reason or another it never became all-important to them. Thus the novelist Dazai Osamu, two years Takami's junior, had his day of juvenile radicalism, but it was only one of a rich store of devices with which he sought to destroy himself. Had he, before his apparent suicide in 1948, confessed to secret fellow-traveling, the effect would have been of ludicrous irrelevance.

What can be said all the same is that Takami's confessions of guilt were honest and important, that he was far from alone in the shame that inspired them—and that it would be very hard indeed to find a major writer of a younger generation to whom similar happenings could seem so crucial. He belongs to the last (and most unfortunate) generation of prewar writers. Writers who have emerged since the war have tended to wear their politics more easily. Partly it is because their politics have not been put to a real test of courage. Those who were Communists but are no more are ex-Communists because they have told themselves that they are or because the Communist Party has told them that they are. But the change would seem to go deeper. Political commitment itself does not seem the portentous matter it once was. Indifference to politics and out-and-out hostility to political organizations come nearer being proper and even stylish literary positions than they were thirty or forty years ago.

Along the vague line where superior journalism blends into literature there are to be found numbers of writers whose concerns are intensely political. Even for them, however, the commitment does not seem the momentous matter it was for people like Takami. Commitment there is, but there are ambiguities and ironies and contradictions (a favorite word), and it is not as if they were joining a priesthood to break the vows of which would mean damnation.

Let us take, for an example of a committed one, Hotta Yoshie, a very admirable journalist whose best reports are called novels. He is just over a decade younger than Takami, and that decade made a great difference. By the time he was out of college the Pacific War, as the Japanese call it, was on, and there was no radical Left to which to commit oneself. That there was no underground is a fact for which the Japanese intelligentsia might choose to reprove itself, but does not. Commitment had to wait until the end of the war, when there were no "thought police" on hand to press reform upon the committed. It was in fact Hotta who gave the word "commitment" —he used the English word—currency among Japanese intellectuals. This he did in a novel called *Alone in the Plaza*. The action takes place in Tokyo during the Korean War, and the theme would seem to be the helplessness of the individual caught in the black currents of international conflict and conspiracy. Hotta's own position is clear enough: peaceful socialist conspiracies have more to be said for them than bellicose capitalist conspiracies. Yet the loneliness and the helplessness are nearer the heart of the novel than the peaceful socialist cause itself. Hotta has been remarkably faithful to his commitment in the decade and a half since. Despite the Sino-Soviet rift, which has given pause to many Japanese radicals, he continues to be a diligent worker for pan-Asianism (or Afro-Asianism), a cause not so ecumenical as to embrace South Korea, South Vietnam, Taiwan, or Israel.

His most recent ambitious work, serialized in 1963 and 1964, is called *Sphinx*. The action moves from Cairo to a number of European cities, principally Paris, Bonn, and Geneva, and the main characters are a lady and gentleman of Japan who are deeply involved with the Algerian FLN. Despite the more cosmopolitan nature of the contents, the theme is much the same as that of *Alone in the Plaza*. As in that novel, Hotta's own preference, his commitment, is not at all hard to discern, and its expression is not always pleasant. A rasping note of anti-Westernism runs through the book. Americans get off fairly well, perhaps because they do not have a very large part to play. When they do appear they are in the Graham Greene mold, blundering, good-natured, naive, and too muscular for their own good. The French, Germans, and Italians are frequently designated by expressions that would go into American English as "Frogs," "Heinies," and "Dagos." Many a sigh is heard for the plight of the Algerians, who must get their arms from Europeans, who will forever be uncomprehending and unreliable Europeans. Hotta even manages to get in a dig or two at the Vatican City. But it is those erstwhile allies, the Germans, who fare worst. They are all fat pigs, with pronounced Nazi inclinations when they are intelligent enough to have any rational inclinations at all.[1] One has no trouble seeing why they are sorted out for special treatment: Hotta has a guilty conscience about Japanese attempts to leave Afro-Asia behind and join Europe, and the Tripartite Alliance is the most conspicuous documentary evidence of one such unhappy attempt. Although no Italian character is prominent in the book, Italians are called Dagos more frequently than French are called Frogs, and the reasons may be similar.

Sphinx is not much of a novel, and it is to Hotta's credit that he does not take it all that seriously. In his postscript he likens it to a quaint nineteenth-century Japanese novel, or tract, called *Strange Encounters with Elegant Females*. *Strange Encounters* does not waste much time over characterization and verisimilitude, for it must race about making contact with every nineteenth-century liberation leader from Kossuth through Parnell and Garibaldi to Arabi Pasha. So it is with *Sphinx*. Yet it is an interesting book, and much of the interest is in the evidence it gives of what commitment is like these days. Mr Hotta's own political preferences are quite open, but he does not pretend to know everything and to have final answers. Here we have his hero meditating upon certain sinister international events of his knowledge:

> There was no telling what might be happening backstage while a war was going on. Dark, shady movements behind the principles and the morals and the like of a country or society— it was when he came against such matters that a kind of excitement swept over him.
>
> The dark, shady movements—if from piddling everyday morals and principles they must be called evil, then let them be evil—caused the cogs to advance a bit, or applied the brakes to keep them from advancing; and that was history.

To be sure, this is not an open statement of belief on Hotta's part, but a soliloquy attributed to one of his principal characters. When characterization is as thin as in this novel, however, a reader has few doubts about when an author is speaking for himself. Just as Hotta does not seem to be happy in the company of Heinies, so this would seem to be his own view of history. *Sphinx* would be a very different book if, given the same characters and incidents, it had been written by an orthodox Chinese. It would also be a different book if it had been written by a Japanese proletarian novelist of thirty or forty years ago. Hotta, it may be noted in passing, makes his political views clearer in his writings than do numbers of his comrades in the fellow-traveling or communist Left. *The Woman in the Dunes* and *The Face of Another*, both by Abe Kōbō, have been translated into English and therefore provide easily available testimony to this fact. Abe was a member of the Communist Party (he has since been expelled) when he wrote both novels, but the reader is likely to think of Kafka or Beckett long before he thinks of Mao or Stalin.

Novels like *Sphinx*, whose interest so frankly depends on concern with immediate political movements, are not likely to outlive the political movements; if they are remembered at all, it will be as amusing period pieces, like *Strange Encounters with Elegant Females*. This does not necessarily mean that writers seeking immortality should shun politics. Yet it does seem to be a fact that Japanese novelists who deserve to be taken seriously as novelists, so far as nearness permits us to judge, are not as disposed as they were in the period between the wars to let politics take over their writing. They are suspicious of organized political movements as their literary fathers were not. They do not propose to abandon themselves. Sometimes they seem committed to the accepted intellectual line of the moment. Though badly shaken by the Sino-Soviet split and the Indonesian reversal, they continue to be vaguely "neutralist" and "liberal" and to hold the United States more responsible than most countries for international unpleasantness. Yet even such novelists have a way of appearing, in their novels, either indifferent to or hostile to the fashionable view as an organized movement. Other writers are downright hostile to the view itself. Hostility to the anti-American vogue does not necessarily have as its reverse friendliness to America. It is usually able to find other backing.

Ōe Kenzaburō, who is perhaps the most promising writer his age, is an example of a novelist who when he is not writing fiction seems to be strongly attracted to "liberal" causes, but who for the most part writes novels that are either non-political or anti-political, in the sense of rejecting crusades of the sort liberals are expected to join.

When Ōe goes in for polemics and pamphleteering, he sounds somewhat to the left of the Russians, and he once revealed to an American reporter that his favorite reading included I. F. Stone's newsletter. When he describes his reasons for taking the trouble to write novels, however, he sounds as far from political causes as a novelist could be:

> Ever since, one morning fifteen years ago, I read of the outbreak of the Korean War, I have sensed, continuing, deep, and certain, the shadow of an enormous something behind the visible world. Not once has it seemed to be giving way. . . . It is not that the writing of novels dispels this obscure sense of crisis or sets a compensatory process in motion. It enables me to resist. That is all. . . . By continuing to write novels, I but keep at arm's length a lunatic something.

Ōe has written stories on political themes, but even then his major concern might be described as anti-political. The most considerable of them is a short novel called "Seventeen" (the title is in English), published in 1961. In 1960 a seventeen-year-old member of a right-wing organization assassinated Asanuma Inejirō, the secretary-general of the Socialist Party. The incident obviously gave Ōe his idea. Most of the action takes place on the hero's seventeenth birthday and the day following. He is desperately lonely, much given to masturbation, and tormented by the self-loathing that goes with it. His family is no help. His father is a schoolteacher of the live-and-let-live persuasion (taught to him by the Americans, we are given to understand). He has no friends except an alley cat he has named Gang (again in English). Gang's most admirable characteristic is his gangster-like ruthlessness. "A splendid scoundrel he is. . . . I was once shaken to find him eating a white cat he had killed. But even then he was calm and grand, a really splendid figure." In complete despair over his academic and athletic ineptitude, the lad joins a right-wing organization.

At which point the story collapses. Ōe sees his hero into the organization and shows us how he behaves—and yet somehow does not. There is no immediacy in the narrative once the birthday and its aftermath are over. It is clear enough that Ōe does not approve of right-wing organizations. The leader of this one is pure, concentrated hate, and some of the slogans the hero has drilled into him ("I am His Majesty's child") are inanity itself; but Ōe fails to convince and to move when he describes these groups. It has been said that right-wing threats frightened him into giving the story a hasty ending. Perhaps it is so; but it also seems possible that he found himself with uncongenial material on his hands and wanted to be finished with it. What he really wanted to describe, it seems possible, was not the evils of political reaction but the terrors of adolescent loneliness and of the initiation into adulthood that must follow them. That, in any case, is what he succeeds in describing. Down to its unfortunate turning point the story is very moving.

Some of Ōe's more political stories from the late fifties are remarkable for their cool discernment. They suggest that even in those intensely political days, when relations with the United States were coming up for review, the apparently committed may not in fact have been all that committed. They too wore their political ideas with a certain jauntiness. The following is a passage from a 1958 story:

For the most part he was immersed in his studies, but from time to time he was taken with an interest in politics as with a fever. He was too discriminating to lose himself in political activity, and he would have been ashamed to. A day of co-operating with the organization was a day of leave from his conscience, a vacation replete with happiness. For the organization itself, to enlist his cooperation was to hire for a day an activist free from official scrutiny. He cooperated, and now he thought it all very amusing.

Contempt for organizations and crusaders is not merely noted in passing, it is the heart of the matter. In "Our Day of Fighting," the story just quoted, unthinking commitment leads to a most delicate predicament. Two students (one of them the "he" of the quotation) are sent by an organization—the Communist Party, it may be supposed—to distribute leaflets at the gate of an American base. The Korean War is in progress, and the leaflets encourage American soldiers to desert. Suddenly the last thing anyone expected happens: a soldier *does* desert, and the lads find themselves *in loco parentis*. They turn to the organization for help, but the organization does not think itself sufficiently organized at this point, and so they are on their own. The comic possibilities of the situation are enormous, but Ōe is not always up to such possibilities. He has a way of introducing violence when it seems inappropriate, and this time the violence results in the death of the American. His views on the merits of the organization and its workers are clear enough all the same.

In another 1958 story, "Human Sheep," the crusade against crusades is followed through to a more compelling conclusion. The story opens on a crowded bus. A number of Japanese are subjected to great indignities by a number of American soldiers. No one protests and no one resists. At first the story seems to be a run-of-the-mill anti-American atrocity report, of which there have been many. But then it becomes apparent that the villains are not the Americans at all, but the Japanese bystanders who fail to resist while the moment for resistance is present, and resist in a manner most objectionable after it has passed.

When the narrator, one of the mistreated ones, gets off the bus, he is pursued by one of the bystanders, a schoolteacher, who insists that he go to the police. The narrator wants only to be left alone with his shame. The teacher will not hear of it. The story comes to a harrowing end with the narrator facing a night of hopeless flight, determined not to give his name and address to this righteous person who is determined to have them. It seems likely that Ōe had in mind the propaganda use to which scarred Hiroshima maidens have been put by the Japanese Left. His symbols are susceptible of application to crusades in general, however, and a disengagement from immediate political issues marks most of his significant fiction.

Ōe's fiction is not, like Hotta's, concerned principally with factions and movements. Its concern is rather with lonely individuals trying to find themselves. More specifically, it is concerned with the pains of growing up. An act of initiation is necessary, a cruel spanking for the offense of having been an infant; and in the punishment an awareness of adult company is achieved. In *A Personal Matter*, one of Ōe's most ambitious attempts at long fiction, the hero is a young schoolteacher whose first child is deformed. He hopes it will die, indeed seeks to have it killed; and he dreams of running off to Africa, where, in a life of delicious adventure, he will show himself that he is a man. An encounter with a childhood friend whom he betrayed in the dawn of adolescence and thereby started on the path downward to male prostitution makes him see that a proper initiation must take place elsewhere than in African adventure. "There are only two honest alternatives to this fleeing from my monster of a baby: strangle him with my own hands, or take responsibility for bringing him up." He takes responsibility and, in a weak ending, that is that. The conclusion suggests a return to the family that is rather startling, because one does not expect it from the pen of a young "liberal." The pursuit of identity by modern Japanese youth, as fiction has told us of it, has been in the opposite direction. Some critics have suggested that Ōe has here written an allegory upon the emergence of Japan itself into international maturity. Such a reading is certainly not impossible; but Ōe made clear the essentially solitary and withdrawn nature of the crisis in his choice of a title.

A disconcerting split between "liberal" commitment for purposes of essay-writing and engagement and withdrawal for purposes of fiction-writing is to be observed in the case of Ōe Kenzaburō. There are other writers about his age in whose cases the two are more congenial. In both stories and essays, Ishihara Shintarō, born in 1932 and so three years Ōe's senior, speaks for freedom from ideological commitment and the acceptance of a very personal sort of commitment. He came, or more properly exploded, into prominence in 1955 with a lurid story the title of which has been translated "Season of Violence." The translation is free, since the Japanese means something like "Season in the Sun," but it is apt. The action has to do with an increasingly conspicuous product of the Japanese economic miracle, the hot-rod set. A group of well-to-do youngsters spend a summer of fighting, racing, and fornicating on the wealthy Shōnan coast, south of Tokyo, and their abundant energies bring on the death, following an abortion, of one of their number. Ishihara was held to speak so persuasively and authoritatively for alienated, affluent, and bored youth that the class of which he wrote immediately came to be known as "the sun tribe."

Ishihara pushes mistrust of righteous causes much farther than Ōe, who seems a little schizoid on the subject. Here, in 1966, Ishihara gives his view of the left-wing "peace" movement:

> I have been critical of the actions of writers in our recent peace movement, of the self-deception and vicarious participation to be detected in them; and that has been both because I have been suspicious of their motives and because I have suspected their "acts" not to be acts at all. If I may be permitted to use again two verbs I have already used, they have been engaged but not committed.
>
> I may seem to be expressing myself in a superficial manner; but what did they serve through those acts, and to what extent were they endangered? To what extent did they feel the truth that every real act comes home to the actor, that for every real act a price must be paid?

The anti-rational and anti-idealist strain is obvious, but it is also paradoxical. Ishihara is with one half of his heart on the side of intellectuals, though not "liberal" intellectuals. He has said that the rational act is superior to the pure physical act. And yet it is in the pure physical act (there is great emphasis on purity) and the willingness to commit himself completely to it, and thereby lower himself, that the individual finds his identity. In Ishihara as in Ōe one detects an element of masochism, not to say of latent homosexuality.

Ishihara's first long novel, perhaps his most successful thus far, was published serially in 1956 and 1957. The hero is an intellectual, a novelist, who by being an intellectual is removed from "pure action." He must seek it vicariously. The two persons with whom he feels a bond of companionship, and then only when he is alone with them, are a prizefighter and a professional murderer. The title, *Crevasse*, is supposed to symbolize his alienation from everyone else, including the movie actress with whom, physically, he is most intimate. The actress for her part finds the nearest thing she knows to fulfillment in the embrace of the fighter, who sometimes bloodies her nose before embracing her. Upon hearing of this last propensity, the hero feels "strangely envious of a person who can express himself only in violence."

Here are further thoughts on the boxer, Kamishima: "What had he shown them if not the act right for a man? Tatsumi had made a wager when he went out to die on that mountain. Here there was not even that, for the cause was lost. Knocked down to get to his feet again, getting to his feet to be knocked down again, Kamishima had been faithful to himself."

Tatsumi is a mountain-climbing acquaintance, killed on the descent from a particularly daring climb. "No doubt he had asked for it. Swept away by the avalanche, struggling desperately as he fell over the cliff—had he been able to find himself?"

The hero has little patience with professorial theories and systems —it was they that sent him down the slightly more adventuresome way of the novelist. He has a reactionary brother who is more unequivocal in a similar aversion. "I dislike intellectuals. They are pigs, pigs wallowing in the mud of ideas and words, getting their nourishment from the mud. They may not like it, but they have no choice. They can't get out." The brothers argue, but are really on the same side. At the end of the book the second brother goes off to participate in an assassination. Thereupon the hero feels unprecedented "love for his brother, as human being, as friend." Ishihara's brother is a movie star who has not, to public knowledge, participated in any assassinations. The novel is uncomfortably autobiographical, however, and there can be little doubt of affinity between novelist and hero.

Africa figures in the wishful fantasies of the Hotta hero and the Ōe hero, and it is important too in the world of the most striking of recent Ishihara heroes. But there is a difference between Ōe and Ishihara (just as there is an obvious difference between both and the busily engaged Hotta): in the end Ōe does not allow African adventure to substitute for an initiation nearer at hand; in the recent Ishihara novel Africa provides an awareness of self that cannot be recaptured in the more womanized world of Japan. *Action and Death*, published in 1964, is set in Egypt during the Suez invasion and in Tokyo at some unspecified time thereafter. The hero is a young Japanese businessman, who, by himself and in the Egyptian cause, scuttles a ship to block the canal. Back in Tokyo he has a very strenuous love affair with a lady who is representative of advanced young Japan, but the ecstasy of that moment in the canal will not return. Among the Japanese lady's faults is her excessive skill in bed. The hero always feels—the description is baldly erotic—that he is being sucked in by voracious femininity.

The act of heroism may have something to do with the Egyptian cause in the abstract, but it has more to do with the hero's individuality and masculinity, his finding of himself in the act and in its immediate stimulus, the embrace of an Egyptian lady. Here we see him back in Tokyo, just released from the embrace of the Japanese lady:

> Now, as if trying to regain something lost, he stood in the gathering dawn and sought to give reality to the hot numbness he had felt then, in an act that now passed belief, deep inside a skin chilled to freezing. . . . What he had seen there alone in the dark water, in the circle cast by the revolving light, was the image of Farida, he had felt her tactile presence. And his own, so keenly that the awareness was akin to pain.

This intentness upon finding one's proper self in "pure action" brings strong echoes of Hemingway. Indeed both Ōe and Ishihara are much in Hemingway's debt, and Ishihara sometimes sounds almost like an imitator. His defeated boxer speaks in cadences embarrassingly reminiscent of Hemingway's defeated ("The Undefeated") bullfighter: "I'm not in luck. That's how it is. The first two rounds were mine. A lucky punch. That's what it was, a lucky punch."

If withdrawal and disengagement from the causes that so moved Japanese journalism in the fifties and Japanese novelists in the twenties seems a conspicuous feature of much that is best in contemporary Japanese fiction, it has its more aggressive side. Enough has been said already to suggest that withdrawal does not mean gentle receptivity and solitary meditation. Zen was not quietism for the medieval Japanese warrior, and the way to self-realization is not quietism for his modern fictional descendant, who is not without resemblances to him.

One notices the frequency with which Japanese are portrayed as guides and redeemers for the retarded and underprivileged three-quarters of the world. In the rather embarrassing climax of Hotta's *Sphinx* we learn that Japan commands the attention of the newly emerging forces not so much because of technology and material prosperity as because of a moral preeminence bestowed through Hiroshima and Nagasaki. Hotta's characters behave from the outset as if their superior powers of discernment and freedom from petty self-interest gave them the right to command. The situation is even clearer with Ishihara's cosmopolitan hero. Hotta's people behave like redeemers, Ishihara's man quite frankly takes the title for himself. If the critics are right in thinking that Ōe, with his constant concern for the trials of growing up and being initiated, is giving symbolic representation to Japan's rise from international insignificance, then matters would seem to be more open with Hotta and Ishihara. It is perhaps worth remarking that neither the Ishihara hero nor the Hotta hero is above resorting to deceit if his aims seem to call for it. In *Action and Death*, the young gentleman of Japan is able to get to the banks of the canal and so to scuttle his ship by flashing his neutral passport. In *Sphinx* the young lady of Japan is able to act with impunity as an FLN courier because she carries UNESCO credentials. Japan would seem to be exercising its leadership by taking advantage of a certain want of responsibility.

One notices the extraordinary incidence of violence. It is so frequent that it almost comes to seem like a silly convention, an annoying mannerism. Ishihara is the worst offender. For no very good reason, one feels at first, his *Crevasse* ends with two murders and a strong suggestion that a third is on the way. Ōe, though he brings *A Personal Matter* to a comfortingly positive—and really not very convincing—conclusion, loves to write of what might be called vicarious murders or symbolic murders. The hero of *A Personal Matter*, though he grits his teeth and finally takes responsibility for the monster he has brought into the world, has been guilty of the spiritual murder of a childhood friend. In the concluding sentence of "Seventeen," the seventeen-year-old hero, participating in the 1960 riots, learns that a girl has been trampled to death by the fevered crowds, and the news brings on "the orgasm of a rapist."

But perhaps even in Ishihara's case it is not, after all, "for no very good reason" that murders take place at such a brisk rate. The second murder at the end of *Crevasse* arises from the first, and the adumbration of the third murder has the function of making explicit a contempt for left-wing intellectuals and a sympathy with right-wing activists. But the first murder is the important one. Only twice is the hero able to bridge the crevasse of the title. One of his partners in the bridging, the professional murderer, is the victim of this first murder. The other, the prizefighter, is the murderer. The hero is of the company, participant in the ultimate act. The sense of having conquered the crevasse comes when he is with one or the other of the two men, and cut off from the world. With the professional murderer it comes first during a walk on a foggy night. With the fighter it comes when the two are out on a boat together. The description of it is of utter bliss:

> He was fearfully happy. He thought that absolutely never before had he been so happy. He took Kamishima's hand and they laughed and gasped and laughed again, and he groaned out something:
> "Now I am here," he said, "completely with him."
> Now he knew himself in the world Kamishima knew in the ring, a world from which he had thought himself disqualified, in which he had thought himself incompetent.

Man of action with man of action, fused, in a world women do not enter—it is a situation with obvious homosexual implications. More important, it is a proto-military situation.

Ōe is somewhat different in that he does not allow his most substantial hero, in *A Personal Matter*, the satisfaction of a proto-military crisis. He lets him dream about it, however: "If I had been to war, Bird sometimes thought, I would have a clear answer to a question: am I a brave man or not? The thought came to him before a quarrel, an examination, it had even come to him before his wedding. And, alas, he had never had a definite answer. Now he wanted to try himself out in Africa, so remote from the everyday. That could be his own individual kind of war."

Enough examples have been cited to make the point. Many more could be. And what do they all signify? It would probably be unfair to say that young Japan is spoiling for another fight. Sometimes a person does have a suspicion, however, that the effects of too much peace are making themselves felt.

(1966)

1. I cannot resist introducing a personal note. One of the most piggish Germans, an unregenerate Nazi who is suspected of being a police agent and whose sympathies are with the OAS, is named Seidensticker. Since Hotta and I are personal acquaintances and since our political views are rather far apart, I cannot but suspect that something besides chance explains his choice of so improbable a name.

THE "PURE" AND THE "IN-BETWEEN" IN MODERN JAPANESE THEORIES OF THE NOVEL

It used to be that Shiga Naoya was the god of the novel—or of the *shōsetsu*, which is not quite the same thing. Now, to judge from advertisements in the newspapers for this or that six-foot shelf of modern Japanese literature, he has become the god of "pure literature" (*jun bungaku*). It is not easy to know whether this change means that he has risen or fallen in the pantheon. The opposite of pure literature is not, as one might suppose, impure literature. It seems to be various things at the hands of various critics: mass literature, or popular literature, or the literature of entertainment, or *monogatari* literature; and between pure literature and non-pure literature lies something known as in-between literature (*chūkan bungaku* or more commonly the *chūkan shōsetsu*). Perhaps, then, Shiga Naoya, although reigning over a more rarefied heaven than heretofore, reigns over a smaller one.

But the impulse to mock comes easily, and already I have taken on a mocking tone. To the Western reader the only distinction of any importance is that between literature and non-literature, between, let us say, a pair equally addicted to autobiography, Thomas Wolfe and Norman Mailer; and the pure half of the expression, the *jun* or *junsui*, becomes meaningless.

There are Japanese critics who would be happy enough to join in the derision. Muramatsu Takeshi, back from a trip abroad some years ago, expressed wonder at the diligence of the Japanese critic who, in addition to keeping his head above the flood of new writing, found time to debate with his fellows the state of affairs with pure literature.[1] Also some years ago, a very young critic, Etō Jun, with the brashness and self-confidence that seem to be the mark of emergent Young Japan, called a middle-aged critic, Hirano Ken, an incurable romantic, a perpetual youth, a boy who never grew up. The chief characteristic of the perpetual youth, said Etō, is a loss of touch with reality; and the occasion for his remarks was an elaborate critical edifice raised by Hirano having to do with the nature and vicissitudes of pure literature.[2]

Yet what at first seems a silly distinction can sometimes teach us something. It can tell us about the values assigned by other people even if we cannot accept them ourselves. We can, like an anthropologist, observe the strange practices by which others attain to feelings of high pleasure. We may even be able to answer that most difficult of questions raised by students, and indeed by colleagues, and by one's own younger self: what in the world do the Japanese see in Shiga Naoya?

The expression *jun bungaku* (pure literature) is as shifty and elusive as most critical terms, but it obviously has reference to something admired by the critic who makes serious use of it. I propose first to look at a series of critical confrontations that seem to have led to its becoming a part of the critical vocabulary, then to look at instances of its use in recent criticism, and finally to see what can be learned from these occurrences.

Recent investigation shows that the expression was in use as early as the last decade of the nineteenth century.[3] Indeed it was used by the man who is generally held to be the pioneer theoretician of the modern Japanese *shōsetsu*, Tsubouchi Shōyō, in his debate with Mori Ōgai. For him the distinction between the pure and the non-pure seems to have been generally the same as the famous distinction in his "Essence of the Novel" (*Shōsetsu shinzui*) between the modern and the non-modern, the non-didactic and the didactic.

Kitamura Tōkoku, the leading critic of the mid-Meiji school called "romantic" by the Japanese, also used the term, and in a sense designed to establish the purity of himself and his friends. For him the pure had reference to literature whose purpose was to satisfy the demands of self-awareness, without reference to the practical or the ethical. In opposition to it stood the popular, the *tsūzoku*, which category in Tōkoku's day included principally domestic and historical novels of considerable didactic intent, ancestors of the newspaper serial. Tōkoku and Shōyō were thus at one in their rejection of

Tokugawa didacticism, and Tōkoku pointed the way to later theories of purity with his emphasis upon the self. To each critic the pure seems to have been generally synonymous with the modern. Or as Young Japan might put it today, purity was anti-feudal.

In the first decade of this century a most interesting exchange took place between two very important literary adversaries, Tayama Katai, who is generally held to be one of the founders of Japanese naturalism, and Natsume Sōseki, a leading anti-naturalist. Katai made two pronouncements to which Sōseki took strong exception. When Katai denounced a certain work by Sudermann as a "fabrication" (koshiraemono), Sōseki replied that the successful fabrication of nature and character was the essence of fiction; and when Katai described "impressionism" as "objective literature," Sōseki replied that the two expressions were contradictory. What he meant, it would seem, was that a random, unshaped collection of small matters observed and experienced by the writer did not add up to a novel. It was just such collections that the naturalists considered the essence of naturalism.

The word *jun bungaku* is not used in the debate, the relevance of which may therefore not be apparent. Yet when we look on the one hand in the direction being pointed to by Tōkoku with his notions of purity as self-awareness, and, on the other, the direction pointed back at by such later believers in purity as Akutagawa Ryūnosuke and Kume Masao, the lines converge on this obscure little disagreement. More and more the notion of what was purest in the *shōsetsu* was coming to have reference to what might be called literary exhibitionism. The novelist who most diligently and unreservedly bared scars and birthmarks in intimate places was the purest and the most modern, for the sum of such marks was taken to be very much the same thing as Tōkoku's whole man fully expressed. Departures from the confessional were, by implication at least, sentimental departures from reality in the direction of the *tsūzoku*.

Or so it was with what the Japanese call "the mainstream." Sōseki, of course, had a very different view of the novel. For him a realistic novel was successful to the degree that its characters took on an illusion of concrete and independent life appropriate to their symbolic function. What he was really doing, therefore, was defending himself against the charge of impurity, of popularization. And what was happening, at the end of the Meiji period, was the jelling of the notion of pure literature as autobiographical literature. The term Yoyūha, originally applied contemptuously to Sōseki and his followers, means something like "the Dilettantes," and strongly suggests that the work they were engaged in was less serious than that which the naturalists had undertaken.

The concept of literary purity thus taking shape in the line from Tōkoku through the naturalists did not have a great deal to challenge it in the early Taishō period. Natsume Sōseki did not long survive the Meiji emperor, and he left no disciples up to the task of carrying on. Mori Ōgai, whose early autobiographical sketches had been praised by Tayama Katai, turned to the past, and his historical writings were reports on real toads in real gardens. Not even Katai could have thought them fabrications. Nagai Kafū, such a fine figure of a lad in the years after his return from America and France, was falling into glum, middle-aged silence, and there are those of us who think that Tanizaki Jun'ichirō never got started until after the earthquake. The Shirakaba faction reigned over the land, and autobiographical fiction was accepted very much as the air people breathed. It was the distilled essence of literature, the abstraction of literature, so to speak. Shiga Naoya was its god.

Very curious is the case of Arishima Takeo, the one man among them who, in his practice as a novelist, might have called himself an heir to Natsume Sōseki. Arishima's most famous critical work is probably "A Declaration" (Sengen hitotsu), published in 1922, a year and a half before his suicide. It is a declaration of despair. Class warfare had come to Japan, and Arishima found himself offside. What was needed was proletarian literature, he said, and only a proletarian could produce that.[4] The implications for his writing were to deny the power of the imagination and to turn him in upon himself; and so in the end he was not far from his fellows and the naturalists who preceded them in denying authenticity to anything except the most personal of literature.

By the time of Arishima's suicide a new generation had come to the fore, a generation of storytellers, Akutagawa Ryūnosuke, Kume Masao, and Kikuchi Kan (or Hiroshi). Fabricators all, by Tayama Katai's standards, one would have thought. And yet with them too matters proved to be curious. Especially so was the case of that second famous suicide among modern Japanese writers, Akutagawa. The indications are that in the end Akutagawa felt dissatisfied with and even guilty about his modernized versions of *monogatari* and *setsuwa*, so far removed from everyday life. His most famous critical writings came even nearer the end of his life than had Arishima's. The last installment of his "Literary, Much Too Literary" (*Bungeiteki na, amari ni bungeiteki na*) appeared in July 1927, the month of his suicide. Although it is not limited to literary controversy, the memorable parts of the series concern a disagreement with Tanizaki.[5] Tanizaki thought an interesting and even a perverse plot the most important thing in a novel or story, and Akutagawa did not. In a key passage he tried to explain what did seem important. It was not that he particularly glorified the plotless story; but the elaborately manipulated plot was not in itself worthy of critical attention. Nor was he in favor of a parading of personal trivia. His ideal was fiction as near as possible to poetry. The purest of fiction was that in which the workings of "the observant eye" and "the sensitive heart" were to be detected. Akutagawa offered as an example of what he had in mind Shiga Naoya's "Flares" (*Takibi*), a little prose lyric that can scarcely be called fiction at all.

It was not until 1935 that Kume Masao got around to saying much the same thing in his "Pure Literature as Avocation" (*Jun bungaku yogisetsu*).[6] Half ironically, Kume argues in favor of writing potboilers for a living and producing "pure literature" in one's spare time. Shiga's work is offered as the "highest peak" of the pure, and a novelist slightly younger than Kume, Yokomitsu Riichi, comes in for a jeer or two. All this professionalism, all this complex plotting—no more of an achievement than the most ordinary popular literature, really, says Kume. "Yokomitsu—do you not find yourself intensely nostalgic for the days when literature was an avocation and you were writing autobiographical fiction?"

Tanizaki's views on the importance of plot make it clear that such theories were not universal. Yet through the decade of the twenties (and Kume Masao, although the essay quoted above came later, was a man of the twenties) there is to be observed a tendency to see Shiga Naoya's quiet prose lyricism as the highest form of the *shōsetsu*. One must add that, although at the time Tanizaki seems to have been thought the winner, one is not sure in retrospect. Tanizaki was not and has not been all that good an advertisement for his own theories. Just at the time of the debate with Akutagawa he was in the process of gestating *Maelstrom* (*Manji*), a novel that would be much improved if its plot were less contrived. *Some Prefer Nettles* (*Tade kuu mushi*), from about the same period, is one of his best works and one of his most autobiographical; and in his most admirable works from the thirties and later, the demands of plot are not so powerful as to forbid extended sorties into the field of the lyrical and discursive essay.

With the passing of Akutagawa, the searcher after theories of pure literature turns most readily to Yokomitsu Riichi. Yokomitsu was the principal theorist of the school known as "Neo-Sensualist," which fact means for practical purposes that he was the writer of whom anti-Marxist critics expected most. The Marxist or proletarian school harkened back in its theories to the didacticism from which Shōyō and Tōkoku had rebelled. The proletarians had themselves not been entirely successful at resisting the blandishments of autobiographical fiction, but their ideological grounding did at least seem to offer promise of an alternative to Shiga's sort of purity.

Yokomitsu became an advocate of the "in-between" or "amalgamated" novel (*chūkan shōsetsu*), which he chose to call by another name. He had every right to feel that he had been caught in the middle. Although the proletarians had fairly well been pushed off the stage by the mid-thirties, the proletarian voice in literary criticism had not been smothered. Yokomitsu's *Coat of Arms* (*Monshō*, 1934), an attempt to present as objective fiction the inner struggles of the vacillating intellectual, was sharply attacked by the proletarians for what in fact it was, too overt in its demands upon the reader. In 1935 the most revered of anti-Marxist critics, Kobayashi Hideo, made as if to join hands with the Marxists. In a famous essay on autobiographical fiction,[7] he argued that Japanese devotees of the form had learned about manner but not matter from the French, and that the "Neo-Sensualists" were the last of the journalizing epigones. The proletarians, he said, must at least be given credit for ideas strong enough to encompass the techniques imported from France. (In passing, Kobayashi made another remark of considerable relevance to our story: that most Japanese literati would be inclined, secretly if not publicly, to put *Madame Bovary*, *War and Peace*, and *Crime and Punishment* in the category of *tsūzoku*.)

Tacitly accepting the judgment that Shiga's sort of purity was very pure, Yokomitsu set out to establish something of substance in the reaches between stratosphere and swamp. Although his most famous essay on the subject came out some weeks before the famous Kobayashi essay, the sense of being caught in the middle, not pure or popular or proletarian, indeed not much of anything, is everywhere apparent. The essay is called "Theory of the Pure Novel" (*Junsui shōsetsuron*). Despite the name he chose for it, the "pure novel" of the title amounts to very much the same thing as the *chūkan shōsetsu*. In his next novel, *Family Council (Kazoku kaigi)*, Yokomitsu attempted to put his theories into practice. Again, unfortunately, the critics were right in finding that the demands upon the reader were too explicit; but more important for our purposes is the fact that his theory of the *junsui shōsetsu* did not deny the claims of the more traditional *jun bungaku*.

Few thinkers have outdone Yokomitsu in the drawing of fine distinctions. In his "Theory of the Pure Novel" he notes five concepts of literature: pure literature, art literature (*geijutsu bungaku*), the pure novel, mass literature (*taishū bungaku*), and the popular novel (*tsūzoku shōsetsu*).[8] It will be seen that they do not appear to be mutually exclusive. Only the first, third, and fifth need concern us. The traditional distinction between the first and the last, according to Yokomitsu, is that the one does not allow waves of sentiment and abhors the chance or accidental, the other loves both. The one stems from the tradition of the diary, the other from the *monogatari*. The time has now come to bring the two together—for is there not plenty of accident, plenty of sentimentality even, in *Crime and Punishment*? The *junsui shōsetsu* in Yokomitsu's theory is the combination of the two, the introduction into *jun bungaku* of contrivance and emotion, one gathers, whose aim is other than to preach or to amuse. It is Shiga's austerity—his "rigorism," as another critic has put it, making use of the English word[9]—plus a plot and a strain of non-solipsist humanity. As foreign examples of what he has in mind, Yokomitsu offers *Tom Jones* and *The Charterhouse of Parma*, both of which, he says, would probably have been labeled "popular novels" had they been written in Japan.

Yokomitsu did not succeed in producing a Japanese *Tom Jones*, and it is not easy to see how his "pure novel" could have been made into an amalgamation of the popular and Shiga's "purity." The delicate "I" of Shiga's writings would be sent back into the blue by the first whiff of Tom Jones. What is more to the point, however, is that both Kume and Yokomitsu, the one longing to return to it, the

104

other chafing at its restrictions, admitted the existence of the "pure" in literature. If such earnest but unsuccessful works by Yokomitsu as *Coat of Arms* and *Family Council* were cast into the pit of the popular by Kume, and no questions allowed, then most of Sōseki's works and many of Tanizaki's and Kafū's could have expected no better treatment.

At the time of his essay, however, Yokomitsu thought that the two of them were part of the same band, and that along with them were, among others, Osaragi Jirō and Hirotsu Kazuo with their notions of elevating the popular novel, and Kawabata Yasunari with his theories on letting a little fresh air in upon the literary world.

Probably no two would have agreed on exactly what works beyond those of Shiga Naoya would qualify as pure. The temptation would perhaps have been strong to say: "I'll call your books pure if you'll call mine pure." For the whole notion of pure literature, it must be confessed, has about it something introverted; it suggests writers writing about writers for the sake of other writers. It suggests the *bundan*, the literary world, tight and cozy and turned in upon itself.

At this point one is inclined to say, "So matters were on the eve of the war," and jump over to the noisy years since 1945. Pure literature was there, and popular literature, and the unfortunate Yokomitsu suspended between. Even if the story is artificially limited to critical debates, however, matters are not so simple. Literary terminology is never very precise in Japan, and debates have a way of evaporating before it is entirely clear what they are about; and other critical terms were meanwhile being tossed about, to attempt a definition of which would in each case require as many words as have already been given to *jun bungaku*. There was, for instance, and continues to be a much discussed but badly defined something known as the "art novel" (*geijutsu shōsetsu*). The term would seem to refer to anything not obviously fugitive and ephemeral and not of use in class warfare.

All the same, so matters were, in a vague and general way. Among those who stemmed from Tsubouchi Shōyō and anti-didacticism, the views of Akutagawa and Kume were of compelling force, and even people like Yokomitsu, who tended to think that there had been enough purity and more would mean asphyxiation, paid implicit homage to them.

Since the war the talk has continued. As should be apparent from the remarks by Etō and Muramatsu noted above, there has been some tendency on the part of younger critics to dismiss the whole notion of pure literature as not very useful. To middle-aged critics, however—those who got their start back in the days when proletarian literature was collapsing and people were wondering where to go next—it still seems very much worth talking about.

There have been successors to Yokomitsu Riichi in more than one sense. The critical Left has sometimes seemed rather near him in acknowledging the presence of something called pure literature, even when not wishing to pursue it. Thus Takeuchi Yoshimi, a strong supporter of the New China, seems in some devious way to think pure literature one of the crimes of Western cultural imperialism; but he seems to agree with most critics his age that the expression does describe something.[10] Others seem to be Yokomitsu's heirs in the cause of developing the regions between the pure and the popular. Perhaps Nakamura Mitsuo is among them. His advocacy of a new "political novel," a revival of a mid-Meiji genre, may be seen as an attempt to turn the novelist away from Shigaesque introspection.[11]

Itō Sei (or Hitoshi) has offered a touchstone or two whereby to distinguish the in-between from the pure. Inoue Yasushi, who of recent years has shown a great fondness for historical fiction, is offered by Itō as one of the more promising of the in-betweeners, and the magazine *Shōsetsu Shinchō* is called their home ground. A glance at its table of contents suggests that writers about the same age as Itō and Inoue and only slightly younger than Yokomitsu are its mainstays: people like Ishikawa Tatsuzō, Inoue Tomoichirō, Funabashi Seiichi, and Niwa Fumio. Itō also tells us that the detective story, heir to autobiography in the case of Minakami Tsutomu, and to social consciousness in the case of Matsumoto Seichō—that tireless raker in the fetid muck of the American Occupation—opens up a bold new in-between prospect.[12]

Hirano Ken, offering an example or two of what dwells up there in the pure, also offers a memorable example of what does not. On high are Shiga Naoya and the Tanizaki of *The Mother of Captain Shigemoto* (*Shōshō Shigemoto no haha*), but *The Makioka Sisters* (*Sasameyuki*) is the worst sort of popular literature. The expression actually used by Hirano is not *tsūzoku shōsetsu* but rather *fūzoku shōsetsu*, which is translated in Kenkyūsha's Japanese-English dictionary as "genre novel." It is most often used disparagingly to refer to a novel wanting in character, intellectual content, and social implications, and given over to superficial descriptions of what people wear and eat and powder their noses with.[13]

Of all postwar critics, Hirano and Itō have probably had the most to say about pure literature. Both participated in the liveliest postwar debate on the subject, and it was Hirano who started it. In 1951 he wrote an article for the *Asahi Shimbun* felicitating the literary magazine *Gunzō* on its fifteenth birthday. In a day of in-between novels, he said, *Gunzō* was notable for its dedication to *jun bungaku*.[14] He made very clear what he meant: pure literature had centered upon the "I-novel," the *shishōsetsu*, and had come upon bad days in the years since the war. It was by way of becoming a historical concept.

In response to attacks upon this theory—Takami Jun, a middle-aged novelist with roots in the autobiographical tradition, as much as called him a snake in the grass[15]—Hirano amplified it at great length.[16] His brief history of pure literature was not all that brief, and it is considerably too complicated to be described here. In a general way he divided the literature of the thirties into three categories: pure literature, the literature of entertainment, and something known as the literature of "actuality." The English word, in *katakana*, was used to designate this third leg of the tripod.

The way to the literature of entertainment—generally, popular literature—was pointed to by Tanizaki with his emphasis on plot and suspense. Pure literature meant, of course, the canon of Shiga Naoya and his disciples, especially Ozaki Kazuo, in the thirties a genial chronicler of impoverished but happy domesticity.

And "actuality"—that seems to be what the proletarians were after until they got enmeshed in Russian-style orthodoxy. The main literary tragedy of the thirties, says Hirano, was that the writers of pure literature, who should have embraced "actuality," disdained to do so; and that was that for pure literature, and the revival of "actuality" has become the main task of postwar writers.

It cannot be said that Hirano is a paragon of lucidity, and the foreign reader may take comfort in the fact that Japanese readers seem to have trouble too. In a dialogue between Hirano and Matsumoto Seichō, published in *Gunzō* in June 1962, Matsumoto asked Hirano to define once and for all what he meant by "actuality." Hirano answered that it was very simple and talked on for a closely printed page, concluding his discourse thus: "I but use 'actuality' tentatively to refer to the problem of how to discover something more universal, something that does not immediately fall into patternization." And so the problem begins and ends in a peculiar Anglo-Japanese jargon, for the last word is the English "pattern" made abstract by the Japanese suffix *ka*. Having listened intently (one may suppose), Matsumoto replied, "*Naruhodo*," or something like "Well, now." The dialogue moved on to topics not of such immediate interest to us.[17]

Itō Sei was among Hirano's politer and more sympathetic critics. He expressed general agreement with Hirano's survey and analysis, although he preferred the word *dōtoku* (morals, ethics) to Hirano's "actuality."[18] And he saw dangers in too much emphasis upon the "pure." For one thing, purity, as seen in the line from Shiga Naoya to Ozaki Kazuo, had meant the cutting away of progressively more from the ken of the pure novelist, until such rich fields as sex were turned over to people like Tanizaki.[19]

For another thing, Itō was aware of a certain professional risk in being too staunch an advocate of the pure. If one were to trace the tradition back to the Heian period, he said, not Murasaki Shikibu but rather Sei Shōnagon would be seen to stand at its head—and indeed in their own day it was she of the two great ladies who was thought the nearer to representing serious literature. And following the lines back again to our own degenerate age, might we not find that writers called "popular" are the true heirs to the *monogatari* tradition? And might they not be producing masterpieces? And might we not be laughed at for all future generations, even as we laugh at the warped taste of the Heian period, for failing to recognize them? A nod in the direction of Minakami and Matsumoto, then, by way of hedging.[20]

The fragmentary story related above is not congenial to brief summary. The notion that there is such a thing as *jun bungaku* seems to have been one of the accepted notions of the thirties, and critics who had their beginnings then still talk of it as if it were an isolable substance. They do not agree with one another on precise definitions and often do not even attempt them; and sometimes, as we have seen in the case of Hirano Ken, one cannot be entirely sure that they are agreeing with themselves. Still, they tend to look upon literature as lending itself to meaningful description as it approaches or departs from purity, and where the substance has been isolated with the most success is to be found an essay-like, highly personal, and frequently lyrical style most closely associated with Shiga Naoya.

These glimpses of the theory and its history may have seemed more striking for what has been left out than for what has been included. The idea of pure literature does not offer a really satisfactory theme for reviewing and summarizing modern Japanese literature because it demands such an eccentric point of view. The reader will have wondered, perhaps, that so much has been said of Yokomitsu Riichi and so little of his more talented colleague, Kawabata Yasunari; that mention is made of Ozaki Kazuo, an Agnes Repplier of the modern Japanese novel, and nothing of Dazai Osamu, a writer who also came into prominence in the thirties but whose autobiographical inclinations were more demonic; why jewels and flummery should all be mixed together. The theory fails to come to grips with the question of what fiction is and what distinguishes it from non-fiction, and so comes dangerously close to casting such persons as Tanizaki and Sōseki into the land of the non-pure or the semi-pure or the merely amusing.

The notion of pure literature is inadequate and perhaps even silly, then; but still it tells us something. The most important thing it tells us, I suppose, is that judgments of contemporary literature that may seem queer to us have venerable antecedents. By our lights the Japanese may not be the most perceptive people in the world when it comes to distinguishing fiction from non-fiction. They have read lyrics in prose and in verse, however, and they have read tales (*monogatari*); and the former genre has often seemed the superior. Better the *Narrow Road to the North* (*Oku no hosomichi*) than the whole prose corpus of Saikaku, better a sheaf of vignettes by Sei Shōnagon or whoever wrote the *Tales of Ise* (*Ise monogatari*) than Murasaki's grand structure.

And so perhaps we can go before our classes and say: "Students, Shiga Naoya may seem like a drink of water to you; but to those who have long sipped of *zuihitsu* and *haibun* and the *utamonogatari* and diaries and travelogues he is Jove's nectar itself." And then, perhaps, we can go on to the fascinating question of why the Japanese should have put relatively so much more emphasis upon confession and delicate lyricism and so much less upon meaty drama and narrative than we have. Or perhaps we shall have to call in the sociologists and the psychologists to do it for us. They have begun to give us appetizing bits on what essay and autobiography say about the proclivities of certain writers; but they have not yet begun to tell, so far as I know, why the impulse toward exhibitionism and self-exposure should be so strong in the first place.

(1966)

1. In "Theory of 'Pure' Literature" (*"Jun" bungakuron*), *Bungakkai*, XV (1961), 12: 85–91.

2. "On Wasted Youth" (*Seishun no kōhai ni tsuite*), *Gunzō*, XVII (1962), 4: 160–69.

3. The information on early uses of the expression *jun bungaku* and on Sōseki's disagreement with Katai comes from Senuma Shigeki, "Modern Concepts of Literature and How They Have Changed" (*Kindai no bungaku gainen to sono hensen*), *Gunzō*, XVII (1962), 2: 150–60. The essay in which Shōyō uses the expression *jun bungaku* is called "Three Schools of Fiction" (*Shōsetsu sampa*), to be found in *A Compendium of Modern Literary Theories (Gendai bungakuron taikei)*, I (1955): 96–102.

4. *Library of Modern Japanese Literature (Gendai Nihon bungaku zenshū)*, XXI (1954): 417–20.

5. Excerpts will be found in *Gendai bungakuron taikei*, III (1956): 336–59.

6. *Gendai bungakuron taikei*, V (1956): 287–89.

7. "Theory of the 'I-novel'" (*Shishōsetsuron*), *Gendai bungakuron taikei*, V (1956): 299–316.

8. *Gendai bungakuron taikei*, V (1956): 288–99.

9. Muramatsu, *"Jun" bungakuron*: 87.

10. See the article on "People's Literature" (*Kokumin bungaku*) in *A Dictionary of Modern Literary Debates (Kindai bungaku ronsō jiten)*, (1962): 358–61.

11. "Further Thoughts on the Political Novel" (*Futatabi seiji shōsetsu o*), *Chūō Kōron*, LXXIV (1959), 5: 281–91.

12. The discussion of Matsumoto, Minakami, and *Shōsetsu Shinchō* will be found in "Is 'Pure' Literature Possible?" (*"Jun" bungaku wa sonzai shiuru ka*), *Gunzō*, XVI (1961), 11: 180–87; and the remark about Inoue in *Gunzō*, XVI (1961), 12: 172, in the course of a panel discussion with Hirano Ken and Yamamoto Kenkichi.

13. *Gunzō*, XVI (1961), 12: 161, in the course of the same panel discussion. It is curious that Hirano also expresses admiration for *Maelstrom*, one of Tanizaki's more contrived novels.

14. *Asahi Shimbun*, September 13, 1961.

15. "A Protest against Attacks on Pure Literature" (*Jun bungaku kōgeki e no kōgi*), *Gunzō*, XVII (1962), 1: 192–200.

16. See, for example, his very detailed introductory remarks to the panel discussion referred to above; see also "Final Remarks on the In-Between" (*Chūkan no shime-kukuri*), *Bungakkai*, XV (1961), 12: 137–45.

17. *Gunzō*, XVII (1962), 6: 140.

18. On p.160 of the *Gunzō* panel discussion referred to above.

19. "Is 'Pure' Literature Possible?": 184.

20. Pages 170 and 171 of the panel discussion referred to above.

ON KAWABATA YASUNARI

Everyone who writes about Kawabata Yasunari tells us, no doubt rightly, that the crucial events in his life happened very early: he was a child, in his own phrase, "without home or family,"[1] and, again as he himself has put it, he has had the mind of a wanderer ever since. He lost his parents in infancy, and his grandmother and his only sister, whom he never really knew, died not long afterward. He was fourteen when, in 1914, his grandfather died. From the following year he lived in a middle-school dormitory, and in 1917 he left his native Osaka to enter the First Higher School in Tokyo. Insofar as he has had a permanent abode since, it has been in eastern Japan: the Izu peninsula, Tokyo, and, since 1936, Kamakura. He has written very little about Osaka, although in recent years Kyoto has caught his fancy.

For some writers a sense of identity with place is essential. For others, homelessness is the big fact, the beginning of it all. Kawabata's writing practices suggest a positive longing for that condition. More than thirty years ago he remarked upon the fact that so much of his writing—more than half of it, he said—had been done at inns. The near fiasco of the Nobel lecture, which was still being reworked in a hotel room at the hour appointed for its delivery, suggests that the practice has not been abandoned. As it is with the creator, so it is with the creations. Even when they have homes, as has Mrs. Ōta of *Thousand Cranes* (*Sembazuru*), Kawabata characters are seldom seen in them. The most notable character of the early Kawabata is a wandering dancer on the Izu peninsula. The most notable recent characters are two old men, one of whom, in *House of the Sleeping Beauties* (*Nemureru bijo*), is seen only at inns and apparently has mainly unpleasant memories of home, while the other, in *The Sound of the Mountain* (*Yama no oto*), feels cut off from his nearest blood relatives, and dreams of two unattainable women, his daughter-in-law and his sister-in-law, the latter dead many years, in an old home that Kawabata chooses not to take him back to. During the years from 1928 to 1936, when Kawabata lived in and wrote of Tokyo, he described the places that most interested him as "islands in a distant sea."[2] The novelist Mishima Yukio, in one of the most perceptive of critical essays on Kawabata, has called him "a perpetual traveler"—a sort of Japanese Flying Dutchman who enjoys and profits from the role.

Kawabata's earliest surviving work is called "Diary of a Sixteen-year-old" (*Jūrokusai no nikki*). Though not published until 1925, it is, Kawabata has assured us, virtually unchanged from the form in which it was first written, in 1914, when, by the Western or "full" count, he was not yet fifteen. His diary for the weeks preceding his grandfather's death, it is an extraordinary work for a fourteen-year-old. The clear eye, the restraint, the curious mixture of pathos and coldness, of pity and loathing, have in them much of the mature Kawabata and suggest an extraordinary and disturbing precocity. This is not, one feels, the kind of boy it would be pleasant to have taking a close look at one. Here are the last lines, written about a week before the grandfather's death (the conversation, in the Osaka dialect, of course suffers from translation, but perhaps something of the cold pathos and the lack of boyish sentimentality survives):

> "I'm going out," I said, running out of the house at some minutes past seven. When I came in the door at about ten, Grandfather was calling for Otsune as if he could not wait a minute longer.
> "What is it?"
> "Where is Otsune?"
> "She's gone. It's ten."
> "Did she give me anything to eat?"
> "Of course she did."
> "I'm hungry. Can't you give me something to eat?"
> "There's nothing in the house."
> "Oh? That's too bad."

It was not as ordered a conversation as this. The same fixed, stupid things were repeated over and over again. What I said to him would go in one ear and immediately out the other, and he would ask the same question again. Is he losing his mind?

Kawabata's earliest important fiction, which appeared in the early twenties, is of a most unusual kind, collections of tiny short stories, or perhaps vignettes might be the more appropriate word, that are called in Japanese *tanagokoro shōsetsu*. Literally "palm-of-the-hand stories," the expression might be translated as "vest-pocket stories," and the form, which to my knowledge no one else has made such considerable use of, might be called the prose equivalent of haiku. Sometimes these little fragments, the shortest of which could be translated into two or three hundred words of English and the longest of which would run to no more than perhaps fifteen hundred, are further fragmented into episodes no more than a sentence or two long, and call to mind less haiku than *renga* (linked verse). A striking example is a little story called "The Moon" (*Tsuki*). It is about a young man who has trouble losing his virginity, and all the women who attempt to aid him in that endeavor.

One woman, standing beside his pillow, sank suddenly and roughly to her knees, and, throwing herself upon his head, breathed of his scent. . . .

And another woman, washing his back in the bath, clutched at his shoulder with a hand that began to tremble violently.

And another woman, sitting with him in a winter room, suddenly jumped down into the garden, and, rolling over face up on the bench in the pergola, held her head tight between her two elbows. . . .

And another woman, coming into his room with her sewing late at night, sat still as a rock while she waited for him to come back; and, red to the ears, in a hoarse voice that caught in her throat, offered the strange lie that she was borrowing his electricity.

If this was Kawabata's point of departure, he has in many ways not departed far. We already have the Kawabata eroticism, chilling in its transience. We have the deftness of characterization, with these anonymous women, each allowed her one sentence and made to move on, floating up with remarkable vividness. We have, in each brief appearance which invites rejection, the Kawabata loneliness and refusal to believe in love, and the sense of emptiness that he himself has described as Buddhist in its origins. We have the emphasis on women, frequently overwrought women. We have the virtuosity of style. A certain strain will be noted in the endeavor to make the last episode what it is in Japanese, a single sentence.

And, probably most important, we have the loose form, a stringing together of episodes with no clear beginning, middle, and end, which again calls to mind *renga*, and has been favored by Kawabata throughout his career. He has said that some scene or person, perhaps no more than a passer in the street, will catch his interest, and he will invent an incident to match it or him; and that incident may or may not call to mind a second incident, and the process may or may not be repeated. It is a concept of fiction likely to seem less strange to someone reared in the tradition of the *renga* and the discursive essay than to someone used to the well-shaped Aristotelian poem; and yet it has its modern, even avant-garde, aspects too. Is this not essentially the shape of a "happening"?

Kawabata's reputation was really made by a long story, or novelette, "The Izu Dancer" (*Izu no odoriko*) of 1926. It tells of a higher-school student who, going through the period of despondency that seems to be expected of higher-school students, takes a walking trip down the Izu peninsula, and in the course of it encounters a party of strolling performers. He is greatly attracted to the little dancer of the title. At first the attraction is sexual, but then, in a passage exceedingly famous but untranslatable because of the subtle use it makes of onomatopoeia, he sees her naked and realizes that she has not yet reached adolescence. His relief and pleasure are boundless, and as he continues down the peninsula with her the despondency goes away. At Shimoda he leaves them, to return by boat to Tokyo.

The story is brighter than most Kawabata, strays nearer the borders of the sentimental, and comes closer to affirming the possibility of love. In other ways it is very representative. It was long in gestating. Kawabata did walk down the Izu peninsula with a group of strolling players, but it was when he was a higher-school student, eight years before the story was finished. In a sense it is unfinished, and so stands at the head of the impressive list of unfinished Kawabata stories. He has said that he meant to add passages of natural description but never got around to them. Given his way of moving from one episode to another by free association, it was sometimes not easy for Kawabata himself to say whether or not one of his stories was finished, and it was frequently impossible for the world to know whether or not he would suddenly add another episode to a story the world had long thought finished.

There has been much speculation as to why the very young virgin should play such an important part in Kawabata's writing. Mishima has offered the interesting theory that it is because she is the epitome of the unattainable. Once she is attained, she becomes, of course, something other than the object of the yearning. Kawabata's eroticism is of a curious kind, having in itself something of the preadolescent. Even when the union is consummated, as it is not in "The Izu Dancer," there is a standoffish quality about the male partner, as if he were not entering into the act but savoring it with a cold eye and hand.

Even in this brightest of Kawabata stories, the melancholy Kawabata themes are present: the loneliness, the homelessness, the unquenchable yearning. And there is the nothingness, the emptiness. "The lights went out," says the last paragraph of the story, "the smell of the sea and of the fish in the hold grew stronger. In the darkness, warmed by the boy beside me, I gave myself up to my tears. It was as though my head had turned to clear water, were falling pleasantly away, and soon nothing would remain."

The translation, which is my own, is somewhat misleading. The word "nothing" is not really right, and the original has reference, in the last sentence, to "sweet feelings of pleasure, as of having nothing left behind." It seemed a touch too sweet in translation. Kawabata insisted, in his Nobel lecture, that the nothingness or emptiness of the East has little in common with the bleak nihilism of the West. Certainly there is an element of the positive in the sadness that so pervades Kawabata's writing, as if it were to be sought after, a sort of enlightenment, and not fled from.

In the mid-twenties Kawabata was a member of a group to which was attached the label Shinkankakuha, usually translated "Neo-Sensualist School." Actually it was a very disparate group, scarcely to be called a school at all. Its members did have in common, however, an interest in European avant-garde movements, Dadaism and surrealism and the rest. We are frequently told that the eccentric images, the sudden transitions, the obscurities of "Neo-Sensualist" writing are to be traced to such sources. There are some Kawabata works of which this is clearly the case. The most conspicuous example is "Crystal Vision" (Suishō gensō, 1931), an imitation of James Joyce. It is another on that list of unfinished works, and one is glad, for it resembles *Ulysses* less than the dreary interior monologues of "Strange Interlude." It is possible to see European influences in "The Izu Dancer" too, as for instance in the image of the leaky head which I have quoted; but when Kawabata is in good form, the new is also very venerable.

Another work, and a far better one, from the period of the unfortunate crystal adventure should be mentioned, because it is one of Kawabata's major "at-home" works, a novel about a city in which he was actually living. The Scarlet Gang of Asakusa (*Asakusa Kurenaidan*) is yet another unfinished work, the merest introduction to its subject, Kawabata has said. It was published between 1929 and 1935. The material is flamboyant, having to do with Asakusa entertainers and thugs. The heroine, who lives on the periphery of the entertainment world, seeks revenge upon her sister's betrayer, and presently has it by transferring from her mouth to his a substance which the dictionaries tell us is arsenious acid. The two most striking things about the book are the fragmented, episodic structure and the poignant lyricism. The characters in this "at-home" novel are wanderers too, and the roar of Asakusa becomes a muted call from one of those islands in a distant sea. And it is the Asakusa of the years after the earthquake. If specific incidents, other than his lonely boyhood, are to be held to account for the Kawabata sadness, the earthquake of 1923 and the defeat of 1945 must surely be among them.

Kawabata has described how he went about gathering his material: "I passed whole nights, any number of them, in the park, but I only walked around. I did not make the acquaintance of any of the delinquents. I did not speak to the vagrants. I did not go into any of the cheap restaurants. I made the rounds of the thirty-odd shows and took notes, but always from the audience. I did not talk to the performers, and only at the Casino Folly did I go backstage. I did not go into any of the cheap inns around the park, I did not go into a bar."[3] The aloofness of the writer is in the book too.

From the same period comes Kawabata's best short story, "Of Birds and Beasts," published in 1933. A year later Kawabata announced a great antipathy for the story,[4] but it would seem to have come back into his favor, for it is included in a lavish Nobel commemorative collection of his works, said to have been selected by Kawabata himself. It is about a man who rejects human attachments and keeps birds and dogs for companions. Scarcely a story at all in the Western sense of the term, it is a collection of little vignettes about the man's birds and beasts, interlarded with fragments about a dancer with whom he has had an affair and who has gone into a sad decline. Nowhere is Kawabata's refusal to believe in love more apparent, for the other side of the rejection of human affections is affection become cruelty, warping and torturing the birds and dogs in the quest for ever purer strains.

Formally, it is of great interest. If as a narrative it looks like an almost formless stringing together of small episodes, another Kawabata prose *renga*, on another level it is very tightly organized, perhaps the best illustration of the dexterity with which Kawabata manages time. It begins and ends at almost the same moment, and in between are flashbacks sometimes so complicated that the reader has to take out pencil and paper to decide whether everything is coming out all right. He may be assured that everything is.

Kawabata has said—the remark is reminiscent of what Faulkner said about *Sanctuary*—that in "Of Birds and Beasts" he set out to bring together the ugliest material he could think of. Ugliness there certainly is, and indeed a fascination with ugliness is apparent in much of Kawabata's writing. "I am drawn to dirty beauty," he remarked in the 1934 essay in which he banished "Of Birds and Beasts" from the canon.

Yet there is another side, a note of affirmation that makes the sad and the ugly in Kawabata so paradoxical and so Oriental. Near the end of the story the hero, if so determinedly anti-human a figure can be called a hero, recalls an occasion on which he and the dancer thought to commit suicide together. The woman's figure with her hands together as if in supplication drove thoughts of suicide from his head. Here is Kawabata's description of what it was that so suddenly changed him: "He was struck, as by lightning, by the joy of emptiness." Here we have it again, emptiness become affirmation, something to be striven for.

I have not changed my mind a great deal since I wrote the introduction to the English translation of *Snow Country*, and would refer the reader to it. I do not think that today I would be reminded so much of haiku by the book as of *renga*. It is quite obvious that Kawabata cannot have known where he was going when he started to write, any more than a group of poets know where they are going when they sit down to compose a *renga* sequence. The first chapter was intended to be a short story, and the last chapter is based on an actual event that had not yet happened when the writing was begun. I might also think of *The Tale of Genji*, both because of the sadness that pervades the novel and because of the structure. The *Genji* is so full of hesitations and new departures as to make it impossible to believe that Murasaki Shikibu had the whole work in her head when she started writing. And I might think of the *zuihitsu* lyrical essay. The narrative element in *Snow Country* is slight at best, having to do with an affair between a Tokyo dilettante and a hot-spring geisha, and at one point Kawabata breaks it off completely to give us an extended prose lyric about silk weaving.

I might be less inclined to describe the Kawabata style as terse than I was in 1956. In *Snow Country* it certainly is. In other works it can be repetitious and somewhat too heavily loaded with adverbs and rhetorical questions and qualifications. The terseness of *Snow Country* is to be accounted for by considerable cutting and reworking during the dozen years that were required to produce it. The original version began with reminiscences about Komako, the rustic geisha, and the present opening, with its evocation of the whiteness of the snow country, was buried some distance inside.

A few words might have been added about the curious nature of Kawabata's eroticism, and the way it has of intensifying loneliness and isolation by stopping at the surface. In *Snow Country* more than in earlier works one is aware of the remarkable part the sense of touch plays in Kawabata's writing. If some computer were put to work counting up and classifying the sensual impressions, it would probably find a disproportionate number of them to be tactile. The most famous such impression comes very early in *Snow Country*, with the case of the remembering finger. Kawabata characters are particularly fond of the feel of a firm young breast. Perhaps psychologists can trace the proclivity to infantile deprivation. In any event the way Kawabata characters have of pressing against each other and never achieving a union adds much to the sadness, the chilly lyricism, of the Kawabata world.

More might have been said about the geisha Komako as the most Kawabata-like of Kawabata characters. Kawabata's successful characters are as curious as his eroticism. They constantly seem to be falling into and becoming part of the natural setting, as in the striking examples of Komako in the snowy mirror, and the eye of the other girl, Yōko, superimposed upon a light in the mountain darkness. Mishima has aptly likened the Kawabata character to ectoplasm, working its way to dissolution in the monochrome sadness of life. And yet how vivid they are, Komako and Yōko, as they appear in flickers and flashes. Kawabata somehow manages to endow ancient sadness and insubstantiality with modern assertiveness.

Although the composition of *Snow Country* spanned the war years, no new part of it was published during the war. Kawabata's principal wartime writing was of a battle far from the battlefields. In 1938 there occurred, over a period of six months, a Go match between the great master, Honinbō Shūsai, and a younger challenger. Shūsai had never been defeated. He was old and ill, and this was to be his last match. He lost it. In 1940 he died. Kawabata covered the match for the *Tōkyō Nichinichi* and the *Ōsaka Mainichi*. In 1942 he began to write of it with touches of fiction. He continued to do so down to 1954, when the work that bears the title *The Master of Go* (*Meijin*) was finished. Kawabata indicated particular affection for it among his works. It is an extraordinary work, evoking with remarkable power the harshness of battle, the absolute commitment of the fighter, and the loneliness of defeat.

Perhaps Kawabata's affection for *The Master of Go* has to do with the fact that a similar loneliness was very much with him in the years after the war. "Since the defeat," he wrote in 1947, "I have gone back into the sadness that has always been with us in Japan. I have no faith in the appearances and the manners of the postwar world. Perhaps I do not believe in reality. It seems likely that I will move away from the realism that is the basis of the modern novel. Perhaps I have never been there."[5] A certain departure from realism is to be noted in Kawabata's last works. Yet the sadness is not a desperate throwing over of everything. It is rather an intensifying of something that had been present all along. Later in the same essay Kawabata says, quite in the spirit of "the master" himself: "The sadness of

Saturday Wife,[6] the pathos of the *Genji*, are softened by a Japanese kind of consolation and succor. . . . I have never experienced pains and sorrows of the Western kind. I have not once seen in Japan emptiness and decay of the Western kind.''

For some years, beginning in 1949, Kawabata was simultaneously at work on two of his major novels, *Thousand Cranes* and *The Sound of the Mountain*. The latter was at length, in 1954, brought to what Kawabata apparently considered a conclusion. *Thousand Cranes* was brought to what seemed a suitably bleak conclusion in 1951, with the disappearance of all the women in the hero's life save the one he cannot stand. Then in 1953 Kawabata brought a couple of them back and apparently intended to produce *Thousand Cranes: Part II*. This last must definitely be put on his list of incomplete works.

Thousand Cranes is centered upon the tea ceremony and upon quasi-incest. The hero has an affair with a widow who was his father's mistress, and when she commits suicide his affections are transferred to her daughter. The latter flees him, and at the end of the 1951 version seems to have disappeared completely, only to come back in 1953. All the while, a second mistress of the father, a mean and ugly woman, keeps intruding herself upon the scene, exuding venom and jealousy, trying to run people's lives and trying also to make a profitable business of the tea ceremony.

Kawabata objected in his Nobel lecture to the Western insistence upon reading *Thousand Cranes* as an anthem to the ageless beauty of the tea ceremony. It is rather, he said, a warning against the vulgarization into which the modern tea ceremony has fallen. Certainly there is more in it than ageless beauty; but surely too there is more in it than the didacticism suggested in the Nobel lecture.

It is possible to see the book as a parable upon the fragility and evanescence of makers of tea and the durability of the vessels with which they make it. Life is brief, art is long. But if these vessels are a symbol of durable beauty, there is also in the book a symbol of durable ugliness. Much the most vivid character is Kurimoto Chikako, the second of the two mistresses. ''And only Kurimoto is left,'' says Kikuji, the hero, at the end of the 1951 version. She, as much as Kawabata's beautiful women, is the eternal Japanese woman, reminding one of the morbid side of the Japanese aesthetic tradition, and of Kawabata's fascination with spoiled beauty, or, as he called it, dirty beauty. Chikako has an ugly birthmark on one of her breasts, a cancer-like object clutching at the heart of sensuality. One of Kikuji's most vivid childhood memories, and perhaps the most vivid detail in the novel, is of Chikako busily trimming the hair that grows from it.

The workings of a morbid sensibility are to be seen all through *Thousand Cranes*, and the stimulus is strongly tactile. The novelist Ibuse Masuji has said that the feel of Shino pottery, which figures prominently in *Thousand Cranes*, gave rise in Kawabata's mind to Mrs. Ōta, the lady who commits suicide. Certainly it is Shino that reminds Kikuji most vividly of her. "The very face of the Shino, glowing warmly cool, made him think of Mrs. Ōta." The word translated as "face" is "skin" in Japanese, suggesting much more immediately a caress, a hand wandering over a breast, than does the English. Earlier we have been told, with a characteristic mixing of the senses, that as Kikuji kneels before the dead woman's ashes he cannot see her face but can feel her touch, as of music. There is a coldness in this reduction to the tactile, making one feel that the poor woman has committed suicide because of a relationship that never really came into being. She has been destroyed by feelings of guilt for a love that was not there. Perhaps one can see in *Thousand Cranes*, a more difficult book than *Snow Country* to find the "meaning" of, the concrete expression of that disbelief in postwar manners and appearances.

The Sound of the Mountain is another "at-home" novel. It is set mostly in Kamakura, where Kawabata lives. The central figure is an old man, Ogata Shingo, who is far more strongly drawn to his daughter-in-law than to either of his own children. She is, once again, the object of a yearning that cannot be satisfied. There is another object: when he was young, back in his real home, Nagano Prefecture, he was drawn to his wife's sister, now dead, and married instead a woman toward whom he seems to feel little except somewhat derisive amusement. The novel is a stringing together of brief episodes, tending toward the lyrical, in typical Kawabata fashion. The action, such as there is, has to do largely with the unhappy affairs of the younger generation and so reminds one of the last chapters of the *Genji*. The Ogata son has a mistress. In the course of the novel his wife has an abortion, her way of emphasizing the essential sterility of their marriage. The mistress becomes pregnant, refuses to have an abortion, and goes off to the country, carrying with her testimony to another love that never came to be. The Ogata daughter packs up and comes home to mother, and her estranged husband attempts suicide. Shingo dreams of going back to Nagano to see the autumn leaves, which have deep associations with his dead sister-in-law; but the novel comes to a quiet stop before even this fulfillment is allowed.

One scarcely needs to beat the drums to announce that this is very much in the main Kawabata line, in its form and in its content. It is another prose *renga*, and it is bathed in a classical sadness. And yet it is also a very modern book. The denial of romantic love is modern, and so, in a way, is the formlessness; and nowhere is Kawabata's skill at characterization, at giving the illusion of individual life, more beautifully in evidence. Characterization is an art in which the Japanese showed little interest from the eleventh century to the end of the nineteenth. Each of the five major characters in *The Sound of the Mountain* comes strongly to life, and this despite the fact that the dialogue is sparse and that the mode is strongly lyrical. One of the five, the mistress, has a single scene, but she is allowed to make supremely good use of it. It is often said that Kawabata is unable to depict male characters. Certainly it is true that most of his writing centers upon women, with men acting as foils. This probably has less to do with a want of skill, however, than with a want of interest, brought on by the obsessive Kawabata themes and preoccupations. Neither the father nor the son in *The Sound of the Mountain* can be described as anything but a successful venture in characterization.

Kawabata's best writing in the sixties saw the withdrawal from realism predicted shortly after the war. *House of the Sleeping Beauties*, a short novel serialized in 1960 and 1961, tells of an old man who spends four nights in the strange house of the title. It is a bordello with a difference, allowing him the company of young girls who have been drugged into a sleep from which they cannot be awakened. The rule of the house is that he can do anything with the girls except injure them or deflower them, and it is assumed in any event that he is past being capable of the latter offense. By the now familiar method of free association, descriptions of how the girls look and feel and smell are mingled in among reminiscences, mostly of women, and short dialogues with the unpleasant woman who acts as procuress and housekeeper. Toward the end of the story we learn that another aged guest has died of heart failure in the course of a night with a sleeping beauty, and in a conclusion which Mishima, with his knack for the right word, has described as suffocating, one of the beauties dies and is dragged downstairs by the housekeeper. In "One Arm," a short story which was serialized in 1963 and 1964, a man has converse with the detached but still living arm of a young girl.

A man incapable of acting as a man, in bed with a girl who is incapable of responding; a man passing the night with the detached extremity of a girl: clearly we have eroticism as dehumanized as it can be, the Kawabata denial of love pushed as far as it can go. In *House of the Sleeping Beauties* especially, the eroticism becomes a quest for extinction, which again must be understood, or felt, in a Buddhist sense. The method of free association has never been used with more boldness and originality. One does not think of James Joyce, as in earlier Kawabata works, but of Kawabata himself, and the Japanese tradition of the discursive lyric. The extreme fragmentation takes one back to the earliest Kawabata. Some will perhaps have noticed and been mildly surprised by the description of "One Arm" as a serialized short story. The first installment, a very short story, was apparently intended to be complete in itself, for there was no indication at the end that it would be continued; and then several more very short stories were added, as in a collection of vest-pocket stories.

Yet Kawabata the modern writer is also in evidence, especially in the deftness of the characterization. The keeper of the house of the sleeping beauties appears in only the briefest bits of dialogue, but she is beautifully done, a new version of Chikako, the eternal nasty woman. Even the five sleeping beauties and the detached arm have an abstract sort of individuality.

Something should be said of the third Kawabata novel that was available to the Swedish Academy. *Koto*, literally "old capital," appeared in 1961 and 1962 and has been translated into German as *Kyoto*. I do not think it very good Kawabata. It is somewhat sugary and tells one that a touch of the morbid keeps the best Kawabata short of sentimentality. It is not wholly without interest, however. It contains some beautiful evocations of the evanescent, of what seems to be dying in Kyoto, and Kawabata's habit of feeling his way along and letting background create character and incident is very much apparent. The two central figures, with whose romantic difficulties the main action of the novel is concerned, are twin sisters. When he started writing, Kawabata has told us, he did not know that there would be twins. It seems that he was strongly drawn to the Nishijin weaving district, where the action begins, and then to the cedar groves of the northern hills; and so he invented a northern-hill twin, estranged in infancy from the Nishijin twin.

Summary at this point would come down to a listing of all the elements that make Kawabata such a unique mixture of the classical and the modern, so eminently qualified for the Nobel Prize. It seems better to let Kawabata talk about himself. He is also a very good essayist and critic.[7]

Here he is in 1947 writing on what the classics mean to him:

> During the war, on the train to and from Tokyo, and in bed during blackouts, I read *The Tale of Genji*. . . .
>
> I had reached the twenty-third book, about midway through the long romance, when Japan surrendered. It was a strange way to read the *Genji*, but it left a deep impression on me. It sometimes surprised me to see, there on the train, how completely absorbed I was in the *Genji*. I might well be surprised at the disharmony between me and the train, loaded with the baggage of refugees and victims of the bombings, making its way irregularly through the charred ruins, in terror of another bombing; but I was even more surprised at the harmony between me and a work a thousand years old.

And here is an earlier statement, from 1934:

> I believe the Oriental classics, and particularly the Buddhist scriptures, to be the greatest of the world's literature. I respect them not for their religious teachings but for their literary fantasies. For fifteen years now I have had in mind the plot for a story to be called "Song of the East." I have thought that I would like it to be my swan song. I will sing the classic Eastern fantasy after my fashion. I may die without having written it, but I wish to have it known that I wanted to write it. I have been baptized in and have tried my hand at imitating modern Western literature; but, at heart an Oriental, I have not once lost my direction these last fifteen years. I have thus far told no one of this fact. It has been the happy secret formula of

the house of Kawabata. Among the great Western realists, there have been some who, approaching death after great trials and agonies, have finally caught sight of the distant East; and perhaps I am playing there with a children's song in my heart.

Here he is, in 1934 again, on the chilly, aloof nature of his eroticism:

Hayashi Fusao has remarked upon the strangeness of the fact that the author of *Chirinuru o*[8] has a boy's longing for the female body; precisely by virtue of the fact that it seemed so strange, I thought that the remark struck home. . . . I have not, like the proletarian writers, a happy ideal, I have no children, I cannot become a miser, I know the emptiness of fame; and love is more than anything my bond with life. But I do not think I have ever held a woman's hand in a manner that falls within the meaning of love. . . . But is it not more than women that I have not held hands with? Is not life also thus for me? Is it not thus with reality? And perhaps with literature too? Am I a sadly fortunate man?

Here he is in 1933 describing the work of a painter friend who has recently died; and, as we see at the end, the description could be of Kawabata's own work:

There is no reason that I should understand surrealist painting; but if there is something old in Koga's "ism" pictures, I take it to be the fault of the ailment that is ancient Oriental lyricism. Far beyond the mirror of the intellect flows the mist of a distant longing. It is difficult for the amateur to see in a painting a rational structure or reasoned argument or philosophy; but faced with a painting by Koga, I see first of all something like a faraway longing, a dim, empty expanse. It is an affirmation beyond emptiness. It therefore has a bond with the heart of a child. His paintings are often like stories for children. But they are more than that. They are the clean, fresh dream of childlike surprise. And they are saturated with Buddhism. . . . Although he put much of the spirit of Western culture into his work, a children's song of Buddhism always flowed through the depths of his heart. That is why, in his brightly beautiful, childlike watercolors, there is a warm sadness. I have this old children's song in my heart too.

Here, in 1934, is the homelessness:

I do not wish to visit the West. I wish rather to visit the lost countries of the East. Probably I am a citizen of a lost country. No other people have so moved me as those endless lines, as if going into exile, of refugees from the fires after the earthquake. I have quite lost myself in Dostoevski, and I have not taken to Tolstoi. Perhaps because I was a child without a home and without family, melancholy wandering thoughts never leave me.

Here, in 1947, is the paradox, the strange fact that the homelessness itself brings one home:

In those days it was with me the reverse of the usual: I received not a few letters of consolation from soldiers in foreign countries. Some were from people I did not know, but most of them were the same. The writer had chanced to come upon my works, and had been filled with thoughts of home, and wanted to offer his thanks and best wishes. My writing seemed to make people think of Japan. Perhaps the *Genji* brought me a similar homesickness.

And here, finally, written in 1947, is a description of a painting by the late Tokugawa artist Uragami Gyokudō, a description which captures the sadness of Kawabata's own writing:

It was a sad, lonely picture, in which the thin, somehow drab red of the leaves and the color of the evening sky seemed to be fading away into each other. It had in it the loneliness of the late Japanese autumn itself. . . . Though it seemed to be a clear autumn day, the mistiness of the Japanese sky was in the painting, perhaps to make one think of the chill of dew. The sadness of traveling alone over mountain and moor, at the end of an autumn day, sank to one's very bones.

(1970)

1. "My Life as a Writer" (*Bungakuteki jijoden*), 1934.

2. *Ibid.*

3. *Ibid.*

4. *Ibid.*

5. "Sadness" (*Aishu*).

6. A novel by Oda Sakunosuke, unfinished at his death in 1947.

7. The quotations are all from three justly famous Kawabata essays: "Eyes in Their Last Extremity" (*Matsugo no me*, 1933), *Bungakuteki jijoden*, and *Aishu*.

8. A story published in 1933. The title, which might be translated "They Fall," is a phrase from the *iroha* poem which contains, without repetition, the whole of the *kana* syllabary.

MISHIMA YUKIO

We will have to wait for tidings from another world, or perhaps for a reincarnation in this one of a sort that he himself seems to have put much stock in, before we can know with what feelings Mishima Yukio had his last say to the soldiers under that late November noonday sun, turned to go back into the general's office, and then disemboweled himself. To judge from the recording of his last exhortation, it cannot have been with a pleasant warmth as of being sent on the way by friends. Some of the soldiers shouted chidings for past misdeeds, some suggested that he go take a cold shower, some merely called him a fool; and Mishima's own voice is scarcely to be heard above the raucous comments. Photographs of the assembly he addressed are dominated by the blandly amused sort of face the chimpanzee must see through the bars of his cage. The newspaper reports are agreed that Mishima's own face was blanched as, abandoning the effort to outshout them all, he left the balcony.

He must have been disappointed at the want of acclaim with which he was seen off. But was the ultimate outcome of the day's affairs a result of miscalculation? Some think so. Some think that he really hoped for a military rising and could not more completely have misjudged the mood of the country boys who join the army, or, more properly, the Ground Self-Defense Force. Others think that the shame of having faced the country boys and been jeered made the shame of having to face the world again more than he could bear. Either theory would lead to the conclusion, or at least the strong implication, that he expected to be among the living when the sun went down.

The burden of the evidence is that he did not. His last messages seem to say quite clearly that he saw suicide as the reasonable conclusion to what he had undertaken. So does the declaration he distributed to the troops that last noontide. His mature view of the Self-Defense Force, as remembered for the newspapers and magazines by his friends, would seem to be such that he cannot have expected many to come forward from its ranks and join him.

Another view is that, victim of the temporary depression that comes at the end of prolonged artistic endeavor, he was not himself. It is true that on the very eve of his death he sent off the last installment of his last work, a massive and very impressive tetralogy called *Sea of Fertility*, and it is also true that he had earlier expressed great apprehension about his state of mind, about the void that was certain to open in his life, once the tetralogy was finished. Yet he did not dawdle over it, as he probably would have had the apprehension been deep. Quite the reverse: his editors had not expected the fourth volume to be finished for some months, and were astonished at the size of the last installment and the speed with which it had been produced. The end of the tetralogy, which he was fond of calling his "life's work," may have provided the occasion for his suicide, but the suicidal impulses must have gone much deeper.

The final statement distributed to the troops hints, or may be construed as hinting, that Mishima had hoped to have more company than he did in that last demonstration. As it reaches a conclusion, he describes the long period of time (four years, he says it has been) that he and the little drill troop the papers have called his "private army" waited for the military to declare itself and so provide muscle tone for the flabby physique of postwar Japan.

> But we will wait only thirty minutes more, the last thirty minutes. We will rise together, and, for what is right, we will die together. We will die to take Japan back to its true self. . . .
>
> Now, even now, we mean to demonstrate for you the existence of values higher than life.
>
> Not freedom, not democracy. Japan. Japan, land of the history and the tradition we love.

Even here it seems necessary to interpret the "we" as having reference only to Mishima and his immediate attendants, and perhaps among the latter only to the single youth who did in fact join him.

Early in the statement there is a summary of what has gone wrong with postwar Japan: economic growth has been everything, the spiritual realm has been forgotten; hypocrisy, self-interest, individualism have proliferated; larger responsibilities have been abdicated, left to foreign countries; the land and its tradition have been sullied. "In the Self-Defense Force, we have hoped to find, even now, a last remnant of the true warrior spirit, of the true Japan."

It summons back memories of a great deal, this all-absorbing passion to rectify, this concern with principle so intense that beside it Thoreau's night in jail seems pale and womanish indeed. It reminds one of various nationalist risings and conspiracies of the past century and especially the army revolt of 1936. Running through them all and especially the last is the same concern with greed and hypocrisy, the same conviction that "right" is immediately apprehensible to the unsullied heart, that he who throws away all for the sake of what is right wins all. And the crucial importance in Mishima's last statement of the word here translated "right" brings an old Chinese tradition to mind. The word is *gi* in Japanese, *i* or *yi* in Chinese; and in an idealistic and optimistic strain of Chinese thought, or feeling, which the Japanese have found very congenial, it stands for a transcendent order of which we are aware so long as we do not allow our natal purity to be clouded—so long as greed and hypocrisy and materialism and all those other things are not allowed to get in the way.

There is another sense in which it can be argued that Mishima's plans got out of control and he would as soon not have committed suicide. He had been rehearsing the virtuous suicide for so long, it may be argued, that the time had come to put up or shut up. He was beginning to look a little specious in the eyes of his drill troop, whose respect was important to him. That problem aside for the moment—essentially it is the problem of how seriously all the talk about right and purity is to be taken—the rehearsals of suicide in his writings seem very immediate and on the whole convincing. The first overt rehearsal, though the dream of martyrdom had been with Mishima from the start, comes in 1960, with a harrowing story the English translation of which is entitled "Patriotism." "Concern about the State of the Nation" would be more accurate, but one would not wish to impose it upon any story. The hero is a young army officer who commits suicide after the 1936 rising, and Mishima himself played the lead with almost too much gusto in the very popular movie version.

But the most apposite rehearsal comes in *Sea of Fertility*. The tetralogy covers a sweep in time from before the First World War down to yesterday. Formally, it centers upon the theme of reincarnation, which Mishima has told us he borrowed from a late Heian romance. In the second of its incarnations, the protagonist ectoplasm is made manifest in the person and deeds of a young man who, in the fevered patriotism of the thirties, does not hesitate to do violence for what seems to him right. Toward the end of the second volume he is on trial for having participated in an abortive attempt at righteous violence. Under examination by the presiding judge, he explains his motives at length, and the resemblance to Mishima's own last statement scarcely requires comment.

> Yes. I wanted to carry out the principle of the unity of knowledge and action, the main principle of the school of Wang Yang-ming. "To know and not to act is not yet to know." Knowing of the corruption around us, of the dark clouds that close off the future of Japan, the poverty of farm villages and the sufferings of the poor; knowing that the origins of it all are in corrupt government and in an irresponsible moneyed class whose interests are served by the corruption; knowing that these are the roots of the growth that cuts off the light of His Revered and Benevolent Majesty; knowing all this, I find it evident that to know is to act.

In response to a request from the judge for a less abstruse statement, the youth describes a wish of long standing to emulate the young of the Meiji Restoration, for whom swordsmanship was more than a pastime, and proceeds to a detailed accounting of the humiliation to which the nation has been subjected since the London Treaty, and of social injustices brought on by the greed of the ruling classes.

> I have believed that the dark clouds which mask heaven must one day be swept away, that a clear and radiant Japan must one day emerge. But waiting does no good. The longer we wait the darker are the clouds. . . . And who then will take upon

himself the responsibility for the grand mission, go up and speak to heaven with his own death? . . . *A pure and resolute act is necessary to bring heaven and earth together.* [The underlining is in the original.]

And, as his eloquence reaches a climax:

> Loyalty is to throw one's life away and seek to be in accord with the great heart. It is to rend the clouds and ascend to the center of the sun, of the great heart. This is the whole of the vow which my fellows and I made to ourselves.

The expression "great heart" is, in the very elaborate context, by no means as emptily rhetorical as it may sound here, with the context stripped away. It has reference to the emperor as head of the mystical Japanese state, and has much in common with the "true warrior spirit" and "true Japan" of Mishima's own last statement.

The judge is much moved, and the young man receives a suspended sentence; and then he does go out and kill a rich man, ostensibly as punishment for a desecration of the Great Shrine of Ise, where the imperial ancestors reside. The volume ends with a lyrical description of his suicide, in the dead of night on a cliff overlooking the sea.

> Isao took a deep breath and rubbed his abdomen with his left hand. Then, closing his eyes, he brought the point of the dagger against it with his right hand, gave direction with the fingers of his left hand, and pressed with all the strength of his right arm.
>
> In the moment the dagger entered, the sun rose glowing red behind his eyelids.

Wang Yang-ming was a heterodox Confucian thinker of Ming China, and it is to the concept at the center of his philosophy that the young man alludes as he begins his apologia. The optimistic and genially romantic tendencies of Wang Yang-ming and his school were naturalized by the Japanese and given a more wildly romantic aspect. Young Isao, in the declamatory remarks that so move the judge, makes reference to young men of the Meiji Restoration. If the origins of the Meiji Restoration are pushed back to the arrival of Commodore Perry, then the young man who comes to mind as perhaps the intensest and most accomplished of them, and certainly the one who made the greatest name for blind dedication, is Yoshida

Shōin. In his early twenties when Perry arrived, he tried to smuggle himself aboard one of the American ships that he might go abroad and learn more of the enemy. Apprehended, imprisoned, and released, he continued to agitate in the cause of fealty to the emperor. By 1859 the shogunate had had enough, and he was put to death.

Robert Louis Stevenson presently learned of his unusual career, and in *Familiar Studies* wrote an essay about him.

> He was not only wise and provident in thought, but surely one of the fieriest of heroes in execution. . . . He failed in each particular enterprise that he attempted; and yet we have only to look at his country to see how complete has been his general success. His friends and pupils made the majority of leaders in that final Revolution, now some twelve years old; and many of them are, or were until the other day, high placed among the rulers of Japan.

Yoshida came from a Japanese school of Confucian purism that originated in the seventeenth century. The founder of the school, Yamaga Sokō, repudiated all the neo-Confucians of the Sung and Ming, including, presumably, Wang Yang-ming; yet his emphasis upon codes of behavior suggests strong affinity, and when he tells the samurai that studies unaccompanied by practical results diverge from the principal message of the Confucian sages, he is very near Wang and his "unity of thought and action." Yoshida's own favorite Confucian seems to have been not Confucius himself but Mencius, and Mencius's notions of a primordial purity to which we must return are basic to the doctrine of purity made manifest in action. Yoshida had a very practical idea of what learning should be, and its end was to set an example. If the example must be at the price of life itself, so be it. "I knew that if I did as I have done, this would be the result," he said in one of his last poems, composed as he was awaiting execution.[1]

And so through various risings and assassinations and attempted assassinations and other diverse incidents of a patriotic nature, down to Mishima. The tradition of suicide by way of example and edification may not be an entirely lovable one, but it is old and powerful, and Mishima, educated in a day of heroics and left to survive in a day of meliorism and sentimental liberalism, belongs at the end of it. Or so one would judge at the moment, though it may be that, like

Yoshida, he set a more impressive example than one can know.

It will seem, perhaps, that too much is here being made of an oration by a fictitious hero. There can be little doubt, all the same, that Mishima's sympathies are with Isao. A strange Mishima collection published in 1966 under the title *Voices of Dead Heroes* and including "Patriotism" as well as a play and the generically indescribable title piece, a sort of rhapsody, concludes with an essay called "The February 26 Incident and I." The "Incident" is the army rising of 1936. "Literary ambitions quite aside," says Mishima toward the end of the piece, "there can be little doubt that I have carried deep within me a wish to console the spirits of the heroes who have ruled me for so long, to clear away the calumny that surrounds them, to rehabilitate them. . . ."

> The reign of the present emperor breaks cleanly in two with the defeat of 1945. For me who lived through the break there is an inextinguishable desire to seek out the grounds for my own continuity, for a logical consistency. . . . I find myself caught up less upon the new constitution, defining the emperor as a "symbol," than upon the emperor's own renunciation of his divinity.

After meditating upon the tragic consequences of the emperor's efforts, back in the thirties, to be a constitutional monarch, Mishima concludes with two rhetorical questions and an answer that is really a third question:

> Was constitutional monarchy ever really possible for Japan? Those statesmen of the Western persuasion, the heedless young army officers—which of the two was in the final analysis right? Japan would seem to have succeeded admirably in a crass kind of Westernization; and one wonders whether in the years that lie ahead Japan will succeed as well with Westernization of a spiritual kind.

Mishima's displeasure with the "liberal" intellectuals who have dominated postwar Japanese journalism was quite open. He would have no part of their imported bromides. He was a complicated man, and one of the great puzzles about him will always be that a man who seemed to enjoy the company of Americans and Europeans, who was something of a Westernized dandy, and who littered his books with Western accessories and appliances should in the end have declared himself an unregenerate believer in the Japanese martial spirit. At least one explanation is that they, the self-styled liberals, were for him the un-Japanese xenophobes and he the true heir to the Japanese spirit in his energetic and sometimes daring pursuit of the most flamboyant new Western styles. He hated the liberal orthodoxy, in any case, and during the fifties, when the professional intellectuals seemed to be running as a pack and their liberal dogmas offered the safest formulas for selling books, he went his own way. There is scarcely a suggestion of the political in his writings during the decade. He may have been driven to his final act, ironically, by the impotence of the intellectuals. He had hoped, he said more than once, that left-wing disturbances in 1970, when Japan could for the first time legally denounce the Security Treaty with the United States, would be of sufficient proportions to force the government into a less ambiguous defense policy. Nothing emerged to make the government other than satisfied with ambiguity, and so the time had come for something dramatic on his side.

Yoshida Shōin made himself clear : he hoped that his death would inspire others to act. He thought of himself as the posthumous leader of a movement. Did Mishima? He did not, like Yoshida, contemplate assassinating anyone, and his followers were forbidden to inflict bodily injury upon the general they had in their power during the final balcony scene (though it has been reported that among those excluded from the scene were some who had more violent ideas). It is hard to believe, and most of the evidence above argues against the likelihood, that he expected immediate results. He knew the sybaritic youth of the land too well for that. What, then, of the long run? That is of course anyone's guess, though there are already intimations that the purity of his motives, if not precisely the script, for that last scene is being offered as an ideal to strive toward. He came, in any case, from a tradition to which suicide as grand gesture, as protest that may not be ignored, is no stranger; and one can imagine, whatever the hopes of his eulogists, that to be remembered as the last embodiment of the tradition would have been enough for him.

What rather brings the argument up short at this point is not the initial objection that his plans went awry but the possibility that what he did may have been not self-immolation at all but a grand act of self-gratification. Here his curious proclivities must come into the discussion. His writings fairly exude narcissism, as also did his spare-time activities, so to speak. He posed for the most extraordinary nude and near-nude photographs. The last English translation of a Mishima work to appear before his death has on the dust jacket a picture of Mishima clad in a loincloth and a head band and those garments alone, and the flap bears the credit line: "Jacket Design by Y. Mishima." It is hard to believe, unless he was one of the most talented and thoroughgoing pretenders who ever lived, that he was other than captivated with what he saw in the mirror.

He made a cult of youthful masculine beauty. He went in for boxing and swordsmanship and body-building, and his horror of old age, the destroyer of it all, is voiced repeatedly in his work, both through symbol and in explicit declaration. There is, for instance, a short story called "The Peacocks" (1965), the very title of which seems a touch symbolic. The central incident is the mysterious slaughter of a flock of peacocks, and the central figure, who is first a middle-aged man and then, in a sequence resembling the second act of a Nō spirit play, his own youthful self, is the presumed assassin. Fascinated by the peacocks, he meditates upon the contrast between their plumage and their drawn and wizened faces. He concludes: "Only through their own destruction could the peacocks be made perfect. The brilliance of the plumage sustained the life in them, drawn taut like a bow, aimed at that one point, the slaughter."

The title of *Tenth-day Chrysanthemums*, the play in *Voices of Dead Heroes*, is more explicit. It has reference to something that is no longer needed or someone who has outlived his day, the Festival of the Chrysanthemums coming on the ninth day of the ninth lunar month. The hero is a man who has lived to be old when he should have died in the 1936 rising. In the essay that concludes the volume Mishima makes very explicit indeed the horror such a prospect arouses in him: "Among the notions I have not been able to rid myself of is that of old age as forever ugly, youth forever beautiful. The knowledge that comes with age is forever murky, the action of youth is forever clear. We decline, we grow worse, the longer we live. A man's life is but a falling backward into decay."

To the narcissism and the cult of youthful beauty must be added the cult of "love-death," of eroticism joined to death and especially to suicide. Mishima has said that the Japanese have taken the love suicide to heights no one else has reached, and (he was half jesting, but one senses a deep seriousness all the same) that it is one of their principal claims to what their "image" abroad has so frequently denied them, originality. A preoccupation with death astonishing in one so young runs through even his earliest works, and the union of self-destruction and sexual joy has its most explicit statement in "Patriotism."

And Mishima's homosexuality must also be added to the complex, and the fact that, like the medieval warrior, he chose to die in an exclusively masculine setting, with young men to help him die and, if they so chose, and one of them did, to die with him. Put all these cults and tendencies together, and there it is: the case for the prosecutor who would argue that Mishima died not to startle the world into a new awareness of an old, honorable, neglected, and perhaps dying tradition, but to taste of the ultimate joy and avoid the horrors of showing the world a haggard face and a sagging body.

So it may be that even the writings of Mishima's last decade, which seem so honest in their espousal of tradition and nationalism, take on a cynical cast. Mishima warned us of irony in, for instance, the title of *Sea of Fertility*, borrowed from one of the barren seas of the moon; but if the tetralogy itself is part of a grand pose, then the irony is such as to make one stand still in admiration. Whatever may be the case with his last writings, the novels of his middle period, the decade of the fifties, have come to look rather different in the light of his final acts. I myself have long held that their most apparent qualities are excessive cleverness and deplorable evidence of a willingness to pander to the reader. Now, perhaps, they may be seen as exquisitely planned and elegantly executed nose-thumbings at that very reader. Probably the best of them is *The Temple of the Golden Pavilion*. A very annoying book on first reading now, suddenly, comes to seem rather delicious. It may be that in the precious explications of a Zen riddle Mishima is out-Zenning them all, suggesting through the very preciosity and sophistry of the words the meaninglessness of words without action.

(1971)

---

1. Mishima killed himself on the anniversary of Yoshida Shōin's execution. It has been averred, but not firmly established, that he was aware of the fact.

SEA OF FERTILITY

The tetralogy *Sea of Fertility* (*Hōjō no umi*) occupied Mishima Yukio for upwards of the last five years of his life. He would seem to have begun making detailed plans for it toward the end of 1964, and the last installment bears the date of his death, November 25, 1970. The very last episode seems to have been written some months before his death. The tetralogy was to have carried the name *Moon Banquet* (*Tsuki no utage*). This rather neutral title had already been changed for the ironically suggestive *Sea of Fertility* before the first installment appeared in the magazine *Shinchō*. Borrowed from the Mare Foecunditatis of the astronomers, it suggests an expanse with an appearance of fertility but after all barren.

Completely engrossed in his plans for the novel and at least the first stages of the writing, Mishima was fond of describing it as his "life's work," in such a way as to suggest strongly that there would be nothing for him to enjoy and seek to conquer once it was out of the way; and so a great sense of emptiness as the end came in sight has been averred as one of the reasons for his suicide. He was fond of saying, wryly but with a suggestion of earnestness, that it was one of the most unread works of our day. He had reference of course to serial publication, and it must be admitted that the meanderings of the huge novel were somewhat intimidating when they came in small fragments. A great Mishima boom followed immediately after his death, and, like a great many other things he wrote, *Sea of Fertility* became a best seller. Yet not everyone who buys a book reads it, and the remarkably small amount of critical notice which it has attracted suggests that it continues to be, relative to the attention it deserves, among the unread works of our time.

The action covers almost two-thirds of a century, a time span so ambitious as to call to mind *The Tale of Genji*, which covers almost three-quarters of a century, and in the canon of modern classics perhaps only Shimazaki Tōson's *Before Daybreak* (*Yoake mae*) can compete. The theme of transmigration was borrowed, Mishima himself has told us, from *The Tale of the Hamamatsu Councillor* (*Hamamatsu Chūnagon monogatari*). The two works bear little resemblance in plot, however. Because characters in the *Hamamatsu* are reborn with memories of earlier lives and in intimate relationships with characters who appeared in those earlier lives, the complications are enormous, beyond even the most outrageous contrivances of W. S. Gilbert. The plot of the Mishima story is much simpler. Each of the successive reincarnations is allowed a volume in which to do his thing and go his way, with little reference to earlier lives. There are thus four protagonists, and there is a long-lived deuteragonist who sees all but the last go their several ways, and who observes and comments rather after the fashion of the *waki* in the Nō theater, by which Mishima was strongly influenced.

The action begins in 1913, when both the first protagonist and Honda, the deuteragonist, are eighteen, and ends in 1975, or just under five years after Mishima's own death. For purposes of the tetralogy itself, 1975 or thereabouts is an immovable date, since each of the protagonists is allotted a life span of two decades, and only the last fails to catch the signal and go; and so one may suppose that when Mishima began writing the novel he had no notion that he himself would die in 1970. He wrote and talked of suicide in such a way as to make his own suicide seem inevitable, and 1975 would have brought his fiftieth birthday, an event toward which he looked with horror; and it seems not at all unlikely that, a decade or so ago, when he began laying plans for the tetralogy, he had 1975 in mind for his own suicide.

The first protagonist, Matsugae Kiyoaki, is the son of a titled family modeled upon that of the great Saigō Takamori. He dies, in a somewhat improbable fashion, because of an impossible love. His soul finds reincarnation in Iinuma Isao, the son of his manservant. Isao is caught up in the perfervid nationalism of the thirties and dies for an impossible ideal, pure dedication to the Japanese family-state presided over by the emperor. The third reincarnation is a

Siamese princess who, in the years just after the war, dies for—well, it is not possible, somehow, to say that she dies for much of anything, since her death is accidental and seems rather gratuitous, and since it is from about this time that Mishima's original intentions for the tetralogy seem to waver. We are given to understand, somewhat fleetingly, that she dies for an impossible commitment to things of the flesh. The fourth protagonist, Yasunaga (later Honda) Tōru, is an utterly cynical and self-seeking representative of postwar youth whom Honda adopts in the belief that he is the fourth reincarnation of the central spirit, and who raises doubts, never resolved, by refusing to die when his twenty years are up. He has the three moles on the left chest that have identified the previous three as proper reincarnations, and he was born at just about the time of the Siamese princess's death, but the most important fact in his biography would seem to be his refusal to die at twenty. In the second and fourth books Honda is intent upon joining his destinies with persons whom he takes to be authentic reincarnations, although in the fourth he seems to conclude that he has been misled. Isao, the second protagonist, is implicated in a conspiracy, discovered by the police, to assassinate a number of important financial figures, and Honda resigns from the bench to serve as his lawyer. In the fourth book he adopts the protagonist and seeks to make him over into a bland mediocrity not likely to let his passions and his distinction from the common herd lead him, as his predecessors have been led, to an early death—and then finds, apparently, that they were not his predecessors at all. The third volume forms a strange blank. Honda is here most completely given over to the ratiocination and the preference for observing over acting that distinguishes him from at least Kiyoaki and Isao, and the Siamese princess fails to come forth as much of a presence at all. The fourth volume is yet stranger, though it succeeds far better as a novel, perhaps better than any of the other three save only the first. It seems founded upon confusions so considerable as to make one wonder whether Mishima might not have lost interest in or control over his work.

Mishima put a great deal of thought into the tetralogy before he began writing. It is a complex work, despite the essential simplicity of the plot. Motifs and themes are intricately woven in and out, and there are echoes back and forth among the several volumes, some of them rather obvious, some very delicate. The philosophical grounding of the work is subtle, receiving its most open statement in the third volume, as Honda, after a visit to Siam and India, pursues the niceties of Yuishiki Buddhism.

Mishima's original scheme works out rather well through the first two volumes, in that the devices which join them are intricate and elaborate, relying largely on dreams. There is little doubt either in Honda's mind or that of the reader that Isao is Kiyoaki's reincarnation. As a novel the second volume is not the equal of the first. It would be hard to find a Mishima novel that might be described as flawless, and often the flaws are to be attributed to the exuberance of Mishima's imagination and to the fact that it was a rather florid sort of imagination, more appropriate, perhaps, to a dramatist than to a novelist. One sometimes feels that he was happiest when writing for the Kabuki stage. He delighted in improbabilities and non sequiturs such as are the very essence of Kabuki but do not seem quite as much at home in the novel. There are also extravagances in *Spring Snow*, the first volume, as when at the end the hero is brought back from Nara to Tokyo without benefit of medical advice despite the fact that he is known to be suffering from pneumonia. The Kabuki audience delights in this device for assuring that he will die, and this invitation to start weeping; but the reader of the novel is accustomed to the more probable. The details to which one might take exception in *Spring Snow* are minor, however, and such as a stern but sympathetic editor could have corrected without much trouble. On the whole Mishima is successful in evoking an atmosphere of courtly grace and a hero who is destroyed by his longing for the unattainable. Kiyoaki is a wonderfully apt symbol for Mishima himself. He too was lost in pursuit of the unattainable, his counter-self.

Though it is tightly intermeshed with *Spring Snow* and though the reader is given no cause to doubt the validity of reincarnation for fictional purposes, the second volume is by no means as successful. When, a decade or so before his death, Mishima began restating the grounds for his traditionalism and making his sympathy for the extremism of the thirties into the material of his writing, one could applaud without oneself having much sympathy with nationalist extremes. For the first time Mishima seemed to be writing about something he really believed in. Yet the hero of the second volume remains an unconvincing abstraction. When, early in the book, he announces his intention of one day killing himself, he sounds like Mishima saying again something he has already said several times, but not like a teenage boy answering a rather casual question from a man he is meeting for the first time. Here, perhaps, lies the key to his inadequacy: he is too close to Mishima to take on a life of his own. It is often the case in modern Japanese autobiographical fiction that when a hero is speaking for his creator a certain abstract stiffness comes into his utterances. Mishima was never an "I-novelist" in the sense of limiting his characters to what he himself had done and said; but in this instance he approached uncomfortably close to auto-biography.

The second volume may be less satisfying fiction than the first; but the two are closely joined, and on an intellectual and conceptual level Mishima seems to be holding to his original ambitious plans. It is with the third volume that the joinings seem to weaken. All the signs are that the Siamese princess is a proper reincarnation. The last words spoken to Honda by the second protagonist, in a drunken delirium, predict that the two will meet again among southern roses, and indeed it is in a Siamese "rose palace" that Honda first meets the princess, still a child. She was born at the proper time, she is able to answer questions about her previous incarnations, and she has the three crucial moles, though (and what one is to make of the fact is difficult to say) they are not clearly visible except when she is sexually aroused.

But there are suggestions that Mishima may have grown uncertain about or perhaps bored with the whole idea of transmigration. The third volume is actually two stories of about the same length, and the first is hardly a story at all. Honda, who is a barrister after having resigned from the bench to defend Isao, is in Bangkok as the book opens, representing a Japanese trading company in a damage suit. The time is just before Pearl Harbor. He meets a princess who is the daughter of a prince he has known in the first volume. From her ability to answer questions about Kiyoaki and Isao he concludes that she is their reincarnation, even though he is unable to detect the three crucial moles. He then goes to India, and he spends a large part of the war studying Yuishiki. So ends the first story, rather more a meditative travelogue and a philosophical disquisition than a piece of fiction.

The second story is set in Japan in the years after the surrender.

The Siamese princess comes to Japan as a student and Honda sees something of her; and then he hears, through a twin sister who makes a rather startling appearance on the last pages, not so much as having been mentioned before, that the princess died in Bangkok at the proper age of twenty, victim of a poisonous serpent.

Of all the four volumes this third was changed most from Mishima's original concept. There was to have been a good deal about Siamese politics, apparently, and the princess was to have been a symbol of and to an extent a defender of tradition. In fact she emerges as very little of anything at all. She spends much of her time eluding Honda, and when she does appear, fleetingly, she has almost nothing to say. Her biggest scene, it is rather sad to have to say, takes place beyond a wall and a peephole. She is engaged in homosexual love with a friend of Honda's. If she has dreams we are not told of them, and so the device that served as the principal binder between the first and second volumes is absent. It is clear that she is of great physical beauty, but she is not enough of a physical presence, even, to deserve ranging beside the other three protagonists. Mishima seems to try at least twice in the fourth volume to establish her significance, once when Honda is giving Tōru lessons in how to be bland and inoffensive and so avoid the early death of his predecessors, and once when the lady who has been the princess's lover gives Tōru a dressing down. But it is too late. The princess is simply not where she should be, at the center of and giving life to the third volume, which is sadly wanting in life.

What went wrong? Japanese novelists have never been very good at depicting foreigners except as clowns and as villains, and perhaps Mishima blanched and lost courage at the responsibility, undertaken of his own volition, to depict a foreigner as neither grotesque nor evil. Had he succeeded in the endeavor and made of the princess a person wholly given over to the demands of her uncommonly beautiful and demanding flesh, and therefore condemned, like her two predecessors, to an early death for having gone against the leveling tendencies of nature, then she even more than Isao would have been an embodiment of Wang Yang-ming's unity of thought and action; and so, one suspects, Mishima would have been troubled by a very deep contradiction. He may have thought of himself as a follower of Wang Yang-ming and in his last years at least held the Wang Yang-ming ideal as his own, but it was always with an intellectual sort of apprehension. The ratiocinative tendency and his aversion to it are both very apparent in the fourth volume. It was perhaps the contradiction he had most in mind when he sought to make himself over into his own opposite.

There is another contradiction, most apparent in the religious discourse that has the effect of making the first half of the third volume only tenuously fictional. Yuishiki Buddhism is a subtle and complex doctrine. With its central tenet that only consciousness is real and that each moment represents a new disposition and meeting of seeds from the "warehouse," the *ālaya*, it would seem to be at least doubtful that the spirit remains an entity bearing with it intimations from past lives and casting shadows ahead into future lives, in the manner we find so elaborately posited in the first two volumes. Mishima is on record as saying that he began from somewhere hereabouts to lose faith in the idea of reincarnation; and it may be that the lifelessness of this third volume is due more than anything else to his own uncertainty about the grand scheme with which he began. At the very end, with the quite gratuitous appearance of a twin sister to inform us of the death by reptile venom of the princess (itself a rather gratuitous and melodramatic way to have her die), it is almost as if Mishima were resorting to melodrama to cover his own uncertainty—and, having come a dangerous and unrewarding way, falling into the theatrics with which he was always most comfortable.

The fourth volume is yet more puzzling. Mishima's early notes for the tetralogy seem to tell us rather definitely that the fourth protagonist is to be a counterfeit, in the sense of not being a reincarnation of the central spirit. What he is supposed to represent is, in Mishima's work notes, couched in technical jargon, and the question of whether or not the whole idea of transmigration is being called into question is a mysterious one. Apparently the young protagonist is meant to be Honda's alter ego. He is the only one of them to marry and has become Honda's adopted son, and so the perpetuator of the Honda line. Thus he is close to Honda as none of the others are. Among Honda's more striking characteristics has been a penchant for rational analysis, and the tendency is remarkably strong in Tōru as well.

It is one of the reasons (Mishima's work notes, indicating his intentions in the matter, are of course the first and most important

145

reason) for concluding that he is a counterfeit, an impostor, not a reincarnation of the proper ectoplasm. None of the other three has been much given to intellectual endeavor, and indeed anti-intellectualism has been among their stronger claims to distinction. Another is that he does not dream and so cannot contribute to the sort of weaving back and forth through dreams that holds the first two volumes together. He is still living at the end of the last volume, even though his twentieth birthday has passed. Mishima has made early death a private convention along the way, on the grounds, presumably, that nature may be expected to lose no time in extirpating its own most exceptional products. There is the strong possibility that he was born too soon in any case to be a perfectly documented reincarnation, though Mishima seems here to play with our curiosity and introduce an element of suspense such as might be acceptable in a play but does not seem entirely appropriate to a novel. At this point he introduces the wildest improbability in the whole long tetralogy, for he would have us believe that Honda has great difficulty in ascertaining when the princess died. Is one to believe that it would be even slightly difficult for a well-placed Japanese to learn when an important member of the Siamese royal family died?

There are other matters to confuse the issue and in the end leave the reader feeling rather puzzled. Tōru is about the right age even if we never learn whether he is precisely the right age or not, and he has the three moles on his left chest. There are strong suggestions that he has glimmerings of memory from another world, and the suggestions are equally strong that it is a tropical world of passion and violence (where better than Siam?). In one of the most curious scenes, Tōru observes the passage of a nameless old man through snowy streets and is reminded of a woman's shorn hair by a bundle which he drops and fails to retrieve. The scene is mystifying unless it harkens back to the first volume, in which on a snowy day the hero's lover becomes a nun.

One is puzzled further to understand why, if he is a counterfeit, Tōru is such an extraordinary young man, far more vivid than his predecessor in the third volume and perhaps the strongest character in the whole tetralogy. He is an utterly cynical and selfish person, so cold and self-contained as to approach, though stopping precariously short of, the incredible. He has long considered the three moles his private sign that he stands apart from the race, and he also seems to consider himself an incarnation of evil for whom none of the ordinary rules applies. The whole improbable revelation that Honda, for whom of course the moles are equally significant, means to adopt him seems to affect him not at all. The next day being a holiday he goes to a movie and takes a stroll along the beach, and apparently gives the matter no further thought. He keeps a diary, certain excerpts from which we are allowed to read, and it is a most remarkable document from the hand of an adolescent, revealing a heartless and astonishingly self-conscious arrogance and suggesting rather more strongly the mature Mishima himself than young boys of one's own acquaintance. To Honda the successive incarnations of the central spirit are all extraordinary persons whom nature drives to their own destruction. Why, one wishes to ask, is this young man, so much more extraordinary than at least the Siamese princess among the earlier incarnations, to be thought counterfeit? And what difference does it make, since he is so extraordinary, whether he is counterfeit or not? The suspicion is not absent that Mishima, having lost interest or confidence in his earlier plans, has taken the escape nearest at hand, returning to the cynical young person he has always been so supremely good at portraying.

The word "angel" in the title also suggests something extraordinary, and the five marks of the decay of the angel, in Buddhist writ a mortal being, are all present, or strongly presumed to be. Is the point that the angel with whom Honda has kept intermittent company through much of his long life is dead or dying? Is it that the whole idea of transmigration has become empty and meaningless, itself an illusion? Even if the answer to these questions is positive, it is hard to think why the reader should be kept in doubt, and indeed kept in suspense by false leads, as if the action had descended to the inferior level of the detective story. Might it be that Mishima lost his sense of direction somewhere along the way?

The first volume of the tetralogy approaches being a masterpiece; the last scene of the fourth is very beautiful. Elsewhere the signs of uncertainty are painful. Mishima seems to have wanted to give Wang Yang-ming's insistence upon action the symbolic reality of fiction; yet empty cerebration emerges triumphant. Honda, an intellectual sort if ever there was one, was supposed to be the *waki*, the deuteragonist, and yet here he is finally at the center of the novel, the last beautiful scene completely his, the protagonist his alter ego as none of the others has been. The novel was supposed to be about transmigration, and yet here at the end we are left with strong reasons for thinking that the laws of transmigration are, like all laws, illusory; but if that is the point, there is no good reason that we should be teased and left in doubt.

All in all the evidences of uncertainty, of wavering purpose, are strong indeed. Might it have been an uncertain and disappointed man, if he still gave a thought to literature, who went to his suicide that November noon? But perhaps, with action at length dominant over the ratiocination that proved so stubborn and unwieldy to the end and brought such ambiguities and contradictions to the last novel, he gave it no thought at all.

(1973)

KOBAYASHI HIDEO

Kobayashi Hideo does not have great admiration for the idea in the abstract. It is the idea embodied in the act that interests him. In a 1940 essay called "The Newness of the Crisis" he thus describes crises in the careers of the sixteenth-century generals Toyotomi Hideyoshi and Oda Nobunaga.

One can list all manner of reasons for Toyotomi Hideyoshi's failure in Korea. The final, unshakable reason is that the planner of the invasion, Hideyoshi himself, was in terrible error. It was not a passive sort of error, having to do with the fact that he was senile. He was not senile. The plan itself bespeaks excessive vitality. The error arose from the fact that he faced entirely new circumstances. His rich knowledge was useless. It was worse than useless. It stood in the way of correct judgment. One may say that correct knowledge, drawn from rich experience, was itself responsible for mistaken judgment. . . .

Whether or not we have geniuses like Hideyoshi among us today, there can be no doubt that for us the China Incident is without precedent, as the Korean invasion was for him and his followers. . . . New ideals are very fine, no doubt, but there is something not quite right about all these pat, lucid theories of a United East Asia. I cannot help feeling that they must have made rather easy writing. Our new theorists feel secure in the dexterous application of old theories and methods to a new situation. Untroubled by doubts, they prepare a new fish with an old knife, and probably fail to notice the real newness of the fish. . . .

True logic is in life itself. Logic is not a tool or a weapon for expatiating upon the shape of life. That is specious logic. Gazing up at a mountain one day, Hegel muttered: "So it is, entirely so". . . . No doubt Yamabe no Akahito, gazing up at Fuji, muttered: "Entirely so."

Let me give an example from history. The Battle of Okehazama was for Oda Nobunaga a crisis. He had nothing that could have been called a guiding theory, a principle of leadership. . . . A young man of twenty-seven, lord of a minor fief, he was faced by the grand army of Imagawa Yoshimoto, confident after a succession of victories. The conclusion of the war conference was that there was no hope in open combat, that withdrawal to the castle confines was the only possible course. Only Nobunaga disagreed. It was unthinkable, he said. And so what alternative did he propose? He did not answer. The useless talk went on and on, and it was very late. Nobunaga announced that he was sleepy and that everyone should go to bed. So it was, grumbled the elders, that the mirror of intelligence in the end was clouded over.

Had the mirror in fact clouded over? I think not. Only Nobunaga had seen to the heart of the crisis, to a determination of what had made it a crisis. To withdraw and await a siege was not the answer. Such, we may imagine, were his thoughts. He arose before daybreak, armed himself, had breakfast standing up, sent someone out to blow on a conch shell, and galloped forth from Kiyosu Castle with five attendants. When he passed Atsuta he was at the head of a band of some three hundred. It is said that, singing a high, clear song, he was riding sideways, holding to the rings of his saddle. He had no doubts. When he reached the line of his earlier withdrawals he was at the head of some three thousand men. Yoshimoto had fought all night and was resting after a victory. The Okehazama battle was not a strike in the dark. It was the boldest of attacks in broad daylight. Nobunaga took advantage of a lull in the rains at about two in the afternoon. Yoshimoto heard a disturbance in the rear, it is said, and ordered a horse from a man who had come running up. The man was Hattori Koheita, one of Nobunaga's followers. . . .

The Battle of Nagashino shows very clearly that Nobunaga

was a thorough and painstaking strategist, and it is clear from his treatment of the Christians and the Ikkō sect that he was an unrelentingly and cruelly suspicious man. To find in his behavior at Okehazama the psychology of the fatalist or the gambler misses the point completely. We moderns have a tiresome way of equating a state of decision with this or that psychology. It is, rather, a leaping of the spirit at a moment when theory and belief are one. As for psychology, well, you may ask psychologists and novelists about that.

Did Nobunaga have a theory? I shall be brief. He was not acting in desperation. He had a firm theory. It was not a theory that lends itself to easy articulation. . . . He looked directly at the crisis, and allowed no plausible theories to intrude themselves between the crisis and the mirror of intelligence.[1]

The following, with minor deletions, is the entry for Kobayashi Hideo in *A Short Dictionary of Japanese Literature*:[2]

KOBAYASHI HIDEO. Critic. Born January 1, 1902, 77 Shiba Shirogane Imasato-chō, Minato-ku, Tokyo.

CAREER. Kobayashi graduated from Tokyo University in 1927, taking his degree in French. . . . The subject of his graduation essay was "Arthur Rimbaud." He has been at the forefront of the critical world since his essay "Various Garbs" won a prize in the *Kaizō* competition in appreciative writing.

ACHIEVEMENT. With French symbolism as his point of departure, he has been thoroughly critical of the autobiographical elements which, a residue of naturalism, have been present in much of modern Japanese literature, and he strongly attacked as a one-sided distortion the materialist and historicist view of literature present in the proletarian writing of the late 1920s. It may be said that with him modern Japanese criticism came into being. . . . From the years of the China Incident into the war he became increasingly interested in Japanese history, writing highly original essays which give the Japanese classics a new and freshly human interpretation. He has undertaken a study of Dostoevski toward understanding the workings of the modern mind. Drawn also to the visual arts, he has written widely on art, and he has written a study of Mozart.

It is a good entry, giving the facts succinctly and without nonsense. To bring it up to date, one might wish to mention, beside the studies of Dostoevski and Mozart, a lengthy study of Motoori Norinaga, the great eighteenth-century scholar of the Japanese classics, which has occupied him for the last several years, and to give it a certain immediacy one might wish to remark upon his very great influence and popularity. The heart of the matter is in the lines crediting him with the introduction of "modern criticism" to Japan and putting him "at the forefront of the critical world." Whatever "modern criticism" may be, one is happy that it is not in this instance qualified by "literary," and whether or not he is the first modern, one happily accepts the suggestion that he is an original.

Kobayashi won the *Kaizō* prize for "appreciative writing" in 1929, and the reviewing of fiction consumed a large part of his youthful energies; but through his long career he has been a broader sort of critic, more of an Arnold than a Coleridge. Perhaps he might be called a cultural critic. The expression has a hollow sound, as if it were a direct translation from the Japanese; yet if there can be cultural historians there can be cultural critics too, people who may be immediately interested in the arts but whose broader interest is in tradition and morals. Kobayashi became specifically concerned with the Japanese tradition during the war years, and since the war he has become a sort of wise man, a reigning sage, to whom large numbers of people are prepared to listen when he tells them how to behave and what to be interested in. Looking for his counterpart in the United States, one may think of Walter Lippmann. Because of the too obvious differences the comparison seems almost ludicrous. Kobayashi is not much interested in politics, and he does not make daily pronouncements. Yet the function as a kind of resident moralist and wise man is similar.

We have had our classical wise men, our Franklins and Thoreaus, whether or not we have wise men among us now. The Japanese have had a long series of them, people whose philosophies, the antithesis of the Teutonic, fill not volumes but sentences, but who have many interesting and worthy things to say about many processes and happenings, and whose responses do somehow add up to a philosophy, very Japanese in its pragmatism and distrust of systems. As a pragmatic moralist Kobayashi is somewhat reminiscent of Ninomiya Sontoku, perhaps the most famous wise man of the late Tokugawa period, who held that virtue consists of and results in raising bigger crops, and whom Kobayashi admires. Commentary upon writing, said Sontoku, bears the relation to life that the icicle hanging from a mass of ice has to water flowing through the fields. "That man is a fool who takes it as it is and does not propose to melt it with the warmth of his spirit." Kobayashi once said: "Ideology is not thought. It is the shadow of thought."[3]

For Kobayashi the greatest of vices is conceptualizing. It is the sort of thing the intellectuals, the *interi*, go in for under the influence of the West, and it is barren and stultifying. His earliest writings may seem too clever by a very great deal, and one may sometimes feel that he could have made do with fewer words; but criticism too can sometimes be literature, and wise men are sometimes what we call creative writers. Franklin and Thoreau are in all the standard anthologies of American literature. The modern Japanese preoccupation with fiction has pushed poetry off into a cramped, rather obscure corner, and made some non-fiction honorary fiction and ranged much of the rest with journalism. We who make it our business to introduce Japanese literature abroad have neglected non-fiction. Not much has been translated save when it is written especially for the edification of the foreigner, in which case it tends toward simplification, prettiness, and condescension. The neglect is deplorable, for Kobayashi, at least, is a better writer than most of the novelists who have occupied the translators.

The deepest reason for his superiority is that he is so much of his place. A man of cosmopolitan erudition, he avoids the cosmopolitan dandyism that makes so many Japanese intellectuals so very tedious. Never rejecting the West and only rarely seeming defensive or querulous, he was a nationalist in the days when almost everyone was, and through the fine years for cosmopolitan dandyism that followed the war he went on being a nationalist. A sense of deep roots has kept him from seeming merely parochial, and he has expressed directly what some of the finest Japanese writers have expressed through the symbolic medium of fiction.

If the entry in *A Short Dictionary of Japanese Literature* does not say anything that is seriously in error and says numbers of things that are right, it does not quite come out with the rightest thing of all, that Kobayashi has little admiration for abstract ideas. In 1943, when Japan was a cacophony of jingoistic ideas, to which numbers of important writers were giving as noisy expression as ever did a cultural commissar, Kobayashi thus described his state of mind and summarized his career:

> These last months, upon some slight provocation, I have become engrossed in the visual arts to an extreme that astonishes even me. . . .
>
> Not since I first became interested in literature has an idea moved me as an idea. It may be said that an aversion to ideology has been the one principle of my critical writing; and now I have come to feel that even the aversion has been too weak. I have resorted to polemics, which are proof of the weakness. Today I cannot even think of polemics. I no longer believe in words that hit other words and give off sounds like soap bubbles.[4]

The same year, at the Second Convocation of Greater East Asian Writers, he said this about "the common task" (*keitai*) of writers:

> A writer is not a deliberator of, a commentator upon, or a propagandist of ideologies. A writer is an artisan who concentrates everything on the actuality which is the work he is writing. . . . We hear loud voices ordering us back to tradition. Behind them is nothing of living tradition. They have all forgotten the simple fact that tradition is not a concept but a thing. . . .
>
> When I say that tradition is a thing, I mean that it is an entity. . . .
>
> Attempting to grasp tradition through concept, to expound it as concept, is playing with shadows. Such is not the way of the true writer. If it is the way of the critic, then it must be called a very low way and a dangerous way.[5]

These remarks are fraught with displeasure at the whole idea of the convocation, at which Kobayashi appeared only to please a friend, but the thoughts are not new ones, made for the occasion. If Kobayashi's prize-winning essay of 1929, "Various Garbs," seems rather too clever, one may excuse it on the grounds that such is the way with prize essays and that there is deep earnestness beneath the archness. It is a statement of the concerns that have not through all the decades since ceased to be Kobayashi's:

> I have no right to protest against the armor in which, after their several ideologies, our critics have armed themselves, save to say that though it may offer security it must be rather heavy. What I do find difficult to accept is the impatience. They will not wait for the object under scrutiny to reveal its destiny.[6]

> Though I do not know whether our favored myths are constructive or decadent, I am not really convinced that our young proletarian writers are pursuing their studies of human fate so that they may soak their writings in the blood therefrom, or that dreams of doubt have assailed our young epicureans with such swiftness as to leave them bewildered and reeling.[7]

> Art does not show us a world of truth and beauty apart from the world in which we live. In art the marks of human passion are most clearly on display. Eternal concepts of art are the curious inventions of aestheticians. Art may be divinely inspired and it may reveal the extraordinary and make spirit manifest, but it must never be without the smell of humanity. . . . Empirical aestheticians can organize systems which correctly encompass the art that has come into this world, because for them art is among the expressive devices to which history has given birth; but for the artist it is neither an object of feeling nor an object of thought. It is action.[8]

> I believe that I have gone through the various garbs to be found in our literary world, or at least the more important of them. It has not been my wish, in the search for something else, to evince contempt for garbs. I have sought to have faith in all of them, because I have so little faith in any of them.[9]

In the same year, 1929, in an essay on Shiga Naoya, probably Kobayashi's favorite among modern Japanese writers, there is an emphasis on art as act and the same distrust of cogitation:

> Shiga does not think and he does not feel. Above all he acts. . . .

He talks in intimate detail of his life, and the result is not gleanings in the form of confession or the hopes which are his reasons, but perfect expression, independent signs of human passion. . . .

His perceptions are direct indeed, like the cobra swaying to the sound of the flute, or the wings of the ptarmigan turning white with the advent of winter. The immediacy of the awareness does not permit of hesitation in the choice of words. They are found before the ripples have reached the edge of the pond.[10]

About a decade later, on the eve of the war, the emphasis and distrust are present once more:

An artist knows himself in the act of creating and not through the species of dreaming known as self-reflection. Michelangelo faces a piece of marble and takes up his chisel, and as the chips of marble fly it becomes clear to him what he has been thinking and feeling. When presently David emerges he sees that David is himself. . . . The writer believes in words with form and not in formless thoughts. Everything is for him a contest with things that have shape. He is the work that has shape, and the self as the reason sees it is a superfluity. . . . Nature and man are the forms apprehended by the eye and the ear. . . . There is no need to think of invisible truth beyond the form as it is; and to hold that the elements which make up the form are more important than the form is mischievous meddling.[11]

They are there again in a postwar essay on Miyamoto Musashi, a swordsman, artist, and folk hero whose career centered upon the early years of the seventeenth century, perhaps the mutest and most hushed of all periods in Japanese literary history:

In Miyamoto Musashi's code for solitary action is this tenet: "I have no regrets for any of my doings". . . . It is a kind of paradox, and it does not mean that, thanks to unfailing prudence and care, he has had none of our ordinary regrets. It is not so shallow. What Musashi means, in the jargon of our own day, is that self-reflection and clearing of accounts with the self are hollow shells. . . .

The "historical vision" so popular today is in Musashi's

terms not vision but sight, denoting criticism or comment from a specific point of view. Musashi's "vision" is a firm denial of point of view. It denies categories in reality and embraces reality itself.[12]

Culture, the concept, can be known only in the act of creating; but the monkeys known in our day as "men of culture" [*bunkajin*] peel tirelessly away at the sections of an onion.[13]

The most important thing in a work of art, we are thus told in several ways, is irrelevant to what it can be said to be "about." The most important thing about an artist is something other than what he thinks. So it is too with the critic: "Whoever has been my subject, I have not taken the easy way of abstracting his thought from his writing. . . . Mr. Shiga is the writer who most completely rejects abstraction. That is why he is so difficult to talk about."[14]

Elsewhere Kobayashi has said that for him criticism is not a process of "dispelling the darkness in another" but rather of educating himself.[15] A novel, he has said, does not teach us anything. "The reader of a novel may hope to learn all manner of things about the customs and ways of the world, the feelings and thoughts. In fact he gets from it nothing beyond his own understanding of the world. A good novel improves as the reader improves."[16]

These remarks dismiss a great deal of criticism. All the world over, but perhaps more in Japan than in most places, inferior works receive endless attention, and works not of the very first order, perhaps, but still better than the works so amply criticized, are neglected. The proletarian writers of the twenties and thirties have received endless comment despite the fact that there is not a single proletarian novel worth commenting upon, and the reason is that the theory of proletarian literature offers the richest material for disputes and opinions; yet Kikuchi Kan (or Hiroshi), a much better novelist than any of them, is called "popular" and "vulgar," perhaps because there is so very little to be said about his better novels. "My, but that was a good story." So much can be said, and not much more.

Kobayashi often seems rather close to the great contradiction in the works of the late D. T. Suzuki, who announced his conclusion first, that nothing can be said about Zen, and then wrote volume after volume. Critics and wise men too must earn their keep, and whatever may be the case with Dr. Suzuki it may be said of Kobayashi that his best writing has the immediacy which he asked for in a work of art.

If art is act, and what is asked of it is an immediacy that does not require the mediation of thought or concept, then concept is the great adversary. Were one to commence indexing Kobayashi's collected works it would soon become apparent that "concept, hostility to" is a useless heading, for it includes everything, even as does "Kobayashi Hideo, collected works of." A dislike of abstraction is everywhere, and so is a belief that art is concrete, a child of nature which must never forget its parent. In the case of literature, and especially of fiction, which has so dominated modern Japanese literature, Kobayashi's dislike of abstraction and concept takes other guises: a dislike for psychology or "psychologism," for the psychological analysis that calls itself realism, for cogitation and ratiocination, for a kind of observation that fails to apprehend its object as a whole, for a numbing "critical awareness."

> Thus Dreiser describes Clyde's face [as he murders his lady friend in *An American Tragedy*]. It is Clyde's face as described by Dreiser. We have seen many detailed specimens of psychological description, and do not find it particularly remarkable. Even if Dreiser had been so kind as to give us an even more detailed description of Clyde's face, I doubt that we would have seen that face before us.[17]

> The difficulty of psychological novels is not in the detail with which material similes are applied to psychological objects or psychological similes are applied to material objects. It has to do with whether or not the analysis is posited upon a whole, with whether or not a sense of unity controls the writer's powers of analysis. It is the only problem worth discussing.[18]

> The great weakness of our new novelists is that they lose sight of nature as the greatest artist.[19]

> I grow weary of incomprehensible characters one after another, women who because they are excessively addicted to excessively complicated psychological encounters are incapable of ordinary love, men who because their heads are so full of ideology have lost track of their hearts; but if fictional char-

acters who lack immediacy are in the broadest sense comical, then nothing is fuller of comedy than our recent fiction.[20]

Even with words like "good" and "bad," which are significance only [and not concrete reference], the writer must have an immediate apprehension of form coated over with the grease and sweat of long history. When the grease and sweat are removed the words are no more than tools for cogitation. It is in this context that we understand what we are so often told, that there is no literature without tradition.[21]

The most useful touchstone I have found for separating the genuine from the counterfeit in modern literature is in the presence or absence of psychologism. Sometimes I almost think that if I find a writer who is living with all his strength in the present moment and is painfully aware of the difficulties of creating literature in the present moment, I do not care a great deal whether or not he writes. Of course what I find all about me is too much writing. I do not propose to do anything about this flood of writerless writing. I shall but write monthly reviews filled with plausible lies.[22]

Human destiny has been lost in the astonishing flood and parade of phantasms, psychology and character and the like, that have been invented by the modern mind.[23]

In a word, the influence of nineteenth-century European literature led to an irresponsible overuse of humanity. The legacy of the Meiji naturalists, if we may use a fiscal simile, produced an unprecedented inflation. That is but natural when one gives the matter a moment's thought: the poisonous antidote for the poison of foreign teachings obscured the ethical strain that had its roots so deep in Western culture. All manner of foreign skills were isolated and reproduced, and as a result of very clever application of analytic techniques in the observation of human character there emerged in the guise of depicting humanity a trackless chaos.[24]

Is it not ridiculously arbitrary to think that observation is surer and keener than respect, sympathy, fellow feeling and affection?[25]

Modern love stories, all of them, are for me the ultimate in boredom. The morals of love have been replaced by the psychology of love. Love should be a sort of petition or plea. To psychologize is to mechanize, and this fact the psychologizer understands least.[26]

But I do not like this view of things [the view which sees Mozart as confident in his own powers and contemptuous of the human race]. It may be plausible, but it is somehow flabby. I detect symptoms of confession, reflection, and psychological analysis. I see victims of the poison which so suffuses nineteenth-century European literature. . . . The loneliness is a most cleverly fabricated concept, and no more, to be used, as the occasion demands, for self-defense or for self-loathing. Confident that he has it, this one glares about him at the world. Certain that he is its prisoner, that he suffers.[27]

I want to call Mozart the great realist among musicians, but I do not want to be misunderstood. No doubt I will be. How much humanity have "modern realists" in fact salvaged from life? To what extent have the techniques of observation in which they so pride themselves succeeded in laying humanity bare? . . . [28]

The modern Japanese novelists for whom Kobayashi has had the highest praise have been Shiga Naoya and Kikuchi Kan. In both cases it is because he senses an immediacy which is the antithesis of concept, cogitation, and those several other things.

Shiga, who was born in 1883 and died in 1971, wrote a handful of little pieces that would be called superb short stories in the context of any literature. His longer writings are so strongly autobiographical that one may doubt whether he should be called a novelist at all. Like most other people, the Japanese have a way of remaking a borrowed word or concept. *Shōsetsu* is the word they applied late in the nineteenth century to the concept of fiction or the novel, but very often works that do not seem very fictional or novel-like are called *shōsetsu*. For the Japanese, Shiga is a writer of *shōsetsu*, but for us he may not be a novelist.

Kikuchi was born in 1888 and died in 1948. He first came into prominence as one of the company that also included Akutagawa Ryūnosuke. In his early years he too showed strongly autobiographical tendencies, but the reference works tell us that from the years after the First World War he shifted to "popular" fiction, in which the autobiographical element is slight. In modern Japanese literary history and criticism, "popular" is a pejorative word. Its opposite is "pure," which usually indicates the fondness of a critic or historian for autobiographical fiction. It is certain, in any event, that Kikuchi became very popular, and as editor of *Bungei Shunjū*, the monthly magazine that has best succeeded in combining quality with mass appeal, he became the most powerful figure in the *bundan*, the literary world. The young Kobayashi was among his protégés.

Kobayashi wrote two important essays about Shiga. The first, his earliest important monograph, contains the memorable similes likening him to a cobra and a ptarmigan. In perhaps the most illuminating passage, Shiga is contrasted with Chekhov, not so much to the disadvantage of Chekhov as to that of critics who think the two similar:

> Some time ago, when Anton Chekhov, like photography, was in vogue, Mr. Shiga was frequently likened to him. I have told myself that I must avoid all reference to appraisals of Mr. Shiga's work which have failed to grasp his essential nature—which is like saying to an elephant, "Your nose seems a bit too long." So I have told myself, but the very enormity of this particular misconception makes it fit my purposes rather nicely. . . .
>
> Chekhov's view of the world became fixed when . . . he was still in his twenties. From then until his death he sang from memory, and he sang elegies. His view of the world, a fascinated ennui, precisely fitted his work. . . . The laughter of this most universally self-conscious of writers was always ambiguous. It emerged from a mixing of the great and the trivial in humanity. His mouth was twisted as he laughed, and so the laughter is always intellectual and moral.
>
> In Shiga, by contrast, we have a sort of supreme egoist. He fascinates by the most individual act of the most individual self-awareness. The world view is not important. The act is. His song has always been of the present and of signs of the future;

161

memory, in the true sense of the term, is wholly absent. There is never in his writing, as there always is in Chekhov's, a suggestion of scenes beyond those immediately present. Present scenes are alone in their elevated solidity, which has in it the weight and feel of the powerful doer.[29]

Early in the essay (a good thing about Kobayashi is that although it may sometimes seem that he does not quite know when to stop, he seldom wastes time in coming to the point), there is a succinct description of the immediacy that is so desirable, and there is an attack on "psychology" remarkable from one so young in a day when it was so fashionable:

"Classical" is a vague, ambiguous word, but if it signifies a deep harmony between emotion and reason, then Mr. Shiga is a true classicist.

He is aware of no distance between thought and act. . . .

What is destroying our nervous systems is not morbid neurosis but an excess of concept. The cerebrum is encroaching upon the other parts of the brain. Our nerves function in a state not of physiological alertness but of conceptual intricacy.[30]

Some pages after the cobra and the ptarmigan comes another natural image, followed by a passage that is perhaps somewhat difficult to accept:

His [Shiga's] spirit does not know drama. His pains are the growing pains of a tree.

People weep when they read *Reconciliation*, and that is because the naturalness of the work attacks their tear glands with a powerful force. If there are those among you who do not weep, it is not because you have run dry. Your not very competent brain matter has been too hard at work. It is easy to make the conceptual ones weep sentimental or nervous tears. . . . The greatest art, all of it, has caught the cry of nature.[31]

This is not easy to accept. *Reconciliation*, describing a young man alienated from his father and presently their reconciliation, is among Shiga's most autobiographical writings, verging on the confessional. Kobayashi does not like confession. The difficulty is not to be evaded by urging an immediacy in Shiga's case which is worlds away from the self-pity, the hesitant ruminating, and the special pleading of most confession. Kobayashi is inconsistent, and that is that.

There is a worse difficulty: that one's tear glands refuse to respond however insistently one urges them. In other words, *Reconciliation* just does not seem like a very good story. It seems rather ordinary, another case of adolescence and the recovery from it. One's immediate reaction is not consistent with Kobayashi's.

So be it: there are few critics all of whose judgments seem unconditionally acceptable. Perhaps the critic has his blind spots, or perhaps his reader is sporadically benighted, or excessively cerebral. It may be the mark of the superior critic that even when the judgment itself is difficult to accept the reasons for it seem interesting— which is another way of saying that the critic is a writer of substance in his own right. It is so with Kobayashi. One notes with approval the insistence upon art as act, whether *Reconciliation* is a good story or not.

Kobayashi may have been uneasy about the fact that sauce for the goose did not always seem to be sauce for the gander. Private, autobiographical, confessional writing was all right for some people but not for others. In 1931 he wrote a very unfriendly review of a long novel called *The Anjō Brothers*, by Satomi Ton, who was born in 1888. It was the extremely private and personal nature of the novel that Kobayashi objected to, the fact that Satomi wrote too obviously to assert his own claims against his family. The same thing might be said of such Shiga works as *Reconciliation*. To this possibility he addresses himself:

> Every character in the novel and every situation is a function of the self-awareness of the character called Shōzō. . . . I found it impossible, despite the skill with which the several characters around him are described, to feel the admiration that comes from the setting of several living, breathing individuals into competition one with another.
>
> In a truly superior novel the characters have their own independence even when they do not depart from the author's own theories of life. . . . Running through *Reconciliation* is a powerful sense of life, and above the flow, the eye of the author is cold and unmoving. . . .

With Mr. Shiga the feeling for life is an unconscious flow. It is a self-evident absolute, and to interpret it and comment upon it is folly. However disturbed, beyond the flow, the psychology of the author may be, the density of his style does not vary. The characters that come under his scrutiny are all depicted with the same accuracy. . . .

With Mr. Satomi the feeling for life is something that must always be interpreted, it is a means for self-improvement, an adversary he does not for a moment forget.[32]

Shōzō is full of the conceptology of sincerity. One cannot be sure, when sincerity explodes, whether the explosion will be pretty or nasty.[33]

Mr. Shiga too has strong likes and dislikes, and a strong sense of the ugly. . . . The object of his distaste is never twisted, however, because the distaste is a kind of immediate reaction that needs no interpretation or analysis. It is identical with the act of seeing. . . .

Shōzō's weakness is to the end intellectual, not so thoroughgoing that unhappiness is imposed upon him. When he tells us, therefore, that he is a complete shambles, he is telling us very self-consciously of his hopes, with self-consciousness his point of departure.[34]

The little aphorism about "sincerity" is worth noting. It introduces another sturdy antipathy, for improvers and meliorists.

The second Shiga essay was written in 1938. Much had changed in Japan in the decade since the appearance of the first, but Kobayashi's admiration for Shiga had not.

Upon rereading an author after a considerable passage of time, one often receives a strangely different impression, for better or for worse. There is nothing of the sort in Mr. Shiga's case. I reread *Reconciliation*, for instance. I am moved as I was before. The tears are the same. I am confronted with a kind of simplicity that quite defeats me.[35]

The Collected Works of Shiga Naoya is one of the more expensive of recent luxury editions, but I am told that it is selling extremely well. I doubt that many people are reading it as autobiographical fiction. Some will find an explanation for the good sales in the reactionary mood of the times. Not a progressive myself, I do not overlook the fact that there is truth in reaction too. Probably ninety percent of Mr. Shiga's readers are quite unaware of critical debates about autobiographical fiction. They find in him a certain freshness that is wanting in more recent fiction, and that is all. . . .

We apprehend a man by affection. We may observe with a cool eye, but observation is not enough to make him interesting and attractive. Affection, friendship, respect are needed, the agents that make the observed image step forth and announce itself.[36]

For the modern intellectual nothing is more remote than the word "happiness," and he has ceased to think his unhappiness his own responsibility. . . .

Our writers and thinkers seem to have fallen hopeless victims to ideological insomnia. Just as the chief cause of insomnia is the effort to sleep, so moral truth eludes the seeker because of the diligence of a quest based on evidence alone. . . .

Put Mr. Shiga's A Dark Night's Passing in such a world. . . . One does well to see that the moral quest is not what the modern intellect understands by the term. Mr. Shiga's hero does not know the nature of the morality he is seeking. He only knows that the intelligence to know is not the intelligence to achieve. He will have none of the game of which the modern writer is so fond, to translate mental anguish into words and then stumble over the words. His anguish comes from life itself and does not need the mediation of words.[37]

Again the judgment is interesting even if one cannot accept with any enthusiasm the concrete awards which it makes. A Dark Night's Passing is another strongly autobiographical work, considerably longer than Reconciliation, and it suffers from the usual maladies of autobiographical fiction: formlessness, querulousness, and an inability to give the thinly fictionalized writer fictional validity. The paradox is the same: one may be interested in what Kobayashi says without being much interested in what interests him. The sharp remarks about intellectuals are pertinent to modern intellectuals everywhere, but most especially, perhaps, to the Japanese interi, who always seem to feel that they are neglecting their responsibilities unless they talk and look like Werther. If "anti-intellectual" may be taken to mean not "opposed to that which is intellectual" but rather "opposed to the intellectuals, the *interi*," then that is what Kobayashi is, and therein lies a good part of his power to persuade.

It was in 1937 that Kobayashi wrote most admiringly of Kikuchi, who had already for some years been the most powerful figure in the *bundan*, patron of a number of people who called him an unrefined caterer to popular tastes. Early in this essay, that Satomi Ton who was found not to be Shiga Naoya's equal is found not to be Kikuchi's. Again the matter has to do with the good and bad in autobiographical fiction:

> I am filled with unqualified admiration for the recent writing of Mr. Satomi Ton, in which he becomes a sort of observing eye; but when I compare [his recent work with that of Kikuchi], I become aware of a far greater originality in the latter. One cannot understand Kikuchi's autobiographical writings unless one sees that they were written by someone who felt no need for a mirror with which to paint a self-portrait.[38]

> Kikuchi is the first writer for whom the social quality of fiction is a matter not of the head but of the body. He feels it with the very center of his being. . . .

> It was of course the mood of the *bundan* that forced him to think himself a slick, popular writer. The most important difference for him was that writing newspaper novels was several times as hard as writing "pure literature." And his newspaper novels are none of them inferior and may be superior to the "pure" literature of his early years.[39]

This is curious, one thinks on first reading. Because there is so much reading matter in Japan, one sometimes accepts the advice of literary critics and historians in arranging priorities, deciding what to read first and what to read later or perhaps never. It is a relief to be told that the first and eighth imperial anthologies of court poetry are the good ones and the others do not really matter, and it is a relief to learn that a prolific modern writer is, save for his early writings, popular and vulgar. The great danger of course is that injustice is done. Conventional views consign certain writers to undeserved oblivion. Critics and historians perpetuate the opinions of earlier critics and historians, and it all comes to seem like a grand lottery. There are some winners and some losers, and no one thinks of contesting the results once they have been announced.

A rereading of Shiga Naoya's more ambitious works did nothing to resolve the disagreement with Kobayashi. *Reconciliation* still seemed rather thin and unconvincing. In Kikuchi's case there can scarcely be said to have been a disagreement in the first place. Accepting the conventional wisdom, one had not paid very much attention to him.

In fact Kikuchi is a rather good novelist, and indeed "his newspaper novels . . . may be superior to the 'pure' literature of his early years." Concept has been allowed to obscure the clarity of the critical eye. All tangled up in the concept of "pure literature," the critics and historians glorified a few writers of autobiographical fiction at the expense of almost everyone else. Then too there is the penchant of critics to talk about people whom it is easy to talk about, people whose writings have abstractable "meaning." About all that can be said of Kikuchi's "vulgar" writings is that they are very good stories, presenting interesting and believable people in interesting if sometimes rather unbelievable situations. There is a touch of the vulgar from time to time, but then there is in Dickens and Dostoevski too. It is hard not to disagree sometimes with the best of critics, for the immediate appraisal from which discussion proceeds is irreducible; but a good critic sometimes teaches one a few things, and jars one out of laziness and inattention. For one lazy reader, Kobayashi performed the service in the case of Kikuchi. The *bundan* once thought the great Natsume Sōseki rather slick and vulgar too. History, or some other mysterious process, has righted the wrong. It has yet to do so for Kikuchi, who is still dismissed in all the reference works as vulgar, despite Kobayashi's persuasive efforts in his behalf.

Kobayashi quotes a very interesting remark by Kikuchi which perhaps suggests why it is that the characters in one novel are interesting and those in another are not: " 'I had thought to have my hero and heroine marry somewhere along the way, and had even thought of subtitling it *A Marriage*; but not even fictional characters will do what they do not want to do.' How much greater is the difficulty for you, parents of the world! Do not force your children into unwanted marriages."[40]

Of other important modern writers, Kobayashi's view has been equivocal. An early (1931) essay on Tanizaki Jun'ichirō is not hostile, certainly, though there is more than a suggestion that the "diabolic" Tanizaki might be something of a poseur; but Tanizaki's works do not, somehow, quite contain what Kobayashi wants from a novelist (and from a historian too): sympathy and affection. But though Tanizaki's ostentatious decadence may be suspect, his freedom from doubt and crippling self-analysis pleases Kobayashi.

> For all the startling abnormality of these carnal experiences there is in them no scent of morbid decay, no shadow of death or despair. The tone is altogether healthy and resilient. Emptiness and doubt are forbidden to touch carnal experience. An absolute faith in that experience shines forth.[41]

> He discovered a devil but he did not discover diabolism. . . . Usually the devil and the heretic have their beginning in rebellion against the world, but his start from obedience. They have not learned the first lesson in sneering at the world. Their essence is an inability to resist the demands of the heart, whatever those demands may be.[42]

Kobayashi's opinion of the most gifted writer among his immediate contemporaries, Kawabata Yasunari, is elusive. Kawabata was some two and a half years older than Kobayashi, and three years his senior at Tokyo Imperial University. Kobayashi's most extended remarks about Kawabata, written in 1941, make it clear that he dislikes the conventional view of Kawabata, but again the strong affirmation so evident in the Shiga and Kikuchi essays is wanting.

> People like to talk of the cold reason and the beautiful lyricism in Mr. Kawabata's novels. It is the talk of bemused fools. He has not written a single novel. The things that interest a novelist—what happens in everyday life, how we become involved with and submit to social systems and customs and the like, what sort of entanglements arise between two people of divergent beliefs and tendencies—one sees how indifferent he

is to them if one reads his works with even a little attention. He is without the ability to differentiate two men or two women.

Disqualification as a novelist is enacted at the very center of his being. . . .

We need not be surprised that he never tires of reading compositions by young boys and girls. His nature demands it. The physiological man rather than the social man. . . . He has come to sing a sort of song written by physiological man bereft of the clothing of society. His perceptions may tell him that it is a kind of inverted romanticism, but to no avail. His genius pulls him along. It pulls one half of him from "The Izu Dancer" to *Snow Country* and the other from "The Funeral Expert" to "Of Birds and Beasts."[43]

This at first seems like rather faint praise, and again one has trouble accepting the immediate judgment from which discussion proceeds. *Snow Country* is a novel, and the two women who dominate it, Komako and Yōko, are very clearly differentiated from each other. *The Sound of the Mountain*, not yet written when Kobayashi was writing, is remarkable in that not two but a half dozen characters are sharply and vividly differentiated. But Kobayashi is not reprimanding Kawabata for not being a novelist. "One sees how indifferent he is" to the preoccupations of a novelist. True to himself, as a genuine writer must be, and no victim of sterile concepts, he wrote something else—erotic children's stories, perhaps. (Or ghost stories, in the erotic Tokugawa tradition? Once when Kawabata had commented laconically, as was his way, upon the teeming presence of vivid characters in Western fiction and their absence from Japanese fiction, someone made the objection that Komako, surely, is rather vivid. Kawabata replied: "*Obake desu yo.*" Which might be translated: "She's a spook.")

In a very famous Kobayashi essay called "Evanescence" there is a glimpse of Kawabata which one does not forget and which suggests that Kobayashi might have made rather a good novelist himself: "I once said to Kawabata Yasunari, who laughed and did not answer: 'A living human being is a poor makeshift. You never know, even if it is you yourself, what he is doing or what he is going to do or say. He is not worth the trouble of watching. A dead man is very fine by comparison. How can he be so clear and strong? He is the real human being. The live one is a brute by way of becoming human.' "[44]

One can see the two of them, the elegantly loquacious sage expounding a theory of history and historiography, an injunction against turning documents and analysis against the quiet and perfect dead, and the novelist, so fascinated with death that it was almost his only subject, silently smiling.

Kobayashi's view of certain other important modern writers has been openly hostile. Of Akutagawa Ryūnosuke he has been trenchantly critical. In Akutagawa's writing he has found an amalgam of all the wrong things, analysis, psychologism, cynical intellectualizing that does not grant its object integrity:

> Most critics see Akutagawa as the epitome of the modern intellectual, the incarnation of his destinies. I disagree completely. This extraordinarily clever man, an essayist who left behind delicate discourses and was not able to portray a single human being—it is very doubtful that in the end his human insights were superior to those of the naturalists whose names are so much less exalted.[45]

> The new novel was born of opposition to those lyric poets the naturalists, who imported the objective, naturalist novel of society and transformed it into a personal, subjective prose poem. It is easy to see why the new novel sought to concern itself with thought and concept, but not a single novelist saw the endeavor to a conclusion. Even with the remarkably talented Akutagawa, intellectual articulation was, like his life, but fleeting.

> And so we had a strange phenomenon. The semi-intellectual Akutagawa, striving to apprehend mankind with clever, alert words, was seen as a realist who, albeit on a small scale, described man as he is, more of a realist, indeed, than writers contemptuous of the intellect. Yesterday's intellectual was no stronger a realist than the naturalists of the day before. Like them he was a sentimental poet. What made him seem like a realist was the cloak of paradox he wrapped himself in.[46]

A favorite technique of Kobayashi's is to set off two figures against each other, one an object of praise and the other of blame. In a 1941 essay called "History and Literature," Akutagawa is found on the losing side of a comparison with the American journalist Stanley Washburn. At first it may seem somewhat curious that a little-remembered American should come off the winner in a contest with one of the most highly esteemed of modern Japanese writers; but the comparison is convincing, and it tells a great deal about Kobayashi's view of history, literature, and life:

I recently read Stanley Washburn's book about General Nogi. . . . A war correspondent for the *Chicago Daily News*, Washburn knew and was deeply impressed by the general during the siege of Port Arthur. He is said to have written in anger when the report of Nogi's suicide reached America and was held to be incomprehensible. His book is in the form of memoirs and not an organized biography, but I felt myself in the presence of the real Nogi. Though there must be a great many biographies of Nogi, I doubt that there are many which so give the feel of the man.

I remembered that Akutagawa Ryūnosuke too had written about Nogi, a story called "The Shogun". . . . I reread it and thought it wholly uninteresting. I asked myself why Akutagawa had thought it worth writing, and why twenty years ago it had interested me.

I can imagine that Akutagawa's feelings were far from simple. One thing is clear, however: he wanted to oppose the hero Nogi with the man Nogi. Indeed his aim is open and undisguised. With the view that a man inflated by popular hero-worship may by cool examination be reduced to human stature, he describes the monomaniac cruelty in Nogi's eye as he orders enemy spies put to death, and his tears at a foolish amateur theatrical about a holdup, staged by his men in camp. Because this sort of dissection is in the final analysis no different from inquiries into the matter of the general's weight, Akutagawa's technical dexterity, ever more dexterous, runs counter to his intentions and produces a caricature. In the closing passages a young writer, also a sort of caricature, comes on stage and provides us with this information: the general's last emotions, as he is about to kill himself, are not incomprehensible to us of the new age, but we do find it impossible to understand why he paused to have a commemorative picture taken. "A friend of mine committed suicide the other day, but he did not have time for a picture." No doubt this is meant to be biting sarcasm.

Washburn's book is simple recollection, without the help of a remarkably observant eye. The monomania and the childlike simplicity are not overlooked. He describes how the general's face, like a steel mask when he is poring over a map or giving orders, takes on an expression of Punch-like delight when one of his poems is praised. What makes Washburn different from Akutagawa is that he sees the extraordinary tragedy which an extraordinary spirit had to enact, and all the details take their place in the light of that perception. He does not forget the tragedy to toy and sport with the general's humanity.

There were fifty thousand combat soldiers in Nogi's Third Army at the beginning of the siege. There were almost sixty thousand casualties by the time the city was taken. The Ninth Division, of which Nogi as division commander is said to have known the name of every soldier, received replacements two and a half times over and had only eleven line officers who fought all through the siege. . . . The general's attitude, says Washburn, was indescribably cold, and the command for the assault on Hill 203 was like the order for tomorrow's horse, as if he had become a sort of war machine; but as the horrible days dragged on, wrinkles spread over his face like scars. No one, even if he tried very hard, could fail to see what the general was enduring in silence.

The strange device known as history hits extraordinary men as if it were aimed at them and subjects them to extraordinary trials. It would indeed be incomprehensible if a man who has survived such trials were to feel driven into a corner and commit suicide like one of the young literary persons we see about us. . . . For a man like Nogi, suicide was the end of the grand wish, and there was time for a commemorative photograph and all manner of other things. The view that the man who cannot find the time is more human seems to me very strange. If it were the sport of a writer now gone it would not matter, but it began as a sort of whim or fancy and gradually spread, and became a psychological cordon of which, much of the time, we are not even aware.[47]

In the essay in which Kobayashi expresses a low opinion of Dreiser's psychological description, Dreiser is compared unfavorably with von Sternberg, who did the movie version of *An American Tragedy*. Dreiser is constantly playing to his audience, and "he does not so much describe an incident as comment upon it."[48] Von Sternberg is more direct and immediate: "He does not try to win the populace over to the truth. He tries to see how the populace has whitewashed the truth."[49]

In the same essay Dreiser's psychological realism is compared with Dostoevski's: "Beyond Dostoevski's great powers of analysis, nature is always visible, the culmination of analysis in the irreducible forms of creation. What he most wanted was not analysis but synthesis."[50] Dostoevski and Mozart are the two Europeans about whom Kobayashi has had the most to say, much more than about any Japanese save Motoori Norinaga, and in both cases the tone is warmly affirmative.

In another telling comparison Dostoevski is paired with Ernest Renan: "The way of Dostoevski was wholly unrelated to the way of Renan. Dostoevski was ignorant of the weapons, the sensibility shaped by erudition, the emotions and affections ordered by observation, which Renan put so skillfully to use in humanizing Christ. Dostoevski never ceased to be the peasant looking up at the heavens in astonishment."[51]

A rather similar comparison, for all the difference in time and place, finds the late Heian poet Saigyō beside his contemporaries Shunzei and Teika:

> "An autumn evening. A snipe starts up from the marsh.
> He too is moved who has thrown off all attachments. . . ."

This is said to have been one of Saigyō's favorites among his own poems. And this was Shunzei's favorite among his:

> "Twilight. Upon an autumn wind that chills,
> The call of a quail. The village of Fukakusa."

There is a subtle but unmistakable difference between the man who knows life and the aesthete.

"An autumn evening. No flowers across the scene
Or scarlet leaves. A reed-thatched hut by a strand."

Whatever the appearances, this last poem, by Teika, has in
it almost nothing of Saigyō's poetic world. Side by side in the
Shinkokinshū anthology, we have in Saigyō's poem a poet, and
in Teika's a gourmet, telling us that this is not quite right and
that is not quite right either. I shall not even bother to quote
Jakuren's poem, the third of the famous "autumn three."
To put them in a neat group is to perpetuate an egregious error.[52]

To be political, among the *interi*, has often meant to associate
oneself with each new shift in the political fashions, and such shifts
are often violent. Kobayashi has not been that sort of writer. In a
1940 essay he quotes with approval some remarks by the novelist
Hayashi Fusao about the *tenkōsha*, the "apostates," intellectuals who
gave themselves over enthusiastically to the radical movements of
the twenties and when those movements were no longer quite the
thing gave themselves over as enthusiastically to the nationalism of
the following decades:

> One day Hayashi Fusao came calling.
> "The *tenkōsha* have real talent," he said. "You see them
> everywhere in the new political movements. They keep things
> moving. They have things their way. But there is something
> not quite right about them. They seem to be going well
> enough now, but their weak points will be showing one of
> these days."
> "What is wrong with them?"
> He thought for a moment and then said: "They are without
> sincerity."[53]

The word translated "sincerity" is *seii*, which suffers from the
fact that it appears so often in Japanese criticism as to become a
mannerism and presently to seem almost a travesty. "Sincere self-
reflection" has long been very popular. What Hayashi is saying is
that the *tenkōsha* easily substituted one enthusiasm for another and
that nothing ever really seemed to belong to them. As for his pre-

diction about their unreliability, he could not have been more correct. Another enthusiasm came over them with the surrender, and we had the phenomenon of the *bunkajin*, the "man of culture," talking endlessly in the newspapers and magazines about peace, democracy, progress, and the iniquities of American imperialism. Kobayashi has had harsh things to say about the *bunkajin*, of which the following is a terse example: "It is said that modern intellectuals are skeptics. I think this is playing with words. I doubt that there is a precedent for intellectuals who are such superficial believers."[54]

Kobayashi was not in the years after the war among the noisy exponents of democracy. He has been suspicious not of democracy itself but of the things that are done in its name: "While we are busy proclaiming that democracy is the taking of power by the people, the monster known as organized political power will no doubt destroy us. Mussolini called fascism an advanced form of democracy."[55]

He has been suspicious of politicians, and much concerned that they be kept in their place: "Politicians are the supervisors and orderers of culture, but not its makers. Not one single convenient scientific or artistic tool has ever come from their hands. They are users. They cannot know the long patience and the delicate working and shaping that is creation, or the joy and sorrow of the creator."[56]

Kobayashi's suspicion of politicians was not new with the coming of peace and democracy, nor has it been the fastidious withdrawal from the immediate workings of politics, the refusal to be sullied by association with any act of government, that has been a part of the orthodoxy of the *bunkajin*. In this suspicion has been an awareness of limits and a devout hope that politics may be persuaded to stay within those limits. It was apparent in a day when politics seemed to have burst forth uncontrollably:

> There is talk of an "emergency." The danger that faces the Japanese nation is quite properly described as an emergency, but there is no such thing as the ideology of an emergency. There are only the thoughts which we have painfully built up day by day. That is the truth we must always have before us. There are policies for an emergency, but there are no ideas or ideologies.
>
> Politics forever require policies with which to meet social

change. Accommodation is the inevitable rule of politics, but it is not applicable to the world of letters, or more widely to the world of the spirit and spiritual culture. A blind attempt at application can destroy the groundings of literature and culture. . . .

The important thing is not that the China Incident has produced new external circumstances. It has but brought under a strong light the virtues and defects already present in the Japanese. The incompetence of the bureaucrat and the stupidity of the politician and his cultural policies are nothing new. The difficulties that have come upon us have but made them evident. . . . The courage and endurance of the Japanese people and the real strength of the Japanese economy have also become evident.[57]

A distrust both of politicians and of faddish intellectuals finds itself most at home with a kind of conservatism that is very different from the radical nationalism of the war years and before. If there were numbers of important writers and intellectuals who shifted violently with the times, there were others who, essentially conservative, had little to say about politics, fell silent during the war years, and thought culture and tradition matters best left to their own devices. Kafū and Tanizaki are the striking examples. Their junior by two or three decades, Kobayashi was rather like them. Like Kafū in particular, he was as distrustful of do-gooders as of politicians.

I have objected only to sentimentalism disguised as logic, and to the romanticist wearing the mark of progress and enlightenment.[58]

Most of all I dislike the benevolent malcontent. He seems the most beyond helping.[59]

It is impossible to know what these large, folded hands will do, but they seem resolved not to move themselves in behalf of social welfare. The eyes look at nature, the hands take the painter's brush. Are they [Umehara Ryūzaburō's nudes] not almost self-portraits?[60]

The expression "malcontents" really signifies people who do not get on with themselves. They think that their trouble is with others or with the environment. . . . To the strong spirit a difficult environment is still an environment. It is what it is. There is nothing wanting in it. One does not fight an inadequate adversary. . . . In the power to live there is a power to see external accident as internal necessity. It is religious. But it is not empty musing. This is a truth very difficult for the extravagant malcontents known as social improvers to grasp. They have not once sought to visit the true site of human happiness and unhappiness.[61]

Mozart did not set himself a goal. His freedom is not to be mistaken for the freedom which resides in the heads of "liberal" thinkers. The latter has in fact no dwelling. Half-realized anxiety that liberty as a concept establishes only another concept is the bed from which their skepticism grows.[62]

Kobayashi's distaste for the *bunkajin* began long before the word, a postwar neologism, had been invented. He is suspicious of people who take a righteous view of culture and think themselves professionally qualified to do something about it. Culture and tradition are not materials for the politician and reformer to work with, nor are they friendly shelters to which, when the weather is bad, the writer returns. He cannot, for he has never left them. "Mr. Tanizaki's view that we should return to the Oriental classics is not a convenient something to be passed from hand to hand. He is but telling us of the route he took as he matured. History moves inexorably to destroy tradition. Inexorably, the individual matures as he comes to a true discovery of tradition."[63]

In "The Living Eye for History," a remarkable essay written in 1937 when the China Incident began, Kobayashi looked back admiringly and nostalgically to the Meiji period as a day when the "living eye" had not weakened. The expression seems to mean something like a sense of the whole which is not diffused by contemplation of the parts. In the Meiji period it was there. In the years since, historians have lost their way in a wilderness of historical materials and surrendered to a materialist view of history. As for the rather startling turn of history known as the China Incident, Kobayashi is very impatient, in another 1937 essay, with materialists who hold that the war contravenes a historical necessity of which they are the chosen witnesses and notaries:

I am no blind believer in nation and race, but I want above all to avoid the malady called historical inevitability. Let persons of leisure go on arguing forever that Japanese nationalism is mystical and anti-rational. I expect nothing at all from the intellectuals, sick from overfeeding on ideology, unable even now that a war is on to forego the pleasure of adverse criticism based upon a rationalist view of history, unable to enunciate clearly because fearful of being called reactionary for so much as indicating a willingness to shoulder a gun should the occasion present itself. . . .

The greatest lesson of history is that the real makers of history have had no faith in predicting the future. They have been strongly tied to the present. . . .

It should not be sacrificed to predictions for the future. The prophetic light comes only to them whose undeviating purpose is to face and come to terms with the present. History most definitely does not repeat itself.[64]

If there was a reluctance to join in easy criticism of the war, there was also a reluctance to join the radical nationalists in rejecting the West. In a report upon a 1938 trip to Manchuria Kobayashi takes exception to the view that receptivity to Western notions and things has led to an impasse and that something else is needed. At the end of judicious imitation must come understanding, which is its own justification. Meiji leaders saw clearly that the only way to overcome the Western adversary was to understand him. It had become a cardinal rule, and whatever the demands of the Incident, they were not sufficient to require modifying the rule.

He who believes that Western thought has obliterated the Japanese spirit sees only the form and has overlooked the subtle workings of the spirit. In the subtlety is the modern Japanese. . . .

The Japanese people have disposed of the China Incident in silence. That is the chief characteristic of the Incident. No doubt the demagogues it has produced are under the delusion that their methods have prevailed. This is the sort of delusion of which demagogues are victims.[65]

Kobayashi's immediate reaction to Pearl Harbor is easily misunderstood unless seen in the context of his quiet conservatism and his refusal to demand the extermination of the Anglo-American vermin and the obliteration of all their works. It was a demand made by numbers of erstwhile "liberals." Early in 1942 Kobayashi described certain emotions aroused by the attack:

On New Year's morning I saw a newspaper photograph of the attack on Pearl Harbor. "The Destruction of the American Pacific Fleet: It Will Shine in the Annals of War." The huge letters of the caption leaped up and assaulted the eye, but the picture itself was utterly quiet. Like a scale model, a neat row of seven ships sent out little puffs of white, and black like the ink of an octopus. No, I told myself, I must not be misled by appearances. It was the picture, untouched, of a flaming hell in which some thousands of men were trapped. I said it over and over again, but to no avail. No one has ever before taken such a picture, I said, and the effect was not to excite me but to restore my calm. My imagination refused to move further. I should think that everyone who saw the picture was assailed by similar emotions, by a kind of confusion in which an utterly astonishing photograph was not astonishing at all. . . .

The wide sea shone under a beautifully clear sky. . . .

There is a passage in, I think, the Lotus Sutra: torment to the eye of the unenlightened is heaven to the eye of the Buddha. I am not quoting exactly, but such is the import. I doubt that it is merely a simile. We must necessarily think it a simile because we are weak. Though I do not wish to be understood as saying that men in battle have the eye of the Buddha, may we not imagine that they see with an extraordinarily clear eye, free of ordinary distractions? They will not want to talk much when they come back. They will be displeased at the literature and literary journalizing that pour forth in the beautiful name of stirring the nation to resolve and valor, at useless mouthings about the extraordinary nature of war. . . .

Literature of war, theories of war, they cannot cloud the eye of the one who fights. Is it not the ultimate point to which the powerful soul of Tolstoi reached as he wrote *War and Peace*? Is it not the terrible idea that war and peace are the same?

Proceeding from criminal psychology, modern man has put together a strange affair known as the psychology of war. The causes of war are not in warlike men. Human life itself is war.[66]

There is nothing of the jingoist in this, and if the Anglo-American vermin are present at all it is as agents working upon a conscience which, in the urgency of the moment, has refused to behave properly. The quiet moment in history is the important thing. One wants to characterize this essay, only two pages long, as a prose lyric. It speaks in its quiet way with an eloquence only inferior to the complete silence of Nagai Kafū. The initial impulse to dismiss it as another piece of wartime ranting comes to seem foolish.

Kobayashi did not fall completely silent during the war years, but he spoke in subdued tones. There were other prose lyrics. Always a traditionalist, he now turned explicitly to the Japanese classics. His essay on Saigyō, written in 1942, has already been quoted from. In a 1942 piece on *Essays in Idleness (Tsurezuregusa)*, Yoshida Kenkō is held to be a Montaigne before his time, not only earlier than Montaigne but more incisive. There were also wartime essays on the Kamakura poet Minamoto Sanetomo and on *The Tale of the Heike*, and there was a fine prose lyric on the Nō play *Taema*. The controlling image is the Nō mask, bespeaking a healthier day when masks were left in place and inquisitive analysis did not rage uncontrolled.

The following is a full translation:

I saw Manzaburō perform *Taema* on the Umewaka Nō stage.
Under stars, through the last of the snow, I was walking a night road. Why did the dream-shattering sound of flute and drum linger on in my ears? Had not the dream been shattered? White sleeves waving, gold crown glittering, the maiden Chūjōhime still danced before my eyes. It was not the lingering aftermath of pleasure. It was utterly different. What was it, what shall I call it, two white feet starting up to the sound of the flute? Zeami quite clearly had a name for it: Taema. Do I believe in him, Zeami, the man, the poet? The question came to me, and startled me.
Priests on a pilgrimage to the Taema Temple hear a part of

its history from an old nun who chances to be attending services. She tells them how Chūjōhime, in retreat at Taema, had a vision of the Buddha Amida. In the course of her story she becomes the Buddha, manifest as a nun who was Chūjōhime's escort, and vanishes, and Chūjōhime herself appears and dances. Music and dance and song are reduced to the barest essentials. The music is like a cry, the dance is little more than a walk, and the song is like ordinary prayer. It is enough. What else is needed? I seemed to be muttering to myself. I felt as if I were being subdued by a simple, persistent flow of sound and form. Though at first one of the priests looked like someone who might be good at mah-jong.

Staff in hand, wearing a gray-violet cloak, an old nun appeared at the passage to the stage. There were only glimpses of brown eyes and nose beneath a pure white cowl, but in them was a strange, unearthly quality. I could not turn my eyes away. It was not as if I had glimpses of a Nō mask, but somehow as if the forms of two or three dead kittens, perhaps, were showing through a kerchief. I did not know why such an image should have come to me. As I had expected, the old woman did not do or say much of anything. I could not hear the muffled voice very distinctly, but the point seemed to be that intoning the holy name does as well as anything. Her main purpose, it seemed, was to have priests and audience observe the mask.

The corpse of a kitten—a ridiculous simile. Is the face itself then to be dismissed? The entr'acte came, there was a stir through the hall. Why had everyone been looking at that odd face? Purposefully twisted contrivance. But the power of the impression was not to be doubted, it was no delusion. Why could I not take my eyes from it? There were all manner of faces in the room, but not one of them was a face from which I could not take my eyes. Every last one of them seemed uneasy and bored. I could not be sure what sort of doltish face I myself had shown them all, and could hold no one responsible for the face he showed; and we were all pleased to read all the faces. It is very amusing and very foolish. When did we fall into this nonsense? Not so very long ago. The stage before us was evidence that until yesterday there were people who held that it was more important to wear a mask than to wear clothes.

Remove the mask, let us see the face, screamed modern civilization, running off it did not know where. Rousseau confessed not one thing in his *Confessions*. The womanish spite of which neither he nor his reader was aware spread limitlessly. I somehow felt, during the entr'acte, that I was chasing a nightmare.

The lovely form of Chūjōhime moved diagonally across the stage, like a flower flung from the mud of history. That thoughts about life and death should take so simple a form! I thought I saw how it could ignore social progress. Things hovered about the lovely form and went no further. Nothing was permitted inside that solemnly contrived mask. There, without doubt, was Zeami's "flower."

What is the modern view that makes Nō appreciation so fashionable? The question is a profitless one, a useless tax upon my energies. But that punishment had come seemed certain, punishment for staring at one another. We do not choose to recognize it, that is all. Historians feel comfortable in calling it a day of disorder, the healthy Muromachi period, when there was not the slightest doubt about the transience of this world and the eternity of faith.

It is not far away. For I almost believe it. And I ascertained, and saw nothing dubious in it, what Zeami thought beauty to be, in a day free from the arrogance of needless concepts. There is the beautiful "flower," and not the beauty of the "flower." "At the end of the count, at the end of contriving, you must see that the flower does not disappear." Modern aestheticians who fret over the ambiguity of the concept are deluded. Amend the concept with the movements of the flesh, Zeami said, for the latter is far subtler and more profound than the former. Were he among us he would perhaps want to say: it is well to let a mask hide the useless expressions of a face that is forever imitating useless concepts.

I walked the night road, looking at stars and snow. Where are the snows of yesteryear—no, I must not fall into that sort of thing. I looked again at the stars, and the snow.[67]

What modern man most fears, said Kobayashi in 1949, is silence. "That is the reason for his loquaciousness. . . . Critics are always making demands of the modern novel . . . but if I were required to make a demand myself, it would probably be in behalf of what is most wanted—silence.''[68]

It is easy to say that the man who has written such volumes of stuff has no right to be talking. It was easy for the *bunkajin*, when they were having their noisiest day, back during the anti-American demonstrations of 1960, to ridicule the prime minister for saying that he sensed the ''voiceless voice'' of the masses behind him. He was right, as the refusal of the electorate to be budged one small inch by the demonstrations later made clear; and Kobayashi has behind him a similarly voiceless voice, of awesome venerability. In chastising the modern novelist for his loquaciousness, Kobayashi was doubtless saying that there has been too much talk of things, and too little awareness and evocation of things.

Because an insistence upon concreteness has always distinguished good literature from other verbal exercises, it is not saying much of anything to say that the best Japanese writers have always so insisted. They have been unusually firm, however, in their distaste for cerebration. The first and greatest of Japanese novels, *The Tale of Genji*, is probably also the most meditative, but its musings do not rise above the level of elegant common sense, and nowhere does it approach the speculative heights of Dostoevski's Grand Inquisitor. Japanese criticism has preferred the simile and the touchstone to the system and the rule; and Japanese philosophy, which *does* exist, though it may sometimes seem rather shy and elusive, has more in common with Benjamin Franklin than with Kant or Hegel.

The expression ''voiceless voice'' brings something important into the confines of two unremarkable words. There is always something vaguely embarrassing, when it is not mischievous or downright ludicrous, about attempting to describe what it is that makes the Japanese so Japanese. A Tokugawa nationalist ''thinker'' seems merely amusing, in a naive, whimsical way, when he finds Japaneseness in a kind of purity, and thereby theorizes away the obvious superiority of Chinese medicine to Japanese with the statement, not easy to prove, that there were no diseases in Japan before China intruded upon the scene to sully things. The amusing can become cruel or grotesque when reduced to a program. When Japanese intellectuals rail away at Japanese ''fascism'' they are coarse propagandists, discarding from their argument all the vast differences between

Japanese authoritarianism and European. Yet there are undeniable and cruel points of similarity, and perhaps chief among them is the racism in the radical Japanese nationalism of earlier in this century. It derives very directly from those amusing Tokugawa nationalists: it is what programs did to their ideas. Transformed into a program not by an organizer of movements but by a radical individualist, it can lead to the grotesquerie of Mishima's suicide.

So it is too with the beauty of Japan. There is something about the Japanese way of doing things. Some may feel one way and others another about a heap of stones that calls itself a garden, and some may have doubts about the virtues of tropical architecture when the winds come sweeping down from Siberia; but almost no one can fail to sense something very unusual about a good Japanese interior or about the Ise Shrine. Attempts to describe this beauty become the bleatings of slick magazines and the manifestos of haiku clubs, and attempts at propaganda are sometimes a little revolting. What is more unlovely than the sight of a bulky party of tourists at one of the Sen family's tea afternoons?

That wisest of Japanese books, *The Tale of Genji*, mentions "the Japanese spirit" only once. It is at the center of a very charming scene, in which there is no attempt to define it, but in which it seems to stand for a kind of accommodation, a common-sense way of applying Chinese erudition. Genji has decided to send his son to the university. His mother-in-law objects, because it means denying the boy, her grandson, the fun and new ranks and offices which his friends are having and getting. Genji argues that a knowledge of precedents can be useful when the going is difficult, and that the Japanese spirit is more successful with than without it. The old lady, who has been urging a kind of elegant hedonism—her view of the Japanese spirit, though she does not use the word—is convinced, and the boy goes off to the university. For neither of them is Chinese erudition the really essential issue, but Genji urges its usefulness, and his mother-in-law presently accedes. The boy immediately indicates his willingness to defer pleasure and do as he is told, and so we may get on with the story, confident that the Japanese spirit has prevailed.

If attempts to schematize this Japanese spirit can sometimes lead to the savage, the grotesque, and the revolting, then perhaps an intense verbal reticence that approaches a kind of muteness is of its very nature, and schemes and programs are what it most dislikes. The distrust of concept that runs through all of Kobayashi's writing comes to seem important, and what he has to say seems more significant, because less subject to the exigencies of the moment, than all the tons of printed matter turned out by the modish *interi*.

At the very least it is hard not to think, upon looking back over the last half century or so of Japanese writing, that Kobayashi is on the side of the heavies against the lights. Those two grand old men who fell silent during the war, Tanizaki Jun'ichirō and Nagai Kafū, had both been intensely distrustful of the journalizing *interi* long before the crisis came. They were at work on the firm accumulation of non-intellectual substance that has given them their claim to immortality even while those most intellectual of writers, the proletarians, were putting together an ideological haystack. The lyrical eroticism of Kawabata Yasunari still seems very close, and the portentous psychologizing of his friend Yokomitsu Riichi seems very remote and dated. One can see, if one tries, why the latter once seemed important, but would as soon not make the effort.

The Shirakaba group of Shiga Naoya, so warmly admired by Kobayashi, gives another fine example. Chronological accounts of modern Japanese literature tend to be cramped, schematic affairs, arranging singularly dissimilar writers into "groups" because of accidents of birth and youthful friendship. So we find in the Shirakaba group Shiga, Satomi Ton, of whose Anjō family Kobayashi so disapproved, and Mushakōji Saneatsu, the Shirakaba ideologue. Perhaps the most important thing about Shiga is his massive indifference to ideas. And right beside him in the Shirakaba group is Mushakōji, as well provided with the tenets of glib optimism as ever was a graduate of an American school of social work. Shiga's longer works may arouse several responses in several readers, but his best short stories have a kind of irreducible purity that quite properly made them classics while Shiga was still alive. By comparison Mushakōji's most substantial efforts are no more than the sand that swirls about the monument. Shiga made more noise during the war than Tanizaki or Nagai Kafū, and some of it is rather shrill; but he seems very subdued indeed beside Mushakōji, that Western-style meliorist screaming for the extermination of the Anglo-Saxons. Although Mushakōji was not among the "apostates" about whom Hayashi Fusao expressed misgivings to Kobayashi, a very similar instability and want of "sincerity" is to be observed in him.

The heavies are the ones who abstained from intellectualizing, the lights are the ones who overindulged. Enjoining them all to silence, Kobayashi becomes intellectual mentor to the best of them, though he would doubtless think the role a ridiculous contradiction. Indeed it is rather contradictory, to be eloquent in the cause of silence; but it is a contradiction central to many of the best things the Japanese have thought and written.

(1975)

1. *The Collected Works of Kobayashi Hideo* (hereafter cited as *Works*), Tokyo, 1955–57, VI: 11–16.

2. Shinchōsha, 1955.

3. *Works*, VI: 30.

4. *Works*, VI: 175–76.

5. *Works*, VI: 207–8.

6. *Works*, I: 105.

7. *Works*, I: 108.

8. *Works*, I: 109.

9. *Works*, I: 116.

10. *Works*, I: 12–13.

11. *Works*, VI: 28–29.

12. *Works*, VII: 162–63.

13. *Works*, VII: 165.

14. *Works*, I: 122–23.

15. *Works*, II: 54.

16. *Works*, II: 75.

17. *Works*, II: 68.

18. *Works*, II: 70.

19. *Works*, II: 71.

20. *Works*, V: 208.

21. *Works*, VI: 30.

22. *Works*, VI: 72.

23. *Works*, VI: 86.

24. *Works*, VI: 89–90.

25. *Works*, VI: 92.

26. *Works*, VI: 112.

27. *Works*, VI: 238.

28. *Works*, VI: 247.

29. *Works*, I: 118–19.

30. *Works*, I: 120–21.

31. *Works*, I: 127.

32. *Works*, II: 12–13.

33. *Works*, II: 15.

34. *Works*, II: 16–17.

35. *Works*, IV: 130.

36. *Works*, IV: 141.

37. *Works*, IV: 143–44.

38. *Works*, IV: 43.

39. *Works*, IV: 47–48.

40. *Works*, IV: 49.

41. *Works*, I: 255.

42. *Works*, I: 258.

43. *Works*, VI: 108–9.

44. *Works*, VI: 123.

45. *Works*, II: 59.

46. *Works*, II: 171–72.

47. *Works*, VI: 86–88.

48. *Works*, II: 64.

49. *Works*, II: 67.

50. *Works*, II: 69.

51. *Works*, VI: 146.

52. *Works*, VI: 164–65.

53. *Works*, VI: 39.

54. *Works*, VII: 165.

55. *Works*, VII: 169.

56. *Works*, VII: 169.

57. *Works*, V: 209–10.

58. *Works*, III: 161.

59. *Works*, VI: 113.

60. *Works*, VI: 214.

61. *Works*, VI: 249.

62. *Works*, VI: 251.

63. *Works*, II: 218.

64. *Works*, IV: 86–87.

65. *Works*, IV: 187–89.

66. *Works*, VI: 114–16.

67. *Works*, VI: 117–19.

68. *Works*, VII: 177.

REDSKINS IN JAPAN

QUESTION: I'm not very well acquainted with American literature, but a while ago you mentioned Dreiser's name in your explanation. I think that with Dreiser, what is called "social realism" has been the drive of his work. Then after that, T. S. Eliot came out—Eliot was more interested in the humanistic movements—"new humanism" movements. You, Mr. Faulkner, would then come after that—I mean the order would be Dreiser's social realism, next Eliot's humanism, and then your new way of handling the human mind. This is how I understand you, and I would like to know your reactions to this understanding.

FAULKNER: I agree with you. . . .

QUESTION: Speaking of [poetry], mention was made, Mr. Faulkner, the other day, of the difference of American literature and French literature. There are a number of similarities between French and Japanese hardships. Edgar Allan Poe is popular in France, so he is in Japan, or at least used to be, because Poe's artistry is exquisite. His finesse appeals to our sensitivity as well as the Frenchman's. At one time in Japanese literature, poets used to sing long poems resembling somewhat Walt Whitman in the volume of the voice and in the representation of nature. But our population increased and it became accordingly smaller, our poets came to sing only [shorter] poems. However, the names of poems are of secondary importance. The poet may sing of the Rocky Mountains or sing make-believe, provided the poem is good. Your literature, allegorically speaking, is of a larger piece, feeling at home in the vast ocean, but ours is of a small fish living in a big stream. That is what I think.

FAULKNER: I agree with that. . . .

QUESTION: Mr. Faulkner, what tobacco do you smoke?

These are excerpts from a most entertaining book called *Faulkner at Nagano*. It is a literal transcription, insofar as one is possible from tape recordings, of Faulkner's intercourse with the Japanese when he made his visit five years ago. The excerpts are a little unfair. The dots indicate among other things passages in which Faulkner tries to break through. He himself had nothing to do with putting the book together. That he should be required to have nothing to do with it seems to have been the one condition he set upon its publication. R. P. Blackmur, who came to Japan a year later, was so delighted with *Faulkner at Nagano* that he wanted to write an essay called "The Book in the Absence of the Author" or something of the sort. I do not know whether or not he ever did.

Although the quotations may not be entirely fair, however, they are in generally the right spirit. They touch upon a truth: when the Japanese read American literature, they read it in a way that would probably be acceptable to the French but may seem perverse to Americans. That progression from Dreiser to Faulkner with a brief Eliot interlude, that nod in Poe's direction—it is the voice of one who knows that America is a tough, hard-boiled place, populated by redskins and less conspicuously by their pale, fragile victims.

It would be wrong to say, as people sometimes do, that America has succeeded in exporting only its vulgarity. Yet the fact is that when the Japanese have had a taste of French or pre-Soviet Russian literature they tend to surrender to the habit, while with American literature they remain very choosy. They seek out the redskins and, *pace* the Poe gentleman, they prefer a bold and even reckless brush to exquisite finesse.

Every year the *Mainichi* newspapers survey the reading habits of up to fifteen thousand people. The preferences of the pollees always turn out to be strongly Japanese, with the first foreign writer, usually Tolstoi, appearing just below tenth on the list of favorite writers. The steadiest American performers are Margaret Mitchell and Pearl Buck, who frequently turn up in the middle teens. A

French writer usually appears down around twentieth. For some reason it has to be a living French writer. Gide promptly dropped from the list when death made him less current. Hemingway caused a brief flurry when *A Farewell to Arms* became a moderate best seller. No other American writer (unless we may call Julius and Ethel Rosenberg writers) has ever been serious competition with the two ladies on the *Mainichi* survey. Indeed *Gone with the Wind* has been far and away the most profitable translation into Japanese since the war.

The *Mainichi* goes into further detail on student reading habits. The first American writer to enter the student's consciousness is Mark Twain. *Tom Sawyer* is popular with fourth and fifth graders, in fact the only foreign book they seem to like. In the middle schools (the equivalent of junior high schools) Twain is succeeded by Harriet Beecher Stowe and, among the girls, by Frances Hodgson Burnett, if she may be called American. In the high schools Tolstoi, Pearl Buck, Margaret Mitchell, and some very current Frenchman make their first showing, and reading habits are set for life.

The *Mainichi* survey aims at a cross section. It must be supplemented by evidence which suggests that among serious readers American literature is not in it with French and pre-Soviet Russian.

The Japanese are properly known as the most avid readers of foreign literature in the world. In the most respected of the "libraries," the uniform paper-bound editions that sell for the equivalent of fifteen to thirty cents a copy, there are over six hundred foreign titles (exclusive of the sections on philosophy and the social sciences, which are almost entirely foreign), as compared to less than a hundred titles from the Japanese classics and just over three hundred from modern Japanese literature.

The series in question, the Iwanami Bunko, was founded just over thirty years ago. About a third of the hundred oldest foreign titles are French. English (including four volumes of Shakespeare) and Russian literature together make up about a third of the rest. There are but eleven American titles even if one stretches a point and calls Hendrik Willem Van Loon, Lafcadio Hearn, and Frances Hodgson Burnett Americans. Here are the eight unquestionably American titles: *The Autobiography of Benjamin Franklin* (number twenty-two, after *Madame Bovary*, *Crime and Punishment*, and *Anna Karenina*), *Huckleberry Finn*, *The Prince and the Pauper*, *The Scarlet Letter*, *The*

Black Cat and other tales by Poe, *Little Women*, *Daddy-Long-Legs*, and O'Neill's *Days without End*.

A decent enough beginning; but one reaches the end of the six hundred and feels that something has been overlooked. A few writers are fairly well covered. Mark Twain and Hawthorne appear three more times each, and O'Neill, the only modern American author Iwanami cares about, appears a total of seven times.

There is almost no poetry: only *Leaves of Grass* and a volume of Sandburg, which tend to be read as social documents. Whitman had a considerable vogue in the twenties, when the Japanese were having their first flirtation with radicalism. The exquisite artistry of Poe is represented only by his tales. Henry James is there with *Daisy Miller* and *An International Episode* and nothing else. *Moby Dick* at length appears among the last hundred titles. The list ends rather as it began, with books by Turgenev, Gorky, and Stendhal. I have not thought of a single nineteenth-century Russian or French book that is not on the list, though no doubt there are some.

The *Publisher's Yearbook* for 1958, which lists all books published or reprinted in 1957, has thirty-two pages of what we might call Anglo-Saxon fiction, American and English lumped together. French fiction alone covers twenty-two pages, and Tolstoi and Dostoevski between them about five pages. The most conspicuous writers in the Anglo-Saxon section are Erle Stanley Gardner (about a page), Agatha Christie, and Ellery Queen. There are ten individual entries for Hemingway, including three separate editions of *A Farewell to Arms*, and there is a ten-volume edition of his collected works. There are three editions of *The Scarlet Letter*, *The Murders in the Rue Morgue*, and *Tom Sawyer*, and two of *The Good Earth*. Howard Fast, usually to be found in *Publisher's Yearbook* under the auspices of firms like Dialectics House, is missing, fallen from grace. James is in there again with *Daisy Miller* and *An International Episode*, and, because of the movie, *Washington Square*.

In 1958 there was an ambitious attempt to educate the Japanese reading public to a wider view of American literature. It was not successful. A very moderately priced twenty-volume series, brought out by Waste-Land House, offered a number of hitherto neglected American writers, including James and Fitzgerald. The public did not rise to the lure. The Hemingway volume sold best, because people are always willing to read Hemingway, and the Sherwood Anderson volume next best, not because people are willing to read Anderson but because a number of universities have started using *Winesburg, Ohio* as a text, and students need a trot. James did very badly, Fitzgerald even worse. Rather high hopes had been held for Fitzgerald, who was discussed at Blackmur's seminar; but fewer than five thousand copies have been sold.

There is reason for believing nonetheless that American literature is growing on the Japanese, whereas the European literatures are simply there, fixed canons that will always have their readers. Certainly this is true of Russian literature. Except for Gorky and more recently Pasternak, Soviet literature has very little following, as, by the way, has contemporary Chinese literature. French literature is still capable of stirring up flurries, but it would be hard to think of contemporary writers besides Sartre, Camus, and Françoise Sagan that people know much about.

With American literature matters are somewhat different. The Iwanami Bunko carries O'Neill and O'Neill alone among modern writers, but its less revered but very successful rival, the Shinchō Bunko, has suddenly added a rash of American titles to its list. Among the first four hundred titles, which include nine by Tolstoi and thirteen by Maupassant, are to be found only *Moby Dick*, *Uncle Tom's Cabin*, *The Naked and the Dead*, a volume of Poe tales and a volume of poems, and some Louisa May Alcott. The last hundred fifty titles, on the other hand, are almost a third American—*The Good Earth* is there, of course, and so are Steinbeck, Erskine Caldwell, O'Neill, Hemingway, Tennessee Williams, and Mark Twain, Jack London, and Dos Passos. But there is still no Fitzgerald.

To summarize, only the ladies seem able to fight it out with Tolstoi and Françoise Sagan for the wider audience. For the reader who wishes to dip a little deeper, American writing seems to divide into three groups: the classics up to the Civil War, the Mark Twain people, and the Henry James people.

The classical canon has for the most part been translated, and *The Scarlet Letter* and *Moby Dick* have been translated repeatedly. These last two find their way into Japanese lists of Great Novels with the dutiful regularity that is to be observed the world over. Yet they seem to have made no impression upon Japanese writing.

Among the classical authors, Whitman and Poe are special cases, to be touched upon in a moment. It is safe to say of the rest that they are far more widely praised than admired. I have never had a student express enthusiasm for *Moby Dick* without the faint reddening at the ears that makes Japanese lies the most engaging and transparent in the world; and I have not found a student who could even bring himself to lie about *Walden*.

The Mark Twain people, on the other hand, are read with some enthusiasm. Twain himself is the first foreigner to make the student's acquaintance, and his hard-boiled, axe-swinging successors are responsible for that growing list of American titles in the Shinchō Bunko. One suspects too that they are responsible for a highly un-Japanese touch of the laconic that has begun to appear in Japanese letters—for the splendid opening sentence of a recent Japanese novel, for instance: "Everyone was yawning."[1] There are gaps, to be sure; as an eminent Japanese professor pointed out not long ago in the *New York Times*, even specialists find Faulkner impossibly difficult. Like Melville, he is more praised than admired. Japanese taste, moreover, is not always American taste. Steinbeck is admired beyond his deserts, and there is a tendency to take Saroyan more seriously than he takes himself. Every year brings graduation essays on "Time in the Works of William Saroyan" or "The Transcendental Optimism of William Saroyan."

Yet, with these qualifications, it is the redskins who are American literature to the Japanese.

The James people and their products, except Daisy Miller, are ignored.

In seeking to explain why the Japanese read what they do, one must first note a tendency to admire things for non-literary reasons. The Japanese have not to my knowledge found existentialist glories in American murder mysteries, but they are not a people to feel qualms about putting literature to work for politics. Along with those metaphysical graduation essays on Saroyan, there are always essays on "Dreiser and Naked Power." Before the Fall there were always essays on Howard Fast, and generally someone comes around with "Meliorism, Mass Culture, and Lanny Budd."

All of this points to a reading of American literature similar in nature to Parrington's: the praise and blame are dealt out as the paraphrasable content of an author's work approaches or departs from a fixed idea. The idea here being somewhat different from Parrington's, however, the readings too are different in detail. When Japanese put American literature to work for politics, they find in it evidence to support the double idea with which they belabor contemporary America: America is the land of the materialist and the machine, and America *used to be* the land of the democratic dream. This leads to a certain inconsistency, since by implication there was once a time when the machine and the materialist (the enemies of Poe) and the democratic dream (Whitman's, surely, if anyone's) lived side by side; but it helps account for the attention given the only two classical writers who receive much attention.

If Parrington dismisses Poe, the Japanese, like the French, make too much of him. Unlike the French, however, they are not much interested in his poetry, and they are interested even less in his poetics. On one level he is admired for the Rue Morgue chill, which puts him in a class with Erle Stanley Gardner. On a higher level, it is less because of his "finesse" and his "exquisite artistry" that he is made much of, one feels, than because he is the perfect symbol of sensitive American spirit destroyed by brutal American matter. He leads that procession of American saints and martyrs the rear of which, for the moment at least, is brought up by Dr. Robert Oppenheimer.

If Poe is the man who was destroyed by materialism and Naked Power, Dreiser is the man who fought them to the end. Dos Passos has enjoyed a considerable vogue for similar reasons; and if, as seems to be the case, the vogue is passing, that may be because he has given up the fight. Steinbeck, on the other hand, may no longer write with the fire he once showed in the cause of the Okies, but he still has a place in his heart for Mexicans and little people.

Then there is the other half of the idea: America used to be a much nicer country than it is now. Here, of course, Whitman comes in, singing the body democratic. It has already been noted that Whitman, almost alone among American poets, has had his admirers in Japan. That he should also have a following in the Soviet Union and that he should have had his principal Japanese vogue in the twenties, their first Red Decade, seem to be closely related facts. Whitman has been enrolled in the proletarian movement. A certain simplification has been necessary. The nature of that mystical "Walt" busy chopping everything up for its maw does not come under consideration, nor, on a less obscure level, do the misgivings Whitman came to feel about the democracy he was singing. America once had a proletarian bard and his dream, and has no more. That is enough.

A second and considerably more important explanation for the Japanese choice in American literature is the fact that it must be put into a foreign language. In spite of the enormous time and expense that go into teaching them English, few Japanese read English with ease and pleasure. On the other hand, they have this last century been the most industrious readers of translations in the world. They tend to be rather lenient toward their translators, not expecting miracles from them. Whereas most people would complain of a translation that was too full of exoticisms, Japanese often complain when a translation does not keep reminding them every sentence of the way that it *is* a translation. They like their translation to be literal. Now and then one comes upon a translator who feels that if he has something eminently readable in a foreign language he need not mind taking liberties in the effort to make eminently readable Japanese of it. He is the exception, however. The foreign book may expect to pass through the hands of a literalist. Some things do better under his ministrations than others. Some things he has the good sense not to try at all, and some things his literalness is even able to improve upon.

The terse, direct statement does fairly well, though within limits. "Call me Ishmael" is a trifle too terse, and results in locutions like "Suppose we make it Ishmael," or "I am the worthless one known as Ishmael." The same can be said for the remark of Gatsby's that so delights Mr. Trilling: "In any case it was just personal." On the other hand, Hemingway's "But they killed you in the end. You could count on that" does very well indeed. Japanese can be to the point when it has to.

Dreiser is somewhat better in Japanese than in English. The barbarity of his style disappears, and his wordiness slips very naturally into Japanese wordiness. When not being disciplined by Hemingway, Japanese is among the least terse languages in the world.

The translators have no doubt been wise to stay away from the Jamesian interplay of style and meaning. One shudders to think of the hard, black Sino-Japanese nouns that would be lined up by a sentence like this: "Our doubt is our passion and our passion is our task." As a matter of fact I did once see such an attempt, faithful to James's sentence, abstract noun for abstract noun. It translates back into English roughly thus: "Our suspicion is our fire and our fire is our homework." This means nothing at all. I have asked several hundred students, and they have told me so.

Fitzgerald, for all his apparent simplicity, presents some of the very worst problems. A non-literalist could have made passable sense of the James sentence by accepting the nature of the Japanese language and putting the verbs to work harder at digesting the Sino-Japanese nouns. But what could one do with Gatsby's unique use of the word "personal?" And what could one do with the splendid list of people who came to Gatsby's house in the summer, the Stonewall Jackson Abrams of Georgia and Beluga the tobacco importer and Beluga's girl and the rest? The Japanese reader, faced with a list of names as hopelessly foreign as a list in a botany text, turns the page and wonders why the book is thought well of in America.

At this point a doubt arises. Is not the language of *Huckleberry Finn* equally subtle? Is not the language of "The Short, Happy Life" also? So it is; but Mark Twain is a liquor with altogether more body than Fitzgerald. He can still please even after the literalists have finished with him. As for Hemingway, it is true that he is in the final analysis a drink no headier than Fitzgerald; but his disciplining of the language is a disciplining to fit the act precisely, not to bring in all sorts of other acts, as when Mr. and Mrs. Abrams and Mr. Beluga visit Gatsby's in the summer. He does not evade the translator as Fitzgerald does.

Interested in Japanese friendliness toward *Huckleberry Finn* and the fact that I had never been able to find a student who could say that he really liked *Moby Dick*, I once sat down to look at the translations.

There are three widely circulated translations of *Moby Dick*. All of them come a cropper over "Call me Ishmael." All are riddled with unspeakable technical terms. The American reader may not have a very clear idea of what stunsails and braces are, but they are somehow a part of our collective memory. The great days of sailing ships are not a part of the Japanese tradition, and the pious literalness of the translations means the introduction of ideographs which one vaguely remembers having seen somewhere but does not have the faintest idea how to pronounce. The effect is a little as if the translator *from* Japanese were to permit this sort of thing: "And then we sat down to a delicious repast of *zensai*, followed by *chawanmushi*, *sashimi*, *kuchitori*, *nimono*, *nakazara*, and some of the best *aemono* I have ever had in my life."

Melville's grand passages suffer grievously from this literalness. Even in English he can be bombastic, but sometimes he manages to roar and swell like the sea itself. A small example will suggest what happens in translation. When Moby Dick is first sighted, he is described as "set in a revolving ring of finest, fleecy, greenish foam." Now fleece happens not to be a part of the Japanese tradition. It becomes "high-grade wool." A sea like high-grade wool is, to say the least, an obscure image. A few lines later, "the soft Turkish-rugged waters" become exactly that: soft waters like a rug from Turkey, than which few things can be more alien to the Japanese.

It is undeniable that *Huckleberry Finn* too loses something in translation. Emmeline Grangerford's file of "cases of patient suffering" from the *Presbyterian Observer* becomes a lot of clippings about indispositions from a publication with an odd foreign name. The same Emmeline's ode to Stephen Dowling Bots loses from not being rhymable in Japanese ("measles drear, with spots," to rhyme with Stephen Dowling Bots). Deprived of the discreet remove which dialect gives it, moreover, Huck's apology to Jim comes dangerously near being sentimental, as do the remarks which occasion it; and like "Call me Ishmael" the wonderful last sentence is a bit too terse. "I been there before" becomes merely "I've already had that experience."

But what survives in translation is still rollickingly good. Now and then one comes across a sentence that seems to have been intended from the start for translation into Japanese: ". . . and by and by you could see a streak on the water which you know by the look of the streak that there's a snag there in a swift current which breaks on it and makes that streak look that way." The splendor of that first "which" is lost in translation, but the circularity is thoroughly Japanese.

Compared to Ishmael, Huck is directness itself. The Missouri twang is gone, to be sure, but Huck's is still the unaffected voice of the new continent.

The unaffected voice of the new continent—this brings us to

another point. Neither of the above explanations is enough. An ideological reading of American literature can hardly account for the popularity of Twain and Hemingway; and, on the other hand, if people were clamoring for James, one could be sure that translators would take him on and, whether intelligible or not, *The Awkward Age* and *The Sacred Fount* would presently find their way into the cheap libraries, beside *Daisy Miller*.

It will be remembered that Gide too was uninterested in James. "It goes without saying . . . that I am aware of all the importance of H. James; but I believe him more important for England than for France. England has never sinned up to the present by too much good cooking; James is a master cook. But, as for me, I like precisely those great, untrimmed chunks that Fielding or Defoe serves us, barely cooked, but keeping all the 'blood-taste' of the meat. So much dressing and distinction, I am satiated with it in advance; he surpasses us in our own faults."

Countries prefer what they find most distinctive in the literatures of other countries. To Gide, James was too French. To the Japanese he may not be too Japanese, exactly, but he is not what they think most distinctly American. Why, then, go to the enormous bother of reading him when much the same thing is more accessible in other literatures, and is in those literatures, notably French literature, the real thing of which he is but a derivative? In vain one points out to students that James's realism is wholly different from Stendhal's, and that, compared to Julien Sorel, Millie Theale seems as innocent of a social milieu as Natty Bumppo, as much alone as Huckleberry Finn. In vain; they will not read James, for he is not a hard-hitting, continent-breaking American. He measured out his life with coffee spoons.

It is interesting that the Japanese sometimes make a similar though reverse complaint about foreign readings of their own literature. Why, they ask, has that fine, grim novel about exploited peasants on rocky northern farms never been translated? Is no one interested in the slice of Japanese life that won the Ladies' Peace Prize last year, the one that opens with the scullery maid bent double from morning sickness? Let people read *that* if they want to know about Japan.

These questions too are in vain. The few Americans who read modern Japanese literature are more likely to be interested in haiku and snippets of Zen than they are in specimens of Japanese naturalism, which differ little from problem novels the world over. Whatever the wishes of the Japanese themselves, to us they will always be fragile and intuitive.

The Japanese are an island people, and a troublesome language barrier has made them far more insular than the island people to whom they are often compared, the English. Their attitude toward the outside world has always been ambivalent, distrustful and at the same time fascinated. One is tempted to speculate: behind the fascination is there a racial memory of the vast spaces from which life came to their small islands—a memory of the continent as the first home?

The continent excites them in any event. Here is a passage from a recent short story, autobiographical in nature: "I longed for something vast, dim, ineffable, that corner of the universe in a Chinese landscape where the clouds gather, beyond endless masses of rock and water and forest. I was immoderately fond of anyone from the continent. . . . Students always seemed to have secret missions toward building a new Orient, and Chinese restaurant keepers had . . . slim-waisted beauties hidden away in secret chambers."[2]

The Chinese have not done much recently to satisfy that longing for the vast and ineffable. They do invite a few Japanese over for a ride and a feast now and then, and the Japanese almost without exception come back to tell how they felt at home again as they watched the tanks and missiles roll past the Gate of Heavenly Peace. In literature, however, the Japanese have had to take their continental vastness where they could find it, and the People's Novel of the New China has not been much help. Thrown in more than ever upon their narrow islands, they have recently turned to producing the continental image for themselves. Historical fiction about the empty reaches of Inner Asia, the shifting nomad empires and the city-state oases, has been much in vogue.

Among writers continental by birth, Pasternak has helped a little where the Chinese have failed. *Dr. Zhivago* was a mixed critical success in Japan, but everyone who read it seems to have been taken by the lyrical evocation of the Russian landscape. Huckleberry Finn too has been a help, and the Nick of the Hemingway northern-woods stories; and Faulkner in his primitivist and relatively comprehensible moods, as in "The Bear."

Here is something wholly wanting in Japanese literature, which may try to present rough people but which, except for historical fiction, must put them in miniature, carefully trimmed landscapes. Even the barren farms on which peasants are defeated in proletarian novels seem no harsher than rock gardens. There was a brave attempt to find a wilderness a couple of years ago when an important novelist (he it was who longed for "something vast, dim, ineffable" in his younger years) wrote a long, long novel about the hairy Ainu and his forests and lakes; but it was not a success. The wilderness evaporated into the sort of talk one hears in Tokyo derivatives of the Deux Magots. Like Nick in *The Great Gatsby*, the major characters are self-conscious observers, and the self-consciousness shuts them off from the primitive dream.

Forever talking and forever creating miniatures, the Japanese find in Huck Finn and Hemingway something they could not have created for themselves. Even when they try to write of people near the earth, something goes wrong. The rough, earthy people seem etiolated. The scullery maid in that slice of life has an air of having been too long lived with.

The Japanese look to Twain and Hemingway for something they do not find in Europe or Japan, and away from James, whose fastidious trimming can be found in one place or the other—or so it is believed. There is a sense, however, in which the Twain people, and particularly Hemingway, are precisely the people with whom the Japanese have most in common: they share a suspicion of the intellect. It may irk the Japanese to be thought intuitive, but one can say that the characterization is one they have asked for. Ever since Okakura Tenshin first dazzled the ladies of Boston with his "Teaism," the Japanese have lost no opportunity to tell us that we are coldly rational (or "scientific") and they are warmly intuitive. If by "intuitive" is meant "having a tendency to denigrate the rational," then they are in fact rather it. Zen intuitivism *is* important in their culture, however one may feel about their efforts to export it; and they have not, on the whole, been given to erecting great rational edifices.

Neither has Hemingway. When a people that wants to love French culture but has never quite been able to suppress a distrust of reason comes away from a bout with Proust, therefore, Hemingway's emphasis on the act and how it feels must seem very familiar and very restful. One does not wish to suggest that the Japanese are wholly unintellectual. They are as a matter of fact rather good at forcing the world into a rational pattern, most commonly a Marxist pattern; but even then the apocalyptic act waits at the end of the argument, as when "Trotskyite" students occupy Tokyo Airport by way of dissuading the prime minister from taking off for Washington.

The alert reader could, if he wished, find disorder and violence in James too—Stephen Spender found it "beneath the stylistic surface, the portentous snobbery" of *The Golden Bowl*. But in Hemingway it is never out of sight. Nor is it ever quite out of sight in Zen and the country of Zen.

The Twain people thus have it over the James people both when they are nearest the Japanese and when they are farthest away. On the one hand they do not overstress reason; and on the other they stand for the great, untamed continent, strange and fascinating to the native of the overcultivated island.

The word "hard-boiled" has been taken into the Japanese language. It describes American literature, and Hemingway is its image. Here is a translation of the definition in a leading dictionary: "Hard-boiled: of literary works, a method of describing incidents, usually of an extraordinary nature, with an attitude and style that are cruel and unfeeling, and admit no mixture of sentiment. Descriptive of cold, cruel writing, such as Hemingway's 'The Killers.'"

This calls for a word about something one cannot talk of with any certainty. Hemingway can be a rather sentimental writer, after all, and Steinbeck almost always is; and Mark Twain is not a writer innocent of ideas. To this objection one can answer that the Japanese would not appear to admit the complications.

Mark Twain's dark determinism, a sampling of student reactions would suggest, is lost sight of in the wish to make him the spokesman of the new continent, and the violence of, say, *Huckleberry Finn* is given an affirmative value he cannot have meant it to have. Japanese students are rather good at returning the teacher's opinions when they write their examinations, but the lecture on *Huckleberry Finn* never seems to take. The book is described as an optimistic one and a happy one. No amount of lecturing can dim the memory of the innocent expectation with which the student approached *Tom Sawyer* some ten years before.

The sampling suggests, again, that the Japanese are not upset by Hemingway's occasional sentimentality, indeed do not even notice it. This is not surprising, since they do not seem to notice what strikes the foreigner as sentimental in their own literature. Perhaps in fact it is not sentimental—that word refers to a response that is emotional out of all proportion to its stimulus, and what is one to say when the people best qualified to judge are aware of no imbalance between stimulus and response? One can say, however, that the Japanese have too long been accustomed to the boldly expressed emotion, the racking Kabuki sob and the equally racking laugh, to find anything embarrassing about Robert Jordan and his little rabbit or the Colonel and his Daughter.

To round out the story, it must be added that chance and the sharp trader account for some things. Thus no deeper significance need be read into Iwanami's partiality for O'Neill than that the company has been unwilling to pay the prices demanded by brokers for rights to other authors. Thanks to an omnivorous experimental theater, O'Neill has been around since long before the brokers started pushing prices up.

(1960)

1. Mishima Yukio, *Collected Works*, Tokyo, 1974, XI: 9.

2. Takeda Taijun, "The Misshapen Ones," in *A Treasury of Japanese Literature*, Tokyo, 1973, LXVII: 182–83.

TOKYO

It does not take long to become an Old Resident of Tokyo, only a little more than the two years considered standard by the diplomatic corps and the foundations. Then begin the years of trying to show newcomers the city. There can be few cities in which this particular duty of the Old Resident is more trying: for there is almost nothing to show.

The newcomer who wants to be shown the city has probably come in at night, because transpacific planes have a way of coming in at night. He is up early the next morning, and he wants to see the city. None of the tricks that would work in a European capital will work here. Unless there is a special exhibition, the museums are not impressive. Too much of the best art is in provincial temples and private collections. The traditional theater is good, but a couple of afternoons will take care of it. The Westernized theater is sometimes very good, but why take anyone to see *The Merchant of Venice* in Japanese, even if Portia happens to be the leading actress in Japan? The visitor's chief impression will probably be that the Japanese leg was not made for tights. It takes a musician to find anything in traditional Japanese music the first dozen times or so, and as for Western music—it may be very good, but why come all the way to Tokyo for it? Or sports, unless it is the enormous *sumō* wrestlers, who perform only a few weeks a year? The Japanese are fine baseball players, but the New York Yankees are better. There are always the tourist industries: dancers whose bosoms show with impossible clearness under their kimonos, and sukiyaki restaurants whose delicate bowls of rice would send an Oriental stalking from the room.

And there are the geisha, very expensive and very hard work. You have to entertain them, not the reverse.

There are few sights. The palace moat, once the inner moat to Edo Castle, is much as it always was, except for several six-lane avenues cutting across the part of the old castle grounds that is now a public park. The escarpments inside the moat present to the north a face of venerable masonry, now a mossy gray-green, and to the south a soft expanse of hand-trimmed grass, surmounted by pine trees that trail off in the misty, indecisive way Japanese pines have. We are told that the first Tokugawa shogun faced a hostile north and had friends behind him to the south; hence the grassy embankments. In any case, the variety is fortunate. Here and there an angle tower survives, and, except for the gold-buttoned policemen, some of the back gates to the palace could be as they were when the last shogun turned it over to the emperor in 1868.

And where do you take the newcomer next? There are some late and architecturally undistinguished pagodas, and a scattering of florid gates where the daimyos had their mansions. The tombs of the shoguns, now sooty and weed-grown, are on a chilly autumn afternoon an impressive testimonial to the impermanence of things; but you have to know the chink in the wall and the unpadlocked gate, and sneak in when the policeman is not looking.

The newcomer begins to look puzzled. What about temples? Almost none worth showing, except as a lesson in how not to use a building material. Some of the larger ones destroyed during the war have been rebuilt with the last details of the wooden bracketing reproduced in concrete, and the whole painted over with vermilion lacquer, as though to keep away termites. Views? The visitor has already had the best view, coming into Haneda Airport at night, and all you can offer now is the Ferris wheel atop the Takashimaya Department Store, from which he can see block after insubstantial block stretching off toward the harbor. "It really is better at night," you say, but without conviction. The Old City, the Intramuros? Tiny fragments here and there: a few houses below the Yushima Shrine, and a few more on a strange little island in the harbor where the same fisher families have lived for centuries.

The truth is that Tokyo is not really an old city, and it is moreover the most impermanent of cities. Very little in it goes back more than thirty years. The city was destroyed once in the earthquake and fire of 1923 and again in the bombings of 1944 and 1945. Depreciated at the standard rate, a house that has been standing since before the earthquake is probably now below zero, and the owner has a terrible time borrowing money on it. If its history can be traced back much before the turn of the century, he is likely to find that he has a monument on his hands, and must submit to busloads of children (being educated the Dewey way) and commissions for the preservation of cultural properties.

It is with relief that one admits defeat—Tokyo takes getting used to—and sends the newcomer off to Kyoto. There, without the help of the Old Resident, he can find temples and gardens, and geisha with engagingly false Kyoto accents. In Kyoto the geisha walk about the streets and pose on bridges and under wisteria arbors, pretty as postcards. In Tokyo they whisk from one engagement to the next, and you would never know them except for the fact that they are the only people in the city who still use rickshaws.

The Japanese have two solutions to the problem. The first is to go looking at sites and graves. "Literary Tour" or "Historical Tour" in hand, they go hunting for the site of the temple from which, in 1657, a burning kimono flew off in the wind, set fire to the city, and killed eighteen thousand people; or the house from which, tradition has it, the pathetic heroine of a Meiji novel saw her student-lover off for Germany. The city is rich in sites, major and minor, and all carefully labeled; but you are likely to find only a placard before a bicycle shop: "In the space between this sign and the public lavatory to the east, the novelist Ichiyō wrote her masterpiece while selling hardware to support her mother and sister." Then there are graves: graves of statesmen and graves of literary men, and even graves of villains, such as the greengrocer's daughter who, in 1683, tried setting fire to the city because she hoped in the excitement to meet her lover. How the Japanese dote upon graves! Some of them are indeed very beautiful, and when the cherries are in bloom the cemeteries are probably the most attractive parts of the city. However, charming though the newcomer may find the story that goes with it, the grave of Oshichi the greengrocer's daughter bores him.

The other Japanese solution is to show off the modern parts of the city, and the sort of places an American would visit in Washington. Time after time in novels one is taken on the standard tour: the Diet

Building, the War and Navy Ministries, the Double Bridge for obeisance to His Imperial Majesty, headquarters of the Guards Regiment, the Yasukuni Shrine (roughly equivalent to the Tomb of the Unknown Soldier), the outer gardens of the Meiji Shrine (Lincoln Memorial?), and so on. Of the ministries, mostly red brick and peeling concrete, the only thing to say is that they look even worse on the inside. There is a certain sphinx-like fascination in the crouching, ungainly Diet Building. Cartoonists delight in showing it as a jack-in-the-box, with a new procurement scandal or police law springing from the squat steeple. But there is no point in taking the visitor to see it. He will have seen more than enough of it from wherever he looks by the time he leaves Tokyo.

As for the business and entertainment districts, they teem with life and they are brilliantly lighted. The most interesting building is still the Imperial Hotel, which dates from before the earthquake.[1] It is hard to know what Frank Lloyd Wright had in mind. The Imperial is the most aggressively unfunctional of buildings, full of blind corridors and staircases that terminate in locked doors, and only the *real* Old Resident knows how to find his way from the front door to the parking lot in the back. To say that the Imperial Hotel is either beautiful or ugly is somehow to miss the point. It is interesting. Among the other modern buildings, few are as interesting as the sewer and subway excavations interminably going on before them.

Every new foreign style has left its alluvium. Foreign-style buildings are not as perishable as the old wooden buildings were. Tokyo Central Station is supposed to be Renaissance, but I cannot be sure that it is. It is red brick, and it wanders from an octagonal tower through a rectangular tower to another octagonal tower. There are gravely unadorned buildings that look sometimes like the Chicago Sullivan style and sometimes like ocean liners. Since the war there has been a great vogue for bright, modern buildings, all pastels and glass. The pastels tend to look tired after a few seasons in the rain. As for the glass, one shudders. Some day there will be an earthquake, and rubbernecking middle-school children in from the country will be decapitated by the score.

Tokyo does indeed take getting used to. Its charm is not on the gray, formless surface. "Where then is the charm?" asks the newcomer. Well, he must walk the streets until he sees for himself. The roar about him is not just the roar of trains and taxicabs. It is also the roar of sinews and blood. A good Buddhist, in the days when the species survived, might have described Tokyo with mild disapproval as smelling of meat; Walt Whitman might have said that it had the fine, clean smell of armpits. Tokyo is a stewing mass of people, and there are no beautiful, dead surfaces to distract one from the vitality once it is known.

Tokyo stands on an obvious site for a great city. At the head of Tokyo Bay, it commands the land and water approaches to the largest level area in Japan, the Kantō Plain. It took some centuries for the virtues of the site to be recognized, however. In the eighth century, when Nara was far too pretentious a capital for a sparsely populated little island kingdom, and on through the Middle Ages, when Kyoto must at times have been the largest city in the world, the Kantō Plain was harsh, semi-wild frontier country, the land of unruly warriors and winter winds from Siberia. The most famous early literary reference to it is in a poem by a courtier who couldn't wait to get back to Kyoto. In the late Middle Ages, when the great Nō dramatists gave Japanese medieval gloom its most subtle expression, they saw the Kantō Plain as the murkiest outer edge of a very murky world. In one of the most moving of the Nō plays, a mother discovers her child's grave on the banks of the River Sumida, and the pathos is heightened by the fact that she has searched to the harsher ends of the earth.

In the fifteenth century, exactly five hundred years ago, a local dignitary built a castle on hills overlooking the bay. Even then, the center of power in northeastern Japan lay some distance to the south. In 1590, the man who later became the first Tokugawa shogun arrived in the Kantō district and proceeded to fortify Edo (the name of Tokyo until 1868). In 1608 he established his shogunate there. The court was left behind in Kyoto and encouraged to study tde tea ceremony, which it did with reasonable docility for the next two centuries or so. The military nobility, on the other hand, were required to maintain establishments in Edo, where the shogun could watch them. They occupied the hills over the bay, and land had to be filled in to take care of the commoners. With the hills and the reclaimed flats thus divided by a rigid social line, the plebeian became assertively plebeian. He cleared his speech of effete diphthongs, and set about cultivating an Edo manner.

For the first century of the shogunate, residents of Edo must have been hard put to think of it as civilized. The seventeenth century was a happy time for Japanese literature and art, but considerably happier in Osaka and Kyoto than in Edo. One of the most famous of seventeenth-century artists rather brusquely refused the shogun's invitation to come to Edo. The military lords and the warriors must have sometimes found themselves wishing that they were in a position to do likewise. There is a wistful note in the Kyoto place-names one finds scattered around central Tokyo.

By the eighteenth century, the great day of Edo, the island culture (these were the centuries of isolation) was beginning to look a little overripe. One has the feeling that the city came upon the scene too late. The old cliché about America might be applied with some truth: that it moved without transition from barbarism to decadence. The literature of the eighteenth and early nineteenth centuries, when Edo had become the unquestioned cultural center of the country, has a warmed-over taste, and even the color print went into a sharp decline after a brief flowering in the late eighteenth century. With qualifications, it might be described as a plebeian afterglow of the great Kyoto decorative schools of the sixteenth and seventeenth centuries.

It is hard to imagine that Edo ever made its mark as one of the beautiful cities of Japan. Even when, for a few years, it happened to be free of earthquakes and fires, the Siberian winds must have given it a gaunt, weatherbeaten look. The arched bridges and the courtesans strolling across them in flowing summer kimonos were no doubt charming, and the gallants rowing up the canals on their way to the pleasure quarters were no doubt dashing; but the heart of the city was still a windblown flat, hard and dusty in the winter, often inundated in the spring and fall, and alive with mosquitoes in the summer. Then, as now, the city must have been a difficult one to show visitors. One can imagine the "child of Edo" (so we must call him, for so he called himself) showing the visitor from Kyoto the flowers of Edo culture and the gray, formless surface, and finally telling him to go wander about the streets if he would discover the real charm of the city.

It was the famous Edo manner that the visitor must find. Today the most ill-tempered remarks about Tokyo are received with equanimity. Indeed people seem to enjoy them. There is one convention, however, to challenge which is to risk displeasure: that Tokyo men are men, and Kyoto women are women. (Kyoto men are of course beneath contempt. Little is said of Tokyo women.) Two centuries ago, the child of Edo required that substantially the same convention be accepted. He held that he himself was sufficient justification for the city. It pleased him to come back from Kyoto and find that the dried sardines of Edo were much more fun, such a finer, manlier crunch, than the spineless delicacies of the emperor's capital. It pleased him to offer salted crackers as almost the only dish Edo produced with surpassing skill. The child of Edo had *iki*—call it aplomb, dash, spruceness—and the *iki* might have been dimmed if the city and its culture had been more splendid.

On the whole, the Edo commoner was successful in creating the impression that what was in Edo was good, for it had *iki*, and he himself especially so. Perhaps there *were* mosquitoes in Fukagawa as late as the middle of January. Where else would you find such brave mosquitoes? The Osaka merchant became a country bumpkin. He may have had money and a fine business sense, but he lacked the *iki* to be noted immediately in any Edo carpenter. And Osaka speech was not for men, but for women and children. The Edo shopkeeper managed to make a show of contempt for even the military nobility. The Yamanote, the hills where the great ones had their mansions, became the "Note," much as the Americans become the "Ame" today. *Iki* dominated the city's notions of beauty and ethics; and it was a concept imposed with triumphant success by the townsman making the best of his dried sardines and salted crackers and dirty, windswept city.

It was also a concept that had its limitations. It would be a great mistake to see the hearty Edo townsman as the equivalent of the hearty English yeoman. His assertiveness, if the word is not too strong, was a question more of manner than of principle. After all, even he would have had to admit that a successful display of *iki* depended on the fact that his city was the shogun's capital. There may have been a few intellectuals who, if they had pursued their premises far enough, would have come up with conclusions highly unsettling for the shogunate; but Edo was not a threat to the shoguns as London and Paris were to the kings. The child of Edo wanted mostly to keep things going as they were.

So, with half its mind, did the whole country. There were pressures for change from within, and there was a growing realization that the country would one day be opened. The Russians were coming down from the north, disturbing emissaries appeared in Nagasaki, and finally Perry was in Edo Bay itself. But there was also a longing to snuggle deeper into the comfortable island burrow. Conservative, xenophobic Edo, which claimed perfection for itself and its spruce manner, seemed to live the desire more intensely than the rest of the country. Even Kyoto was less involuted, as can be seen by the way it set about making itself a tourist center once the emperor had left the city for good. One of the chief worries of the Edoite during the disturbances that brought the emperor to Edo and made the city Tokyo, the Eastern Capital, seems to have been over the closing of the Kabuki theaters for a few weeks.

But the changes did come, and soon "enlightenment" was the rage. Tokyo led the country in the rush to catch up with the world and be enlightened, as though its mission were to step up the two contradictory forces pulling at the Japanese. In Kyoto and Osaka, the burghers themselves turned to face the problems of the new day. In Tokyo, there was a split, and Tokyo is the better symbol of the country, which often seems to be running forward and backward simultaneously.

One of the most common characters in the popular comic monologues is the *wakadanna*, the "young master" who has a surplus of Edo *iki* and a talent for ruining the family business. The child of Edo likes to think that there is much of the *wakadanna* in his makeup, and that he is no match for the Osakan when it comes to business. There seems to be a great deal of evidence to support the belief. When the changes came, it was not the old resident of the city who took advantage of them. The new ruling clique was from the far southwest. It was Osaka that finally came to dominate Tokyo journalism. Two of the three largest newspapers in the city today are comparatively late arrivals from Osaka, and one finds with surprising regularity that the more pestiferous of the journalizing intellectuals are from Osaka or still farther south and west. In the early years of this century an Osaka theater syndicate began to move into Tokyo, and today it dominates the legitimate stage and controls a very large chunk of the movies. Restaurants that offer Osaka cooking have driven Edo cooking into a few unobtrusive little pockets. The glamorous pleasure quarters beloved of the Edo townsman are now the tawdriest accumulations of bawdy houses (you pay by the hour). The elegant geisha districts of modern Tokyo grew up nearer the ministries, for the convenience of the rustic samurai who were the new bureaucrats. Even baseball is dominated by Osaka and the western prefectures. The Tokyo Giants would be forlorn indeed if they lost their Osaka players. The Osaka Tigers could get by very well without Tokyo.

All in all, the old Edo merchant class did not make much of a showing in the new Tokyo. The novelist Tanizaki Jun'ichirō, himself a member of the class, has described them as "the defeated." He has little sympathy for them, and thinks that they asked for everything they got; and yet even as he tells it, the story of the diaspora of the Edoites to the southern and western suburbs—far from the flats through which they once strode with such aplomb—is very touching.

Yet the child of Edo is still very much a part of the city, for it is a city of nostalgia. There are those two opposite urges, we must remember, and even as it bustles energetically toward the future (leaving the Edoite to run for the suburbs) it looks to the past with a sorrow that is sometimes sweet and sometimes bitter (and invites the Edoite to indulge in what he is best at, reminiscing). Since little survives except sites, most of what is written about the city is an untranslatable mishmash of place-names.

There is a class of professional reminiscers who seem to make a good living at the work. They do not have to be old. They only have to be children of Edo, born somewhere in the plebeian flats, and they do not have to reminisce about the distant past. The city changes so fast that the flapper era and the era of the assassinations have melted pleasantly into the eighteenth century. Even though the true son of Edo was thoroughly dispossessed by the time flappers and popular music and taxicabs arrived, he has managed to assert his dominion over the whole of the past. It is he, and not the late arrival from the provinces, who must tell how it was when straw-colored streetcars came to the Ginza.

Some of the journalist-reminiscers are very good, and one first-rate novelist, Nagai Kafū, has made the changing city his subject.

Actually he does not quite qualify for the work he has chosen, because, though a native of Tokyo, he is not from a merchant family; but he behaves as the true Edoite should. He seems able to control his material only when he is writing of a Tokyo that is dead or dying. Sometimes he tries describing the city as it is at the moment, and when he does he only reports. It is difficult to describe the power of his best works. They are full of empty houses and people who do not belong, and more often than not it is late autumn; and behind everything is the most impermanent of cities, its dead past so palpable because such a short time away.

While the child of Edo reminisced, the city was off about other business. The emperor had arrived, the country was open to the barbarians, and Japan must not be left behind. The Japanese have a terrible fear of falling behind. It nagged at them through the centuries of seclusion, and now it exploded in a mad rush to catch up. The day of the New Men had come, the day of the intellectuals and the entrepreneurs. While the entrepreneurs were probably more conspicuous in Osaka than in Tokyo, the intellectuals, who must gather and digest new ideas for the country, were concentrated in Tokyo. In the ideas poured, at first English empiricism, then darker influences from the Continent: Rousseau, who as always clouded the air; Nietzsche and Hegel, who, by doing their bit for German nationalism, also did their bit for Japanese nationalism; and later Marx, whose message did not really strike home until after the Russian Revolution, but who is today the young person's guide to economics.

One may occasionally wonder whom the intellectual leaders were leading. The government went its own way, caring for but one idea, the divinity of the emperor. If Hegel found a warmer welcome than most of the barbarians, it was because he could be accommodated rather successfully to what the government had in mind. The new intellectuals did much that was ridiculous, moreover, and in their rush to learn they set a standard of superficiality that prevails even today. They found the West at a time when its artistic standards were not in every way of the highest, and they failed to discriminate between what was good in the West and what was probably far better in Japan (the theater, for instance). When they started to react away from the West, as inevitably many of them did, they

212

could be equally immoderate. The silly cliché about the spiritual Orient and the materialistic Occident is a part of the legacy they have left us as a result.

That they were brave and energetic and filled with a missionary zeal, however, is impossible to deny. Japan might be very spiritual—Japan *was* very spiritual—but circumstances had shown that something was lacking, and it was up to them to discover what. Followers of Locke, Hegel, the Presbyterian missionaries, and the Black Dragon Society were alike in their determination to save the country. Without meaning to imply that superficial ideas somehow become admirable when held with boyish enthusiasm, we might not be too far from the point in suggesting that again it was the manner that was important. A distinction between the content of the intellectual baggage and the energy with which it was shouldered does in any case reveal a curious incongruity.

The tired, inert young man who is the intellectual in Meiji fiction, the intellectual's portrait of himself, seems to bear no resemblance to the young man we actually see piling up new ideas. In the novels, all is darkness and bewilderment, and young persons groping and straining and dutifully cracking up. How then to explain the way they did scribble, most of them? Whether it was the enlightenment they were writing of in thirty volumes, or the "Japanese spirit," their energy belied their claims to nervous exhaustion. One feels that they must have gone well with the city they swarmed in upon—a city confused, cluttered, only superficially modern, never quite sure (to this day) whether its populace should walk or be provided with enough streetcars, but through it all buoyant.

Today the intellectuals really do seem tired. The face shown the world has at length come to coincide with the self-portrait. The incongruity has moved on a step, however. It remains to puzzle us when we look at the city. Tokyo is supposed to be intensely depressing. In novels with titles like *Streets without Sunlight*, we learn that it is a city of wanderers in a world that will not have them. Perhaps to some extent it is. Certainly the suburbs that extend endlessly to the west are very dreary. There live the intellectuals, and there Communists are elected to the ward councils, evidence no doubt of rootlessness.

But if anything is true of the teeming flats to the north and east, it is that they are *not* cold and dark. Life there is far from idyllic, of course. There are gangsters and dope peddlers, and hardly anyone has a room of his own; but if one were to walk across the city from west to east with an instrument sensitive to such things, one would with very little doubt find a steady rise in good spirits. The delivery boys and the barmaids probably wish they had lots of money, but they do not have the look of people who are tired of life or who want to be someone else. The contrast with the sluggishness of Manila or the surliness of Hong Kong cannot be overlooked.

It is a city of the young, who persist in being hopeful ("having a dream," the Japanese put it) when everyone tells them to despair. They leave school and set up businesses of their own, and in an over-cartelized country that means being almost recklessly hopeful. Tokyo has acquired half a million people per year since the war, and today the Tokyo-Yokohama area and the far north are the only parts of the country where men outnumber women. These statistics, given life, mean that young people are pouring into the city. The newspapers love to carry stories of vanished hopes, but again one feels that it simply is not so. Either the young men and women on the Ginza and in Asakusa are consummately gifted actors, or they like what they are doing. If they are to be criticized for anything, it is for enjoying themselves too much. "Oh, go out and build a bridge somewhere," you occasionally want to say to the young man with the guitar.

The novelist Tanizaki, who hated the old city and was pleased to see it disappear in 1923, has written of his plans for the reconstructed city.

> Well-ordered streets, and gleaming new pavement, and a flood of automobiles, and block towering upon block in beautiful geometric patterns, and elevated railways weaving their way beneath, and subways and streetcars, and the stir of a great, nightless city, and pleasure facilities rivaling those of New York and Paris. The people of Tokyo would live in the Western manner, and the young, both men and women, would wear Western clothes. . . . Views of the reconstructed city passed numberless across my mind, like flashes in a movie. Evening gowns and tails and tuxedos, and champagne glasses

floating by like the moon upon the sea. The after-theater crowds late at night, with the beams of countless headlights crossing and clashing on the darkly shining streets. Vaudeville, a swirl of satin and gossamer and legs and artificial lights. The seductive calls of streetwalkers, cutting in and out of the lights of the Ginza and Asakusa and Marunouchi and Hibiya. The secret pleasures of Turkish baths and beauty parlors. Grotesque crimes.

There are many Japanese who will say that Tanizaki's dream has come true. To them, Tokyo has taken the place of Shanghai as the gaudy pleasure center of the Far East. It is an enormous cancer, strangling the rest of the country. Even Yokohoma, only a few miles away, has the look of a ghost town. The country's foreign exchange goes to buy automobiles for Tokyo, the honest laborers of the nation must build more hydroelectric dams so that Tokyo can have more neon lights.

In Shinjuku and Shibuya, which prosper as transportation centers for the western suburbs, the number of movie theaters almost doubled in the single year 1956. The jam of foreign automobiles is indeed evidence that the government, mad about free enterprise, has exercised less control than it might have over foreign exchange reserves. There are too many restaurants, too many bars, too many television towers, too many baseball stadiums, too many well-groomed young ladies whose source of income is doubtful, too many thoroughbred dogs.

Still, it is hard to think of Tokyo as merely a city of pleasure. Cities of pleasure ought to stay open all night. Tokyo closes tight by midnight, so that the dancing girls and bartenders can catch the last train home. The public transportation system has little sympathy for people out debauching. It is for people who work. On both the downtown loop line and the line to the western suburbs, there are no trains between one and four in the morning, and there are more trains between five and six in the morning than there are between eleven and twelve at night. Even in the grosser pleasures one notes a certain restraint that makes it hard to think of the city as abandoned to sin. There is an enormous amount of drinking, and an enormous amount of vomiting on public vehicles, for the Japanese cannot hold their liquor; and yet drunkenness is not a social problem. Alcoholics are comparatively rare. There are erotic shows which the touts call "French"; but one does not have to see many to note that they are carefully ritualized, as though by following the rules the performers managed to preserve their dignity. There is little doubt that the police could stop the erotic shows, but have concluded, with much justice, that they do not matter. Now and then, for the record, a few performers are taken at random and fined; but I have an acquaintance who once stopped at a police box to ask where he might find a "French" movie, and was obliged with fairly exact directions.

It is often said that Tokyo is not a city at all, but an overgrown village. In a sense, not necessarily derogatory, this is true. Possibly because most of it is so ramshackle, as though put up for only a summer, there is a feeling in even the most crowded parts of the city that the rice paddies are not far away. In Nagai Kafū's best Tokyo novels, the dirt and waste of the city are described with a farmer's eye for the passing seasons, and the great annual festivals follow the rhythm of the farms. Even in Asakusa the buses must stop while the portable shrine for the spring festival weaves its way down the street—at first sight to avoid the oil smears, actually for no better reason than that shrines have always been carried thus. The elders complain that the young have gone flabby and do not give the god the bouncing he has every right to expect; but probably they were making the same complaint a hundred years ago when the feckless *wakadanna* overslept on festival day.

There is nothing surprising in the discovery that modern celebrations with a strongly secular tinge (the stimulus today is not awe but drink) were once fertility rites. So, we are told, was the May-pole dance. Still the matter seems rather special when one looks at Tokyo. The urban populace has not been cut off from the farms as in most Western cities. It is second and third sons who go to the city or surplus daughters who are sent off to be maids or courtesans. Whole villages have not been uprooted, as in nineteenth-century England. This is not of course to say that everyone has a farm to go home to in hard times; but sanctions of a very ancient order do nonetheless seem to operate to keep the city under control, or at least its poorer districts. The largest Communist strongholds are not in the industrial slums but in the white-collar suburbs. Japanese laborers *ought* to be revolutionaries, just as tenant farmers ought to be, and a massive peasant conservatism seems to explain the fact that they are not.

Some forty years ago Thorstein Veblen described what he called "the opportunity of Japan." For a time, he said, an industrial state would be able to make use of feudal loyalty patterns; but only for a time. Industrialization would inevitably destroy those patterns. He may have been right. The authority of the family head, on which the whole structure was based, is no longer what it once was, and there is much talk of juvenile delinquency, not to be dismissed even though much of it seems alarmist. When and if the last of the old sanctions go, there is no telling what will happen. Today they are no longer strong enough to send young men off to die for the emperor, but they are still strong enough to preserve the essential steadiness of what may on the surface seem like a mad, jangling city. The jangle is over by midnight. By eight o'clock in the morning, even if it is Sunday, not one person in a hundred is still in bed.

I for one would not be sorry to see the gaudier entertainments go. It would still be the same city without them, and the righteous would have less to frown about. It would still be a great stew of people even if they all lived in tents, and it would go on living with added intensity the split, contradictory life of the country. Tokyo has not really changed much from the years before the pastel-and-glass buildings began to go up. The Tsukiji Fish Market was very nearly the best show in town then, and it is very nearly the best show in town now. Noisy, undecorated, wholly unperfumed, quarrelsome in a genial way, the Tsukiji Fish Market might in fact be the answer to the nagging question of where to take the recent arrival. The only trouble is that you have to be there by six o'clock in the morning.

(1957)

---

1. This has now disappeared.

THE BUSINESS AT HAND

Dear Sir:

The gloomy rains continue, and things feel damp and clammy to the touch. I trust that your efforts to keep your spirits from flagging have met with success.

As to the business at hand:

You must forgive me, a stranger, for writing to you without proper introduction. I am a third-year student in the Liberty Hill Girls' Higher Seminary. I am nineteen years old, twenty-one years old by Japanese count. My hobbies are literature, philosophy, and television. I am 5.1 feet tall. I enclose a snapshot, taken last spring at the athletic meet, when I had fluctuations and was not feeling well. I think I would like to exchange ideas with a foreign gentleman, and when I went to the American Cultural Center and said I thought I would like to they were kind enough to give me your address. You must forgive me for writing to you without introduction.

I think I would like to exchange ideas on literature, philosophy, society, and television. Please let me know when I can see you. I shall take but a few minutes, provided I am feeling well.

Take good care of yourself in this damp weather.

Hideko ONO (age nineteen)

July 11

At last there are breaks in the clouds, and the early summer sun beats down. I urge you not to let the weather debilitate you.

As to the business at hand:

218

I think I need have no doubt that you feel keenly your duties to scholarship, and that you maintain a tight and learned schedule. It was therefore very good of you to agree to see me, if only for a few hours. The afternoon and evening were among the memorable ones of my life. Indeed had you not reminded me I would probably have missed the last train. Oh, scatterbrained me!

I am now firmly resolved to acquit myself of my duties to scholarship. I was particularly impressed with your views on education reform, and on Japanese plumbing. I said to myself: "There is a person who knows more about our culture than we know ourselves."

By the way, I checked with my mother about the recipe just to make very sure that I had it right, and she pointed out one rather important point which I (scatterbrained I) had overlooked. You must use white vinegar, not yellow vinegar. If you use yellow vinegar, the taste will be the same, but the color may call up unpleasant associations.

Uncollected as always, I forgot to ask how you feel about women's rights in Japan. How do you feel? You must forgive me for putting the question so bluntly, but, alas, I have rather strong feelings myself. You may have lulled yourself into thinking that women have equal rights in Japan. Have you? No, they have not. Japan is still very feudal. My own father is excessively feudal. He has a number of children I have never been introduced to. My oldest brother (I assume he is my oldest brother) is also very feudal. He locks his desk. This is evidence, do you not think, of morbid, feudal suspicions, and the nature of the family system.

Perhaps when next we meet for a few minutes we can exchange ideas on women's rights. Do you not think that we must work together to destroy the family system? I do. Perhaps when next we meet I can tell you of the part I mean to play. It will be a poor part, but, well, Japan is a poor country.

Now that we have become friends I think I must tell you why I am nineteen years old and only a third-year student in the Liberty Hill Girls' Higher Seminary. I believe that there should be no secrets between friends. Is that not the essence of anti-feudalism? The truth is that I was suspended for a year, because of what I can only describe as a measure of public-mindedness. I knew what the physical education instructor was doing, and I said so, in an open letter which I posted on all the bulletin boards. But it is too disgusting.

I start having fluctuations at the thought of it.

Take care of yourself in this warm weather.

Hideko

August 12

The days grow warmer and warmer, and my limbs grow heavier and heavier. I hope you manage to keep yourself at your valuable work.

As to the business at hand:

I continue to meditate upon the profundity of your remarks at our meeting. You have a great deal to say not to me but to the whole Japanese nation, and I hope your natural reticence will not keep you from speaking out. Please feel free to say nasty things about us, and especially about feudal remnants we have not yet succeeded in uprooting.

By the way, white vinegar is sometimes a little hard to come by (Japan is a poor country), and I hope that want of it has not caused you loss of sleep and weight. I think I should like to present you with a small bottle, which my mother ordered from Kobe. My mother sends regards, although you must forgive her for doing so without introduction.

Would you like to meet my sister? She is two years older than I and rather old-fashioned, indeed much too Japanese. Something must be done for her. When I told her about the physical education instructor, she said she had no idea what I was talking about. Can you imagine it? And she already nineteen years old at the time, and, in ways which it would be tasteful not to discuss, less subject to fluctuations than I am even now, and certainly less than I was last spring. Will you help me with my plans?

I enclose my sister's snapshot. If you look on the back, you will find all the necessary information about her. I forgot to mention, however, that her hobbies are music and rock climbing. She plays the trumpet. The neighbors say she is very good, and, not qualified to pass judgment myself, I can but accept the statement.

Take care of yourself in this increasingly warm weather.

Hideko

August 21

The great heat has come, the city sizzles. I pray that you are keeping yourself on guard against the assaults of the summer.

As to the business at hand:

As always, I think I found it far more worthwhile talking to you than spending my time in silliness. I come away from a talk with you bearing such a rich harvest. How different from my father, who, when we see him at all, only growls feudally. I feel more confirmed than ever in my mission, and again I urge you not to be parsimonious with your wisdom. Bestow it liberally, you have so much to give.

As the hours passed and the time for the last train came (I did not forget this time, but thank you for reminding me anyway), and the moments of silent meditation became more frequent, I saw with an intuitive insight that you could be counted on. We Japanese are an intuitive people, and it does not take much of a hint to make us see the truth. What was that pungent Americanism with which you characterized your relatives? Anyway, I saw with an insight, as we looked meditatively at our fingernails, that you agreed with me about the feudal family system. "Ah, ah!" I said to myself. "Ah!" Now everything will be all right, for you are at my side. My sister is not the cruelest victim of the system, perhaps, but it has not allowed her ideal fulfillment, and we must begin where we can. Japan is a poor country.

From your remarks about the Tokyo subway—why, why can I not remember those biting Americanisms? I must buy a tape recorder. Anyway, from your remarks on the Tokyo subway, I gather that you do not object to surface transportation. I know, moreover, that my sister's pulse rises—no, I cannot in any honesty pretend to know anything of the sort. I have never taken her pulse. All I can say is that she squeals with delight when she sees a cliff and starts wriggling into her climbing pantaloons. Oh, oh! Oh! I have just used an Americanism. I found it on page 2260 of Kenkyūsha's *New Japanese-English Dictionary*, 1931 edition. I am ashamed of not having the 1954 edition, but on these barren islands of ours we must learn to do with little. Anyway, I enclose two second-class tickets to Matsumoto, together with a schedule which I trust covers most eventualities. There have been a number of landslides lately, but I think you will be spared. The opportunity to have her exchange anti-feudal ideas with you is so golden that we must take the risk, be it great or be it small. Do not let the roar of the train in the tunnels interrupt your discourse, or, if it must, try to have the tunnels coincide with the moments of silent meditation.

By the way, I noticed that your peony looked rather dejected in the afternoon sunlight. Peonies, as you know, require rich soil, and, since you are sensible enough (I remember *that* earthy Americanism) to have no truck with Japanese flush toilets, the remedy is simple. All you need is a dipper with a long handle. Perhaps I can help you until you get the swing of it. Against the distant possibility that you do not have a dipper with a long handle, I shall try to remember to bring some chicken manure when next I come. My youngest (I assume) sister keeps chickens, and it will be no trouble at all. I shall wrap it up in a crepe kerchief.

Did you find the white vinegar helpful? My mother sends her regards.

Take care of yourself in this hot weather.

Hideko

August 26

The days grow shorter, and the morning and evening breezes begin to bring a touch of coolness. I feel secure in the knowledge that you have found new vigor.

As to the business at hand:

I think you were as disappointed as I was. I hope that you did not wait too long at the station, and I hope too that you had the sagacity to choose the air-conditioned waiting room. Or did you perhaps make the trip by yourself? My own disappointment, I fear, was more than disappointment. It approached disillusionment, the end of belief. I had thought that only men were feudal, but my sister refused to listen to my most closely reasoned arguments, with an obstinacy that must be labeled feudal. I can see now that the roots of the problem lie deeper than I had thought.

I had hoped to come inquiring after your peony before this, but to have one's plans go astray is cause for retreat and sincere self-reflection. By the way, if you have run out of chicken manure and still do not have a long-handled dipper, a little linseed cake laid not too close to the stem will fill the gap, though not, alas, with the vigor of animal substances. My mother sends regards. Do you like daffodils? I have dug all ours up, and my mother insists that I find new homes for them. I cannot understand her—she will not learn. We went through exactly the same thing last year when we had kittens, and of course we ended up by throwing them away.

Well, as I have said, this is a time for sincere self-reflection, by me and by all of us. Are we to cut away the infected part or are we not? Are we? Are we not? It gives me strength to have you at my side.

Take care of yourself in this time of shifting temperatures.

Hideko

September 12

The fields yellow, and the noonday sun is weaker. Since the autumn effluvia frequently bring disorders to the body, I urge you to treat yours with consideration.

As to the business at hand:

We are having a pleasantly noisy time. My youngest (I think) sister is having hysterics, I suppose you would call them. And for very little reason that I can see. She has locked herself in the closet, silly thing, and she bangs and bangs, and screams and screams. My oldest (I am fairly sure) sister, who is very methodical, is having her hour on the trumpet. My brothers are out streetwalking, and my mother is asleep, and my father too. I suppose he is snoring, though I cannot hear him. I sit here watching him breathe, and it is the oddest thing. I have great trouble writing. Have you ever tried humming a waltz while you are playing a march? That is exactly how it feels. His lip flutters every time he breathes out. I am sure he is snoring. I fear that you will find my writing transparent and vulgar. It is inelegantly legible at best, try though I may to improve it. While my youngest sister has not been too successful at describing the reasons for her hysterics, and while her performance is a trifle exaggerated, I must say that I too was shocked at one point. "The trouble with you is that you just don't want to grow up," my father said to her. Think of it! The indelicacy of touching on a subject so intimately personal! I almost wanted to vomit.

By the way, I am bringing the daffodils, because my mother keeps after me. We vibrate so in harmony, you and I, that I think you dislike the watery yellow things too. Still I must plant them, for I cannot lie to my mother; but they will not bloom, you know, if they are buried too deep or if the soil is too rich. I pride myself on being the least demanding of persons, but I really must ask you to buy a long-handled dipper.

How refreshing it was to read Mrs. MacArthur's remarks in the newspaper this morning. Do you realize your good fortune in belonging to a nation of dedicated, forward-looking women? But I do not despair. With your help, we too are moving forward.

Take care of yourself in this frequently malevolent weather.

Hideko

September 19

On the hills the plumes of autumn grass rustle in the wind. Autumn scenes fill me with thoughts of things, and no doubt have the same effect upon you.

As to the business at hand:

My plans received a setback, you will remember, but I have at length recovered my determination. I am bringing my sister to see you. Last night she talked in her sleep. I shall not tell you what she said, it was too awful; but it was clear proof that the feudal family system does not answer to a woman's needs. To my suspicion that she too is feudal, I must now add a suspicion that she was not being entirely honest when she said that she did not know what I was talking about when I said that I knew what the physical education instructor was doing.

I am not one to spare myself when it comes to sincere self-reflection. Here in this small breast of mine I have found traces of feudalism! I have interposed complications. I am over-supplied with reticence and delicacy, which are attributes of little use in the fight that lies ahead.

And now that I have seen the fault and overcome it, I shall venture to tell *you* something. I have in the past found you wanting in delicacy. Think of your habit of calling my attention to the striking of the clock, *just* when we Japanese would be silent, savoring the dying echo. "Four o'clock," you are always saying, and "nine o'clock," *just* at the moment of the dying echo. I think that, in the course of our intimacy, I have not once been allowed to enjoy it. "There is the difference between the rational Occident and the intuitive, artistic Orient," I have said to myself each time.

But now I see. Your want of delicacy is in fact a virtue. *You* have no Japanese reticence. *You* can be counted on to plunge in. So I shall bring my sister to see you. I should have done so earlier. And when I have seen her to your shady study, I shall quietly withdraw, slip into my shoes again (I must remember to wear loafers), and, after planting the hydrangeas I mean to bring with me, perhaps go street-walking for a time. Will an hour be enough? I think you will find her in most respects satisfactory. There are those toothmarks, of course, but you will see upon close inspection that they are the marks of a dog's teeth. I shall not go into the details, save to tell you that, practicing the trumpet on warm nights, she sometimes removes encumbrances to breathing, and that our dog (of an Occidental breed) is very unmusical. And do remember one thing: screaming runs in our family. There is no need whatsoever to be alarmed.

I shall be waiting for a full report. If there is any one thing that the anti-feudal movement has demonstrated, it is that progress must be documented. I know I can count on you for a (let me emphasize it) *full* report.

I hope the daffodils are as I left them. For the time being, I think we need do nothing more about them, though you might let me know if they begin to break through. I think you like hydrangeas.

Take care of yourself in this brisk weather.

Hideko

September 26

Clear autumn days follow one another, and yet showers come up from nowhere. Be not deceived, I beseech you, by the fickle autumn skies.

As to the business at hand:

I find it hard to know at precisely what point along the way forward we have arrived. You must admit that you have been slow with your reporting. My sister, for her part, has shown a tendency not to speak to me. That we move forward is unmistakable, however. Evening before last (I saw it all) my father glanced at her and then looked at her, and said he must think of finding her a husband one of these days, and she looked straight back at him and said she was not going to give up rock climbing for any pair of pants *he* was likely to bring home. Was that not splendid? And all, I think, because of you. Thank you, thank you. By the way, did you notice anything wrong with her? My father did look at her in the strangest—but how I babble on. You must forgive me if I have said anything inappropriate. I make it a practice not to talk about my family.

My family and your family. My line and your line, separated for so many ages that I think your hair has become red and mine black. Then together again. Ah, ah! Ah! There is something about the idea. I tremble before it. Red hair mingled with black, like a fire in the night. How I think I wish you could have been with me, those spring nights when Tokyo burned. I watched it from the mountains, red and black halfway up into Scorpio. But it will burn again some day, and we can watch it together. I must see you. Ah! Your red hair glows before me like centuries of loneliness.

I hope the hydrangeas are taking root. They thrive on exactly the soil that is poison for daffodils. They will bloom and bloom, sending out blue veins that remind me of—I hardly know what. Would you like to learn flower arranging? My mother is very good at it. She can even arrange zinnias. She always sends me into the garden with shears, and waits in the tea room until I have finished. My sister once said she knew exactly how I felt, she felt the same way about rocks. Well, I am babbling on. Do keep your hydrangeas well fertilized, even if the smell is a bit trying. How foolish I felt on the train with that long-handled dipper! I wonder what would have happened if I had surrendered to my impulse to—no, I shall not tell you of it.

Take care of yourself in this unpredictable weather.

Hideko

October 10

In the hills the leaves are turning. The days grow shorter and shorter, and soon we will hear the call of the quail and the wild goose. Do not allow yourself to be plunged into melancholy, I pray you, by the cold, white autumn moon.

As to the business at hand:

I called several times, only to find you away from home. What a pity. Yesterday I knocked and knocked, and when there was no answer I took the liberty of going in through the garden gate to see your hydrangeas. Well! I must say I was surprised. I sniffed and sniffed, and could detect no evidence that they had received any care other than that which I myself gave them some three weeks ago. I said to myself: "Now *there* is the difference between the Occident and the Orient!" I thought it necessary to put more dirt on the daffodils. Not being able to find your dipper, I had no other recourse. The mound over the daffodils may at first distract you (did you notice when we planted them what an odd configuration they made?), but you will get used to it, and, as I have said, I had no other recourse. I took the dirt from under the foundations, where it will not be noticed.

I had the strangest feeling that someone was watching me from your study. Did you notice anything missing when you came home?

I would have brought more chicken manure but for the fact that my youngest sister is no longer keeping chickens. Had I told you? My father used to eat the eggs raw, especially when he came home late at night, and to remark that he wasn't the man he used to be. My oldest sister killed all the chickens and will not allow an egg in the house. I think she is quite right.

Here it is the full moon again. How things have changed this last month! When the moon was last full, we seemed to be marching ahead, with your encouragement and Mrs. MacArthur's. My mother was to be next—a more difficult problem, to be sure, but I was really so very hopeful. And now, will you imagine what has happened? My father arranged for my sister to meet a man with an eye to reviewing him as a possible suitor. We all went along, of course. I think the man seemed to have very progressive, anti-feudal ideas, but he had an unfortunate way of touching the tips of his fingers to his lips, and giggling. My sister, I swear it, looked at him only once during the evening. And will you imagine what has happened? She has agreed to marry him! Yes!

How am I to explain it? Have you kept something from me? Have you deceived me? I would be quick to forgive most injuries, but not this, no, not this.

Well, one thing is clear. I am doing no good along the periphery. I must strike at the heart of the matter, the source of the trouble.

It is very quiet. The moon is shining on the late chrysanthemums, and the crickets are chirping. Usually at this time of the night my sister would be at her trumpet, but she is getting her ropes ready for one last go at the rocks before the snows come. My father, who got home early this morning, has fallen asleep over his newspaper. I wonder why he isn't snoring? Maybe he never snores, and it has until now not been quiet enough for me to know. And yet his lip trembles each time he breathes out.

Take care of yourself in the growing autumn cold.

Hideko

The autumn winds come down upon us, bringing dust from the hills. Do not breathe too freely of it, I advise you most urgently.

As to the business at hand:

We have been terribly busy. Not of course that there is much for me to do. I help my sister make tea for the priests, and that is about the sum of it. Oh, well. I have done enough already. Do you think they will be sufficiently grateful when they find out?

I should so like to be at the crematory. I cannot put down the feeling that I have allowed myself to be maneuvered into an unfavorable position. I cannot help feeling that I may be left behind to keep the tea boiling. Oh, well. I think there will be other opportunities.

Do you remember your profound remark, when first we met, about education reform? "You can't make an omelette without breaking eggs," you said. I have thought about it so often. Indeed I have thought so often these past few days about you, and your red hair. I must see you. I *will* see you.

I think that by this time your daffodils will need additional cover and (you are so lazy) food, essential to their deflowering.

Take care of yourself in this time of chill and darkness.

Hideko

(1961)

SELECTIONS
FROM "THIS COUNTRY,"

1958–1962

The Japan boom, which, as we all know from the papers, has swept Europe and still more America, shows signs of faltering. An acquaintance fresh from the United States said the other night that she had had to flee New York, where everything is Japanese, for Tokyo, where many things are still American; but another acquaintance, still in New York, suggests by letter that the rage for things Japanese may be receding. "Incidentally some Japanese department store has opened a branch in New York all filled with quite appalling Woolworth things."

Broadway is still fascinated with Japan and the Orient. Something about a good-hearted Hong Kong tart named Susie Wong has just opened, and something about a "Flower Drum Song," whatever that might be, is to open shortly. Publishers of translations, on the other hand, seem a trifle cooler this season, and it is reported that a couple of once steady sellers ended the last quarter with more copies returned than sold.

Yet in its untidy way the boom does go on. What does it all come to, though? The most extravagant claims have been made. A publisher's editor rather well known in Japan predicted not too long ago that the Japanese novel would work a revolution comparable to the revolution worked by the Ukiyoe on nineteenth-century art. A well-known translator of haiku has made equally grand claims for his genre. The finest poetic utterance is the utterance in one quick gasp, his argument seems to run, and gasps do not come longer than seventeen syllables. Hence poets in windier traditions must one day become aware of haiku.

Neither poets nor novelists, alas, seem to have been much influenced by Japanese techniques—at least not in a way that can be attributed to the Japan boom. Ezra Pound's ideas of imagery may be a dim reflection of something Japanese, though it is debatable, but they were formed long before the current boomers came along. If there is a Japanese influence on American letters, it would seem to be a matter more of subject than of technique.

On one level, James Michener has made a fortune by modernizing Madame Butterfly and turning her roguish friend B. F. Pinkerton into a martyr. On a slightly higher level, or rather on several somewhat higher levels, B. F. Pinkerton has become a disciple of Zen and a refugee from "the ills of American machine culture."

Jack Kerouac, the most aggressively anti-intellectual of young American novelists, has now turned to Zen, and if the Japan boom can claim credit for Mr. Smith, the hero of Kerouac's most recent novel, then Zen is surely its most important gift to the American spirit. Zen keeps cropping up in very unlikely places. Besides Mr. Smith, there is, for instance, J. D. Salinger's Mr. Zooey Glass. But can the boom as a matter of fact claim the whole credit? Might not all this Zen be more American than Japanese, a new name for an idea that has always fascinated Americans, indeed an idea that brought them to America in the first place?

Kerouac's new novel is a little different from his others. Hitherto he has had his characters beating themselves up in frantic trips back and forth across the country. This time he only has them racing up and down the Pacific coast. At last, in Berkeley, California, Mr. Smith comes upon Zen. Zen with a touch of sex, after which he decides to leave the machine-dominated cities and climb mountains. He also leaves his master, the Berkeley Zen person, to depart for Japan and enter a Zen temple.

A new twist to an old, old theme. One thinks of Jimmy Herf at the end of *Manhattan Transfer*, thirty and more years ago, having a last drink of bootleg gin and heading west into the morning. Now that the West is the land of the AEC, Jimmy's descendants can only turn to the wide-open Pacific. Not interested in Madame Butterfly, they find Zen, which sounds very positive and fits nicely into the three-letter vocabulary of the Beat Generation.

Zen has apparently become a part of at least one school of psychoanalysis. It is rash indeed for a person who knows little about Zen and nothing at all about psychoanalysis to comment upon the development. Still, it might be permissible to ask how great the Japanese contribution has been. The name, certainly, is Japanese, and so is the prophet, Dr. Suzuki, but the way in which the cures (acquaintances in New York have had them) are worked suggests that Zen is just a revival of good old American pragmatic religion. If it makes you feel good to believe something, then by all means believe it, William James said, with at least part of his mind. Zen for mental health would seem to be right in the tradition. Zen came along at a time when conversion to communism was out of the question, and conversion to Catholicism just a little too common.

This may be an excessively cynical view of the case. The evidence is not all in, and possibly Zen and Japanese literature are subtly changing the American mind. At the moment, however, the main impact of the Japan boom seems to be on a lower level. First, and only slightly lower, come the movies. Others will have to say how wide their appeal is; but in my part of the West, a particularly backward and provincial part, perhaps, no one I questioned this summer had seen a Japanese movie. Even in more advanced areas, not quite everything goes. The poetry contest sponsored recently by the Tuttle Company turned up some highly uncomplimentary remarks about Mr. Mifune. (The same contest brought forth enormous numbers of pretty haiku, some of them actually seventeen syllables long, and all of them material for the argument that no one is likely to go much beyond Ezra Pound in that particular direction. Perhaps something innately gross about us will keep us forever remote from the real possibilities of poem as gasp.)

It is when one reaches the level of decorative and immediately useful objects that the impact of Japan is impressive. There are *zōri* and Japanese lanterns everywhere. I even saw men at a big-league baseball game in *zōri*, and in Honolulu almost everyone whose feet showed—who wasn't wearing a mau-mau or whatever they are called—was either barefoot or in *zōri*. As for the lanterns, they are indeed everywhere. A Japanese might find them a trifle funereal or a trifle too suggestive of the teahouse for his taste, but Japanese they all are, undeniably. Then there is Saito's Restaurant, which puts its customers on the floor, charges them ten dollars a plate, and is always packed. There are Japanese ceramics, Japanese sliding doors, low Japanese coffee tables—all of the things that go into gracious Japanese living, in short, except Japanese plumbing and Japanese heating.

Far more than haiku and revolutionary fiction, appliances and footwear are the Japan boom. Those spiritual qualities we keep hearing about have so far not completely demonstrated their exportability.

(Nov. 8, 1958)

OKINAWA'S CULTURE IS TOTALLY CHANGED

I have just been on a trip to Okinawa. Since the announcement that I enjoyed it seems to shock people (they accuse me of being a latent militarist), I shall let that announcement pass, remarking by the way that Okinawa ought to come as a pleasant surprise to people who have known it only through Japanese newspapers and magazines.

There are, fortunately, a number of fairly noncommittal things one can say about Okinawa—things unlikely to reveal one's conviction that the administration of the Ryūkyūs has been pretty shabbily treated in the Japanese press.

There is, for instance, the interesting problem in acculturation presented by the reconstruction of Naha. We have been told by many lamenting Japanese journalists that Naha is thoroughly Americanized. The simple charm of old Naha, which the Japanese apparently loved even though they sometimes chose strange ways of showing their love, is gone. No more long-sleeved, high-haired Ryūkyū maidens pulling the traveler back, no more walks through the quiet tombs of a spring evening, no more hibiscus hedges, no more Kagoshima merchants. Instead, horns, phonographs, dust, glare.

All of these last phenomena are undoubtedly present. But it does not take much exploring to make one feel that an influence not entirely American has been at work.

Naha is laid out on an odd triangular plan. The center of the city is a mile or so from the center of the old city, on hilly land that was before the war fields and tombs. The city was picked up and moved over, in other words; and in the process almost any street plan, however aggressively rational, could have been imposed.

The famous Kokusai-dōri, sometimes called the Miracle Mile, sometimes called the Dirty Mile, seems at first sight to offer promise. It shoots uncompromisingly ahead without a bend, until it ends on a street that wavers off toward the waterfront. This ends, for all practical purposes, on a street that sidles back downtown, to close the triangle. An odd plan for a city, but not necessarily an impossible one, given a certain sense of how to build usable cities.

Here the other influence makes itself felt. Inside this triangle of wide streets, chaos reigns: alleys that lead without warning into creeks and cliffs, or give way to other alleys at angles that bicycles have trouble negotiating; tangles of huts among the tombs; tree stumps, chuckholes, passages gouged through the hillocks but not, apparently, leading anywhere. One afternoon the gentleman I was driving with missed his turn, and we had to do the whole triangle before we could get back for another try—whatever else goes in Naha, U-turns do not.

One more detail, to nail down the influence conclusively: it is virtually impossible to find an address in Naha. "We will all meet at my house," said a lady novelist one afternoon, "because my house is the only house a person can find. I am right opposite the Education Building." Alas, there proved to be two education buildings in the city.

The cabaret section of Naha, again, suggests something not quite American. Many of the cabarets have invitingly foreign names, Latin Quarter and the like. I am told, though I did not actually see it, that there is one called the Club Yes.

The typical cabaret is underground. It is reached by descending stairs and plunging into the darkness. Some moments later, in the glow of Christmas-tree lights, one makes out velvet wall hangings, a large peroxide-haired doll in a glass case, a quilted ceiling, just slightly tattered, boys with Ginza haircuts, and scores and scores of young ladies. Young ladies to pour your beer, young ladies to bare their bosoms and look sultry, young ladies to ask how long you have been in Okinawa, young ladies to recognize expense accounts and be pawed in some still darker corner.

It may be very American. I have not been all over America, and cannot really say that it is not. But another image keeps rising, to blot out the image of America: Shinjuku. Sakurazaka in Naha is exactly like Shinjuku in Tokyo. Smaller, perhaps, and without quite such a supply of austere intellectuals and businessmen to draw upon, but Shinjuku all the way, even down to the mannerisms.

Just as in Tokyo the austere intellectuals gather in Shinjuku bars late at night on their way home from the Ginza, so in Naha Okinawans gather at Sakurazaka late at night before starting up the hill to Shuri or down toward the harbor. What they do earlier in the evening no one was able to explain, since there is no real Naha equivalent of the Ginza; but the Shinjuku rules are scrupulously observed. The bars do not really get under way until ten or so.

The hula hoop has arrived in Naha, the Ogoshi Department Store having just gotten in a supply—from Japan. And not only the hula hoop. All the shops are full of brittle plastic objects in that peculiarly intense Japanese shade of sweetheart pink. Blue jeans are only beginning to come in, but soon they will be the uniform of delivery boys, just as they are in Tokyo. Young Naha ladies, who are irresistible, have a way of slightly overdressing that reminds one of Misora Hibari, the popular Japanese singer. The Okinawan theater, fighting a brave battle against Japanese movies and variety shows, will probably have to retreat yet another step this month when the Shōchiku girls pay their visit.

Though Americanization no doubt comes ultimately from America, it has reached Okinawa after a stopover in Tokyo. Naha is far, far behind the capital. All those thousands of American adolescents have not succeeded in selling blue jeans to Okinawans, but Tokyo is doing the trick.

When the time comes to decide who killed Ryūkyū culture, the war and the American administration will have to take their share of the blame. The centralization of Japanese culture, however, is not to be let off easily. If Americanization is bad, the bad choice was made by Tokyo. The provinces, including Okinawa, are being pulled along.

(Nov. 15, 1958)

STUDENTS AND VISITORS SPREADING GOODWILL

Sometimes one wonders about the exchange of persons, if that is the correct bureaucratic term for the various programs that send people off to the United States on the theory, one gathers, that they will love what they see and come back firm friends of the American way. The theory seems to work better for Russians than for Americans, at least to the extent that it is applied to Japanese. Hardly a soul comes back from the Soviet Union or the New China who is not wholly won over by one or the other of those peaceful socialist nations. A great deal of American time and attention, on the other hand, has gone into the making of the most virulent anti-American feeling.

This is particularly noticeable with the prewar crop of returned students. The most tragic example is probably that of Matsuoka Yōsuke, who graduated from, I believe, the University of Oregon, became a successful diplomat and ultimately foreign minister, took Japan into the Tripartite Alliance with Germany and Italy, and died while under prosecution as a war criminal.

Others have gotten in their digs in less dramatic ways. The late Miyamoto Yuriko, an important novelist who studied in the United States, was the wife of the present secretary-general of the Communist Party, and herself no friend of the United States. Mrs. Ishigaki Ayako, who may not be precisely a returned student but who lived in the United States an awfully long time all the same, has become famous as an energetic exposer of "American fascism."

Miss Matsuoka Yōko, secretary of the Japan PEN, can be counted on to say unpleasant things about the United States when others fail, though it is of course not often that others fail. Messrs. Minami Hiroshi, Tsuru Shigetō, and Tsurumi Shunsuke, for instance, are usually happy to tell us and our fellow readers of *Sekai* or *Chūō Kōron* how much they loved the America of their student days, and how much they wish the benighted America of today could see its way back to peace, progress, and disarmed isolation.

We do not know yet how it will be with the postwar crop. In many ways, things are different with them. For the most part, they do not go abroad under a cloud, as did so many of their seniors, nor do they face precisely the trials of, for instance, Messrs. Tsuru and Tsurumi, who were in the United States during the giddy red decade and who then had their clocks stopped by the war and the Occupation. In a word, more ordinary students are now going abroad under more ordinary circumstances.

Even so, something about the United States seems to make many of them unhappy. Information from more than one university suggests that they are among the slowest of foreign students to adapt. In the process they often develop rationalizations that add to the difficulty. They tell themselves that they have nothing but contempt for the country and its educational system, and are in America only to learn English—which, in turn, they would just as soon not do if they did not have to make a living. Or they build a shell. If the university is not going to help them, well, the fault is not theirs.

Not all of them, of course. Many do very nicely, and many among even the prewar crop came back feeling rather amiable. An outstanding example is Miss Sakanishi Shio, who is certainly as kind to the United States as it deserves and perhaps a little kinder.

One does not want to go on record as having said, even by implication, that student exchange is a failure and should be stopped. Still, a little more attention might be given to the problem of selection. This indiscriminate shipping of students to small freshwater colleges is likely to bring a fair return of Matsuokas, Yōsuke or Yōko.

Another method of exchanging persons, the sending of mature Japanese for relatively short visits, seems to work better, although here again the results can be a little disappointing. The high hopes with which the Asia Foundation sent Mrs. Hirabayashi Taiko to the United States, for instance, proved premature. The trip seems to have made her nervous, not to say angry. She was robbed, she did not get along well with her traveling companion, her feelings were hurt on occasion, and some of the things she said when she came back sounded a little ill-tempered, if she was reported accurately.

Since she is a most estimable person, one cannot believe that much of what happened to her was her own fault. Is something the matter with American guidesmanship? Guided tours of the Soviet Union and of the New China never seem to make people lose their tempers.

Mrs. Hirabayashi's traveling companion, Mrs. Enchi Fumiko, another novelist, came through the tour unruffled, and had interesting things to say about the Negro problem when she got back. This is not the place to concur in or dissent from her observations. The point is rather that Mrs. Enchi saw what she saw and formed her own conclusions about it, free from the fixed notions so beloved of Japanese progressives.

Another important novelist, Mr. Hino Ashihei, has just come back from the United States. He too investigated the Negro problem, than which no problem fascinates the Japanese more, and in addition he went on the sort of literary tour Japanese are always taking in Japan. He visited Poe's last shack in New York, a Longfellow mansion in Cambridge, Mark Twain's birthplace in Hannibal, and some spot in New Orleans associated with Lafcadio Hearn.

Some of Mr. Hino's remarks are a little odd. He seems to draw broad conclusions about American literary taste from the contrast between Poe's neglected hovel and Longfellow's much touristed mansion, and he seems to have been surprised that his New York taxi driver was not able to take him immediately to the Poe site. I should not be in the least surprised if a Tokyo taxi driver were unable to guide me to the site of Bashō's hut in Fukagawa.

But perhaps Mr. Hino's quaintest idea is that the government of Washington is to be accounted for by the Negro problem. The city is directly under Congress, it seems, because there are so many Negroes to be kept in line. The framers of the Constitution were perceptive indeed, foreseeing desegregation as early as 1787.

Mr. Hino too can be a good observer, however, and his conclusions about the race problem are not materially different from Mrs. Enchi's. He seems to have been astonished at finding no barricades in the streets of Little Rock, and, like her, he noted differences in customs and manners that make it hard to pretend the problem away.

(Nov. 29, 1958)

ON TRANSLATING INTO ONE'S OWN LANGUAGE

Dr. Arthur Waley, the British translator of Chinese and Japanese literature, has a most interesting article on translation in the November *Atlantic*. Commenting on a recent translation by a committee of Japanese, Dr. Waley again makes a point he has made before, and a point with which one tends to be in agreement: "The Japanese committee finds it 'regrettable' that Japanese literature has hitherto been chiefly translated by foreigners. I believe, on the contrary, that it is almost always better for the translator to be writing in his own language. It is in the highest degree improbable that a writer will command all the resources of a foreign language even as regards vocabulary, and when it comes to rhythm he is almost certain to be completely floored."

Not only the committee in question has found the practice regrettable. Sniping at foreign interlopers from Dr. Waley down has been one of the national sports of the Japanese. The *Mainichi* not long ago carried an article proclaiming that the good day was coming when translation would be out of the hands of "those people." The Japan PEN, it appeared, was stepping in to suppress them. Though the *Mainichi* article apparently did not express the specific will of the PEN, the secretariat of that organization has never made any secret of its belief that Japanese literature should be translated by Japanese.

It is therefore good to have as respected a voice as Dr. Waley's speaking out again. His statement of the case is, as always, fair and lucid. He does not say, and no one would say, that translations into English by Japanese are automatically bad, translations by Englishmen and Americans automatically good. Mrs. Kondō's translation of *Kokoro*, though not always sure in its use of the colloquial, is in many ways more economical than Edwin McClellan's. William Marquardt's translation of Mushakōji's *Love and Death* is generally inferior to Matsumoto Ryūzō's translation of another (and equally unsatisfying) work by the same author.

But the chances are surely better that a translator will be able to grasp the meaning of a foreign expression and find an equivalent in his own language than that he will be able to choose expertly from among the subtle possibilities for putting an expression from his own language into some foreign language.

A one-for-one correspondence between words in two different languages is rare except when the words refer to objects or creatures which the two cultures have in common. "Dog" is, on the whole, a safe translation for *inu* and "cat" for *neko* when the words refer to Fido and Tabby. When the words take on a figurative sense, the difficulty begins. If *inu* is found in a student newspaper and refers not to Fido but to a police spy, "cur" might be better, although there is probably an exact English equivalent, "fink" or "gink" or something of the sort; and when *neko* takes on implications of obsequious dissemblance, "cat" will no longer do. English cats are not dissemblers. They are but a step away from the jungle, and their claws are bared. I recently came upon a translator who had not learned that in English a person casts valuable objects not before cats but before much untidier beasts.

As one approaches abstract nouns or departs from nouns entirely, the difficulties increase. "Can't you feel gay?" says one drinking companion to another in a recent translation. It just won't do, but how is a person to explain why it won't do? (This remark, by the way, is from a translation not by a Japanese but by an Englishman. Perhaps the English do talk that way, although I have been spared

239

the experience of hearing them.)

"When the two were walking abreast, X started," said a translation in the paper the other morning. The context makes the meaning clear: "X began to speak." Most readers, however, will have visions of X leaping into the air, or twitching, or allowing his eyeballs to protrude. But if the context makes the meaning clear, the translator will ask, then what is wrong with the translation. Well, it just won't do, that is all. "Begin, start, commence, initiate, inaugurate"— they have their places, and you know them or you don't.

The richer and more complex the word, the greater the difficulties. If one of the distinguishing marks of literary style is a controlled use of connotation, then the translator out of his own language is likely to find himself losing his bearings at precisely the point where the literary value of the original begins.

"Gentle, mild, meek, obedient, submissive, compliant, pliable, yielding, dutiful and well-behaved, docile, manageable, tractable, tame," says Kenkyūsha of *sunao*. It is all of these things, no doubt, but when a passionate and contradictory woman says it of her lover at the climax of a novel, it is none of them. The translator has to invent strategies to encompass it. His chances of success are better if he is familiar with his weapons. "Sophisticated," not that it is a particularly good word, is said to have no equivalent in French, and certainly it has none in Japanese. What Englishman or American would be reckless enough to try putting J. D. Salinger into French or Japanese?

The Japanese have a tradition of writing languages other than their own, and they seem to think that their language is alone among the languages of the world in complexity and subtlety. Complex it is, but the other attribute it does not necessarily have in quantities to set it apart. "But how do you manage the nuances of Japanese?" the Japanese are fond of asking, as if other languages did not have nuances, and as if there were no significance in the fact that the word "nuance" had to be borrowed from French.

The problem of levels of usage offers an admirable illustration of the fact that complexity does not necessarily give a monopoly on subtlety. Probably no other language has quite the abundance of levels Japanese has. But we do have our levels too. Who has not had the experience of reading a sober passage of Japanese-English, suddenly to stumble upon a wife become "the little woman," or children become "kids," or a person of indefinite age become "that guy"?

In conclusion a few Arnoldian touchstones from recent translations. Proper names are suppressed to make spotting more difficult.

"Anyway, 'Let's kill X,' I whispered, and very surely did I whisper clenching my teeth, in spite of myself."

" 'Is that so! Ah, you two are conspiring against me and trying to make a fool out of me. Both of you know everything, and I don't. I'm just a laughing stock. Darn it! It's much easier to get along with a total stranger than with someone of casual acquaintance. Say, that girl over there! Come over here! Let's you and I drink together.' "

" 'What do you think of that one? I think it's a mere failure.' "

Although I have not seen it, I am told of a translation in which we learn that "the Japanese abolished summertime in 1954."

(Dec. 13, 1958)

ON UNDERSTANDING THAT JAPANESE SMILE

A columnist in a rival newspaper recently wrote a most unfriendly review of a perfectly harmless book of children's stories. The gentleman, Japanese by nationality, is a specialist in introducing quaint Japanese things to readers of English. He found the English versions of the stories inaccurate. But then a flicker of doubt came over his mind: had the inaccuracies been put there on purpose? Did they serve the function of making the stories less mystifying to the Occidental mind?

A Japanese lady wrote an article on Japanese cooking in an English-language monthly not long ago. As writers of such articles will, she told us that Japanese food is very pretty to look at. Then she seemed to have a flicker of hope: even foreigners, she said, might be able to eat the more extreme products of the Japanese cuisine if they would but persevere and throw away childhood prejudices. The possibility that they might like them immediately was not admitted.

The other morning one of the largest Japanese dailies covered much of page seven with an article headlined thus: "The Japanese

Smile: Foreigners Cannot Understand It." The Japanese smile when they are sad and smile when they are embarrassed, the writer explains, and this puzzles foreigners, who are used to smiling when they are happy and blushing when they are embarrassed and weeping when they are sad. The case is cited of a *Life* photographer who found people laughing during the Fukui earthquake. They were embarrassed, naturally, explains our anonymous journalist.

A famous novel which I once tried to translate is sprinkled with remarks like this: " 'Does that foreigner like Chinese cooking?' asked Etsuko." " 'Bring Mrs. Stolz something she can eat, someone.' He saw Ohana pouring tea. 'Bring a piece of cake for Mrs. Stolz. Take that other away.' " "The Makiokas thought another family with a daughter like Rumi might move into the Stolz house, but the house was designed for foreigners, and most foreigners had left the Far East."

To summarize, the gap between Japanese customs and manners and foreign customs and manners is set off for you to look at wherever you turn. The complexities of children's stories must be eliminated for foreigners, fish must be cooked or perhaps hidden when foreigners come calling, sadness must be accompanied by tears in the presence of foreigners, else the inhabitants of This Country will be misunderstood.

The business about the Japanese smile has been going on for a long time. The Japanese smile bothered Lafcadio Hearn, though he was very shortsighted and perhaps may be forgiven. The Japanese, for their part, have a long tradition of trying to make not only the smile but everything Japanese seem impossibly mystifying to turquoise-eyed foreigners.

Probably the origins of the tradition lie in the Shinto nationalism of the Tokugawa period, when the Japanese as children of the sun had by definition to have things not visible to ordinary eyes. It continued through Okakura Tenshin and those lectures on "Teaism" which so delighted the ladies of Boston a half century ago.

And here, to come down to but yesterday, is the noted Zen scholar D. T. Suzuki showing us how far the Occident has yet to go: "Even D. H. Lawrence and Simone Weil, who are appraised as 'brave men' by Richard Rees, have not in my view really penetrated into the secrets of the Self as they are understood in Zen. It is quite natural that being brought up in a Christian atmosphere they could not transcend their background with all its mythological trappings."

Here is a much-read modern novelist in a confessional mood (the translation is not mine): "Wherever one goes one sees only Occidentals. My cousin always accompanies me and he has made things easy, but somehow I have the feeling that we are looked down upon. . . . Then filled with pride, I chide the Westerners inwardly, 'There is a joy waiting for me in that distant land of mine which you can never taste.' Can anyone match me in the splendor of my spiritual possessions?"

This last quotation is just a little unfair. Among the gentleman's "spiritual possessions" is his beloved, and he has a right to be somewhat enraptured. Still, his remarks are of the same sort as those of the old Shinto nationalists when they looked down upon the world from the Sun Goddess's lap; and at the same time there is a curious insecurity in them.

The Japanese claim to impenetrable uniqueness is in fact highly ambivalent. It is the product of an island culture and of a people who speak a difficult orphan language, and, as this last quotation so admirably shows, it is several things simultaneously: an expression of a certain cultural arrogance, a last defense against nagging feelings of insecurity, a symptom of a suspicion that the whole idea might be the sheerest nonsense.

The much-read novelist just quoted is honest enough to go on and say that he really hasn't been able to talk to any foreigners and therefore he has only his intuition to fall back on. By implication, therefore, he asks a very important question: if national modes of thought and behavior are really so mystifying that only vulgarized versions can be transmitted to foreigners, might it not be that the possessors of those modes of thought and behavior are not in a very good position to understand anyone else's? If they are sure that we do not understand them, can they be sure that they understand us?

The question is a deep, metaphysical one that touches upon the meaning of meaning, and Dr. Richards is not here to give us an answer. Much can be said for the Japanese point of view. The Japanese have been studying us a good deal longer and more intensely than we have been studying them. They may have been mistaken from time to time, like the lady in *Honorable Picnic* who used to wash her husband's shoes, but they have certainly been undaunted. They have moreover been forced to read a stream of drivel about the Orient from Voltaire to Anthony West, enough to make them think that they are indeed the hardest people in the world to understand. Then they have had Madison Avenue blurbists who call *The Makioka Sisters* "a vast and varied picture of the declining glory of a great Osaka merchant family," and *Snow Country* a book "about the possibility of love in an earthly paradise."

Yet the question remains, and it is a fundamental one. This perpetual making over of things so that foreigners can understand them implies that the most diligent and astute foreigner could never penetrate to the essence of the real thing; and if that is true the impossibility of understanding may work both ways, and all the diligence and astuteness of the Japanese in pursuit of the West have done them no good.

It is only a question, and it must remain unanswered. On this uncertain note we may leave the matter, adding that it is not only Japanese profundities, spiritual treasures, and delicacies that the foreigner cannot understand, it is, reasonably enough, Japanese absurdities too. Here is Kanō Hisaakira, director of the Public Housing Corporation, writing in the *Sunday Mainichi*: "The other day I was invited to a study group made up of diplomats from various countries. The theme was 'The Japanese Intellectual Class and Democracy,' and the discussion was most lively and interesting. In general, however, the conclusion was that 'the Japanese are impossible to understand.' Students wave red flags and participate in demonstrations, but they become conservative, upstanding citizens as soon as they discard their student uniforms. This sort of thing must indeed be, to the blue-eyed ones, 'impossible to understand.'"

(Jan. 10, 1959)

SUMO TOURNAMENT VICTORY BY SYMPATHY

The institution of the fix (Webster scorns the word as "colloquial," but what other is there?) is probably common to professional athletics everywhere, and perhaps to amateur athletics too. As they have to so many things, however, the Japanese have given it a twist all their own.

244

In sports introduced from abroad, fixing would appear to be very much as it is in most places, although in proportion to the prevalence of rumors there is perhaps less public outcry than one would expect. It may be, too, that fixing of team sports runs somewhat above the world level. Certainly rumors abound. I have even had the exciting experience of being informed in advance that a baseball game was going to be fixed.

I do not know that it actually was fixed, but it ran remarkably true to form. The pitcher was supposed to tunnel a pair of easy grounders at crucial points in the game. He did just that, and his team lost. Usually the rumors take this form: the Lions and the Braves split the double-header yesterday so that the Lions would have a sure victory to help them on the way to the pennant and the Braves would be in a fair position to finish with the top pitcher of the year and therefore a good drawing card for next year. I do not pretend to have information on how many of the rumors have been based on fact.

In any case, they do not much matter. This sort of fixing is neither a particularly interesting nor a particularly Japanese institution. There is gambling money behind it, whether the fixed is a jockey at Santa Anita or a pitcher in the Kōshien.

The Japanese have a kind of fixing which is all their own, however. It is found in the traditional sports, notably *sumō* wrestling, and it is such a combination of money and prestige and tradition and duty and emotion that perhaps it should not be called fixing at all. The magazine *Bungei Shunjū*, one of the most influential in the country, has published a number of articles on the subject. They have been so outspoken that it is hard to imagine them not actionable even in This Country, with its easy libel laws, unless what they have to say is true.

The world of *sumō* is full of anachronisms. Every now and then there is a reform movement, as when the head of the Sumō Association tried to commit suicide a couple of years ago and was somewhat hastily replaced by Futabayama, one of the greatest wrestlers in history. Criticism of the association had become severe, there were hints of a tax scandal, and Futabayama promised to do away with the anachronisms.

He did away with only one, the traditional *sumō* teahouses, and even they have come stealing back. The teahouses are in effect recognized scalpers whose profits go to important members of the association. They did disappear for a tournament or two, but the newspapers and *Bungei Shunjū* report—I have not been to look—that they have returned.

A more intriguing anachronism has to do with relations between the wrestlers. They are of a sort that many Japanese would describe as "feudal," which is to say that they are in some respects premodern. One would like to think that personal matters fade away the moment two wrestlers face each other in the ring, and that the strongest man therefore wins. Such is apparently not always the case with *sumō*.

Indeed the whole system is based on the assumption that friend and friend or master and pupil outside the ring will continue to be friend and friend or master and pupil in the ring. It is for this reason that two wrestlers from the same *heya* (might it be translated "club"?) never meet each other.

This may possibly bring a reduction in the number of friendly fixes, but it also leads to unfairness. The wrestler from the small, weak *heya* has to wrestle all the powerful wrestlers; the wrestler from the large, strong establishment is spared the duty to wrestle powerful colleagues. Thus Chiyonoyama and Tochinishiki, two of the three top men until the recent retirement of the former, never met, because they were from the same *heya*. Wakanohana and Kotogahama never meet. Shimizugawa, on the other hand, has to take on everyone of any importance at all, and so did Rikidōzan, which fact in part accounted for his leaving *sumō* in favor of professional wrestling.

To show how feudal *sumō* wrestlers can still be, here is Ōkuma Hideo quoting Tochinishiki's views on possible revision of the system: "If a system is adopted whereby every wrestler has to meet every other, then I'll have to meet Chiyonoyama. Why, we ate together when we were boys, and we grew up on the same training ground. Does anyone really think we'd be fighting it out in the ring? If anyone does, he knows very little about the *sumō* world."

It is this sort of frankness that makes one a little reluctant to call the whole business fixing.

Whatever we are to call it, it continues in spite of the system that keeps members of the same club from meeting. The system results in unfairness in the sense that not every wrestler meets the same list of opponents, and, on the other hand, it fails to produce complete honesty, in the sense that the strongest man does not always win.

At this point money and sympathy seem to enmesh inextricably. Sometimes money is there by itself, naked and smiling—Ōkuma tells us that the standard rate for a throwaway among lesser wrestlers is 10,000 yen, and he told us in an earlier article of a wrestler who preferred drink to fame and who would decide, depending on the number of fingers his adversary held up, whether or not to throw the match. Each finger stood for a bottle of sake, it seems, always faithfully delivered.

Just as often sympathy is involved. One wrestler will help another at a crucial moment on the latter's way to the top. He will himself expect to be helped when the moment comes. Or, again, he will give a revered old wrestler the victory he needs to delay for a moment the beginning of the sad road down.

In recent tournaments, Matsunobori seems to have profited most from this last kind of sympathy. After a disastrous beginning two tournaments ago, he finished triumphantly by knocking over all the top contenders in a row, recording a precarious eight victories against seven losses, and thus avoiding demotion. It all seemed very fishy. The impression of fishiness was borne out in the next tournament, when not even sympathy could save him and he was at length demoted. He is doing poorly again this time.

As for wrestlers helping each other to the top, the give and take between Tochinishiki and Wakanohana looked very suspicious to the rankest outsider, and Ōkuma now confirms the fact that it looked suspicious to the expert too. Tochinishiki got to the top first, and, whether from general feelings of sympathy or from pressures within the Sumō Association, he gave Wakanohana a match at just the right moment. Once on top, Wakanohana repaid the debt. Now that both are on top, Asashio is the man to watch.

Ōkuma thinks that Asashio's victory at Fukuoka last fall was arranged. He tells an interesting story. The match between Asashio and Wakanohana on the last day was to decide the championship. Wakanohana's dressing room was empty. All his underlings had gone home. In Asashio's dressing room, on the other hand, everyone was decked out in formal *hakama* for the victory parade.

There is an openness about it all that makes one want to say, "It isn't fixing, it's just *sumō*." Perhaps *sumō*, like professional wrestling, is more a show than a test of strength, or at least a combination of the two. Perhaps everyone knows what is going on, and gets a good lump in his throat because of it. Old Matsunobori—he doesn't deserve to win, but it's nice that everyone lets him.

(Jan. 24, 1959)

PASTERNAK, JAPAN PEN, AND ARTHUR KOESTLER

Since this paper has not been as eager as some of its rivals to follow the details of Arthur Koestler's quarrel with the Japan PEN Center, it might be well to present some of the facts. Before that, however, it might be well to say something about the nature of the Japan PEN. PEN centers rather tend to be assemblies of people who wish they were literary but really are not. Those hours over cocktails at the Pierre give a pleasant literary buzz, so to speak, to people on the fringes of writing.

Such is not the case in Japan. Not every important Japanese writer is a member of the PEN, and not every writer who is in theory a member does much about it. It is nonetheless a highly respected organization. The president, Kawabata Yasunari, is one of the finest living Japanese novelists. One of the vice-presidents is the dean of the literary Left. The secretary, Takami Jun, is also a famous and accomplished novelist. People listen when the PEN speaks. The International PEN Congress in Tokyo two years ago was a sort of national festival. One worries, therefore, when the PEN begins to speak ambiguously.

In December three foreign members of the Japan PEN, Father Joseph Roggendorf, Ivan Morris, and I, thought it necessary to call attention to a certain ambiguity on the part of the PEN in the case of Boris Pasternak. The PEN had adopted a resolution so strangely worded that it seemed to censure Pasternak's defenders more sharply than his assailants.

A sequence of events which it is not necessary to recount here had moreover left us with the unhappy impression that Japanese writers worry a great deal about their own freedom of speech, and very little about freedom of speech in general; or, to put the matter differently, that a potential threat to their own liberty of action, as in proposals to strengthen the police, quickly brings them to a boil, whereas brutal infringement upon someone else's freedom of action, particularly if it takes place in a "socialist" country, leaves them cool as the Antarctic dogs. We wrote a letter pointing this out.

There followed what seemed to us an inconclusive answer, and what no doubt seemed to them an inconclusive answer to their answer—"a thriving exchange of notes," as one newspaper put it. The first letter in the series found its way into a monthly magazine. The *Mainichi* picked it up, and carried a long article summarizing the exchange and very fairly and objectively adding rebuttals from both sides. This in turn found its way into the English *Mainichi*, in which a translation of the article from the mother paper appeared on the day before Koestler was to address the PEN.

He was incensed by it, and wrote a public letter declining to appear before the PEN and stating his reasons in detail. One passage in particular incensed him, a statement attributed by the *Mainichi* to Takami Jun, the PEN secretary. It appeared thus in the English edition: "The Pasternak incident may be a grave problem as Mr. Seidensticker and Mr. Morris say from the point of view of principle. But one must also think of the repercussions that might have been created if a statement were issued by us. I do not know if it is wise to stick to principles always."

This, said Koestler, was the language of politicians, and, since he had announced in advance his intention of avoiding political gatherings, he thought it best to avoid the PEN. He then summarized the facts of the Pasternak case as he saw them, and added that he would probably not be here if European intellectuals at the time of the Spanish Civil War had been as timid in their protests as Japanese intellectuals seem to be now. He was saved from a Franco death cell by protests that were in no way timid.

The next day, Monday of this week, the PEN met, without Koestler. There was a lively discussion, apparently rather hostile to Koestler. Since I was not present, it would be inappropriate for me to comment on the proceedings in detail. Reports on what happened are enough in agreement, however, that a few remarks about the Monday meeting and about the Pasternak question in general might not be out of order.

In the first place, one comes away with strong feelings about the futility of having an argument with the Japanese.

A most astonishing variety of red herrings lies strewn across the path. Thus it is said that the PEN's failure to take a strong stand in support of Pasternak was due to the fact that *Dr. Zhivago* had not yet been translated into Japanese. As if that had the slightest relevance!

One would have a grudging admiration for the person who said: "Freedom of speech is nonsense, individuals are nothing, and I for one feel a certain exhilaration in seeing naked, ruthless force in action." But what is one to say when the position is rather: "I just love freedom of speech, really I do, and I just wish I could find time to read his books and tell you whether he should have it or not."

Reports on the Monday meeting suggest that the red herrings flew like mad, and that no one really got down to considering what the substance of Koestler's charges was, how valid they were, how they should be answered. Someone got up and attempted to get to the heart of the conspiracy, to determine whether the four of us were in league and had followed a careful timetable. Someone else was concerned about the propriety of listening to foreigners at all, since to listen to them would in effect be to acquiesce in improper interference in Japanese domestic affairs.

Someone else thought that it was not protests by European intellectuals that got Koestler out of the Spanish prison, but rather the fact that he was not a Spaniard. Someone else was angry because the second of our letters got into the papers almost before it got into the hands of the PEN. Someone else (this remark was in the newspapers) thought "it was all a mistake."

Several people said that the PEN was not a political organization, so there, Koestler.

But almost no one got down to the simple issues he raised: the fundamental immorality of Takami's *Mainichi* statement, if he was quoted correctly, and the fact that, for what seem to us political reasons, the Japan PEN was not disposed to speak out in support of Boris Pasternak.

People in This Country seldom get down to the substance of an argument. Everything is pre-argument, as in the old debate over whether Article Nine of the Constitution was MacArthur's idea or Shidehara's. The question ought to be whether it is a good or a bad idea, whoever first had it.

Just occasionally, the Monday discussion touched gingerly on the basic issue, freedom of expression and the PEN's attitude toward it. On those fleeting occasions, there seemed to emerge an exaggerated belief in the number of positions it is possible to take on the question of free speech. One would have thought that a person either believes in it or does not; either cares about it or does not.

But at least three members used the word "neutrality," and at least one spoke in sad, self-congratulatory terms of the difficulty and necessity of being neutral.

How is it possible to be neutral? To refuse to speak out for Pasternak is to give tacit support to his tormentors. The pose of neutrality is in effect a withdrawal which amounts to an admission that the withdrawer does not really care about freedom of speech. One might as well say to some stricken island: "Oh, perhaps you do have a cholera epidemic going on, but, lest I compromise my independence, I shall not send you vaccine. I am not one to take sides."

There is a bright spot in the dreary picture, however. On Tuesday the *Yomiuri* quoted the novelist Tamura Taijirō as saying ruefully that foreigners seemed to worry more about matters of principle than the Japanese.

Than which an apter remark could not have been made.

Since the above was written, the PEN has sent a long letter to Koestler. It does not answer his charges, however, and only makes one feel more strongly how hard it is to have an argument with the Japanese.

(Mar. 7, 1959)

INFORMATION ABOUT BABYLON BY TOKYO BAY

At the top of the best-seller lists this week is a fascinating book called *Tokyo*, by Shibata Tokue. Although Shibata is somewhat given to editorializing—he likes to make remarks about capitalism and the ruling classes and the like—his book is what we call a mine of information. Almost everything fit to print about Tokyo is to be found there.

Thus we learn already in the introduction that Tokyo has 15,300, 000 lights and consumes some 5,600 million kilowatt hours of electricity a year. It has more neon lights than any other city in the world. It has twice as many movie theaters as New York. It has sixteen percent of the eating places in the country and consumes fifteen percent of the sake, although its population is only about ten percent of the national total. The tax office thinks, but evidently is not quite sure, that there are 90,000 *pachinko* machines in commercial operation in the city. The number of department stores in the main business districts doubled between 1950 and 1958.

While the more garish consumer services have thus flourished, the essentials have been neglected. Housing space per capita was in 1955 at only about three-quarters of the prewar level. The Chūo Line carries about two and a half times its theoretical load of passengers, the Keihin Line three times.

Then there is the noise, and there is the dirt. Shibata tells us that automobile horns in Tokyo make as much noise in ten seconds as New York horns do in an hour, and that it takes Paris three months to accumulate the honks Tokyo has every five seconds. In the month of January, 1956, an average of 107 tons of soot fell on every square kilometer of Chiyoda Ward in central Tokyo, including, of course, His Majesty's establishment. The Kanda River running past Chiyoda Ward is three times as dirty as the Kanzaki River running through the Osaka-Kobe industrial district.

All this we learn in the introduction. Later we learn much more. A few random examples will have to suffice.

Tokyo is now the largest city in the world, and it has probably had that honor before. Its predecessor, Edo, seems to have reached a population of a million by the late eighteenth century. In 1801 London had 860,000 people, Vienna and Moscow only 250,000, Berlin 170,000.

The growth of the early modern city was steady but fairly slow. It took half a century to accumulate the third million. Then, in the years from World War I to the earthquake, the population suddenly shot up to four million—these were the years of the growing pains so frequently complained about in contemporary fiction. The population was approaching eight million when World War II cut it in half. Immediately afterward it began climbing again, for a time at the rate of about a half million per year. Now the growth seems to be leveling off at about a quarter of a million per year, most of it the result of migration from the provinces.

The population today is thus only about a million above the highest prewar figure, but the distribution has shifted radically. The population of the central wards was in 1955 only about two-thirds the figure for 1940, while in the western wards, Nerima, Suginami, and Setagaya, it had doubled. The center of population had moved a mile or two west, from Akasaka to Yoyogi. Hence that enormous press on the Chūō Line.

With about a tenth of the population of the country, Tokyo in 1957 has 16.9 percent of the automobiles, 14.8 percent of the crimes, 15.2 percent of the traffic accidents, 15.2 percent of the fires, and 15.2 percent of the income. Very decadent, very para-sitical, grumbles Shibata. Tokyo has only about a quarter of the com-panies capitalized at under 200,000 yen, but it has sixty percent of those capitalized at 1,000 million or over. Very Wall-Streetish.

There is a graph to demonstrate what one has always felt about the place: that it is a city of the young. The distribution of population by ages does not produce the symmetrical fir-tree pattern one would expect. There is a sudden flaring out in the early twenties, and the flaring is more pronounced on the male side of the tree graph than on the female. In the older age brackets, women considerably out-number men, but in the city as a whole there are (or were in 1957) 106 men for every 100 women. At the ages of about twenty-two to twenty-four, if I read the graph correctly, there are close to 150 men for every 100 women. This, if one is looking for it, should offer a practical argument for legalized prostitution.

There is information on the traffic problem. Between April 1952 and September 1957, the number of motor vehicles using the streets came near quadrupling. It is calculated that for maximum safety and efficiency no more than 30,000 vehicles should pass a point on a four-lane highway within a twelve-hour period. More than three times that number passed through the Palace Plaza, and nearly three times that number passed Shimbashi, between seven in the morning and seven in the evening on September 16, 1956. Almost 10,000 an hour passed through the plaza in the late afternoon.

Tokyo is woefully behind other cities of the world in the propor-tion of its area devoted to streets. In Washington, a rather staggering forty-three percent of the city has been allotted to the streets.

In New York and Vienna it is thirty-five percent, in Berlin twenty-five percent, in London twenty-three percent. Among Japanese cities, Nagoya, with twenty-two percent, compares favorably with London and Paris. Nagoya was the only major Japanese city to take advantage of the bombings for a thorough replanning. In Tokyo, which just grew, the percentage is 9.2.

The supply of parks is not much better. Tokyo has less than a square yard of park per capita. New York has eighteen times as much, London twelve times as much, Paris more than ten times as much, and Washington more than sixty times as much. The war cut into the already limited park system, and so, alas, did the Occupation. Shibata tells with some glee how a small park at Toranomon was taken over by the Occupation forces and upon its release was made into a splendid garage by "a foreign company."

There is more, much more: information about sewers (Charlie Chaplin is supposed to have remarked that Tokyo would never make a movie, because its chief sensual impact was upon the nostrils) and cemeteries, information about fires and accidents, information about Diet members and tax collectors, indeed everything you need to know about the great stew that is Tokyo. Minus a few of those editorial comments, the book ought to be translated—if only there were someone around to do it.

(Mar. 28, 1959)

MISS LONELYHEARTS, HELP ME! HELP ME!

The *Yomiuri Shimbun* is, to my knowledge, the only major daily that carries a regular Miss Lonelyhearts column. Several experts, most of them ladies, take turns giving advice and comfort to the lonely, weary, and troubled. Very reputable experts they are, too: among them a leading medical journalist who also writes detective stories, an important lady novelist, and the wife of the president of Waseda University.

Two of the experts have assured me that all of the letters are genuine, and one admitted, somewhat shamefacedly, that she answered only the easy ones. What the hard ones must be like defies the imagination.

There is much to be learned from even the easy ones about, for instance, that continuing delight and enigma, the Japanese woman. Sometimes we see her as Basil Hall Chamberlain and the other early connoisseurs saw her: gentle, self-effacing, and long-suffering. Not long ago there was a letter from Wife Who Prays to God, Nagano (the names of the writers are never given). Wife Who Prays to God has had enough. Her sixty-two-year-old husband is having an affair with his niece, who lives with them. Wife has suggested tactfully that the girl find a nice man and get married, but the girl likes it better here, and has now countered with the suggestion that they adopt a son into the family for her. There are certain peculiarly Japanese elements in the case—the adopted husband and the like—but what really startles one is that the affair between husband and niece has been going on for nine years. Only now has Wife Who Prays to God, Nagano, had enough.

The case cannot be considered typical. The expert who replied seemed as startled as I was. Where but in Japan, though, could you find a wife who would put up with this sort of thing for more than nine minutes?

But it is not only the long-suffering wife who appears in these columns. Not long ago there was a letter from a gentleman who wanted to know what to do: his wife worked hard, and on the whole he found her satisfactory; but recently she had taken to spending the night downstairs with strange gentlemen while he himself slept upstairs. "Have you no spine, man?" answered the expert.

Then there is that universal demon, the mother-in-law who in her Japanese incarnation must be at her most savage. The chief difference from the Occidental mother-in-law is that her wrath is directed against her daughter-in-law, not her son-in-law. Maternal grandmothers seem to be fairly well out of the picture. Not long ago Troubled Wife, Yamanashi, wrote in to say that if her mother-in-law had her way Troubled Wife would be without a pot to cook in. Fortunately Troubled Wife is able to borrow pots from her own mother. About all the experts can do in the face of this sort of thing is throw up their hands and lament the scarcity in Japan of homes for the aged.

If the Miss Lonelyhearts columns do anything, they dispel forever the notion that America alone is the country of the over-possessive mother. Here is part of a letter from Distressed Girl, Kanagawa

(Distressed Girl is the child of divorced parents): "I met my father again when I was in my fourth year of elementary school, and was much drawn to his way of living and my brother's. . . . Mother is always taking me to movies and to department stores when I don't want to go, and when I try to refuse she bursts into tears and says, 'You just don't care whether your mother is alive or dead.' " ("You will forgive me for saying so, but you have a pretty stupid mother," says the expert. Experts can be blunt on occasion.)

There seems to be a certain free, informal intimacy about Japanese family life that must be very charming. Y., Tokyo, is living with but not married to a young gentleman. He used to be sincere, but recently he has shown signs of delinquency. (One of the delinquent things he does, by the way, is flirt with communism, a fact which would suggest that communism is not as widely admired by the people as it is by the monthly magazines.) Now his whole family, five strong, has suddenly picked up and moved into the room next door. Y. wants to know whether she should now marry him, not, apparently, because it embarrasses her not to be married to him, but because as the oldest son he ought to be married. Get out as quick as you can, says the expert.

A rather casual attitude toward marriage, divorce, and birth control, it might be noted, makes work somewhat easier for the experts. They can airily recommend divorce or abortion as no Miss Lonelyhearts in the U.S. would dare do. This same casualness causes troubles that could easily have been avoided, however. N., Tokyo, began living with a divorced gentleman five years ago. Then when the time came to register the baby she discovered that he wasn't divorced at all—the "former" wife's name was still in his family register, which N. had apparently never bothered to look at.

Another N., Tokyo, has had so many abortions that she can no longer have children. Suddenly, inexplicably, she has decided that she wants them. What should she do? The expert admits that the case looks fairly hopeless, but recommends adoption. N. has other problems too: her husband has also been divorced, and it seems that he is spending alternate nights with his former wife, so that he can see the children. (Poor N. gets no sympathy from the expert, who suspects that she married the man for his money and now is looking for a way to keep him.)

Adoption is a recurring theme in these columns. The letters only hint at some of the deeper problems it must create. Boys are adopted into families on the understanding that they will one day marry one of the daughters. The time comes, and either the young gentleman in question or the young lady in question rebels. Much of the rebellion is of course the modern way of looking at arranged marriages. Yet it is a little hard to imagine how one would feel as the day approached for marrying the girl with whom one had been reared as brother and sister. Since some sort of ban on incest seems to be one of the few moral principles which the whole human race has in common, the strains of being reared as an adopted husband must be complicated indeed.

A minor reward from reading the Miss Lonelyhearts columns is the light which they throw on the Japanese attitude toward other races. The Japanese are always most pleased to be able to accuse other people of racial prejudice. And what of the Japanese themselves?

Here is part of a letter from H., Saitama: "I am a girl, aged nineteen. When, at the age of sixteen, I went to work as a maid on an American base, I began to date an American soldier, and very soon he proposed marriage. Unable to tell my parents, I could not decide what to do. Then he went home, and we corresponded for two years until, in July of last year, he came to Japan again. . . .

"He is twenty-four, and he says he must marry me whatever happens. I finally spoke to my parents. The whole family is opposed to the idea. They say that it will not look good if I am married to a foreigner, and that I will have no chance of being happy if I go to America. What is more, my brother lost 500,000 yen at the bicycle races last year, and the family wants me to work a little longer. . . .

"Sometimes the American telephones his love to me from where he is stationed, but my mother says that if he really loves me he should show it not by letters or telephone calls but by presents."

To which one can only answer: how very spiritual the East is.

And here is part of a letter from Company Employee, Tokyo: "Three years ago I established relations with a twenty-eight-year-old girl, and two years ago I got her a job at my company. She is far more lively and intelligent than most people. She is also beautiful . . . and I love her with all my heart.

"We were making concrete plans to get married . . . when I happened to run into an acquaintance from the days when she was

257

working in a bar. I learned that at the age of nineteen she became the 'only' of an American, that they lived together for a year, and that she had a child by him. After leaving him she had affairs with four or five other men. In tears, she admitted the truth of all this.

"If it were only a matter of Japanese I would not mind so much, but I cannot reconcile myself to the fact of her having had relations with a foreigner."

(Apr. 11, 1959)

NOTES IN MEMORY OF KAFŪ, TOKYO'S NOVELIST

The novelist Nagai Kafū died one night last week. I never met him, though I saw him wandering through Asakusa once or twice; but the news was strangely saddening. He was the strongest of the few remaining links with the Meiji period, and the Meiji period has a powerful fascination for the student of Japan and of Tokyo.

While a few of Kafū's (one must ask to be forgiven for using his "elegant sobriquet" rather than his family name—the family name does not come naturally in cases like this) colleagues are still with us, the Meiji period itself is still with us; they are the men of Meiji, messy, confused, brave, and energetic. And on the other hand, the Meiji period seems so extremely far away. Knowing someone from it is like knowing someone who fought at Bosworth Field and saw the end of the Middle Ages. So near and so far, the Meiji period is the focus for the nostalgia which, in many ways, a liking for Tokyo amounts to.

"Falling snow; and Meiji is far away," says one of the most famous and most untranslatable of modern haiku. The poet is looking out over the modern city in the snow, we may imagine, and thinking of the city that is gone. This haiku was written before the war. Another whole city has disappeared since, and Meiji has moved several steps farther on its way out of sight. With Kafū's death it seems to recede another sudden, enormous step into the distance.

In his youth Kafū was famous as a philanderer. One of his wives was Fujikage Shizue, the well-known dancer. She left him, she said in the bittersweet little memorial she gave one of the newspapers upon his death, because he was really too given to amorous pursuits.

As for the objects of those pursuits, Kafū listed them faithfully in the diary he kept for half a century. We learn not only their names, but also their particular charms. Thus the entry for May 16, 1936, tells us all about the ladies of the Tamanoi pleasure quarter. Mariko at No. 48 is so bawdy by nature that she sometimes sends a young, inexperienced customer fleeing in shocked surprise. Yukari at No. 73 and Chieko at No. 57 are prepared to perform special services, the nature of which I am prepared to reveal upon request, in a less public place. Taeko at No. 54 does interesting things with mirrors, but charges a special fee. And so on.

In his later years, he was more famous as an eccentric. He disliked people, and especially newspaper reporters and fellow writers, of which species he had many nasty things to say in his novels. Living alone, he could not do what most eminent novelists do, send a battery of disciples to the door to tell callers that the master is indisposed. Instead he would go to the door himself, announce that he was out, and go back inside again. His dislike of people seems to have been compensated for by a peculiar fondness for money. He is said to have had some 30,000,000 yen in the bank when he died, and he always carried his deposit book with him. He recorded in his diaries the price of almost everything he bought. You know exactly where to go, therefore, if you have to know how much nose paper cost in 1925. You also know where to go if you have to know whether it was fair or foul on May 6, 1929. No writer except perhaps Thoreau more faithfully recorded the weather over the years.

He quarreled with almost everyone, including all his relatives. Some fifteen years ago he adopted a son, and promptly quarreled with him. The boy went home to mother. Now it appears that the boy's name was never taken off the family register, and he is heir to the 30,000,000 yen and, if he chooses to press the claim, the copyrights too. There is talk of setting up some sort of fund for the advancement of literature. Having observed rather closely the sort of thing Japanese literary people do when they get their hands on a fund, I hope myself that the boy presses the claim and gets every yen.

It is not as philanderer or eccentric that Kafū will be remembered, however, but as the novelist of changing Tokyo. Tokyo was his great subject from his return to Japan in 1908 (he had been in the U.S. for some years and in France for a few months) until he fell silent after World War II. The Tokyo which is the object of his attentions and his affections is always receding into the past. In his youth it was the Edo of the Tokugawa shogunate, in his old age it became the Tokyo of his youth. No doubt there is a certain amount of perverseness in this; but the city does force those who are fond of it to keep looking back. It changes too rapidly. Hardly anything in it is a hundred years old, and all that is most engaging about it seems on the point of being swept under by war, disaster, and the mad rush to keep up with the world. No one who likes Asakusa and loathes the western suburbs can fail to see what Kafū means.

The young Kafū back from France was repelled by the superficial, confused Westernization of Tokyo. He made it his mission to seek out what was left of Tokugawa Japan, and he found it among the actors, musicians, and geisha whose professions made them custodians of the past. All of them happened to be rather disreputable professions, because the late Tokugawa disapproval of all pleasant things lingered on. A fondness for the disreputable, for outcasts and near outcasts, was a part of Kafū's writing to the end.

Perhaps the finest work of his early years, "The River Sumida," is available in English translation. It is about a desperate boy who wants to become a samisen player but whose ambitious, up-to-date mother wants him to go to the university and become a bureaucrat. A bit inconsiderately, Kafū leaves him critically ill with pneumonia. He has found an ally in his uncle, however, and the implication is that if pneumonia doesn't do him in he can have fun with the samisen.

A number of early novels deal with geisha, particularly Shimbashi geisha. Some of them are very successful, but by the end of World War I the vein was worked out. The war boom was killing the old city—these were the years of the growing pains that both Kafū and Tanizaki have described—and, though Kafū cannot have known it, the earthquake was in sight to deliver the final blow. In 1921 he published a long essay called "Drizzling Rain." It is a confession of utter dejection. For a decade thereafter Kafū wrote nothing of importance. The remnants of Edo were gone, the new city could not fill their place.

From 1931, however, he did begin writing of the new city. His distaste for his material is apparent. The Taishō barmaid is a shabby successor indeed to the Meiji geisha, and, as is usually the way when a novelist too openly takes sides, the reader is put off.

But presently the scene shifts to Asakusa and beyond, outcasts are once more custodians of the past, and the old power returns. *A Strange Tale from East of the River*, the masterpiece of his late years, is a discursive little work, half essay, half novel, about an old writer who finds a conservative prostitute "east of the river" and spends summer evenings talking to her. She takes him back to Meiji, but in the end, as the autumn winds begin to blow, he has to leave her.

Kafū continued to write through the war years. A number of stories that could not be published then have appeared since. The best of them is about Asakusa dancers. It verges on the indecent—indeed there is a downright pornographic version, though I do not know whether or not it is authentic—and hides nothing of Asakusa sordidness; but there is a wistful evocation of changing Asakusa surfaces that is most effective, and makes one sorry to see the hero move away—to the western suburbs, of all places—at the end of the book.

It is not for his social criticism or his naturalistic reporting, but for exactly this, that Kafū will be remembered, for his lyrical evocation of the moods of Tokyo. He will probably never be as adequately translated as less deserving writers. He is too much a part of the city, and therefore lacks what we call universality. One has to know something of the city to guess what losses that tree among the ruins symbolizes. Not likely to find his translator, Kafū is perhaps the best reason one can think of for learning Japanese.

(May 9, 1959)

NOTES ON WAR GUILT

The other night we had an interesting argument about how much war guilt the Japanese feel, particularly toward the Chinese. None of us knew the answer, of course. Probably the Japanese themselves do not. Always more than willing to offer a confident opinion in a loud voice, I took the position that they feel very little. True, there is much talk about all the bad things "the militarists" did in China, and a guilt-ridden book about Manchuria, *The Human Condition* by Gomikawa Jumpei, has recently been an enormous best seller. Yet

I cannot help feeling that all the talk and all the guilt have a certain fabricated look about them. They were put together to make one more reason for being good to the New China.

I have been going through a rat-infested heap of old magazines in search of the articles that have contributed to this impression. The most memorable of them falls with as suspicious a clank now as when I first read it. It appears in the *Chūō Kōron* for December 1954, and it is by Shimizu Ikutarō, a professor in the crown prince's school, the Gakushūin, and a highly emotional pleader of the cause of the New China and similar nations.

Here is a particularly telling passage. Shimizu is describing an apprehensive plane trip from Moscow to Peking. He has just told us how he was able to commiserate with war-weary German-hating Russians by pointing out that Japan suffered similar horrors at the hands of America. "That would do for Russia, but it would not do for China. As I went from Siberia to Irkutsk [sic] and from Irkutsk across the Gobi Desert and approached Peking, I became worried about what sort of face I should put on before the Chinese. What the Germans had done to Russia, the Japanese had done to China, and over an even longer period of time. No doubt I would be met in Peking by Chinese. And what sort of face should I wear when I saw them? There in the airplane I worried the problem over. But at length the plane carried me and my troubled little breast to Peking. We got off, and various important Chinese greeted us with the utmost warmth and consideration. There was of course nothing to make me feel in the least uncomfortable."

His apprehension was not entirely beside the point, however, Shimizu continues. Later on, when he was visiting a happy farming village, he was taken to task by a weather-beaten old farmer for Japanese imperialism. "I was no longer able to look him in the face. I shriveled before him, I stood motionless, looking at my feet. But then he added that he was speaking of Japanese imperialism, that the Japanese people were another matter. Toward the Japanese people he felt as brother toward brother, and he was sure that the Japanese people were at one with him in their love of peace. Japanese imperialism and the Japanese people were two different things. And so I was able to look him in the face again."

Is it uncharitable to feel that the "guilt" here is a rhetorical device to make one melt toward the forgiving Chinese?

Another thing: that remark about how the Japanese suffered at the hands of the Americans as the Russians suffered at the hands of the Germans does not sit very well on one's stomach. It is dangerously near self-pity, and if Shimizu and his countrymen really feel as guilty as all that, might it not occur to them that they perhaps— just perhaps—brought their sufferings upon themselves? If trying to conquer China was a crime, then bombing the chief Pacific base of the country that most clearly stood in the way of that conquest and others was at least a misdemeanor. To argue otherwise is to argue that one should not steal, but one may feel free to blackjack the night watchman who tries to stop one. (The question here is of course not whether a crime was committed, but whether certain professions of guilt are genuine.)

Similar considerations come up every August during the orgy of self-pity that commemorates the dropping of the atom bomb. I felt in 1945 and I feel now that the dropping of the bomb was a hideous error morally and politically; but the way in which the annual festival is turned into an anti-American rally confuses the distribution of guilt, to say the least. There is something exasperatingly simpleminded about the Americans who go off to Hiroshima each summer to ask to be forgiven, and about the Japanese who, with calm, long-suffering, tea-ceremony smiles, forgive them.

One more point, and the tirade is over. Even toward Asians, the "guilt" seems a trifle limited and partial. If one is really conscious of having committed a crime, then one should feel most contrite toward the people who have suffered most grievously. No one has suffered more grievously than Chiang Kai-shek, who might even today be in Nanking and whose government might not have become so venal if he had not had to fight the Japanese and the Communists simultaneously. He may be a congenital tyrant who deserved to be driven from the mainland. I don't know. The simple fact remains that he and his regime suffered grievously from the Japanese invasion.

Again, might it not be reasonable to expect a more charitable view of the Koreans? They are not showing much talent for governing themselves, perhaps; but some of their ineptitude might be due to the fact that they began their experience of the modern world with three and a half decades during which they were not even allowed a try at governing themselves.

(May 23, 1959)

We all know the pat notions abroad about Japan, land of paper houses, land of clever imitators, land where there is something of beauty in even the poorest house. We also know fairly well where the notions came from: on our side, from Pierre Loti and Lafcadio Hearn and the dweller on the Yokohama Bluff, on their side from Okakura Tenshin and Professor Suzuki and the rest.

We also know the pat notions the Japanese have about us. Germany is a land of philosophers and scientists and orchestra conductors, France is a land of artists, England is a land of gentlemen (why have the English so much more than the rest of us succeeded in pushing their ladies into the background?). And America is a land of aloha shirts and race riots and materialism.

We want to ask questions about them, however. Why do the Japanese always seem to have a German conductor around, but never an Italian? Why does the presence of all those foreigners in the School of Paris have no effect upon the monopoly the French are supposed to have on modern art? As for America, the one complaint all the Japanese travelers bring back is about American indifference to good food. But is not indifference to food indicative of precisely the reverse of materialism? And by what processes did these over-simplifications develop?

I have just been reading a book which would suggest that the fixed idea about America, at least, was fairly late in coming. The book in question is the "North American" (by which is meant that it covers the United States and Canada) volume in an ambitious collection of travel literature.

It contains accounts of Japanese trips to North America from the middle of the Meiji period down to but yesterday. The earliest travelers did not like America, some of them, but there is a certain eagerness, an adventurousness, in their writings that sets them apart from their more recent fellows. The latter frequently seem to know what they are going to see before they start out.

The very earliest traveler represented is Katayama Sen, who went to the United States in 1884. He was at the time a Christian, but he was later to help with the founding of the American Communist Party and to end his career in Moscow as Japanese representative on the Comintern. Apparently he was on the verge of starvation a number of times during his stay in America, and yet his reminiscences are remarkable for their lack of bitterness. He tells us what fond memories he has of Alameda, California, but when he proceeds to describe his life there the story is one of overwork and misunderstanding. His schoolmates—for he had decided to study English and the Bible—called him "Catty," and this he took to be a derogatory likening of a Japanese to a cat. He withdrew in high dudgeon.

The recently deceased Nagai Kafū went to the United States about twenty years later. He sent back some lyrical descriptions of nature, which he observed in such places as Asbury Park and Kalamazoo, but in America as elsewhere his chief interest was women: a girl named Stella who sang "Dixie" to him one night in Chicago, a loose little thing named Edyth who almost persuaded him to take her to France with him. In a New York bar, a pert doxy sat down beside him, asked for a cigarette, gave him a prim kiss, and hummed "Will You Love Me in December as You Do in May?" Unfortunately some sailors then caught her interest, and he had to leave alone.

Then there are his descriptions of Chinatown, which do not show America at its most lovely. Here are the broken-down ladies he found lolling in the back streets: "The rags on their twisted bodies barely saved them from nakedness, and their watery eyes were like rotten oysters. It was as if they lived only to nourish the fleas. Their matted white hair like tatters of cotton, they sought shelter from the rain and the dew in the corridors of tenements, under the floors, in public toilets, and they somehow kept themselves alive by doing laundry for the prostitutes."

Not precisely the picture of The American Way that USIS likes to see disseminated. What one likes in these early descriptions, however, is their freedom from preconceived notions.

Though it is dangerous to draw firm conclusions from a single book, and a hastily read book at that, it would appear that the stereotype of America began to emerge not as a result of the Portsmouth Treaty or the Japanese Exclusion, both of which were causes of great resentment, but rather from those troubled days of economic depression, nationalist extremism, and frustrated Marxism, the late twenties and the early thirties.

The first real dose of it in this book is presented by a man who is still very much in the news, the novelist Ishikawa Tatsuzō. A highly emotional and impulsive man, he once told his countrymen that they had much to learn from the New China about the necessary limits to their freedom. He came back from the Soviet Writers' Congress a few days ago, however, apparently convinced that it is not such a bad thing after all to have a government to dislike and to be allowed to dislike. Since he is a most influential man, this new view may prove to be important, a sort of Japanese version of Gide's views on the U.S.S.R. That, however, is a matter of now and later, and the matter for consideration here is one of thirty years ago.

Here is Ishikawa writing of the United States in 1930:

> America, a country which sticks its nose into the problems of the whole world, and, gaining hostility as a result, retires feeling aggrieved—a new country of unlimited violence and high-handedness.
>
> America, a country which flaunts violence under the name of justice, which pushes world armament under the name of peace. . . .
>
> America, which under the banner of mass production boasts of being "first in the world," and marches triumphantly forward as it spreads terror and depression among the economies of the world. . . .
>
> America, which says that *Uncle Tom's Cabin* is a thing of the past and yet practices cruelty upon the Negro, and which has gained the resentment of all colored races.
>
> America, land of contradictions.
>
> America, land of journalism.
>
> America, land of the ready-made.

The details of the stereotype are all there, and others, too—references to bourgeois waste, for instance, which indicate the ideological leanings of the young Ishikawa. On the other side is another well-known novelist, Mushakōji Saneatsu, who was so fervently behind the government in its expansionist scheme that he was one of the few writers to be purged by the Occupation. Taking advantage of the fact that his brother was ambassador to Germany, he made a trip to Europe and the United States in 1936. His notes on the train journey across the United States are mostly complaints about drabness, monotony, sameness, bad food, and a lack of spiritual qualities—at least spiritual qualities communicable to one who does not know a word of English. Here is one such passage: "Westerners are not unpleasant. They are pleased with themselves, however. There is not a person on this train who seems spiritual. No doubt they are very practical people, but there is not one who seems really clever and intelligent."

And mind you, he does not know a word of English.

The far Left and the far Right have a great deal more in common than either is prepared to admit, and the evidence from this book is that between them they created the fixed notion of the United States some two or three decades ago.

Not that there has not been a certain amount of variety since. The young novelist Mishima Yukio, for instance, seems to have gone around looking for characters and found them: a young New York actress who when he met her had had an estimated fifty lovers, a rich young dilettante, also a New Yorker, who was a friend of Tennessee Williams and Christopher Isherwood and a follower of voodooism. If Mishima's story is to be believed, the gentleman went about poking pins in pictures of people he did not like.

(June 6, 1959)

NEW DEVELOPMENTS IN DEBATE OVER COURTS

A number of events recently have reopened discussion of a very touchy and subtle problem, the proper limits upon criticism of the courts. It is a problem in every country governed upon a theory of balanced powers. The dignity of the courts must be preserved if there is to be protection against an arbitrary legislature or executive, and yet the sad fact is the courts are sometimes wrong, and they cannot be above criticism. Few countries have succeeded in solving the problem. Certainly the United States has not. Whenever the Supreme Court has been particularly courageous in protecting civil rights, one can expect the old talk about clipping its wings to come up again in Congress.

The Japanese too have been slow about finding a solution. Part of the fault lies in the courts, which occasionally seem a bit timid about protecting their own dignity. The idea of contempt of court is not wholly unknown in This Country, but it is rarely made an issue of. Some years ago, in the notorious "People's Train" case, the defendants were allowed to occupy the court benches with impunity. There have been threats against the persons of judges and their families, and these too, so far as I know, have gone unchallenged. Judges seem out to show how determined they are that the defendants should have complete latitude.

Occasionally, too, the courts have come up with decisions that impress one as patently silly.

This is not the place to go into the controversial Sunakawa decision, which declared the stationing of American troops in Japan unconstitutional. An impressive legal argument can be put together in support of Judge Date, who handed down the decision. It must be pointed out, however, that the argument is coldly legal, quite refusing to admit practical demands into the cold, self-contained world of the law—quite the reverse, in a word, of Holmes's pragmatic view of law. This sternly legalistic position is certainly an honorable one, perhaps in the final analysis the only position a person can trust. But it was with astonishment, some weeks later, that we found this same Judge Date letting a murderess off with a suspended sentence, apparently because she was a wife and mother, he felt sorry for her, and she had not meant to murder the person she had murdered. She had hoped to poison her husband, and she had poisoned her daughter instead. Where in the second decision was the cold, Prussian legal mind we grudgingly admired in the first?

The Sunakawa decision seen by itself is not transparently silly. To at least one reader of the newspapers, however, the recent Kobe decision on hit-and-run drivers is. The notion that to hit and run is a crime is of course based on the notion that having hit one does not run. One waits for the police to come, and reports what has happened. But to require a person to do so, said the Amagasaki branch of the Kobe District Court, is to violate Article 38 of the constitution, which provides that no person shall be required to testify against himself. If there is a suspicion of criminal negligence, the decision seems to say, then the act of reporting an accident is an act of self-incrimination, and cannot be required.

It follows that when a driver hits and runs and is caught and confesses, he can be taken to task for negligence, but not for having run. So why not run, everyone? You have a fighting chance of not being caught and therefore not even being taken to task for your negligence. "An infringement upon the prerogatives of the legislature," said the traffic gentleman in the National Police Agency about the Kobe decision.

Even though one sometimes feels that the courts are acting imprudently, however, the striking thing is that their imprudence has been mostly on the side of civil rights. In the "People's Train" case and in the Kobe case an eagerness to be on the side of the angels seems to have blinded the courts to the fact that human beings are not angels. Rights imply restraints and restraints must be enforced.

Be that as it may, the last people in the world one would expect to see attacking the courts are the leftish people who profess to worry so much about human rights. Yet they are the ones who really seem out to discredit the courts. A couple of weeks ago the chief justice of the Supreme Court, addressing a national assembly of judges, attacked the practice of launching "popular movements" in attempts to influence cases under adjudication. He objected specifically to the "dramatization" of cases still in the courts, the purpose of such dramatization being to discredit the courts. He did not propose specific countermeasures, but, in rather Japanese fashion, urged "deep reflection."

Two cases of such dramatization immediately come to mind. Hōjō Hideji, in his stage version of the Matsukawa train derailment case, presents the action through the eyes of the chief attorney for the defense, and by the end of a very long and scrappy play the Fukushima District Court and the Sendai Higher Court, which found the defendants guilty, are demolished to the satisfaction of Hōjō and presumably all the leftish gentlemen who have been raising such a clamor.

The other is the Yakai murder case in Hiroshima Prefecture, which the Communist director Imai Tadashi, with a bow in the direction of that Fascist Beast Arthur Koestler, filmed under the title *Darkness at Noon*. Again a court decision is made to look ridiculous, this time a decision finding that a pair of murders was committed by several people, not by a single man, as the defense has argued. It is hard to repress a suspicion that people like Imai are out to get the courts and thereby provoke general unrest. Civil rights but provide the pretext.

On May 26, the *Asahi* carried an interesting editorial about the chief justice's remarks. It pointed out an abuse that he had overlooked. "Although Chief Justice Tanaka did not touch upon it, there is a matter which we believe calls for the deepest reflection on the part of the Bar Association. As a question of professional ethics and common practice, lawyers in foreign countries consider it immoral to plead a case outside the courts while it is in litigation. In Japan, however, it seems to be the practice for the defense attorney to stand at the very head of the campaign outside the courts. . . . May we not ask the Bar Association, as one of the pillars supporting the courts, to work harder as intermediary between the courts and the people?''

Again the Matsukawa case and the Yakai case are the first that come to mind. The chief defense attorney in the former has been most clamorous in his allegations of injustice. Masaki Hiroshi, one of the defense attorneys in the latter, is an even more striking case. He is probably the most widely publicized of all Japanese criminal lawyers, and he is not a man to miss his chances for the headlines. Both in the Yakai case and in the other with which he is most flamboyantly associated (it involves an attack upon a police box in Kyushu), he has written and talked and been interviewed like mad. No Clarence Darrow ever had a better flare for self-dramatization.

The reaction to the chief justice's remarks has been mixed. Sōhyō, Japan's largest confederation of labor unions, of course did not like them. Perhaps the most sober reaction thus far has been an article by Professor Itō Masami of Tokyo University. He tries to draw a line between two conflicting constitutional principles, the independence of the courts and freedom of speech, from the assaults of which the courts are not immune.

He urges contempt-of-court proceedings against those whose actions arouse a lack of confidence in the courts. He would apply three general principles to define legitimate criticism, however: that the criticism should not be an *ad hominem* attack on a particular judge, and should not be designed to exert pressure for a specific purpose; that it should be objective; and that it should be based on matters before the court, and not on irrelevancies.

It seems clear that, accepting this attempt at definition, no court would have any trouble finding Messrs. Masaki, Imai, and Hōjō guilty of contempt. While one does not especially want to see the three gentlemen in jail, one does feel that the courts have been overly deferential, and that a contempt case now and then might not be a bad idea. Today the courts probably have the prestige to see a few controversial cases through. One day they may not.

(June 13, 1959)

LAND OF MORNING CALM AND SYNGMAN RHEE

Today we will have a few notes on That Country, the Land of the Morning Calm and Syngman Rhee, from which I have just returned.

It would be nice not to have to say anything about Korean politics and economics; but to avoid those messy subjects would be dishonest. A word about them, then, and on to more pleasant matters.

The stories one hears about the behavior of the president of the Republic are so grotesque that, if it were not for the cruelty involved, one would be tempted to call him the last surviving example of Gilbert and Sullivan's "peppery sort of potentate." The trouble is not that he is arbitrary and capricious, though those qualities make him less than a lovable man; it is rather that under him the energies of the country seem so hopelessly misdirected.

All those students out marching day after day, mechanically demonstrating against the repatriation of Koreans from Japan to North Korea—if they have that much spare time from their studies, they ought to be out planting trees and building bridges and otherwise making theirs a country which Koreans in Japan would choose in preference to the north. All those policemen out following foreigners and opposition politicians around the peninsula—they ought to be looking into the black market and official misconduct.

The remark one hears most often in Korea, from Americans and Koreans alike, goes something like this: "Korea is a very young country. You have to give it time."

Now, one's sympathies are certainly with a country that never has time to recover from one invasion before another comes, a country that moves from the most vicious sort of Oriental despotism to foreign rule to military occupation to civil war and invasion and partition. One does not wish to preach to such a country. It has already had enough.

Yet retorts to that remark about young Korea come almost automatically. Does Korea have all that much time? Whatever its defects, the administration in the north is moving ahead, and the

271

assumption in the south that there will always be dollars is not the soundest one imaginable for planning the future.

The Republic of Korea moreover impresses one less as a very new country than as a very old country that has failed to throw off its past. The administrative evils of the Yi dynasty (from which, by the way, the president of the Republic descends) are still with us, and until they are overcome it is hard to see how all the dollars in the world can do much about those misdirected energies.

I went off to Korea expecting to find a rather disagreeable people. Instead I was charmed. Nothing, to my knowledge, has been written to prepare one for the humor, the openness, the robustness, the good looks, of the Koreans. Their press notices are among the worst in the world. Partly this is because the world has taken over the Japanese view of Korea; partly it is because people who cluster about military bases are seldom the most attractive of people, and most foreigners who have been in Korea have known only such Koreans.

Here is what Terry's *Guide to the Japanese Empire* has to say about the Korean: "He steals freely when the opportunity offers. . . . The spawn of a low order of civilization, he is untidy and swinish in his habits, and apathetic in the face of work. . . . He is a born dawdler, gambler, and brawler. . . . He is lethargic, purposeless, devoid of thrift or ambition, and he dwells contentedly amidst incredible dirt and discomfort." What is this but the Japanese view of the Korean? One suspects, so inaccurate is his account of the country, that Terry never went to Korea, and hoped, by making it sound completely unbearable, to frighten off travelers who might go and discover the inaccuracy for themselves.

In all sorts of superficial ways, the Japanese have it over the Koreans. They scrub themselves more assiduously, they do not take siestas. They do not pick pockets with quite such practiced grace, they are restrained and soft-spoken.

Yet Terry's description of the Korean is so utterly wrong-headed that one hardly knows where to start correcting it. Koreans do steal, but so do other people. I have three times had my pocket picked while patronizing the Tokyo public transit system—or were the pickpockets all Koreans, as sober-faced Japanese acquaintances assure me? I found, moreover, that once one gets away from the scum around the railway stations, Koreans behave very much like rural Japanese. You deposit your baggage in some public square, announce that you mean to take the three-thirty bus, and come back at three-thirty to find the baggage there and a sort of home-defense platoon watching it, for the matter has become one of public responsibility.

It is true that Koreans are less tidy than Japanese, but I do not find this fact particularly important, and all those rivers full of soldiers suggest that, given the chance, Koreans too feel the impulse to bathe. It is true that they are hot-tempered, but I suspect that this trait has been exaggerated. A certain vehemence in their way of expressing themselves gives an impression of pugnaciousness even when it is absent. Someone comes running up and bawls something in your face, and, as you are preparing to roll up your sleeves, you learn that what he said was, "I am sorry to have kept you waiting."

And even when tempers are clearly and undeniably lost, one suddenly realizes that something has been missing all these years in a country where tempers are not lost. Koreans quite abandon themselves to their rages. Then, presently, the moment comes when they realize that they shouldn't and a most engagingly sheepish expression comes over their faces, an expression one never sees in This Country.

As for laziness and apathy, all I can say is that I simply do not agree with you, Mr. Terry. There is that hour in the early afternoon when the whole country is sprawled out under poplar trees; but, the siesta out of the way, Korean farmers go on working into the darkness even as Japanese farmers do. And you would never find an American bus driver working as hard as that Korean driver did, getting us back from the east coast in that coughing, sputtering bus. And the housekeeper of the friends I stayed with was teaching her children Japanese in her spare time, because, whatever the views of the president of the Republic, she saw that they would one day need to know Japanese, and was determined that the day would not find them unready. What is this if not the reverse of lazy and apathetic? One would not feel so upset about those misdirected energies if one did not feel that real and important energies were there to be misdirected.

I have no doubt that Koreans are as unreliable and difficult to do business with as everyone says they are. The point is, however, that something has been overlooked in the standard descriptions of them. Negatively, Terry's adjectives can be disposed of one by one; positively, the Koreans have something the devious Japanese do not. It is most refreshing to have someone look you straight in the eye and say, "That is the silliest remark I've ever heard." In Japan, the honorifics begin flying at this point, and the compliments about one's impeccable Japanese, and the expressions of wonder that one should know so much more about This Country than even the inhabitants thereof.

I saw a lovely, tear-jerking Korean movie about the assassination of Prince Itō. There was wild applause as the prince fell, and there were sobs from both sexes when the Korean assassin went to his death. To me, however, the fine moment was a brilliant parody by a Korean actress of a genteel Japanese laugh. All the resentment of the decades under the Japanese was in that parody, and all the annoyance of a people that likes to laugh and wishes others did too.

For the great charm of the Koreans is in their genius for comedy. The Japanese simply do not have it, and it is good to know that there is another country so near and so different to go to when, as does happen, I get a bit tired of This Country.

(June 27, 1959)

TIBETAN RIGHTS AND SINO-INDIAN FEELINGS

Going off to some country nearby, one is immediately struck with the fact that there is very little lateral communication among the countries of Asia. People are always talking about "One Asia" and participating in Asian writers' conferences and the like, where they have brief but intoxicating drafts of oneness.

Yet in many ways Asia seems less the vast spiritual commune it likes to call itself than a collection of isolated valleys that know far more about what is happening at some distant center than about what is happening in the neighboring valley. Modest cultural stirrings in Paris are presently picked up in New Delhi and Manila and Seoul and Tokyo; but it takes the next thing to a revolution in Seoul to attract any attention in Tokyo. Or at least it takes some new piece of Korean truculence that touches directly upon the interests of This Country and makes it think sadly of the good days when the Koreans could be kept in their place.

It is becoming clear that the Tibetan unpleasantness did not really bother the Japanese, certainly not as much as the Hungarian unpleasantness. Two facts, or perhaps the face and the reverse of the same fact, help a great deal to explain the indifference: the Japanese, although they profess to fret a great deal about being "the orphan of Asia," do not really know much or worry much about the rest of Asia; and they at the same time feel a strong emotional resistance to any hint that Asia might not be one after all. For if Asia is not one, what happens to the Asian spiritual superiority we keep hearing about? It becomes an imaginary attribute of an imaginary entity.

Somewhat reluctantly, one senses, the monthly magazines are beginning to have something to say about Tibet. There is little sign that anyone is really much concerned about learning what happened there, and, on the other hand, there seems to be an intense, obsessive desire to be reassured that Nehru's Panch Silla (the five principles that make Asia one vast, peaceful community) are still alive and among us.

The July *Chūō Kōron* says nothing about the disturbances proper. It does, however, carry a brief article about the background, by Miss Nakane Chie, a lecturer at Tokyo University. Although Miss Nakane's manner is objective and restrained, her article seems calculated to leave one with the impression that Tibet's independence has for the most part been a fiction, and that the Chinese are therefore justified in calling the whole affair an internal one. She is also careful to point out that the Dalai Lamas exercised political power for a relatively short time, and that Lamaism is based on a system of land tenure both "feudal" and "medieval."

"Irrespective of Chinese advances," says Miss Nakane, "it was inevitable, within the meaning of world history, that the medieval political, economic, and social structure of Tibet would sooner or later travel the way to modernization. . . . The disbanding of the aristocracy and of the monasteries that rest upon the same structure will probably be accomplished, as in the rest of Asia, through land reform." Although Miss Nakane seems to be advising the Chinese to move slowly lest they have a real religious war on their hands, the implication is clear that the goals the Chinese have set themselves in Tibet are proper.

To which Professor Tanaka Michitarō recently gave the perfect answer in the *Yomiuri Shimbun*: when Mussolini moved into Ethiopia, he announced to the world that what he was doing was for the good of a stubbornly backward nation. Ethiopia must one day travel the way to modernization.

Not of course that the two cases are exactly parallel. Everyone admitted that Ethiopia was independent, not everyone admits as much for Tibet. Miss Nakane, for instance, seems to believe that real Tibetan independence, or at least real power in the hands of the Dalai Lamas, was a matter of only a few decades when a highly abnormal international balance kept various greedy hands off.

One would have to know a great deal more about Tibetan history than I do to be able to answer her. One can say with some confidence, however, that the issue is in doubt, and that respectable people are to be found who will argue that Tibet was never any more a part of China than was Korea, say, or Okinawa, and therefore that Chinese operations against Tibet amount to imperialist expansion.

Here, for instance, are some remarks made recently by the Indian statesman Jayaprakash Narayan: "Tibet is not a region of China. It is a country by itself which has sometimes passed under Chinese suzerainty by virtue of conquest and never by free choice. Chinese suzerainty has always been of the most nominal kind and meant hardly more than some tribute paid to Peking by Lhasa. At other times Tibet was an independent sovereign country. For some time in the eighth century Peking paid a yearly tribute of fifty thousand yards of Chinese brocade to Tibet. . . .

"There are some who say that facts of history must be taken into account and if Tibet has sometimes been under China, it is irrelevant to raise the question of Tibetan independence now. . . . According to the logic of this viewpoint, Hungary, for example, having long been a part of the Austro-Hungarian empire should never be entitled to independence."

The July *Sekai* carries a panel discussion on "The Problem of Tibet and Sino-Indian Relations." The chairman, Yoshino Genzaburō, editor of the magazine, poses several questions, among them whether or not Tibet is comparable to Hungary, and whether or not there has been a significant worsening of relations between India and China.

In reply, Katō Shūichi, a physician and journalistic jack-of-all-trades, answers both questions negatively, and gives precise formulation to what is evidently becoming the orthodox "liberal" view of Tibet. Katō does not think that the Chinese have gotten a sufficiently charitable press. In the first place, it has not been adequately emphasized that the whole problem is an internal one and that Tibet is in no way comparable to Hungary. Standing Narayan on his head, Katō argues that Tibet has been Chinese even when the Chinese have not been in a position to assert their sovereignty.

In the second place, he thinks that the Tibetan class struggle has not been as carefully studied as it ought to be. The Chinese have emphasized a conflict of classes, he argues, and the Indians a conflict of nationalities. The Japanese press has tended to ignore the Chinese claim. "Japanese newspapers, as a third party, have given far too little emphasis to the class conflict. They have discussed the problem far too much as one of nationalities. They have hardly touched upon the problem of what stratum of Tibetan society—dividing it, for instance, into a landlord class and an impoverished peasant class—was chiefly responsible for the disturbances."

Katō then makes a point familiar to those of us who watched the Japanese reaction to Hungary, that we must wait until all the evidence is in; and, finally, he offers it as his view that only a few people were involved, and that the Tibetan masses remained undisturbed by the unpleasant happenings. It may be pointed out in passing that these last two points rather cancel each other out. If we do not have sufficient evidence on which to make judgments, how can we judge that the masses remained indifferent? As at the time of Hungary, one detects a certain tendency to eat and have the cake simultaneously.

The members of the panel generally agree that China acted within its rights. On the question of whether or not India is mature enough to see that fact and go on being friendly—of whether or not Panch Silla still lives—there is unqualified optimism from Katō, hedged optimism from the others. It is odd how Nehru, until yesterday the darling of the "progressives," has come to be on the defensive. Since the Chinese have done nothing wrong, the responsibility for any worsening of relations between the two countries obviously rests with him.

(July 5, 1959)

PERSONAL REMARKS ON RELATIONS WITH JAPAN

The time would seem to have come for some rather personal remarks about relations between This Country and me. Somewhere along the way there has been a breakdown in communication, the result, I suppose, of a certain persistently sour note in this column. I have tried to keep it out, but obviously it has crept in. Too many people have noticed it and complained of it.

Since this column first began to appear, something over half a year ago, the remark I have heard most often about it has been rather like the remark we used to make to Italians and Mexicans and Swedes when I was very young: "If you don't like it here, why don't you go back where you came from?" In This Country, of course, it is usually phrased more delicately: "We must apologize for not having made your stay a happier one," or something to that effect.

The trouble is, I do like being here. I like This Country and its inhabitants, or much of it and many of them. Since this column has been what we call a thoughtful one (thoughtful in the other sense—not the sense of heedful or considerate), however, there has really not been much to say about the likable things. Above all I have wanted to avoid Quaint Japanese Customs or My Impressions of Japan or A Foreigner Looks at the Geisha or The Night I First Slept on the Floor.

The major subject has been the Japanese intellectual and his ways. If there has been sourness on that subject, it has been nothing compared to the sourness there might have been had I not continually been reminded that I was a guest of This Country.

It is very strange, but I have on the whole been spared the annoyances with which other people meet. I have found the policemen polite and not overly intrusive, and I have found the Tokyo taxi driver friendly, engaging, and unbelievably honest. I once upbraided a driver for taking me the long way home, and, in my self-righteous desire to determine how much he had cheated me of, discovered that the way he had brought me was shorter than the way I would have chosen myself.

I have found the bureaucracy much friendlier and more helpful than its American counterpart, of which I was a member. I have had trouble with the Immigration Bureau, but it has been largely of my own making. Once when I left the country, the inspector told me that I was free to go if I must, but that a failure to have certain changes made in my re-entry permit might lead to difficulties when I came back, and, given my "important work" (his actual words), he would prefer not to see this happen. I went anyway, and there was trouble. Eventually it was straightened out. In the process I detected no sign of impatience or hostility on the part of the bureaucracy. Another time I was late in applying to have my alien registration amended. What was my excuse, asked the gentleman at the counter. I had none, I replied. He shrugged his shoulders and quietly predated the application.

I have not found Japanese service particularly bad, and I have not been particularly struck with xenophobia in NHK. I have been spared the disagreeable experience of being turned away from bars because I do not look like an inhabitant of This Country. The people who have been turned away have cause to complain. Their experience has been different from mine, that is all. I must conclude that mine has been exceptionally pleasant.

Eleven years in Japan, and not a single brush with an obdurate bureaucrat, not a single impulse to write a letter to an editor somewhere about how that fruitcake from Aunt Edna was detained by customs! One way of avoiding unpleasantness, insofar as it has been consciously avoided, has been to remember that customs officers tend to be fussy in most places and consequently to call Aunt Edna off in advance. Another has been not to own an automobile.

Tokyo is much the most interesting city I have ever lived in, and the most interesting I am ever likely to. Just to be able to wander through it is enough compensation for the trials of life among the magazines and the intellectuals. Sometimes Tokyo seems so given over to pleasure as to be depraved, sometimes it seems the very embodiment of young wholesomeness. No city has greater variety, and no city is in fact so many different cities. You can move on to a new Tokyo as soon as the old one begins to pall, and, in changing cities, you are spared the nuisance of travel.

All of this I like, then, and all of this is reason enough for not much wanting, at least at the moment, to go back where I came from.

What I cannot abide in This Country, and what has been the cause of the sourness, is its "progressive intellectuals." Their capacity for self-deception and the deception of others quite passes belief. To people who have not had to follow their activities in the monthly magazines, I can only say: "Very well, I may be sour, but you do not know what the provocation to sourness has been."

Each time I pick up a new pronouncement by Shimizu Ikutarō or Hani Gorō or Nakano Yoshio or Abe Tomoji, I sit in quiet meditation for a few minutes, trying to muster my resources to get through the thing without retching. I never succeed.

It is difficult to know where the self-deception ends and the willful deception of others begins. (Or perhaps where a canny eye for the market begins, as when progressive intellectuals start turning things out for the progressive students who picket the Anglo-Saxon embassies and buy *Sekai*.) Can these people really believe that what they are advocating is "neutral"? That the sort of "neutrality" which they, along with the Communist Party, keep talking about is not in fact highly advantageous to one of the two sides?

I do not know. I only know that someone is being deceived when a person's every word and action is aimed at helping the Soviet Union, and yet he goes on telling us that he is "neutral." It is not here to the point whether the Soviet Union ought to be helped or not. There are those who think that the Soviet Union stands for peace and the United States for war. I do not agree, but I am not here interested in refuting them. Nor, indeed, am I much interested in the nature of their relations with the Communist Party.

The important thing is rather the enormous fraud and deception in doing the work of the Soviet Union and cloaking it in expressions like "neutrality"; in professing to be worried about human rights and doing everything possible to weaken the countries that are the defense of what tattered rights we have left. At least one knows where a Communist stands: his "neutrality" is utterly cynical, and the whole notion of human rights is to him so much bourgeois sentimentality, designed to hide the slavery that is the true state of the proletarian masses.

You can call an admitted Communist a Communist and go on from there. But try pointing out to the "progressives" what seems to you objective fact, that they are doing the work of the Soviet Union, and you are immediately accused of being a primitive McCarthyite and a CIA agent. Any attempt to cut through to the assumptions behind their argument leads to an outraged severing of relations.

"I don't dislike Red. It's Pink that I can't stand," a very eminent Japanese gentleman recently said to an acquaintance of mine. He could not have put the matter more succinctly. It is the layer of shocking pink that makes one occasionally want to write a sardonic column about This Country. On the whole, though, it is a very nice country.

(July 18, 1959)

MAGAZINES GO ON ASSAILING CATHOLICS

The questioning of a Belgian priest in the case of a murdered BOAC hostess was the signal for the opening of an attack on the Catholic Church that shows no sign of stopping. It has been conducted on all levels, from weekly scandal sheets with details of happy hours spent by Roman collars in love nests, to sober monthlies that accuse the Church of laxness and lethargy in the handling of its Japanese affairs.

The quality of the articles has, on the whole, been directly related to the quality of the magazines carrying them. Now, however, comes the exception. A responsible and highly respected magazine, *Bungei Shunjū*, has in its August issue a piece that takes one straight back to the worst cross-burning days of the Ku Klux Klan. It is by one Takase Hiroi (whom no one seems to know—perhaps he is using a pseudonym), and it is called "The Inside Stuff about the Red-headed Priests."

It is hard to know what nerve or complex of nerves the Catholic Church touches to make the Japanese intellectuals cry so stridently against it. As the *Bungei Shunjū* title suggests, the attack is fundamentally anti-foreign. Again as the title suggests, the Church seems to them clandestine, conspiratorial, furtive. Because of its undeniably close relationship to the Middle Ages, it strikes them as having that most undesirable of qualities, feudality. Because it is unique among religious organizations in having a foreign service, it opens itself to charges of pursuing its interests under the cloak of extraterritoriality. In sum, it fills the insular Japanese with the blackest suspicions.

Whatever its causes, the *Bungei Shunjū* article is a real shocker. The Mafia just isn't in it with the Roman Catholic Church. Here, for instance, is an informant peeking tremulously in at the ritual by which priests "purge" (probably this means "excommunicate") one of their fellows for incontinence: "A foreign priest, kneeling before the altar. The head of the monastery, who is to conduct the ceremony. The attendant priests, mumbling prayers. At length the officiating priest, with his back to the altar, laid his hand on the shoulder of the kneeling priest and tore off his clerical robes with a harsh ripping sound. One could hear the pure white Roman collar fall to the floor. The kneeling priest raised his hands. Taking up a piece of glass, the head of the monastery scraped deep into the two upraised hands, first the right and then the left—then the glass moved from the forehead to the eyes to the mouth."

At this point Takase, as is the way with writers of articles for the Japanese monthlies, seems to forget what he has been talking about. Having described the harsh punishments the Church has in reserve for misbehaving priests, he goes on to describe the ease and apparently the impunity with which "foreign priests" misbehave. Although the documentation is not exactly impeccable, there is an impressive list of cases: devout little Japanese girls who have suffered that most awful of fates at the hands of their spiritual mentors, other devout young ladies whose fate is less clear but whose happiest hours are spent "in the priest's room," hot-blooded young priests who are found serenading under (unless I misread it) the convent window, and so on. There is one rather charming little piece of whimsy: a priest, nationality unspecified, encountered a young lady who made use of the confessional to confess her love for him, and so he stopped being a priest and became a greengrocer instead.

The atrocities out of the way, the article begins to move on to what would seem to be its main burden: that the Catholic Church is an affront to Japanese national honor. We learn that, unlike the Protestant missions, the Catholic missions are dominated by foreign priests and foreign money. We learn that the Church meddles in politics, as when a lady communicant was ordered in the confessional to vote for a certain conservative candidate. We learn that the Catholic Church is a totalitarian organization. By gradual steps we seem to be led back to the seventeenth century, when the Catholic Church was considered a political threat. But in the end Takase remembers himself, and is able to dismiss the Church and all its missionaries with a scornful laugh. He asks a question of them: "You priests with the blue eyes, aren't there things you could better be doing in your own country? And I have heard that the Catholic orders are strangely lax in sexual matters. In the Orient we say that when the individual cultivates himself the country is in order and there is peace under heaven. Suppose you have a taste of this maxim now and then."

However one feels about the Catholic Church, there is something so nasty and self-righteous about this that one wonders for the future of all the Christian missions. They have suffered in the past from a kind of Japanese nationalism that is not yet dead.

A few very pleasant days sunning and diving along the Shima Peninsula have been the occasion for a few more thoughts about This Country and its intellectuals.

In Tokyo, amid the clamor of printing presses, one occasionally has the uneasy feeling that the progressives may in fact be doing what they think they are doing, leading the country into the future. But one only has to step into the provinces to feel how completely bourgeois they (the intellectuals) are, with their fussy Shinjuku bars, their suburban "homes," their ranch-type houses in Karuizawa. Like intellectuals in most places, they are cut off from "the people." The chief difference is that they profess to be speaking for the people; and so they may be even more decisively cut off than the rest of us, since they do not yet realize what has happened.

For another thing, one knows again upon going into the provinces how good it is to meet people who are completely competent at what they are doing. In Tokyo too this happens occasionally. I have twice been trapped into radio interviews with professional baseball players, and each time I have been reduced to awed silence at the man's sheer command of his calling. In the provinces this same competence is apparent everywhere, most apparent, perhaps, among people who work on the sea. The aplomb with which those girls dive into forests of seaweed and come up with octopi—it is truly awesome. One afternoon we lost the anchor. "Hard luck, old man," I said, "but I suppose you can buy another. Shall we go back?" But not those girls: they started diving and soon they had it, and we were able to stay out the rest of the day.

Thus one realizes that another thing one has against the intellectuals is their incompetence. Their function presumably is to think. But when a statement like "Arms make war; therefore Japan should not have arms" passes as tight thinking, well, something is wrong with the people who are doing the thinking.

Finally, it only takes a few days on the Shima Peninsula to make one realize again what a nice country this is. Hating to leave Tokyo to go to the Shima Peninsula, and hating to leave the Shima Peninsula to come back to Tokyo, I started wondering how many places in Japan I have been able to leave without regret. Sasebo, certainly. Just possibly Yokohama, and just possibly Hokkaido, though I am not sure of them. In my native country, on the other hand, the only practical thing would be to count up the places I have ever wanted to stay longer in.

(July 25, 1959)

FADS AND NOVELTIES IN JAPANESE LANGUAGE

Probably it is a sign of approaching middle age when linguistic novelties that would, in one's youth, have struck one as fresh and charming begin to seem affected and pretentious and even vulgar. This does not mean that the fresh rhetoric of a Mark Twain or a J. D. Salinger no longer delights. It is rather that many of the would-be novelties no longer ring true. They seem to serve no purpose other than to divert one's attention from the essential dullness of what is being said.

Thus the sportswriter hopes, by calling a pitcher a moundsman, to take you out to the ball game and make you forget that there is nothing duller than a recounting of the game you saw on television yesterday. And the journalist in general seems to hope that all of those inanimate possessives—Japan's Kishi, Long Beach's Miss Universe and so on—will give you the feeling that you are keeping up with *Time*, the Weekly Newsmagazine.

Here is what that finest of writers on tradition and change in language, H. W. Fowler, had to say about the inanimate possessive: "It begins to seem likely that 'drink's victims' will before long be the natural and no longer the affected or rhetorical version of 'the victims of drink.' The devotees of inflexion may do well to rejoice;

the change may improve rather than injure the language; and if that is so let due praise be bestowed on the newspaper press, which is bringing it about; but to the present (or perhaps it is already past) generation, which has been instinctively aware of differences between 'drink's victims' and 'the victims of drink,' and now finds them scornfully disregarded, there will be an unhappy interim."

The problem, as Fowler suggests, is a very subtle one. It is impossible to prevent change, and silly to resent it, even when it has, to any impartial judge, been change for the worse—when, for instance, a useful distinction has been lost. It was rather nice back in the days when everyone made a distinction between "disinterested" and "uninterested," but most people no longer do, and that is the end of the matter. "Ohio's Governor" may at the moment have about it the sound of one who has read too deeply of the Weekly Newsmagazine or listened too long to the Far East Network, but possibly the day is coming when "the Governor of Ohio" will sound as quaint as "wherefore" and "howbeit" and "withal" do now.

Yet it is perhaps neither silly nor uncharitable to resent faddism, and to feel misgivings about changes which are being pushed so fast that communication seems about to break down.

Fashionable jargon is the great evil of American English. Since this column must eventually be pulled back to This Country, I shall say of American English only that I resent it very much to go back to the United States and find that no one can talk about "our town" any more. It has to be "our community." No one ever buys "a house" any more. It has to be "a home."

It would be presumptuous to feel resentful or fearful about changes in a language not one's own. One can say nevertheless that Japanese is more a victim of faddishness and reckless change than perhaps any other language in the world. A number of Japanese gentlemen middle-aged and above seem both fearful and resentful.

Some months ago Tanizaki Jun'ichirō, a novelist and one of the respected elders of Japanese letters, accused Ōe Kenzaburō, a young novelist who has made something of a splash this last year or so, of illiteracy. For all the flashiness of his style, Ōe has trouble keeping his nominatives and objectives straight. This month three distinguished scholars, gathered in a round-table discussion for an academic magazine, have in effect repeated the charge. Ōe, they say, is so fond of lurid imagery (it seems to derive ultimately from the French) that he often forgets to give his sentences subjects and predicates. He also has a way of using quite ordinary words in a context they were not made for. Thus someone leaps astride a horse and gallops away not "rapidly" but "richly."

More than once I have asked Japanese acquaintances for an interpretation of an Ōe sentence, and have had them throw up their hands and say: "I don't know what it is, but it is not Japanese." Yet he does seem to mean something to the young people who are his chief readers. Perhaps they, like him, were taught to write in a day when other things seemed more pressing than giving a sentence a subject and a predicate. Perhaps, again, Japanese is being changed so rapidly at the hands of people like Ōe that the generations are literally finding it hard to talk to each other.

Ōe may be reckless, but at least he can be given credit for trying to say something that no other Japanese writer of fiction has said. More reprehensible are the out-and-out faddists, the people who can think of nothing new to say but can think of all sorts of chic ways to say it. The three gentlemen who attack Ōe this month also attack another person, a critic named Haniya, for writing not Japanese but a direct translation from French. It is not easy to describe exactly what this means, though the effect is rather like the style of the American Germanist who, an unkind critic said, "let all of his verbs with a dull thud at the end of the sentence fall."

This sort of studied contempt for the Japanese language always seems to make a great hit with students. So does another sort of faddishness, the introduction of as many foreign words into a sentence as possible. In a most entertaining article for the August issue of *Gunzō*, Iwabuchi Etsutarō, who is on the staff of the National Language Research Institute, describes listening to a learned professor with a fondness for English and German. The gentleman seems to be speaking of international reciprocity, and here is what he has to say (the words in single quotes are all in English or German or Latin in the "Japanese" original): "On the question of 'co-operation' in this matter, we would be prepared for 'Mitarbeit' if both sides were on an 'equal footing.' The 'equal footing' is only 'nominal,' however, and 'de facto' one side is 'cardinal' and the other is 'complemental,' and we cannot expect success."

Iwabuchi points out that perfectly good Japanese words are ready and waiting to be used in all these cases. The professor's students might have understood him better had he used them, but the performance would not have been half so grand.

A fondness for foreign words where Japanese words will do just as well seems to be one of the chief marks of spic-and-span, up-to-date, Weekly Newsmagazine Japanese. You go into a restaurant and ask for a glass of *gyūnyū*, and the young lady replies, "You mean milk?" You ask for *gohan* with your sardines, and she says, "Do you, perhaps, mean 'rice'?" Iwabuchi tells another amusing story, of a small boy who went on a *hansuto*. *Suto* is of course an abbreviation for *sutoraiki* or "strike," and since *han* means "half," the young man thought he was going on a sort of semi-strike or slowdown. When informed that what he had actually undertaken was a hunger strike (*hangaa sutoraiki*, abbreviated *hansuto*), he decided that he was not so angry after all.

All of these various details may seem trivial, but they add up to considerable linguistic confusion. Poets are not talking nonsense when they speak of their duty to purify the speech of the tribe. One suspects at times that an inability to call a town a town and a house a house has led to a sentimental flabbiness in the whole of American culture. Be that as it may, it is surely a most serious matter when the inhabitants of a country can no longer understand one another, and This Country, with its linguistic fads and quick change acts, does sometimes seem to be moving in that direction.

(Aug. 8, 1959)

EVERYTHING WILL BE DAIJŌBU, JUST RELAX

I have an acquaintance who is compiling a sort of private Japanese-English dictionary. Much the best entry in it thus far is *daijōbu*, which in Kenkyūsha's Japanese-English dictionary is defined as "safe, sure, all right," but which in my acquaintance's dictionary is defined as "imminent disaster."

A great deal of Japanese history and contemporary Japanese intellectual life is to be accounted for by the *daijōbu* spirit, the tendency to take the sanguine view when most sensible people find the arguments for the gloomy view almost irresistible. True, this spirit served the Japanese very well in their early modern history, when they challenged and defeated two enormous foreign powers. It served them rather less well when, in 1941, they challenged several more powers. Yet the experience seems to have made little difference. If the "progressive" intellectual today means what he says, and is not merely deceiving himself and trying to deceive us, then his view of the international situation is extraordinarily sunny.

As has been suggested earlier in this column, there are grounds for thinking that a wish to mislead does characterize the writings of many intellectuals. There are other grounds, however, for thinking that the Japanese as a nation have a way of taking the sanguine view. I know nothing about business. I have however heard a number of stories about the Japanese trader which suggest that he too is steeped in the *daijōbu* spirit. He will propose to meet deadlines which people familiar with the conditions of Japanese production are likely to consider impossible, and he will airily answer *daijōbu* as the deadlines approach and there seems to be no smoke coming from the factory chimneys.

As for this same airy optimism in the intellectual's approach to international problems, it can perhaps best be illustrated by the conversation a person is always having with the "neutralists." It must be remembered that a desire to conceal the speaker's political inclinations and ultimate wishes for the nation may lie behind certain of the remarks. Taken at face value, however, they add up to sunniness itself.

PERSON: "I have just seen your article in *Chūō Kōron*."

NEUTRALIST: "You read it, did you? I am much moved. You show so much more interest in and understanding of these vital problems than even we Japanese do."

P: "I take it that you are in favor of neutralism. And what does that mean?

N: "That Japan is to belong to no military alliance, but, independent of both sides and at the same time a bridge between East and West, is to work for a lessening of world tensions."

"And you feel that this offers no risks for Japan itself?"

"Quite the reverse. With the lessening of world tensions Japan's position will be secure. Japan will be able to live in the peace for which all Japanese long, since the Japanese, unlike Americans, have known the true horror of war."

"But perhaps I do not make myself clear. There are those who think that too much emphasis on peace is itself risky. A defenseless, pacifist country might be peacefully occupied by one of the communist nations."

"Oh, but indeed, sir, I would be the last person to wish to see that happen."

"You feel, then, that your neutralism contains guarantees that that will not happen. Am I to understand that Japan is to be heavily armed, like such neutralist countries as Switzerland and Sweden?"

"Rearmament means increasing world tensions. Besides, it is unconstitutional."

"An unarmed Japan, then, can be considered free from the danger of attack. And why should this be?"

"Japan is a poor country."

"You mean that no one would want Japan? No one would want the richest country in Asia, and the single industrialized country in Asia?"

"Japan is a poor country. Besides, the Soviet Union and the New China are too busy building their own economies to think about expanding abroad."

"It might be said on the other hand that communism has thus far succeeded in expanding only in the wake of war, and that it might be willing to undertake a cheap and not very dangerous little war for the sake of Japanese industry."

"You Americans. Always seeing everything black and white. Anyway, we would not be able to defend ourselves. How could we defend ourselves in the atomic age?"

"No country could defend itself in the event of war. You fail to see an important reason for having arms: they are in large part meant to frighten off people who could defeat you but might not be willing to make the sacrifice. Don't you see that a foreign power might be unwilling to make the sacrifice which the invasion of an inadequately armed Japan would require, and yet might be quite willing to have the prize if no sacrifice at all were required?"

"I do not think that the New China and the Soviet Union want war. And besides, an invasion of Japan would mean a world war. They are not prepared to risk that."

"Ah, now. What you are saying is that Japan is safe because an invader would face the threat of American retaliation. Japan can afford the luxury of neutrality, then, because the United States is there. But do you not catch a hint of inconsistency in your position? On the one hand you rely on American strength, and on the other you are intent on tearing it down. Your 'neutralism' means a considerable lessening of American strength without a comparable change on the other side."

"We do not need your armed strength. All we need is normal relations with the New China, and guarantees of Japanese neutrality."

In the end, it all comes down to this last remark. There is really no answering it. Perhaps the Soviet Union and the New China do indeed want to live in peace, perhaps a wholly unarmed Japan, without the backing of other powers, would be in no danger, perhaps "poor" Japan would be of no interest to its big neighbors.

Events may one day prove all of these things true, and again may prove all of them false. The point is that the "neutralist" gives the sanguine answer to every question. It should not surprise us that he seems, on the whole, to be at odds with the statesman, whose duty it is as a matter of principle to take the gloomy view. When you may need to be on your guard and then again you may not, it is well to give the greater weight, if you are a statesman, to the former possibility.

But no amount of pointing this out can dim the sunniness of the "progressive" view. The New China wants peace, and that is that. It is in this context that the visit of the vice-president of the United States to the Soviet Union comes as a minor disaster. A clever and, on the whole, self-serving American politician has given the world the impression that tensions are relaxing when in fact agreement is no nearer on any controversial point.

Here is the way the "progressives" have been getting at a person lately.

PROGRESSIVE: "Isn't it nice that tensions are relaxing."

PERSON: "Are they, now?"

PRO: "Why, your own vice-president, who is certainly not pro-Russian, seems to think so."

PER: "I have on the whole not been inclined to think him a reliable guide. And where specifically do you note a relaxing of tensions? The Berlin crisis is about to be solved?"

"Without a doubt."

"How? We are told to give up Berlin. Do you think we will?"

"The Berlin problem will be solved as other problems are solved."

"And what other problems are being solved?"

"Khrushchev will go to the U.S. Eisenhower will go to the Soviet Union, they will talk things over. How nice that will be. And is it not ridiculous that at this point we should talk of rearming Japan and revising the Security Treaty?"

There is no reply. They have it straight from my leader, Richard Nixon, who seems to have been converted to the *daijōbu* spirit.

(Aug. 15, 1959)

EDUCATION MINISTRY TAMPERS WITH WORDS

In a country where everyone from the television singer up to the president of the most important university seems to be engaged in a popularity contest, there is much to be said for an organization that blunders on in the direction it thinks best and cares not that it annoys everyone along the way.

Just as Miss Yukimura Izumi is not necessarily a good singer just because she is popular and President Kaya is not necessarily a good president just because he seems to think that being liked by his boys is the most important thing in the world, so the Ministry of Education is not necessarily bad just because it manages to alienate everyone. This, however, is not the place to pass judgment.

It is enough to say that in This Country of confused and sentimental democracy, where it is sometimes even implied that judges are bad because their decisions are not always popular with defense attorneys, there is something almost heartwarming about an institution as sturdily unliked and unwanting to be liked as the Ministry of Education. It may be assumed, of course, that no one will interpret this statement as a plea for a return to prewar controls and bureaucratic interference.

The Ministry of Education does have a most wondrous faculty for alienating everyone. Its desire for efficiency ratings on teachers has greatly annoyed the Left, its desire for a course in "moral education" has annoyed almost everyone except the extreme Right, and

291

its ideas on language reform, welcomed by much of the Left, have greatly bothered people who on most issues would probably prefer Mr. Kishi and the Liberal-Democratic Party to anyone else in sight.

In language reform, the point at issue is this: should Japan continue to use the complex and inconsistent system of writing, partly phonetic and partly ideographic, that was developed over the last millennium or so; or should Japan rather introduce a system which any first-grader could master, and thus leave the remaining years of compulsory education open for the mastering of other things?

When the question is thus stated, the answer seems obvious: Japan needs a nice, convenient little alphabet. Words are strange affairs, however, that have a life of their own, and a literate populace resists any tampering with them. In English we resist simplified spelling because we like to have the history of a word show on its face. We like to spell "knight" that way even though three of its five consonants refer to phonetic elements long ago discarded. And then matters of pride and prejudice come into play. The English probably continue to spell "honour" and "favour" as they are spelled here because the Americans spell them the other way. (Let those who doubt it read Fowler's article on the subject.)

So it is in Japan with people who take words seriously. When they are writers they resist or ignore the Ministry of Education and go on following a system, if such it can be called, that reflects the pronunciation of a thousand years ago. The Left, on the other hand, has a number of principles which it holds more sacred than purity of language, and one of them is that the New China is always right. The New China is moving boldly in the direction of language simplification, and Japan too must move. We are therefore treated to the amusing sight of the Japanese Left, the Ministry of Education, and the New China all playing happily with the same set of blocks.

To be sure, the Ministry of Education has at no time indicated its intention to discard the old system completely in favor of romanization or some other phonetic transcription. It has limited itself to simplification of the old system: limiting the number of ideographs, and standardizing the phonetic symbols that explain and supplement them.

Recently, however, it has come up with something that has led extreme opponents of language reform to suspect that the ultimate goal is in fact phonetic transcription. Since written Japanese is a highly unstable combination of the phonetic and the ideographic, it has always been troubled by the problem of where the one should take over from the other. No consistent solution is possible.

It may be said, for instance, that the unconjugated part of a verb should be represented by an ideograph, and conjugational endings should be represented by phonetic symbols; but if this principle is applied consistently the way is open to mistaken readings. The past of the verb *arawasu*, "to show," is *arawashita*. Following the above principle, the ending *shita* should go in phonetics, the remainder being covered by an ideograph; but if it is so written no one can possibly know whether it was meant to be pronounced *arawashita* or *hyōshita*. To make quite sure, the element *washita* must be put in phonetics, eating into the element theoretically covered by the ideograph.

So much, at a risk of boring, to indicate the complexity of the problem. Late last year the Ministry of Education came up with a scheme so hopelessly riddled with inconsistencies that its enemies suspect it of sinister intentions: it means to make people so sick of the whole system that they will gladly accept romanization in its place.

Perhaps so. The Ministry's way of doing things can be devious, and the new "system" is clearly leading to great confusion. Indeed there are grounds for suspecting that the intention was to confuse rather than clarify. A dictionary giving the orthography of every word in the language would have clarified, but a statement of contradictory principles followed by a few examples and, as is the way in This Country, a thunderous "and so on"—this can only confuse.

The day may therefore be in sight when Japanese will be read with twenty-two Roman letters—minus the useless *l*, *v*, *q*, and *x*. Whether in sight or not, it or something like it is coming some day. Once the Chinese have romanized, the Japanese will not be far behind.

(Mar. 3, 1960)

TAXI DRIVERS AS INFORMATION SOURCES

A great deal has been said about the Tokyo taxi driver as a noisy threat to life, but not much, to my knowledge, has been said about his virtues as a commentator. Some people have a way of finding talkative taxi drivers elsewhere in the world. I have an acquaintance who swears that a New York taxi driver once turned to him and said: "You would never guess from my suntanned face that my body is a milky white, would you?" For my part, I have always found New York taxi drivers a rather dour lot, given to grunts and acid looks through the rearview mirror. In London that wall of glass makes it quite impossible to determine whether a taxi driver is dour or not, and in Paris it seems best to let sleeping dogs lie.

But the Tokyo taxi driver is always ready for a chat. Indeed he must be among the most garrulous taxi drivers in the world. He does not mind asking questions. One evening—it was the evening the crown princess's condition was made public, I remember—a driver asked me what sort of birth-control techniques I had found most effective. Another evening one of them asked me what sort of excesses accounted for the tendency of foreign gentlemen to lose their hair rather early in life.

Nor do taxi drivers mind being asked questions, and they are worth questioning. In spite of their inability to find an address— and, after all, not even the fire department can find a Tokyo address —they know the city well. They can tell you where the baseball players and movie stars live, and how it is with the girls who were thrown out of work by the anti-prostitution law; and they have interesting things to say about the general nature of the city.

If you ask them what part of the city is the most hopelessly confusing and full of false leads, they will always answer "Setagaya." I have never come upon an exception. This fact demonstrates that Tokyo has grown in a manner rather different from most cities. Whereas in most cities someone begins to plan as the place begins to get big, in Tokyo the impulse to plan has given out as the city has sprawled to the west.

A city can be forgiven if it has at its heart a rabbit warren that is an absolutely unbreakable traffic barrier, but one expects increasingly broad streets and an increasingly rational pattern as one leaves the warren of the old city.

In the far downtown of New York, West Fourth Street crosses West Twelfth Street and there is a Little West Twelfth Street for no reason at all and I think that no one has ever been able to find

First Street or Second Street. Above Washington Square and Greenwich Avenue, however, the grid is solid and unbending.

In Tokyo the reverse is true. The heart of the old city was laid out on reclaimed land, and followed a fairly reasonable geometric pattern, uninfluenced by animal tracks or the flow of water. After the earthquake the pattern was made even more reasonable. But then the stamina of the planners seems to have failed, and after the recent war nothing at all was done.

As the paddies fill up in Setagaya and Suginami, the streets follow the farmers' bicycle tracks, scarcely widened, and no map does more than approximate the eccentricities of the area. I once met a taxi driver who said that one damp night he had been unable to extricate himself from a blind Setagaya alley, and had had to hail another cab to take him home. This was obviously a very humiliating experience, as when a telephone operator gives herself the wrong number.

Since taxi drivers are an important contact with what the progressive magazines call "the people," it is good now and then to question them about more serious things too. Their reactions tend to be very middle-class, and offer little evidence to support the progressive intellectuals who hold that class warfare is becoming more intense. If pressed to tell whether they have any feelings of belonging to a class, taxi drivers will generally reply, somewhat sheepishly, that they consider themselves workers, and change the subject. I once found a particularly intelligent driver who said that his income was such that for statistical purposes it put him in the middle class, and what class did I belong to?

In view of everything the newspapers have had to say about impossibly difficult work loads and the like, it is astonishing how little sense drivers seem to have of belonging to an exploited class. Back in the days when the talk was all of the white-plate drivers who were trying to break in on the big companies, I made it a practice to ask every driver I saw for his views on the problem. Something like two-thirds of the answers were nasty remarks about the white-plate drivers. Generally I was warned to stay away from them—they were people who had been fired by the companies for cheating or carelessness.

Although the Tokyo taxi driver is happy to talk about almost anything, there is one subject on which he does not seem able to give a clear and final answer: why taxis refuse to pick you up. Some will tell you that it is because the driver who does the refusing is waiting for a long trip, others that it is because he is waiting for a short trip. If you ask why he refuses you without asking whether the trip is long or short or into town or out to Setagaya, the answer is usually that the cab must be on call. Why then does he not turn out the light in his windshield?

At this point the answers become imaginative. One driver told me that it might be because the refusing driver was superstitious. Another suggested that it might be because I weighed too much.

(Apr. 3, 1960)

HATE-AMERICA DRIVE HITS BURLESQUE SHOWS

The hate-America campaign has gone about as far as it can go. It has invaded the Asakusa burlesque houses. What realms remain for it to conquer?

The Rokkuza in Asakusa was one of those fine, dirty, off-limits places where, in the early years after the war, a person could go and shiver with Mary Matsubara and the other strip queens. Lately it has shown signs of going socially conscious.

Until last week, the attraction at the Rokkuza was entitled *The Tachikawa Base: Ten Years of Rape*. A fine, rape-filled drama it was, too, just rape, rape, rape for a whole decade. The audiences loved it. On the Saturday night when I went, the house was jammed and enrapt, and the empathy complete. From time to time there were angry shouts from the balcony at some particularly objectionable American rapist, most commonly a Negro. It is hard to know why the run was not extended.

As the play begins, a young man of an apparently disreputable calling is about to be arrested. "Wait a minute, officer," he protests. "I killed Akemi because I loved her." He goes on to tell what happened to poor Akemi, and to give a small political sermon while he is about it. Akemi was raped. Worse: she acquired a loathsome disease as a result, and was rendered insane. The young man is not one of those who, prisoners of sterile ideas, demonstrate against the Security Treaty. He is one who knows from personal experience the

296

horrors of the treaty system. "Damn the Americans. That's why I had to kill my Akemi." Then the flashback begins.

We are in Tachikawa, in a house that rents rooms to disreputable ladies. Poor Akemi, who lost her husband in the war, stays on to help her parents-in-law, the owners of the dreary place. They do not like their business any better than you or I would, but what else is a person to do in Tachikawa? Akemi occupies herself with welfare work among the unfortunate women.

The young gentleman appears. He is a friend of Akemi's dead husband, and he is out of work. He launches himself on the career that comes easiest in Tachikawa, pimping, and he falls in love with Akemi. Her parents-in-law will not have him. He "washes his feet," as the expression goes, and comes back, an honest man, to have another try at Akemi. Alas, the fate briefly described above has overtaken her. Not even the best medical care does her any good. He has to poison her. "Damn the Americans!" (Or perhaps "Damn the Yankees!" might be better. The word used is the contemptuous *Amekō*.)

This recounting of the plot does little to suggest the allurements that lie along the way. The rape of Nanking just wasn't in it. Young ladies, uniformly and conveniently clad in halters and panties, lynch other young ladies for violating the code of the whores, wrap themselves around American soldiers and are wrapped around in return, and now and again have to fight for their honor and fee. One of them gets shot by an MP who assures her that she is no better than a cockroach.

Some very astonishing remarks are dropped while all this is in process. The sexual imagery is completely open, and there is one memorable account of how the young ladies manage to keep from getting bored with their work. There are also little sermons from time to time, some of them masterpieces of dirty invective.

Thus we are told that American soldiers are all stupid clods who think the women no better than pigs, and that the women should learn to think of the soldiers in a similar manner. The invective reaches its shrillest peak, and the play its most tasteless moment, when a young lady is exhorted to forego her penicillin shots. If she does so she will be in a position to infect her customers, and what patriotic young lady would not wish to infect the destroyers of Hiroshima and Nagasaki? "What difference does a little pus make? You can stand it." Thus concludes this particular little sermon. No other line in the play quite reaches the same standard.

It is interesting that here, as in so much of the hate-America campaign, the Negro comes in for a great deal of hostile attention. Negroes are prominent among the rapists (Negroes with Mongolian folds, albeit), just as they are always prominent in rotogravure sections exposing the evils of American bases, and just as they are the implicit target of that Communist-directed movie about mixed-blood children, *Kiku and Osamu*. The implications of this seem to escape the Japanese. If to them the Negro is the ultimate horror of the evil bases then one can only conclude that they share in the prejudice with which they are always taxing the Americans. Indeed it is worse with them because they do not realize that they have it.

All in all, Tachikawa emerges as a place one wishes one had investigated more carefully. The leaflet that goes with the play assures the audience that rape, so rare now that you hardly ever come upon a case of it, was just everywhere ten years ago. You had to pick your way among the bodies, so to speak.

It would be nice to know whether any comparative statistics are available. No doubt American soldiers misbehaved, and no doubt the Occupation did its best to keep the facts from becoming public. Can one really believe, however, that the frequency of the assaults approached that in Nanking and Manila under the Japanese, or Vienna under the Russians?

(Apr. 20, 1960)

CONTRADICTIONS IN TALK AGAINST TREATY

Perhaps the most irritating thing about the noisy campaign against the Japan-U.S. Security Treaty is its ability to eat its cake and have it too. This it is able to do largely because it seems to have two contradictory views of the Soviet Union and the New China, and one view is freely substituted for the other as the convenience of the moment requires.

The argument that Japan would do better without the American alliance, and the closely related argument that it would be better not to rearm—the argument that Japan needs neither allies nor arms

—must be based on some sort of appraisal of the two countries that would be most pleased by the success of such an argument, China and the Soviet Union; and there are two radically different appraisals, each of which, firmly adhered to, could lead to the desired conclusions with no internal inconsistence.

The first, of course, is that the two great powers to the west are so peacefully intentioned that the most defenseless little lamb of a country need fear nothing from them.

Such an appraisal of the situation seems to be based, first, on the Marx-Leninist assumption that wars are brought on by "capitalists," and warlike impulses disappear when a nation contains nothing but "socialists," and, second, on the magic of something known as "peaceful coexistence."

Mr. Nixon visited Moscow, Mr. Khrushchev visited Hollywood, and therefore no one need have arms. This may strike one as a peculiarly Japanese form of logic; but the fact remains that, once the premise about the absolutely peaceful intentions of the two questionable powers is granted, the argument moves smoothly to its ally-less, arm-less conclusion.

The second possible appraisal sees those two powers as powerful to the point of being unstoppable. If it has any meaning at all in terms of the practical alternatives facing statesmen, this appraisal carries a very strong implication that they will one day resort to force.

Since it will be irresistible, one's chances are better the weaker one is. The little lamb is less likely to get hurt than the dog that bites back. Or, to use an overworked metaphor that is thought by some to have in it the Wisdom of the East, the bamboo does better in a hurricane than the oak.

This appraisal of the situation also leads to the desired conclusions about the mischievous nature of arms and allies; but only, be it emphatically noted, if one believes in an inevitable and irresistible onslaught of force; only if one believes that a counter show of force can neither deter nor channel it.

Though one may challenge these premises, one cannot fight off the conclusions once they are granted. But one does, perhaps, have a right to be irritated when one's adversary jumps like a gazelle from one appraisal of a highly controversial situation to what is virtually its antithesis.

A truculent statement from Moscow or Peking is a reason for not having arms and allies, and a sweet call of brotherhood from Peking or Moscow is a reason for not having arms and allies. The fact that the Soviet Union undoubtedly has stronger rockets than the United States is cause for throwing down your arms, and the fact that Mr. Khrushchev has a cherubic face, a ready laugh, and a plain old shoe of a wife is cause for throwing down your arms.

It might be better to say not that the anti-treaty movement is able to eat its cake while having it, but that the Soviet Union and the New China are in that happy position.

"Well, which do you mean?" a person asks that solemn-eyed student, in exasperation. "Do you mean that you are telling your prime minister to disarm before a conqueror who can be neither warned off nor fought off, but who may lend an ear to a call for mercy once he has conquered? Or do you mean that conquerors are quaint old relics of feudalism or something you call capitalism, and that he and his country need fear nothing in the buoyant, classless future you tell them you have in mind? Which do you mean?"

Well, it usually turns out that he means both, and neither; and here a hint of dishonesty creeps into the argument. For that solemn-eyed student, back from scrambling over police trucks, and perhaps walking a little strangely from having had a sharp jab in the groin for his troubles, knows perfectly well that he need make no appraisal at all of the Soviet Union and the New China and their intentions.

He can do so if he wishes, and he generally takes extravagant advantage of the privilege; but an appraisal not of his making has radically altered the situation he is appraising and he has the luxury of wishing this last appraisal away.

This is a somewhat pretentious way of saying something that could be said very simply. It would not be uncharitable to summarize the essence of the anti-treaty, anti-rearmament line in two very simple sentences. Everyone knows that Japan will be defended. Why, therefore, should Japan worry about defending itself?

To elaborate a little: the view on the one hand that the Soviet Union and China are absolutely peaceful, and on the other hand that a bleat from Japan will call down irresistible destruction, are both innocent, academic exercises in rhetoric, because the United States takes an intermediate view.

The American position is that the Soviet Union may one day demonstrate itself to be absolutely peaceful, but at the moment it is not wise to disarm; and that, however warlike the Soviet Union may be, it can be restrained by evidence that war will be costly.

In sum: someone is there, willing to fight for the Republic of Korea, of all places; and so why should anyone else arm? What is really missing in the anti-treaty campaign is this sort of healthy cynicism. One would have a certain admiration for it. But what is one to say of self-deception which seems to think that an argument is strengthened, and not murdered, by accepting two contradictory sets of premises?

(May 3, 1960)

WEAKENING OF CLASS WARFARE IN JAPAN

One of the principal charms of This Country is that very few of the things one hears about it seem to be true. The generalization seldom fits the observable facts or the analyzable data.

Thus one is always told, to begin with a minor matter, that the Japanese scrub themselves before they get into the bathtub. Actually, they usually get into the bathtub first and scrub afterward. Again, one is told (in for instance *Honorable Picnic*) that they are quite indifferent to nudity. Actually, they would appear to be a rather prudish people.

The same refusal to fit the generalization holds with larger things too. It is quite impossible to wander around the streets of Tokyo and believe what the newspapers keep telling us about This Country, that it is a very angry country. Not even the demonstrators look really angry. They snarl into the microphone and make nasty remarks to policemen, it is true, but the whole business has a somewhat fabricated look about it, an air as of posing for the cameras of the world.

The Economic Planning Agency has recently issued a report which suggests that the most cherished generalization of all must go. Japan, it seems, is not overpopulated. The time is coming when the drop in the birthrate will be a serious economic problem, and employers faced with truculent unions will curse Margaret Sanger.

A generalization that has always had a slightly spurious ring to it is the one "proletarian" novelists and "people's" novelists have been throwing at us for a couple of generations: that Japan is a country of deep class resentments and divisions.

Indeed one of the remarkable facts about This Country is that, in contrast to a country like England, class differences are not immediately apparent. The delivery boy on his night out talks and dresses and acts very much like the rich boy from the Keiō Business School. Nor do electoral returns reveal any sharp class antagonisms. The poorer northern and eastern parts of Tokyo are more restrained in their "liberalism" than the white-collar western and southern districts, from which Communists are elected to the city council.

The June issue of the magazine *Jiyū* carries an extremely interesting survey that gives evidence to support these vague feelings. It is called "The Structure and Consciousness of the Middle Class," and it is a detailed analysis of questionnaires on the subject returned by more than seven hundred residents of Tokyo. Though one might have wished for larger numbers and wider geographic distribution, the survey does nonetheless represent a significant beginning.

The striking thing is how little difference there seems to be between people who consider themselves part of the working class and people who consider themselves part of the middle class (the pollees are asked to assign themselves to classes). Although there is some difference in class loyalty to political parties, it is not enough to support the conclusion that the major parties represent two warring classes.

The two socialist parties have the support of forty-eight percent of the laboring-class pollees, thirty-seven percent of those from the middle class. The floating vote and the conservative vote combined take forty-one percent of the laboring class, sixty-one percent of the middle class.

On the question of "class party" versus "mass party" (the great ideological dispute separating the two socialist parties), the two classes are remarkably in accord. Of the laboring class and the middle class respectively, twelve percent and eleven percent favor a class party, fifty-four percent and sixty-seven percent a mass party. The same is true on the question of the good society. Of the laboring class, thirty-three percent would like to live in a radically transformed society (variously described as "socialist," "communist," and "people's"), fifty percent seem fundamentally content with things as they are. Comparable figures for the middle class are twenty-five percent and sixty-nine percent respectively.

Asked how they feel about the emperor, sixty-eight percent of the laboring class and seventy-seven percent of the middle class feel that he should be left as he is, a symbol of the nation. Only thirteen percent of the laboring class and six percent of the middle class are in favor of abolishing the monarchy. The two classes are almost completely in agreement on the efficacy of demonstrations and political strikes (about half of each class thinks that both are useless).

But perhaps the most astonishing of all is the response to a question challenging the fundamental Marxist notion of class warfare. Asked whether labor and capital should make war on each other or cooperate, sixty-three percent of the laboring class and sixty-six percent of the middle class reply that they should cooperate. More interesting yet, fifty-eight percent of those who give such a reply are supporters of the Socialist Party, the platform of which is still framed in the most doctrinaire Marxist terms.

One of the gentlemen who analyzed the survey summarizes the matter thus: "If the existence of opposing classes presupposes one class consciousness distinguished from another qualitatively in its contents and its ideals, then we must conclude that, at least as far as the large cities are concerned, there is no clear evidence of such opposing classes in contemporary Japan. When relatively clear differences are to be observed in matters of political consciousness and related social problems, they have to do not with class but with age and party loyalties."

It is to be hoped that more such surveys will follow. At the very least, it would be good to have one for Osaka, the most radical of the big Japanese cities. Is Osaka's penchant for sending Communists to the Diet a matter of class divisions, or do the gentleman's conclusions hold there too?

(June 2, 1960)

GIANTS TUMBLE AND STUMBLE,
AMITY STAYS WHERE IT WAS

There are many strange notions of how to spread international amity and understanding, but perhaps the strangest is that which involves the import and export of athletic teams. The Olympic Games, of course, have become a minor battlefield in the Cold War. As far as Japanese-American relations are concerned, all that can be said is that we are probably damaged less than the Soviet Union. The Japanese tend to become violent nationalists when they participate in international athletic contests, and a gold medal in the Olympics would probably crowd even a moon landing off the front pages.

Fortunately, therefore, the United States is among their serious rivals only in swimming; and in swimming, photographs make the results incontestable, and a fix is virtually unthinkable. The Russians, on the other hand, compete with them in their other two big sports: gymnastics, in which the judges can always be accused of prejudice; and wrestling, in which the referees can be accused of prejudice, and in which a participant on the point of being disqualified can sometimes be persuaded to throw a match and thus help a comrade along.

An international baseball game probably does not arouse strongly nationalist feelings. A game with an American big-league team is as much an exhibition as a contest, and no great questions of prestige are involved, since the Japanese do not pretend to be the best baseball players in the world. Indeed they seem to take a certain delight in telling a person that their best is good Triple-A. Yet it is hard to believe that anyone was really happy about that first game with the San Francisco Giants.

Myself, I was mortified beyond description. The Yomiuri Giants are a team that has seen better days. On the day that the San Francisco Giants played them, they amounted to perhaps the equivalent of a big-league player and a half. They have one good pitcher, who, however, was a worn-out old man from having had to pitch in nearly seventy games during the regular season, and a very good third baseman, who, however, was limping around on a sprained something or other. Suppose we be generous and say that they came to two major-league players: three-quarters of a pitcher, three-quarters of a third baseman, and the rest of the team to make up the difference.

Against this team the San Francisco Giants were not able to score, and they allowed a run from a dropped fly (by Willie Mays, of all people) that should have been counted as an error but (the scorers of This Country are so forgiving) was not. Well, I was mortified.

And I cannot believe that anyone in the Kōrakuen Stadium that afternoon was really happy. Not even the frog-voiced gentleman behind me who kept shouting vile epithets at the San Francisco first-base coach. Some of them were very vile indeed, having to do with the rather bulgy outlines of the coach, who, in blissful incomprehension, would turn around from time to time and tip his hat. I doubt if even this frog-voiced person, pronounced though his sentiments were, left the stadium happy. It was nice to have the home team win, but a dirty shame to put down money for big-league baseball and instead see Willie drop a fly.

Probably if the results had been the reverse, no one except me, another intense nationalist in international meets, would have gone home happy. The emotions with which people left the sloppy affair at the Kōrakuen would only have been reversed: it was nice to see big-league baseball, but a dirty shame to see the home team lose.

Still one does not really want to say that the San Francisco Giants have done us harm. The sportswriters have been very sweet about trying to explain away their defects, and have refrained from dwelling too much on the increasingly obvious fact that the *Yomiuri* bought a pig in a poke when it arranged to have them come in the first place; and they have, after all, managed to win a few games against the All-Japan team (good Triple-A).

A more real question is whether they have done us Americans any good, and whether affairs of this sort ever do much good. Do they change anyone's mind, make anyone think better of us? The most recent *Asahi* newsreel suggests what the answer is with at least one rather influential group.

It begins by dutifully documenting the first two games. The Giants lost both of them, it is true, and got their single run in eighteen innings on a double error, but one cannot accuse the *Asahi* of malice. One can but accuse the Giants of incompetence. The games would probably have been documented just as dutifully had the Giants won.

American baseball out of the way, the newsreel moves on to American bases. Life beside the jet bases is intolerable, it seems, because of the noise. There follows a series of shots all of which could have been posed two hundred miles from the nearest base : hospital patients lying with quilts over their heads and their legs sticking out ; crying babies ; a gentleman shouting into a telephone ; a lady with earmuffs on ; plaster falling from a schoolhouse wall. Everyone knows that plaster falls from the wall of every schoolhouse within six weeks anyway, and that the phenomenon has little to do with jet planes. Rather it is related to the quality of the plaster and the roar of tiny feet.

The last third of the newsreel shows Mr. Akao Bin, the rightist leader, making a speech. The gist of the speech is that Mr. Asanuma (the assassinated leader of the Japan Socialist Party) was lucky to get off without torture. Behind Mr. Akao are enormous streamers urging solidarity with the United States.

Clearly the takers of *Asahi* newsreels have not been seduced into warmer feelings toward the United States. The overall impression of this latest newsreel is that the Giants are nice, maybe, but the United States is pretty unnice.

(Nov. 2, 1960)

DEMOLAND REVISITED, WITH SPECIAL NOTICE
FOR ITS SCRIBBLERS

Eight months have now passed since the assumption into heaven of Miss Kamba, killed in last year's rioting; but, with the trial of her fellow demonstrators beginning, the old sick feeling comes back each time her parents start hamming it up for the photographers. One sympathizes with bereaved parents, of course, but one feels too that it would be a little more dignified if now, eight months after, Professor and Mrs. Kamba could manage not to look quite so much like two faltering St. Bernards. And one wishes too that the press would give them fewer opportunities for so looking.

Involved in discussions of the Japanese press, I have occasionally had trouble explaining exactly what about its behavior during the crisis so distressed me. Thinking that I might have been a victim of hysteria and that the press might not have behaved so badly after all, I recently went back and reread the files of the *Asahi* from mid-

May, when the issue of Diet extension was coming to a crisis, to late June, when Miss Kamba's shrine disappeared in the night and the violence subsided.

It was a remarkable experience, that rereading. I felt rather as I used to when, very young, I would see Marie Antoinette off for the border, and hope that this time she would get through. All the old irritation and apprehension came back. This nonsense could not be permitted to continue, Eisenhower had to come, why didn't the police use tear gas, and so on. And I am able to say what I have against the Japanese press, or at least against the *Asahi*.

The *Asahi* seemed absolutely determined to keep things going. Or rather, parts of it did. The editorial writers managed to maintain an air of sobriety, which deserted them only once. In the days before May 19, *Asahi* editorials were urging Diet extension "to talk things over." This being the case, one would think that the Socialist resort to force in its efforts to prevent Diet extension might have seemed reprehensible; but on May 20, after the Diet was extended and the Security Treaty ratified, the wrath of the *Asahi* descended upon Mr. Kishi alone. The editorial writers quickly remembered themselves, however, and the air of sobriety returned, with much finger-shaking at both sides, and many invitations to quiet "self-reflection."

In the news columns, meanwhile, the war drums were beating. In the quiet after each demonstration, they would start beating for the next, and the proportions of the demonstrations were consistently exaggerated. On May 19 we were told that a hundred thousand people were going to converge on the Diet. On May 20 the fact that the ratification had been pushed through in the night drowned out reports on how many actually did converge, but thereafter the crowds swelled and swelled.

On May 24, we were told that there would be 150,000 demonstrators two days later. On May 27, the front page trumpeted tidings of "an unprecedented demonstration." Not 150,000 but 170,000 had demonstrated, said the top headlines. In an obscure corner of page 12 was the police figure: 60,000. On June 4 we learned, again in large print on the front page, of 5,600,000 strikers and demonstrators. Once more, those who persevered could eventually find the police figure: something over a million. On June 5 publicity had already begun for a demonstration to take place on June

17. So successful was the beating of the drum that the demonstration was presently moved up two nights, to what was to become the night of the assumption. On June 14 we were informed that the strikers and demonstrators would this time total 5,800,000. This figure was never contradicted, but on June 15, in small print, we had the police estimate: well under a million. On June 18 there were to be 280,000 people at the Diet. On the morning of June 19 the figure had swollen to 330,000. There were 130,000, said the police.

We need not go into the maudlin treatment accorded Miss Kamba (lots of stuff about frail bodies and heavy police boots), or the sentimental pictures of students making common cause with the people (helping old ladies across streets from which all traffic had been evicted anyway), or the headlines about "Surging Wave of People's Movement" and "Fury at Midnight" (stringy-haired girl students looking pretty furious, a person had to admit).

Aside from its insistence on keeping things going, one other thing about the *Asahi* was particularly maddening: its determination to show the anti-treaty movement as a national uprising. "Isn't This Public Opinion?" stormed the *Asahi* when the prime minister said he thought public opinion to be on the side of the treaty. There followed voluminous quotations from the provincial press, designed to show that every cove and glen of the archipelago was having fits about the treaty. Then there were loaded opinion polls. Who, when faced with a question like "Do you approve of the government's action in closing debate and forcing the Security Treaty through?"—who among the people of This Country would not be tempted to answer "No," however he felt about the treaty? "Talking things over" is a national passion, and the mere notion of "closing debate" is repellent.

So even after a cooling period of eight months, the performance of at least the one newspaper seems fairly irresponsible. Pushing through toward the far end of the flame-throwing headlines and news columns, one suddenly comes upon that seven-page declaration of June 17, decrying violence. It is as startling now as it was on June 17.

(Feb. 16, 1961)

PLEASANT TIMES ON YAMATE LINE,
OR LET'S ALL SING HAPPY SONG

My, but we all had a good time the other night. It was approaching midnight, and the counterclockwise train on the Yamate Line was loaded with us Shimbashi people, some in tight trousers, some in tight skirts. There was much genial elbowing and stepping on toes as people at the back of the train pushed to the front, and people at the front of the train pushed to the back.

Then, just as we were about to come into Komagome Station, the train stopped. There was complaining, not unfair, I thought, at the erratic habits of the government railways. Then someone looked out the window and invited the rest of us to do the same. Just below my window a young man lay writhing and groaning by the tracks.

Excitement. The Shimbashi sheen disappeared from our faces and eyes began to sparkle. People began jumping, or being pushed, from the windows. I do not know whether anyone landed on the figure or not, for it was soon out of sight behind the merry crowd. "Help, help!" someone shouted, and there was a roar of laughter. A pity, I thought, that the figure was not sufficiently conscious to join in the little joke at its expense.

But that was far from the end of the fun. News shortly reached us from the front of the train that we had hit a taxi. The writhing figure had been thrown clear, but the driver and a young woman were still inside. "They probably want to be alone," said someone, but the joke was not as successful as the earlier one, because people were by now jumping from the windows like rabbits from a brush fire, and running to the front of the train. A pity. It was actually a better joke, I thought.

Real excitement. I too moved toward the front of the train, though without jumping from the window, for the aisle was by now far less crowded than the tracks. Glancing back, I saw a couple of gentlemen, apparently in the uniform of the government railways, hoisting the unconscious figure from the tracks. They did it rhythmically, rather as though they were preparing to toss a victorious coxswain into the river. Good lads doing their duty, I murmured approvingly, although it did seem odd that they should not wait for an ambulance, and it was hard to see why that five feet of track should be cleared when the rest was a black mass of us Shimbashi people.

The front of the train was just a picnic. A Mardi Gras. The taxi was bent around the left wheel of the locomotive in a perfect *L*, and the driver's seat was just at the bend. An ambulance finally came up. "Help, help!" someone shouted, and there was a roar of laughter. Shimbashi is a humor-loving place. The ambulance attendants had just a little difficulty (not much, really) reaching the scene, because people kept asking to see their permits. Word got around that the writhing figure back down the tracks was an off-duty policeman, and that the woman still in the car was married, but apparently not to him—or so much was to be judged from documents that had spilled onto the tracks. This news really amused us. The sort of thing you would expect from an off-duty policeman.

We did not get much of a look at the woman, because the spoil-sport ambulance attendants got her out of sight in a hurry. This was all right, I suppose, though they might have been a little more diplomatic. They are after all public servants, and their behavior did not sit well with the crowd, which was in any case becoming a little restive. The possibility was growing that we would miss the last Seibu train from Ikebukuro. A number of people said as much, and the replies of the public servants were very undiplomatic. I think I shall write a letter to the *Asahi*.

The taxi driver was at length extricated. He was a lump, sort of. You could tell by his clothes that he was of the masculine gender, but beyond that he was just a lumpy bundle. He did have black hair, so I suppose he was a Japanese. Or a Korean. Yes! I'll bet he was a Korean! That is the sort of thing Koreans do, make people miss the last train from Ikebukuro.

But we took it in good humor. The attendants were behaving in a somewhat more commendable manner, to be sure. They laid the lump by the tracks, and, not bothering to cover it with a blanket—that would have taken time, and done no good—they turned to the task of disengaging the taxi from the locomotive. Perhaps they realized that people had to have something to keep them interested, and not so worried about that last train from Ikebukuro.

There were many good-natured remarks, in any event, as when someone, in a burst of Shimbashi humor, said: "He looks as if he might have been hit by a train." My, how we laughed! It was enough to awaken the dead—but of that I of course cannot speak, for the lump was out of sight behind the good-natured crowd.

The only slightly sour note came when a foreign person marched up and started berating people in a fashion almost hysterical. I must assume that he was berating people, although I could not understand a word he said. He was probably an American, and I only speak English. But I did not spend long reproving him. I am sure that a moment's calm reflection, once he had regained control of himself, showed him the true state of affairs. After all, where else in the world could there be so much fun for so little? Japan is a poor country.

(June 18, 1961)

SEVENTY HAPPY WAYS TO BETTER YOUR ENGLISH, STARTLE YOUR HOSTESS

There have recently been some spicy comments in these columns about whether or not it is possible for us foreigners to communicate and be communicated with in the language of This Country. I do not feel qualified to comment on the subject, although it has always seemed to me at least likely that the Japanese language, if it is an impenetrable barrier keeping us outsiders from looking in upon the Japanese, is also a barrier keeping the Japanese from looking out on the larger world. It may be like one of those mirrors in dirty hotels, of course, transparent from one side; but I would suspect that its opaqueness, if it exists, operates in both directions, and that the people of This Country suffer from it more than we do. I do not know, however. I but pass my suspicions on, for what they are worth.

Whatever may be the case with foreigners struggling to learn Japanese, I have long been an observer, always interested, frequently puzzled, and frequently amused, of Japanese struggles to learn English. The struggle seems at the moment to be reaching one of its periodic peaks of intensity.

It is a pretty frantic affair, though not without its light moments. The other day in a beer hall in Osaka a young gentleman sat down to practice his English on me. After the usual remarks about whether I found life in Japan comfortable and whether I approved of nuclear weapons, he said cheerfully: "Well, nature is calling," and departed.

I wondered where he might have picked up the remark. Now I know, and must give warning that, if the current boom proves effective, his is among the less surprising remarks we may expect from young gentlemen practicing their English.

He learned it from that enormous best seller, Professor Iwata Kazuo's *How to Improve Your English* (*Eigo ni tsuyoku naru hon*). Several hundred thousand copies of *How to Improve Your English* have been sold, and it seeks to improve your English in the direction of, well, slanginess, earthiness.

Thumbing through a copy of *How to Improve Your English*, I found myself thinking of a passage in one of John Espey's delightful sketches of life in prewar Shanghai, the passage in which he describes the electrifying effect on his Chinese primary-school teacher when he used an expression "of jocular disbelief" he had learned from the boatmen on the canals. I thought too of the dear little Japanese typist, back in my brief bureaucratic career, who learned her English from an American with a perverse sense of humor, and who, when taxed by her very proper American supervisor (an ex-missionary) with the narrowness of her margins, said, "Oh, Jesus Christ, Mr. Somebody!" and walked off.

I thought of these incidents because there are going to be some pretty electrified hostesses around Tokyo if Professor Iwata has his way with his hundreds of thousands of readers. Although I may be guilty of a certain descent from good taste in doing so, I feel duty-bound to warn them what to expect.

At the end of Professor Iwata's book is a list of seventy "happy phrases" (whatever sort of company was he keeping when he learned them?) which he particularly commends to the consideration of his followers. Presumably the hundreds of thousands will learn these seventy felicities if they learn anything; and so we may visualize the scene.

Mrs. Something settles down happily with her eager little group of students of English, the occasion being one of her Wednesday evenings. As always, there is intense competition for the attention of Mrs. Something. The debate picks up momentum, and one eager student turns to Mrs. Something and says of another eager student, genially but with obvious seriousness of purpose: "Oh, don't bother about him, Mrs. Something. He's just an ass kisser." I am very sorry, but I feel duty-bound, and there the happy phrase is, number five on Professor Iwata's list of seventy. Professor Iwata explains that phrase number five is a product of capitalism, with its drive to get ahead in the world.

The general purpose of the list, and presumably of the book, although I have not gone through it in any detail, is to teach snappy, slick, slangy English. The other sixty-nine happy phrases include the following: Attaboy!, baby-wife, con game, hangover, joy water, kiss-me-quick, make water, number one and number two (in senses that take me back to grammar school), sexperiment, and varsity man.

I don't know. The hostesses will presently come out of their electrification, but might not the injury to the already sickly English of This Country be irreparable? We all know how we wince when some Japanese starts talking about "the wife and kiddies," and life is going to be very difficult when "Attaboy!" becomes a standard part of Japanese-English.

A better beginning toward "strengthening your English" might be made by throwing away Professor Iwata's book and all books on the problem, and listening instead to English as it is spoken. Then, when progress has reached the point where "lovely bride" as read by an eager student no longer sounds like "rubbery blight," the emphasis might shift to learning absolutely standard English, proper to the point of being prim. Slang by its nature is always changing. It is impossibly difficult to master, and it almost always rankles in any case when it comes from the mouth of a foreigner.

The English of the Filipinos is charming precisely because it is a trifle stilted. I cannot describe how delighted I was with those signs on the campus of the University of the Philippines: "Please do not pluck the flowers." I have a friend who says that once during the Philippine campaign he was picked up by a savage-looking Filipino truck driver. Presently the truck stopped, and the driver said in the softest tones: "It is here that we take our noonday meal."

When the Japanese have come this far, they will have come quite far enough.

Let's not have any more of those attaboys.

And so ends the sermon for today.

(Sept. 17, 1961)

313

The Japan (October) issue of *Holiday* magazine contains a fine and upsetting article on Japanese baseball by Robert Trumbull, who used to be the *New York Times* man for This Country. It is a fine article because it says about everything there is to be said on its fascinating subject, including many things that such aficionados as myself had not known before; and upsetting because, not having had much to say on the matter since the San Francisco Giants came and disgraced themselves last year, I was poised in readiness to write an article of my own. Now that the definitive work is in, there is not much left to do but to cavil and to moralize.

Were I a native of This Country, I could begin with a cry of horror at the rashness of Mr. Trumbull, a green-eyed foreigner, in venturing so near the awful mysteries of the Japanese language. I could point out that he is quite wrong about the origins of the word *chambara*, which has to do not with the sound of drums but with the sound of sword clashing against sword. And I could then proceed to the conclusion that this grave error utterly disqualifies Mr. Trumbull as an expert witness.

But since I am not such a one, I shall do what comes much more naturally in any case to us products of the cold, rational Occident; I shall moralize. There are several places in Mr. Trumbull's article that call for reflection upon what Japanese baseball tells us about the Japanese people.

There is for instance the nature of Japanese baseball crowds. "Under the impact of increasing Western contact, Japanese fans are showing the rude behavior encountered in American ball parks," says Mr. Trumbull. Some time ago I felt confident enough to say exactly the opposite in print: "Cheering sections at amateur and semi-professional games are vociferous. But the crowds at professional games tend to be quieter than in the United States. . . . The player who fails to run out a close play is seldom subjected to the derision he could expect in any American ball park."

This was some time ago. Today I think Mr. Trumbull is probably right. There had been reports, to be sure, of nasty happenings in Nagoya and Osaka, but it took nastiness nearer home, the all-night game at the Kōrakuen Stadium this summer, to convince me that

Japanese baseball fans are indeed losing their manners. The players themselves started losing their manners long ago, and the custom of swinging on the umpire now seems to be firmly rooted. (Japanese will tell you that it is current among Korean players only, but do not believe them, despite the fact that the gaudiest swinger, Yamamoto of the Tōei Flyers, happens to be a Korean.)

Is this a limited phenomenon, associated only with us baseball lunatics, or is it indicative of a change in the populace at large, of a tendency to dispense with ceremony? The latter explanation seems the likelier, and so the matter is of some concern, for a ceremonial code has long done duty in Japan as a substitute for a moral code. It is a little frightening to think what will happen if even this is disappearing.

Mr. Trumbull makes some amusing remarks about the rhubarb: "The traditional rhubarb with an umpire has been translated into Japanese with one embellishment: when the squawking player finishes his row, he turns to the grandstand, removes his cap and bows low from the waist." I have never been near enough to a Japanese rhubarb to know whether it is translated from English or not; but I would have thought it different from an American rhubarb in an important respect not touched upon by Mr. Trumbull: it has some chance of succeeding.

In America a rhubarb generally serves as final assurance that the umpire's decision cannot be changed. The big brawl in the Kōrakuen, however, began when an umpire changed his mind in the course of a rhubarb. He had at first called a runner out, and he then decided that the defending third baseman had been guilty of interference; and so the bottles began flying. The institution of "talking things over" (hanashiai) is so dear to the Japanese, it would seem, that they even take rhubarbs seriously.

One of the conclusions toward which Mr. Trumbull's article seems to be reaching and toward which I have been moving myself might be of some comfort when next I start getting all worked up about Japanese baseball (I always do when the odious Yomiuri Giants have a long winning streak, and I am threatened with acute megrims now that they have won their damned pennant): that Japanese baseball really is not all that good, and so nothing to get worked up about.

Even with the American rules changed to favor the batter, and with badly overworked pitchers, Japanese baseball has never produced a triple-crown hitter, and at the moment of writing it appears that the great Nagashima is going to miss it again this year. It seems likely, therefore, that he would be a pretty dim light in the American big leagues. With this thought I shall try to control my rage as he carries the herd of plow horses known as the Yomiuri Giants to future victories.

Not long ago I wrote a long article on Japanese newspapers for the Japanese-language parent of this paper. In the course of it I said some rather unpleasant things about the *Yomiuri Shimbun*, at least by indirection. They were carried precisely as I wrote them. I chanced along the way, however, to say an unpleasant thing or two about the Yomiuri Giants. This unpleasantness was cut. I wonder: does the *Yomiuri* own the Giants, or do the Giants own the *Yomiuri*?

(Oct. 17, 1961)

SOCIALISTS FORCE NEW APPRAISAL
OF MARX AND ADMIRABLE GIANTS

There is nothing like the Socialist Party of Japan for making a person change his mind about things. It made me change my mind about Marx, and now it is making me change my mind about baseball.

Since I am now known, insofar as I am known at all, as a black reactionary, it might be of some interest to recall that when I first took up residence in this country I was something of an amateur Marxist. It was easy to be such in the United States of a decade or so ago. Capitalism did seem to be racing toward monopoly control, and monopoly capitalism did seem to have all sorts of internal contradictions. Those depressing miles of used-car lots—they were enough to make a person think that maybe the whole gigantic machine was out of control and producing more than it could possibly consume, and so perhaps even giving credence to Lenin's notions of the capitalist need to expand into overseas empires.

In short, much that Marx had said seemed to be true, and maybe everything he had said might prove to be. This, however, was an essentially pragmatic attitude. It amounted to waiting and seeing whether Marx worked out in practice. What was so unpleasant about observing the left wing of the Socialist Party of Japan in action was that it quite stood pragmatism on its head, and thus demonstrated Marx's way of blunting the sense of reality into complete uselessness. His pronouncements were not tested against objective reality. They were reality. Marx shaped the world.

It seemed, during and after the last Lower House elections, that the spell of Marx on the Socialist Party might be wearing off. And now there the Socialists are, back at it all over again. According to Mr. Eda, the secretary-general, the world is torn by a struggle between "socialism" (led by the Soviet Union) and "capitalism" (led by Du Pont). Since the former is a nice thing and the latter an unnice thing, it is easy to see who is really responsible for the Berlin crisis, the Soviet nuclear tests, the unpleasantness in Laos, Mr. Ikeda's low posture, Mr. Ikeda's high posture, and Mr. Ikeda's medium posture.

Perhaps the United States really is responsible for all of these things. Being rather far from the seats of power, I cannot really say. What troubles about the workings of Mr. Eda's head, however, is not the conclusions themselves but the way in which they are arrived at. Everything follows from a single assumption, that the Soviet Union is at the head of the socialist world. It therefore has the sanction of history and cannot be significantly wrong. I have never myself seen any reason for considering the Soviet Union a socialist state other than that it tells us it is; but this seems to be a very compelling fact for Mr. Eda, and, unfortunately for the world, he is a much more important person than I am.

Having turned me away from Marx, the Socialist Party of This Country has now made me turn back and have another look at the Yomiuri Giants, hitherto known as the odious Yomiuri Giants. If a leading weekly magazine is to be believed, the Socialist Party is having a fight with Nagashima, the third baseman of the Giants and the only good player they have.

It all began when Nagashima made some remarks about politics in an *Asahi* interview: "Sure I read the political columns. Berlin, and then what was the name of that fellow that died? Hammarskjöld, that was it. I read all about it. Started getting interested because of the treaty business last year. We're all conservatives, you know. If the Socialists took over, well, baseball, er, baseball, well,

317

we might not be able to call it baseball, you know." This is the nearest I can come to translating Nagashima's remarkable syntax, which resembles that of Dwight Eisenhower, Casey Stengel, and Paul Aurell.

Nagashima's pronouncement so enraged a Socialist member of the Diet, one Mr. Akamatsu, that he allowed himself to be quoted in the same magazine as believing Nagashima to be an imbecile, literally "a super-feeble-minded boy." Baseball, said Mr. Akamatsu with his eye on the sand lot vote, will not be done away with by the Socialists. It rather will be reorganized into happy little clubs. Mr. Akamatsu is an admirer of the Chūnichi Dragons, which organization, it seems, gives its players instruction in politics, economics, and sociology.

I used to sort of like the Dragons myself, but the picture of a shortstop frowning over his Keynes and Schumpeter is such that I will have trouble ever looking at them again with a straight face. As for Nagashima, he may not be the brightest young person in the world, but to me he begins to sound like a pretty nice guy. I will have to think up another adjective for the Giants.

Nagashima goes on to say that he is essentially not a very political person. He has made only one political speech in his life, in support of a Liberal-Democrat candidate for the Diet. How I wish I could have heard that speech!

(Nov. 16, 1961)

OOPS, MY MYSTIQUE HAS SLIPPED, OR WHAT THEY BROUGHT BACK FROM PARIS

It would be a very healthy thing if all the products of "the Japanese spirit" could be subjected to international tests of strength, as judo has just been. No doubt there is much that is admirable about those products. The trouble is that they have a way of getting all smeared over with blobs of mystique that make it quite impossible to discriminate what is good from what is specious.

It did not seem to strike the Japanese as significant, until that sudden awakening at Paris, that their own judo champions had been getting bigger and bigger. In fact they are enormous, and much more terrifying than enormous *sumō* wrestlers because they are all muscle. When accosted by Asashio all a person would have to do would be to get a firm grip on his folds of fat, but that would not work with Messrs. Natsui and Sone.

But the power of the mystique has been too strong, and the people of This Country have gone on pointing out that the grand satrap of modern judo, Mifune Kyūzō, is a small man. He is, to be sure; but he has the advantages of being a pioneer. All credit is due to pioneers. Yet they have certain advantages because they know certain tricks that no one else does. If the tricks could be kept forever secret, no doubt the mystique could be preserved, and tinier and tinier men would be doing what judo champions are supposed to do, using their opponents' weight against them. The ideal judo type would presently be a powdery mummy.

But it is all a little like Norman Vincent Peale and "positive thinking." It might just be possible for a pole-vaulter to vault that extra quarter of an inch because of his prowess with positive thinking, and so win the meet. What happens, however, when all the other pole-vaulters become equally adept at positive thinking?

Even since Paris, the grand satrap has been heard muttering that weight matters only in a negative way, that the heart of judo must not be lost, that he is a small man and look how far he has come. Other commentators have been more honest even when they have sounded a trifle petulant. The Dutchman was no more skillful than they, they have said. He was just bigger.

And so they have admitted that it was all nonsense. Every text on judo begins with a solemn chapter about how judo is unique because no one else in the world has thought of the principle of giving way and so letting your opponent fall flat on his face. No one else has thought of the principle that the bigger they are the harder they fall. Only the people of This Country, and notably the satrap, have thought of it.

Paris and the big Dutchman have demonstrated what the solemn chapters mean: that in judo you try to catch your opponent off balance. As, of course, you do in any other sort of hand-to-hand struggle. There is not a doubt in the world that the tiniest little judo black-belter could throw me all over town; but so could the tiniest little flyweight wrestler. Neither the tiny black-belter nor the flyweight would be much good against Rikidōzan, who also knows a thing or two about catching opponents off balance.

None of this is to deny that judo is a very remarkable form of wrestling. What happened at Paris is healthy because it demonstrates that judo is a form of wrestling and no more. Now we can settle down to producing judo champions whom the mystique has not blinded to the importance of sheer physical strength.

How nice if the blobs of mystique could be similarly wiped away from other manifestations of the Japanese spirit! How nice if, for instance, there could be an international competition in which the pretensions of the modern tea ceremony could be set off from its actualities. Throughout the world there are ceremonies which masquerade behind vast aesthetic and moral principles, but which are in fact beautifully staged occasions for conspicuous display. In such a competition the tea ceremony as practiced so energetically and profitably by the Senke schools would probably rank high, right up there with opening night at the Metropolitan. Shorn of its mystique it would still be very pleasant to look at and still more pleasant to participate in; and we would no longer be put off by all that talk about the Buddhahood in the common clay, and the unity behind the multitudinous, and so on.

And in what sort of competition would we enter Zen? With Norman Vincent Peale and positive thinking, maybe; and maybe too with the philosophy of the young man in *West Side Story*, who advocated keeping cool for purposes of living longer. Again Zen would probably rank rather high, and we would thereafter be excused from taking it seriously as a religion. It would rank high among those secular tonics which, in a time of war (or in New York), help their possessors to kill before being killed, and which in a day of peace help in grabbing up a large share of the profits. Just as judo champions tend to be large, muscular people, so Zen champions (such as the owner of a large Tokyo newspaper which must remain nameless) tend to be very affluent people.

But why enter these peripheral manifestations? Why not have an international competition in which the Japanese spirit itself could be entered, and we could see just how spiritual the people of This Country are? In a way they are unique. The world over people are flagellating themselves for being too materialistic; but the Japanese go right on assuming that they are very spiritual, and that when someone presses them to the precise terms of a contract the person in question is being lamentably materialistic, as no Japanese ever would be.

I suspect that the Japanese would rank rather low in a spirituality contest, but I do not think that this would necessarily be to their discredit. They would come out maybe a cut or two above Moise Tshombe, but far below Dr. Verwoerd, a man who really takes abstract ideas seriously. And so we would see them for what they are, and be happier for having seen: a very materialistic people with a redeeming strain—goodness knows where they got it—of moderation and humanity.

(Dec. 17, 1961)

IN PURSUIT OF ENGLISH,
OR WHO IS THAT LADY ON YOUR CARVING BOARD?

There have been many harsh words exchanged recently about whether This Country could use a fresh supply of American English teachers. (Perhaps the last of them have already been exchanged. I have a knack for rushing in upon a controversy just as it is ending.) In the letters-to-the-editor column of a rival paper, the United States has in effect been charged with cultural imperialism for even suggesting that there is such a need. It has been said that we might better devote ourselves to planning a Japanese Peace Corps to teach other people Japanese, since Japan has so much more to teach the world, and especially the United States, than the United States and the world have to teach Japan.

It is a tricky, metaphysical business, this balancing of one culture against another and deciding which has the more to give and which the more to take. Like everyone else I have my own ideas on the relative merits of Japanese culture, and I suspect that the "mindlessness" which Professor Suzuki is so intent on exporting may not be the attribute of supreme importance in the struggle that lies ahead. The matter need not be made so complex, however. The simple facts of the marketplace can perfectly well determine what teachers go where to teach what languages.

It is a marketplace whose demand works in one direction only. Maybe this is a sad state of affairs, and maybe we ought all to be working to build a demand in the other direction. I do not know, although I suspect that were America to come to me and ask if it should learn Japanese, I would be tempted to reply: "America, if you have all that spare time, go learn French, German, Spanish, Italian, and Russian instead. You could learn them all in about the time it would take you to learn Japanese, and you would find richer rewards waiting at the end of the struggle than you would find after your conquest of Japanese. And besides, you have Professor Suzuki to explain Japan to you; and you would not wish to deprive him of a livelihood, would you?"

As for the situation with Japanese studies of English, I would have thought two facts to be absolutely clear, neither of them having anything to do with cultural imperialism.

First, that the Japanese want enormously to learn English. Why else would a million of them have bought that wretched piece of flummery, Professor Iwata's *How to Improve Your English*? Two hundred million yen from the pockets of a million pursuers of English into the pockets of those unscrupulous purveyors of English, Professor Iwata and his publisher, Kōbunsha! And they got but a small part of the total take for the purveying of English. (One word in defense of Professor Iwata, who has by now acquired revilers enough: I suspect that some of the worst things in the book are not his fault but that of Kōbunsha, the brassiest, crassest publisher in the business.)

Second, that they are not learning English. Not even people who ought to be professionals, such as hotel clerks and switchboard operators, can be counted upon to follow an English conversation when it departs from the "Good morning, did you sleep well?" pattern. What is going to happen in 1964 if the hotel desks have not by then learned to take a message in English, write it down, and put it in Box 1559, as requested, and not in Box 1595 or Box 1995?

It is not surprising, perhaps, given the methods of teaching English in Japanese schools, that the national grasp of English conversation should be somewhat insecure. It is utterly astonishing that the people of This Country do not even seem to be able to read English accurately. I have gone over a number of translations from English into Japanese in the course of the years, and have become convinced that the really accurate translation is very rare. Presumably publishers of translations commission them only from people who are supposed to know both the foreign language and the subject matter well; and if we cannot have a straight reading from them, what in the world can we expect to have from a college student fresh from stumbling through Lamb and Saroyan?

My judgments are sometimes thought unnecessarily hostile. Let me therefore give a few examples from a translation that has recently come to my attention. The translator is a man whose English ought to be above reproach, since he has held an important position in the Japanese Embassy in London. I will first give a retranslation into English of the Japanese translation, and then the English sentence from which the translation was made.

Retranslation: "A series of strange stories mark the island story. Many appalling things were done for the sake of England."

Original: "A series of paradoxes mark the island story. The most appalling evils sometimes worked to the good of England."

Retranslation: "For example, the lengthy and bitter contest between the Roman Catholic Church and anti-papal Christians . . . contributed toward the growth of the nation and provided the strength for enduring the trials that England later faced."

Original: "For example, the lengthy and bitter contest . . . contributed materially both to the growth of nationhood and to the toleration which the British eventually came to practice."

Retranslation: "Again, with the development of centralized power, feudal barons, who enslaved their serfs, had of their own accord to restrain themselves."

Original: "Feudal barons who brutally oppressed their enslaved serfs provided at the same time a necessary check upon the equally vital development of centralized power."

Retranslation: "From the generation before Shakespeare wrote that mercy droppeth as the gentle rain from heaven and Spenser penned his *Faerie Queene*, ministers as individuals were rated no higher than gentle ladies upon carving boards."

Original: "A generation before Shakespeare wrote that mercy droppeth as the gentle rain from heaven and Spenser penned his *Faerie Queene*, royal ministers were not above personally stretching gentle ladies on the rack."

All of these sentences are from a single paragraph. Even with the broadest and most liberal standards for judging translations and ample allowance for slips and howlers, which are bound to creep into any long translation, this seems pretty extreme. I would not deny, of course, that there are excellent Japanese translations and translators, and I have been fortunate enough to come upon some of them. I only say that, given the vast amounts of time and money spent on learning English in This Country, such persons and works seem to be remarkably rare.

(Feb. 1, 1962)

ONCE YOU LEARN ABOUT FOREIGNERS, MONKEYS ARE NO PROBLEM AT ALL

You always bring a real harvest back from a trip to the provinces of This Country. The most recent trip took me to some of the remoter provinces. They are also among the more conservative provinces, and the nature of the organization sponsoring the trip was such that I did not meet many rebels. Indeed about the only ones I did meet were around four or five years old. It was rather a surprise, therefore, to learn that not everyone was pleased with the performance of the Kennedy boy and his baby-wife, as Professor Iwata would say.

More than one dignified, conservative member of the regional gentry had roughly the following to say: "Mind you, I hold no brief for the way the Waseda students behaved. Indeed I thought it outrageous, and am sorry that flogging has gone out of style. But don't you think that it was a little rude of Mr. Kennedy to sit on the table?"

So it goes. This Country is a touchy, tricky old country. You think everything is going nicely, and then along comes some youngster and sits on a table, and, blooey, you are right back where you started again.

It was also interesting to learn that problems worrying the city-dweller, or at least the big-city newspapers, do not always seem of the greatest moment out in the provinces. In return for my train fare, I was expected to make some remarks on "Japan as Viewed by a Red-haired Foreigner" or "Japan as Viewed by a Green-eyed Foreigner," I forget which.

And so, shaking my shaggy red mane and injecting a note of

sincerity into my green eyes, I would go over the problems that sometimes trouble my exotic sleep: the need to do something about the consumer boom at home and cease expecting sincere self-reflection on the part of foreign buyers to take care of the deficit in international payments; the need to do something about developing the public sector of the economy before Tokyo and the tourist centers strangle themselves; the need for an understanding with Korea; and the need to sit down quietly and decide what such expressions as "imperialism" and "decadent capitalism" and "socialism" mean, and to refrain from using them with quite such airy abandon until they have been defined.

At first I arranged my exotic insights thus because I thought that, so arranged, they did touch upon a few difficulties that would one day have to be faced. Then I began offering them intact as a sort of control for a little experiment. The reactions of my listeners were so remarkably similar the first couple of times I pontificated that I wanted to see whether they would continue to be so throughout the trip.

They did. When the question-and-answer period came, there would always be some preliminary queries, polite but not very enthusiastic. Did I not think that the Koreans were just as responsible as the Japanese for the interrupted dialogue, and did I not therefore admit the advisability of a lecture tour of Korea? I would reply that I thought the major responsibility, for historical reasons if for no others, to be with the Japanese; and there would be polite but unenthusiastic nods and murmurs—clearly some people were more taken in by false Korean claims than other people were.

Then there would be a question or two about the public domain, and an answer or two, followed by unenthusiastic murmurs, for clearly the red-haired, green-eyed one paid less income tax than did his listeners, and so had less to lose to the public domain.

These questions out of the way, we would arrive at the one problem that really interested my moderately conservative audiences. Although not unrelated to the last of my four problems, it was a matter upon which I had not directly touched, and one which does not, I think, arouse in the big papers quite the sense of urgency I detected in the provinces.

In every city I went to someone presently got up and said substantially this: "We are very grateful for what you have told us, because you know so much about Japan, and therefore we are grateful, because you know so much. But I would like to have your valuable advice (you know so much) on another matter: what in the world are we going to do about our schoolteachers?''

Then the atrocity stories would begin, about schoolboys lisping anti-imperialist slogans, about schoolgirls on the verge of nervous prostration because their teachers had threatened them with ruin for taking the national achievement tests, about schoolchildren of both sexes indoctrinated by their teachers in ways of circumventing the feudal admonitions of their parents, and, in general, about the role of teachers in interrupting the dialogue between the generations.

There is great anger at the Teachers Union, such that I sometimes found myself tutting and cautioning and advising mature self-reflection. To this advice one gentleman made telling reply: ''But the Teachers Union is not like other unions. A union may have the idea that a plant is not run the way Marx or Professor Sakisaka says a plant should be run; but it does not usually claim the privilege of reorganizing the plant. The only union that does insist on reorganizing the plant before it will have anything to do with production is the Teachers Union. You can't blame us for wanting to sit upon it.''

And sat upon it may well one day be, if my sampling of opinion has any significance.

The really high moment of the trip, however, came when I was viewing the monkeys on Mt. Takasaki, just outside Ōita. About a thousand native Japanese monkeys have been sufficiently tamed that anyone can go up and watch them, and study their social arrangements. Really dedicated students of the problem recognize each of the thousand monkeys, and know where each one stands in the hierarchy, and which are rising and which are falling.

Or so said the gentleman guiding the party next to ours.

One of his wards expressed mild disbelief that it was really possible to tell a thousand monkeys apart.

''Oh, it's very easy,'' said the guide. ''It's just like telling foreigners apart.''

(Mar. 1, 1962)

BOORS, WHELPS, MADAMES AND OTHER GRIST
FOR MILL OF RUTH AND JANE

Is it not about time the *Yomiuri* found itself a Ruth or a Jane, someone to chatter away, on Mondays and on Saturdays, but chiefly on the latter days, about The International Set?

Being a latecomer, however, the *Yomiuri* would have to find someone different, a Ruth or a Jane with a new dimension, someone to chatter away about the chatter behind the chatter, so to speak.

I would not wish the job myself, nor indeed do I think I would be capable of encompassing it. Those huge numbers of madames you have to meet when you do that sort of work—I am afraid they would strike me all of a heap. But I do think I might be of assistance to whoever is found for the work. The following are a few touchstones, a few specimens of the sort of thing that is needed.

There were seven more National Days last week, or was it eight, each commemorating a new crack in the British Empire. Debonair Sir Somebody and petite, austere Lady Something were present at all of them, being very brave, and even managing a smile now and then. But Yours Truly would give a penny to know what their real thoughts were. Sick transit Gloria Monday, as Jane would say. Had a chat with bland Sir Brian Beaune-Hedde, who is a houseguest of the Somethings, and who is connected with the *Express*. He said to Yours Truly: "The *Yomiuri* is a bloody awful paper."

Keep the Home Fires Burning International met on Tuesday at the lovely new Azabu home of the Spencer Turmights. Yours Truly would give a penny to know how big their pile is and all off of used cars, too. The meeting was to introduce new members. Had a chat with petite, loquacious Madame Akudama, who is bravely keeping her home fire burning. Suave Mr. Akudama is out of sight for a few months, you know. They have him up for bribing a public procurator.

Had a chat too with petite, exotic Teeny Turmight, who is also bravely keeping a home fire burning, and who is just about the loyallest petite little dear you could ever hope to meet. Affable Spencer, you know, is said to be out of sight for a few months because he couldn't make his Japanese income-tax return match his American. But Teeny says that isn't true at all. It's just a question of what exchange rate you use.

On Wednesday, a tea at International Culture House, to promote international culture. The Corps Diplomatique was out in full array, including the vivacious Qxstrzas, who haven't been much seen in the International Set since that coup. Petite, swarthy Madame Qxstrza drank tea indefatigably, as did Miss Elizabeth Something. Believe that between cups there was talk of West Irian, but of that Ruth will have to tell you.

Had a chat with intense, energetic Mr. Mizumushi of the staff of International Culture House. He asked if Yours Truly did not think it would be good for international culture if Paul Robeson were to visit Japan. Murmured "yes," so glad to be of assistance to international culture. Also had a chat with Madame Mizumushi. Must have been in a pretty witty mood, because at every remark Madame Mizumushi giggled.

Query: is it true, as rumored, that International Culture House's bill for calls to Peking is simply terrific?

My, what a busy day Wednesday was. Also on Wednesday, at the Industry Club, a meeting of Dog's Life, International, to plan its lottery. Such a lovely charity for dogs. The slogan is to be "Your Pennies for a Dog's Life," and the prize is to be a mink coat.

Had a chat with petite, poised Madame Hanagata, who was very colorful in a kimono of mauve, saffron, and emerald, and just about the darnedest obi I ever saw. She comes from such a lovely family. (Boorish Edward Seidensticker kept whispering in my ear that she is actually the daughter of the scullery maid, but we all know how reliable he is. Don't know why he had to be there in the first place. It is very well to be fond of dogs, you still don't want to have one whispering in your ear.)

Had a chat with her about her family. It seems that she and scholarly Mr. Hanagata were brother and sister before they were married, only they weren't really, because there was something about an adoption, and then his parents lived together before they were married, or was it after, whereas hers lived together after they were married, or was it before, or was it that they weren't—well, Yours Truly didn't get all the details, but Mrs. Hanagata comes from such a lovely family.

Asked her how many brothers and sisters she had. She said much depended on how you defined brother and sister, but if it is important for Yours Truly to know she would go have a look at the family register. Bet Ruth and Jane never get these little insights into Japanese family life.

On Thursday evening, had an interesting dialogue with the Japanese Left at the American Embassy.

"Hello, Left," said Yours Truly.

"Hello," said the Left, not catching Yours Truly's name.

So don't let anyone tell you it's not possible to have a dialogue with the Japanese Left.

Had a chat with boorish Edward Seidensticker. Some of the things he said about some of the other guests, especially petite, thin Madame Masaoka (she speaks such lovely English)—why, Yours Truly wanted to put her hands over her ears. Rumor has it that he will soon be departing these shores, going back to the old Larries and Penates. About time, is what Yours Truly says.

(May 1, 1962)

NO MORE FOR ME, THANK YOU, I'M FEELING QUITE MELLOW ENOUGH ALREADY

I have recently noted signs that I might be mellowing, and so, believing that mellowness in This Country is death, I am going home in a few weeks' time. This is to be my last column. Perhaps life in the United States will be sufficiently unmellowing to send me back one day. Time will tell.

People keep asking what happened. I suppose therefore that the matter is of some interest, not because it concerns a nasty but lightweight columnist, of course, but rather because it concerns someone who took This Country for a decade and a half and then, for obscure reasons, gave up. Those to whom the matter is in fact of no interest are at this point dismissed, with a word of thanks for having been so patient.

The editors of the *Yomiuri* deserve a very special word of thanks. They have been unbelievably patient. Sometimes I have found myself wondering how far I could go before they would start censoring me; but, although their typesetters and proofreaders have dropped a word now and then, they themselves have cut nothing in the more than three years this column has been running.

329

No, the editors of the *Yomiuri* are not dismissed quite yet. I mean to try their patience for a few seconds more, because I have a request to make. Can something not be done about the editorial drivel they so faithfully translate from the Japanese *Yomiuri* every day? Those editorials are easily the worst thing in serious Japanese journalism today, and they are no credit to what I believe to be the liveliest and most intelligent of the English-language papers. I think that if the editorial writers of the Japanese *Yomiuri* could be changed, I might, in return, be able to persuade myself not to hate its baseball reporters any more.

Which, of course, brings me to the heart of the matter, my fear of growing mellow. Perhaps both the editorial writers and the baseball reporters richly deserve to be hated; if so, to begin acquiescing would be to compromise on a matter of principle.

I think a fable is needed to dispel a bit of the fog hereabouts, or perhaps to make it denser, more mysterious. It is called "The Fable of the Meadow Mouse Who Was No Longer Unreasonable."

Once there was a meadow mouse who chanced to tell a friend of his problem. He could not go out of or into his hole except at dawn or dusk, because only then, when the snake outside was changing from day eyes to night eyes or the reverse, could he scamper by without being detected and eaten.

"The snake outside your hole?" said the friend.

"A fat, smiling snake with beady eyes. I can tell when he's changing to his night eyes because they begin to go glassy, and he stops looking like the minister of agriculture and forestry and starts looking, well, torpid, like the director of the Economic Planning Agency. Then's when I scamper back in again."

"How can he be fat if he sits outside your hole waiting for you all the time?"

"Well, he is."

"And how do you know he wants to eat you?"

"I am a student of snakes."

"Oh, be reasonable." The friend was a very reasonable meadow mouse, who had had training in psychology. He had known a paranoiac or two in his time (a student of snakes indeed!), and his theory was that the way to treat them was to confront them with their delusions in all their deludedness. Don't argue, confront!

"Very well," he said, turning to conceal a smile as they stepped into a bar, "there is outside your hole a snake who looks sometimes like the minister of agriculture and forestry and sometimes like the director of the Economic Planning Agency. Two double whiskies, please. What you fail to realize is that snakes are perfectly nice people. I want you to go out there now and make friends with him. I am sure that, like everyone else, he is a fan of the Yomiuri Giants, and that will give you something to talk about."

"But I am a student of snakes."

"Of course you are. Snakes are perfectly nice people. Another double whisky, please. No more for me. I'm driving."

"He scares me. He smiles in the friendliest way, as if an election might be coming up, but I know he means to swallow me."

They sat in silence for a time, broken by sipping and by the smart crack of Nagashima's bat over the *terebi*. The reasonable meadow mouse sensed that the moment had come.

"Snakes are perfectly nice people," he said. "They work hard to support their children, no different from you and me. Drink up, now, and I'll see you as far as the anthill."

"Snakes're perfly nice people," said the first meadow mouse, no longer unreasonable, holding up what he judged to be two fingers to order another whisky. "Perfly nice people."

The sun was still high, but there was a trace of evening coolness in the air when the two parted at the anthill. The reasonable meadow mouse gave his friend an encouraging slap on a thin shoulder and, himself turning right, pushed him to the left.

The tipsy, no-longer-unreasonable meadow mouse disappeared around the anthill, waving his arms and saying, "Perfly wonderful game, snake. Perfly wonderful. Nagashima hit a home run and two doubles, and the Tigers played like a bunch of grannies. Snakes are perfly nice people, I always say."

The reasonable meadow mouse turned away, smiling a self-congratulatory, therapeutic smile.

The snake gulped once, a satisfied gulp, and, looking more than ever like the minister of agriculture and forestry, started off toward the residence of the reasonable meadow mouse.

There we are. I have felt recently that I might be getting mellow, becoming a reasonable meadow mouse. The Japanese are just like other people. They work hard to support their—but no. They are not like other people. They are infinitely more clannish, insular, parochial, and one owes it to one's self-respect to preserve a feeling of outrage at the insularity. To have the sense of outrage go dull is to lose the will to communicate; and that, I think, is death. So I am going home.

(May 16, 1962)